D1799698

Shaping Online Spaces Through Online Humanities Curricula

Julie Tatlock
Mount Mary University, USA

A volume in the Advances in
Educational Technologies and
Instructional Design (AETID) Book
Series

Published in the United States of America by
    IGI Global
    Information Science Reference (an imprint of IGI Global)
    701 E. Chocolate Avenue
    Hershey PA, USA 17033
    Tel: 717-533-8845
    Fax: 717-533-8661
    E-mail: cust@igi-global.com
    Web site: http://www.igi-global.com

Copyright © 2023 by IGI Global. All rights reserved. No part of this publication may be reproduced, stored or distributed in any form or by any means, electronic or mechanical, including photocopying, without written permission from the publisher.
Product or company names used in this set are for identification purposes only. Inclusion of the names of the products or companies does not indicate a claim of ownership by IGI Global of the trademark or registered trademark.

Library of Congress Cataloging-in-Publication Data

Names: Tatlock, Julie, 1977- editor.
Title: Shaping online spaces through online humanities curriculum / Julie
  Tatlock, editor.
Description: Hershey : Information Science Reference, 2022. | Includes
  bibliographical references and index. | Summary: "This book will take a
  strategic look at what we have learned about online teaching and
  learning in the humanities in this unprecedented time of Covid-19 and
  reexamine online learning best practices"-- Provided by publisher.
Identifiers: LCCN 2022007244 (print) | LCCN 2022007245 (ebook) | ISBN
  9781668440551 (hardcover) | ISBN 9781668440568 (paperback) | ISBN
  9781668440575 (ebook)
Subjects: LCSH: Humanities--Study and teaching (Higher) |
  Humanities--Computer-assisted instruction. | Humanities--Curricula.
Classification: LCC AZ182 .S53 2022 (print) | LCC AZ182 (ebook) | DDC
  001.3071/1--dc23/eng/20220401
LC record available at https://lccn.loc.gov/2022007244
LC ebook record available at https://lccn.loc.gov/2022007245

This book is published in the IGI Global book series Advances in Educational Technologies and Instructional Design (AETID) (ISSN: 2326-8905; eISSN: 2326-8913)

British Cataloguing in Publication Data
A Cataloguing in Publication record for this book is available from the British Library.

All work contributed to this book is new, previously-unpublished material.
The views expressed in this book are those of the authors, but not necessarily of the publisher.

For electronic access to this publication, please contact: eresources@igi-global.com.

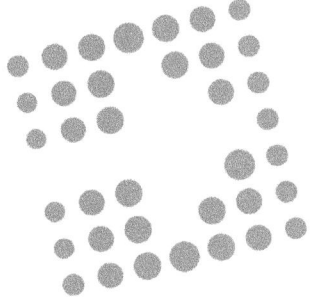

Advances in Educational Technologies and Instructional Design (AETID) Book Series

Lawrence A. Tomei
Robert Morris University, USA

ISSN:2326-8905
EISSN:2326-8913

MISSION

Education has undergone, and continues to undergo, immense changes in the way it is enacted and distributed to both child and adult learners. In modern education, the traditional classroom learning experience has evolved to include technological resources and to provide online classroom opportunities to students of all ages regardless of their geographical locations. From distance education, Massive-Open-Online-Courses (MOOCs), and electronic tablets in the classroom, technology is now an integral part of learning and is also affecting the way educators communicate information to students.

The **Advances in Educational Technologies & Instructional Design (AETID) Book Series** explores new research and theories for facilitating learning and improving educational performance utilizing technological processes and resources. The series examines technologies that can be integrated into K-12 classrooms to improve skills and learning abilities in all subjects including STEM education and language learning. Additionally, it studies the emergence of fully online classrooms for young and adult learners alike, and the communication and accountability challenges that can arise. Trending topics that are covered include adaptive learning, game-based learning, virtual school environments, and social media effects. School administrators, educators, academicians, researchers, and students will find this series to be an excellent resource for the effective design and implementation of learning technologies in their classes.

COVERAGE

- Adaptive Learning
- Collaboration Tools
- Curriculum Development
- Digital Divide in Education
- Online Media in Classrooms
- Hybrid Learning
- Virtual School Environments
- Game-Based Learning
- Classroom Response Systems
- Social Media Effects on Education

IGI Global is currently accepting manuscripts for publication within this series. To submit a proposal for a volume in this series, please contact our Acquisition Editors at Acquisitions@igi-global.com or visit: http://www.igi-global.com/publish/.

The Advances in Educational Technologies and Instructional Design (AETID) Book Series (ISSN 2326-8905) is published by IGI Global, 701 E. Chocolate Avenue, Hershey, PA 17033-1240, USA, www.igi-global.com. This series is composed of titles available for purchase individually; each title is edited to be contextually exclusive from any other title within the series. For pricing and ordering information please visit http://www.igi-global.com/book-series/advances-educational-technologies-instructional-design/73678. Postmaster: Send all address changes to above address. Copyright © 2023 IGI Global. All rights, including translation in other languages reserved by the publisher. No part of this series may be reproduced or used in any form or by any means – graphics, electronic, or mechanical, including photocopying, recording, taping, or information and retrieval systems – without written permission from the publisher, except for non commercial, educational use, including classroom teaching purposes. The views expressed in this series are those of the authors, but not necessarily of IGI Global.

Titles in this Series

701 East Chocolate Avenue, Hershey, PA 17033, USA
Tel: 717-533-8845 x100 • Fax: 717-533-8661
E-Mail: cust@igi-global.com • www.igi-global.com

Table of Contents

Detailed Table of Contents

Chapter 1
Julie Tatlock, Mount Mary University, USA
Paula Reiter, Mount Mary University, USA

The purpose of this chapter is to reflect on the experience of online education during COVID-19 at the university level with a view towards using that experience to guide online education going forward. It is the authors' argument that not only is it unlikely that online education will go back to pre-pandemic levels, but also that it is incumbent on academia to deliberately deliver quality online instruction. The focus in on college-level humanities courses, and the chapter considers both what universities did well during COVID-19 and what needs improvement in the future.

Chapter 2
Julie Tatlock, Mount Mary University, USA
Paula J. Reiter, Mount Mary University, USA
Stepanka C. Korytova-Magstadt, Mount Mary University, USA

This chapter offers several models teachers can use to better engage students in content through the use of creative assignments. It begins with the importance of effective online orientation and building student learning outcomes specific to online classes. That is followed by examples of how to use the traditional discussion forum in new ways to encourage true intellectual exchange. The chapter ends with a series of sample creative assignments that help students personalize and fully integrate complex content.

The need to critically engage learners whether the classroom space is traditional, hybrid, or virtual is one of the most pressing educational issues teachers face today. Engaging learners specifically in an online environment requires the examination of both the content being taught as well as the methods or pedagogical models used to deliver the content. This chapter highlights how both the content, and the delivery can be filtered in ways that are relevant to the learners, that value their home and community assets, and that provide them with tangible touch points to transfer classroom information into the real world to maximize student engagement. The core of this chapter focuses on the use of Socratic Seminars as a means of engaging learning through targeted and purposeful conversations around social justice issues. This chapter demonstrates how the original tenets of Socratic Seminar can be used to present content in a manner that leverages students' cultural and linguistic wealth, develops personal and social identities, and builds critical competencies and global awareness in all learners. Specific connections between justice oriented Socratic Seminar, anti-bias teaching frameworks, and online learning environments are made.

The chapter details how the first-year writing program at a small, highly diverse, private university in the Midwest responded to the pandemic and the social unrest of the time by engaging in a wholesale revision of the information literacy curriculum. The authors aimed to build a pedagogical framework that would acknowledge the power, influence, and lure of digitally but simultaneously would trace its complex biases. In sharing the curriculum that aims to recoup central critical questions—a more holistically imagined, digital curriculum designed to bolster anti-racist pedagogy—this chapter will answer the following questions: What does digital, anti-racist, and culturally responsive information literacy curriculum look like in this moment? and What kinds of methodologies for teaching information literacy might we follow to help make space for the continual evolution required when teaching through an anti-racist, culturally responsive lens?

Chapter 5
DuEwa M. Frazier, Coppin State University, USA

Teaching an online multicultural literature course during the early stages of the COVID-19 pandemic from Fall 2020 to Spring 2021 created an opportunity to engage in reflection on instructional practices and student reactions to diverse literature selections. In an effort to understand how community was created and dialogue maintained between instructor and students, the author sought to reflect on strategies that encouraged critical thinking and ongoing sharing of individual student perspectives during the course. This chapter examines how an online multicultural literature course was created and facilitated for students during a time when college courses were delivered solely through online instruction. The chapter illustrates how the online multicultural literature course was developed with culturally responsive pedagogy in mind to generate online discussion, guide literary analysis, and develop student writing. In examining this process, the chapter highlights instructional strategies that can be utilized by faculty to create engaging online learning communities.

Chapter 6
Hany Zaky, Kean University, USA

Game-based learning is a powerful instructional method to build students' sense of community and cultural awareness. Educators view game-based learning as one of effective pedagogy and learning principles. Therefore, integrating technology in the teaching process is an influential tool that spurs learners' academic achievements and awareness of the learning goals. Understanding intercultural sensitivity in digital classrooms needs the individuals' awareness of subjective and objective cultural dimensions to deepen this integration. Due to the current varieties of offered educational games, educators need to know each game's background, context, and the proper pedagogical approach. The chapter focuses on the impact of technological advancements on building learners' intercultural sensitivity using game-based learning, as an adult classroom instructional technique, toward a more humanistic approach. It proposes the educational approaches to designing, managing, and using games for learning development assurance.

The term "sisterhood" evokes a wide range of interpretations and responses, both positive and negative. Popular culture defines the term in a variety of ways, largely dependent upon and unique to context, authorship, and audience. In Race, Class, and Gender: Prospects for an All-Inclusive Sisterhood (1994), Dill takes on the complicated concept of sisterhood from a critical perspective. In many ways, online teaching is its own complicated sisterhood grappling with challenges similar to those Dill addresses. Dill raises questions that are not unlike the persistent question of how to better attract, retain, and support educators. The chapter explores both the questions as well as associated strategies to further support educators in online environments.

The outbreak of COVID-19 pandemic resulted in large-scale educational disruptions for school-going children around the world. India was among the worst hit, as multiple lockdowns put a sizeable percentage of Indian children, out of school which resulted in accumulated learning gaps, particularly for children coming from marginalized socio-economic backgrounds. To confront this learning crisis and curricular deficits, Room to Read India, a global organization working towards a world free of illiteracy and gender inequality, adopted multiple remote literacy interventions to reach out to children from vulnerable families. The study recommends that a blended hybrid mode of education, incorporating both online and offline mediums of learning, is significant in bridging the digital divide for marginalized children, who do not have adequate access or knowledge about digital resources. It was inferred that successful digital learning for children cannot take place in isolation and a dynamic partnership between teachers and parents is essential to reach out to vulnerable children.

Chapter 9

This chapter proposes an educational transformation project (ETP), remote group work (RGW), to support students' group work in the context of online teaching and learning. An ETP assisted by RGW (ETPRGW) uses critical success factors and areas, natural programming language environment, and a dynamic decision-making system, which can be used to improve the organization's online learning capabilities. ETPRGW supports all phases of an ETP, and its concept is based on existing standards, methodologies, local specificities, and traditional educational practices. Complex educational topics, like information and communication systems (ICS) need particular RGW requirements that force educational organizations (simply entity) to integrate agile collaboration products, educational patterns, educational best practices, and educational services' management. An RGW approach forces the used transformation framework and the related set of existing modules to synchronize all types of transformation activities, like the integration of an automated coordination of RGW activities.

Chapter 10

Although there has been a call for the transformation of the world from the Eurocentric paradigms to a decolonised and decentralised world, the role of technology is still embedded and continues to be at the centre of everything in society. Over the past few years, particularly from 2019 to 2022, since the discovery of the COVID-19 pandemic, the technological interdependency intensified by moving contact spaces to online platforms, private resources to open resources, including the pedagogical space. Despite advances in technology and pedagogy and their relation to education, and the focus on the local and global, the new internet and teaching and learning including its policy still lack serious engagement with blockchain technology and the metaverse, as well as how to effectively utilise it. This chapter address this gap by using Howard Gardner's theory of 'multiple intelligences' to consider the role of blockchain technology and the metaverse as new options for the facilitation of open-ended teaching and learning that has emerged in the age of Web 3.0.

The COVID-19 pandemic has offered many lessons for educators as this event has disrupted the lives of all students and teachers across the world. As all learning moved to some form of online instruction in early 2020, teachers and schools scrambled to modify current courses to move online and then to later design face-to-face courses to an online format. This shift to virtual instruction has not been easy, particularly for those teachers with little online teaching experience and for those courses that have not traditionally been offered online. This chapter offers some advice based on the author's experiences as well as an exploration of the current research, which suggests the best practices for online learning. It also offers three short cases that represent learning experiences that have helped shape the author's beliefs and actions.

Preface

Many of us remember where we were when news of the COVID-19 shut down came. I had just returned from a conference in Boston, the last trip I would take for some time. In addition to the personal stresses of fear and anxiety, faculty around the world were faced with a dramatic and sudden shift to fully online instruction. While online teaching certainly was not new, in many institutions it remained a small portion of overall course offerings. Suspicion as to the efficacy of learning remotely combined with reticence to embrace technology meant that some departments had never offered anything in a purely online format. This is not surprising as change is rarely easily or quickly adopted. But in the Spring of 2020, there was simply no choice. We were going online and we were doing it right away.

As we navigated the enormous challenges both personal and professional, there was little time to reflect on what it all meant for education long term. Perhaps some thought it a stop-gap measure that would not last very long and, once the crisis passed, so too would the need for such massive transformations in teaching and learning. Given the sustained nature of pandemic culture, however, many institution remain at least partially online and certainly online tools were more fully incorporated to life across the academe. It is now difficult to imagine a path back to the pre-pandemic university. If online education on a more massive scale is here to stay, then assessing the experience can help us contextualize what it means going forward. What have we learned about our institutions and the way we teach? More importantly, what have we learned about how our students learn.

No doubt the experience of faculty and students during the pandemic has varied greatly. Some institutions have had a longer experience with digital education than others and access to broadband and computers also varies widely from institution to institution. These differences likely played a large role in how faculty and students experienced education for the last two years. But there are some things that we learned collectively about teaching and learning online. These insights can help us prepare both for the immediate future, where remote learning will continue to be necessary and in the long run, as technology can no longer be avoided in education systems around the world.

It was not uncommon to hear things like, "just put your class online," or, "just use Zoom." Both of these phrases are problematic. Despite historic efforts to cast online learning as simply an extension of face-to-face instruction, there is little truth to the statement. Both formats can be extremely effective in educating students, but they are different and need to be treated as such. This became evident as faculty across the world tried to quickly change content from face to face to digital environments. It was not an easy transition. The go-to answer was Zoom, a word which suddenly became part of everyday life. And, rightly so; it was, for the most part, reliable, and faculty could teach in a familiar way albeit in a different setting. They could lecture.

The question I wanted to ask. Was anyone listening? First, there was the issue of whether faculty could demand that students have their cameras on during "class." Then, the issue became managing classroom discussions via Zoom—seeing all of the students, watching for hand raises, and the chat, and students trying to participate. Dogs and cats often put on a show, and children could be found learning next their parents. I like dogs, cats and children, but chaos is not conducive to a lecture environment. At the time, perhaps, the question of efficacy took second place to simply surviving the first semester.

What faculty quickly learned was that the online space was not the same, even with the greatest of modern technology, something the majority of students around the globe didn't have at their disposal. That should not have surprised us as much as it did. Education has never truly been about the tools, whether that be a lectern or a keyboard. It has always been about building a relationship between faculty and student where information and ideas can pass back and forth effectively. Hundreds of years have gone into creating the right architecture for teaching in the classroom, and thinking that these structures could be easily transplanted was hubris and lacked the same self-reflection humanists praise and try to teach their pupils. I would argue that is the relationship between faculty and students that transcends the physical environments of education, while the structures of any given class—its learning objectives, assignments, and assessments—must adapt to the physical form, or forms, of the class space.

This is not a popular view in many circles. One guideline of the Higher Learning Commission, for example, is that online classes and their face-to-face iterations should have the same learning outcomes. While certainly this is the case when it comes to content, the skills one builds might differ from one format to the next. Perhaps it is time to consider distinguishing face-to-face and online courses more deliberately. This distinction would allow online classes to have some learning outcomes that are appropriate specifically to a digital learning environment. The skills a student gains in online classes should be considered as objectives in online learning environments as they not only shape the quality of student learning outcomes, but also transfer into skills students will use every day in their work lives. If we do not conceptualize online spaces as unique, are we not missing great opportunities to expand what our students take from our classes?

For example, academics have long discussed the ideal classroom where interested students come to learn from the "sage on the stage," in an intellectual Socratic community. There is a great deal of pedagogical research on engaging students in classroom learning. While there is work on online pedagogy, most of it does not take time to talk about what the classroom online should look and feel like. This is largely because the online classroom has not been envisioned on its own terms, but rather as a mirror, however distorted, of the traditional class experience. The ability to individualize online spaces also means that there is, in theory, an infinite number of ways to shape the online classroom. I would further argue that attempts to stylize online spaces have largely been negative in tone. We talk of best practices in a way that assumes we need to uphold certain ideas in the face of online tools. I cannot remember the last time anyone asked me about best practices in face to face classes. The assumption seems to be that they, best practices, will be there simply by virtue of the space we occupy. In trying to make online space conform to a room with only four walls, we are not teaching as effectively as we could and, in fact, we may be hindering student learning.

This text is intended to be a work of diverse scholars reflecting on their experiences during COVID-19 through the lens of their expertise. Each author offers a unique perspective on online education, but all collectively convey that the "space" of needs to be shaped in thoughtful and meaningful ways that may, at times, vary from how face-to-face instruction looks and feels. It also suggests that the critical decisions we make about delivering content cannot happen in a vacuum. We must consider race, gender and class as formulate our courses. As teachers around the world also take time to think about their own response to teaching in the pandemic, the chapters herein offer new ways to think about how we reach all students, regardless of the rooms in which they learn.

Chapter 1. Just Put Your Class Online: The Realities of Going Online During COVID-19

In Chapter 1, Dr. Paula Reiter and Dr. Julie C Tatlock, of Mount Mary University, explore what "going online" looked like at their institution. Both authors have taught online for over fifteen years and bring considerable expertise to the subject matter. They contend that it is incumbent on all those involved in college-level education, including administration, student support, institutional infrastructure, and teaching and learning, were indelibly marked by the experience of rapidly transitioning to fully online instruction. The fact that so many were "forced" to teach and learn in digital space translates into a watershed moment in the history of education and as such, requires significant reflection.

Chapter 2. Using Innovation and Creativity to Engage Students in Online Education

Chapter 2 offers several models teachers can use to better engage students in content through the use of creative assignments. It begins with the importance of effective online orientation and building student learning outcomes specific to online classes. That is followed by examples of how to use the traditional discussion forum in new ways to encourage true intellectual exchange. The chapter ends with a series of sample creative assignments that help students personalize and fully integrate complex content.

Chapter 3. Social Justice Through Socratic Seminars: Promoting Critical Engagement in a Virtual Learning Environment

The need to critically engage learners whether the classroom space is traditional, hybrid, or virtual is one of the most pressing educational issues teachers face today. Engaging learners specifically in an online environment requires the examination of both the content being taught as well as the methods or pedagogical models used to deliver the content. This chapter highlights how both the content, and the delivery can be filtered in ways that are relevant to the learners, that value their home and community assets, and that provide them with tangible touch points to transfer classroom information into the real world to maximize student engagement. The core of this chapter focuses on the use of Socratic Seminars as a means of engaging learning through targeted and purposeful conversations around social justice issues. This chapter demonstrates how the original tenets of Socratic Seminar can be used to present content in a manner that leverages students' cultural and linguistic wealth, develops personal and social identities, and builds critical competencies and global awareness in all learners. Specific connections between justice oriented Socratic Seminar, anti-bias teaching frameworks, and online learning environments are made.

Chapter 4. Tracing Bias in a World of Binary

Authored by Jennifer Kontny of Mount Mary University in Milwaukee, Wisconsin this chapter argues for a revolution on our "information literacy curriculum" which she piloted in her very diverse, freshman writing program. Changes to this foundational curriculum "aimed to build a pedagogical framework that would acknowledge the power, influence, and lure of digitally but simultaneously would trace its complex biases." Her chapter answers the following questions: "What does digital, anti-racist and culturally responsive information literacy curriculum look like in this moment? And: What kinds of methodologies for teaching information literacy might we follow to help make space for the continual evolution required when teaching through an anti-racist, culturally responsive lens?"

Chapter 5. Creating Community Through the Teaching of Multicultural Literature Online

Dr. DuEwa M. Frazier, Humanities, Coppin State University, found in the COVID-19 crisis an opportunity to engage in meaningful reflection on how to best teach a variety of literature in online spaces. The chapter examines how an online multicultural literature course was created and facilitated for students during a time when college courses were delivered solely through online instruction and illustrates how the online multicultural literature course was developed with culturally responsive pedagogy in mind, to generate online discussion, guide literary analysis, and develop student writing. In examining this process, the chapter highlights instructional strategies that can be utilized by faculty to create engaging online learning communities.

Chapter 6. Digital Literacy for Adult Education Beyond Borders

Dr. Hany Zaky of Kean University argues in Chapter Six that "game-based learning is a powerful instructional method to build students' sense of community and cultural awareness." He notes that educators already "view game-based learning as one of effective pedagogy and learning principles. Therefore, integrating technology in the teaching process is an influential tool that spurs learners' academic achievements and awareness of the learning goals." The chapter's overall argument is that it is necessary to include concepts of intercultural awareness and empathy when using games as an instructional technique and offers examples of how this can be achieved in courses geared towards adult learners.

Chapter 7. The Sisterhood of Schooling, Teaching, and Education

Jennifer Schneider, of the Community College of Philadelphia, explores issues and trends associated with online education in the context of Dill's Race, Class, and Gender. In, "The Sisterhood of Schooling, Teaching, and Education", she takes a critical look at the role of "sisterhood" in the context of online education as well as associated ways universities might improve the recruitment and retention of educators.

Chapter 8. Remote Literacy Interventions
With Children During COVID-19

Dr. Pradeep Mishra and Dr. Jannat Fatima Farooqui, both from Research, Monitoring and Evaluation Department of Room to Read, India explores the learning impact of school closures in India which adversely affected more than 321 million students. They content that this dramatic shift to online education resulted "in widened and accumulated learning gaps, particularly for children coming from marginalized socio-economic backgrounds. The learning crisis and curricular deficits were acute for children in vulnerable families who did not have adequate access or knowledge about digital resources." They suggest that the answer to such gaps in digital access is best addressed by a "blended hybrid mode of education." Finally, they note that, "that successful digital learning for children cannot take place in isolation and a dynamic partnership between teachers and parents is essential to reach out to vulnerable and marginalized children in remote and rural areas."

Chapter 9. Educational Transformation Project's
Remote Group Work (ETPRGW)

Antoine Trad, professor and a researcher at IBISTM in Europe and the Middle East, argues that more needs to be done to "support students' group work in the context of online teaching and learning." His primary argument is that "an ETP assisted by RGW (ETPRGW) uses critical success factors and areas, natural programming language environment, and a dynamic decision-making system, which can be used to improve the organization's online learning capabilities." This particularly applies to high level, integrated and complex education areas such as Information and Communication Systems. The author uses his own genuine transformation framework which is based on Artificial Intelligence, Enterprise Architecture, Information Technology, and Transformation concepts; and today he has an academic lead in the domain of Intelligent Transformation Projects.

Chapter 10. Humanities in the Age of
Blockchain Technology and Web 3.0

Dr. Zingisa Nkosinkulu of the University of South Africa, argues that "although the has been a call for the transformation of the world from the Eurocentric paradigms to a decolonized and decentralized world, the role of technology is still embedded and continues to be at the center of everything in society." He also contents that despite the exponential expanse of online education during the COVID-19 pandemic, digital education, infrastructure and administration, still lack serious engagement with blockchain technology and the metaverse, as well as how to effectively utilize it. This chapter address this gap by using Howard Gardner's theory of 'multiple intelligences' to consider the role of blockchain technology and the metaverse as new options for the facilitation of open-ended teaching and learning that has emerged in the age of Web3.0.

Chapter 11. Supporting Student Success in Online Courses: What COVID-19 has Taught Us About Effective Teaching and Learning

Rob Ceglie offers a reflection on how the COVID-19 pandemic impacted Faculty through the lens of his considerable experience in online education and circles back to a broad view of this experience can transform the future of education in positive ways. The chapter also "offers some advice based on the author's experiences as well as an exploration of the current research which suggests the best practices for online learning. It also offers three short cases that represent learning experiences that have helped shape the author's beliefs and actions."

Julie Tatlock
Mount Mary University, USA

Acknowledgment

I would like to dedicate this work to Dr. David Bruce, my partner in life, and one of the best teachers I have had the privilege to know. I also thank my colleague Dr. Paula Reiter, for her brilliance and friendship. Finally, I would like to thank my fellow teachers and my students at Mount Mary University, all of whom inspire me to improve my own teaching through their profound belief in humanities education and its power to transform individuals and the world.

Chapter 1

Just Put Your Class Online:
The Realties of Going Online During COVID-19

Julie Tatlock
Mount Mary University, USA

Paula Reiter
Mount Mary University, USA

ABSTRACT

The purpose of this chapter is to reflect on the experience of online education during COVID-19 at the university level with a view towards using that experience to guide online education going forward. It is the authors' argument that not only is it unlikely that online education will go back to pre-pandemic levels, but also that it is incumbent on academia to deliberately deliver quality online instruction. The focus in on college-level humanities courses, and the chapter considers both what universities did well during COVID-19 and what needs improvement in the future.

INTRODUCTION

We, Dr. Paula Reiter and Dr. Julie Tatlock, teach literature and history, respectively, at a small, all-women's university in Wisconsin. Our student body is the most diverse in the state. The majority are first generation students, and many come from traditionally underserved populations. Our class sizes generally range from 10 to 25. Although our online caps are currently set at a reasonable 15, that number is often around 20 students by the time a semester starts. We have published and presented numerous articles on online pedagogy—both individually and together—and we have been

DOI: 10.4018/978-1-6684-4055-1.ch001

Copyright © 2023, IGI Global. Copying or distributing in print or electronic forms without written permission of IGI Global is prohibited.

teaching online humanities courses for more than 15 years. We have participated in a prestigious research project on digital learning in the humanities and have chosen to base our chapter on our experience and expertise. While a chapter such as this might traditionally begin with a literature review, the pace of change in online learning has been so fast that we feel such a review would not be useful here. All of this is to say that our experience is located in a certain context, but we believe that what we present in this article is widely applicable across college environments.

THE STRUCTURES OF ONLINE LEARNING AT THE COLLEGE LEVEL: DID UNIVERSITIES CHANGE?

Until recently, online instruction at our institution was a small undertaking, with a few departments offering a handful of classes. There was considerable resistance to teaching online; most faculty strongly favored teaching face-to-face. Likewise, students took an occasional online class only if they needed to have the scheduling flexibility to allow an internship or to accommodate a scheduling conflict. Finally, there was a general sentiment that online instruction was inferior to in-person instruction. Faculty scoffed at online classes, and students assumed they would be easier.

All that changed when COVID-19 hit. In the short term, all faculty and students were forced to experience online classes. In the long term, attitudes toward online instruction changed dramatically. Now, many faculty and even larger numbers of students prefer to have classes online for the flexibility and creativity they offer. Our online classes fill first and have long waitlists, and faculty request to be allowed to teach online.

Yet we have not changed much else. In many respects, the university continues to view online classes as supplemental (that is, filling gaps in instruction) rather than as fully integrated into department and university curricula. Although many faculty and students have changed their minds about online education, other changes have not followed. There is a lag in building the structural support needed for a much more robust and sustained online presence. We suspect that this holds true for many other institutions. The current institutional structure does not reflect the much larger role that online instruction now plays at our university. The lack of support structure should be rectified if we want to continue to offer a significant portion of our courses online. This is a challenge for all schools, but smaller institutions with correspondingly small IT departments and lean budgets face an uphill battle.

RECOGNIZING ONLINE LEARNING AS A DISTINCTIVE ENTITY

There are many areas to consider when building this support; the first is academic structure and reporting. Rather than have online classes scattered throughout the university, there should be a dean or director of online instruction charged with oversight of all aspects of online delivery. Such a position would be akin to a dean for graduate studies or a director for accelerated programming. This dean or director would be a voice for those teaching online and would be charged with representing the interests and needs of students taking classes online.

One area this dean or director would be responsible for would be the onboarding of new online students. Before enrolling in their first online course, students would experience a centrally created and administered online skills evaluation and training. This orientation would cover such topics as study skills for online learning, common technical skills (for example, uploading a document), time management in online classes, and how to ask for help and find resources. Finally, students would be evaluated to ensure readiness—technically and otherwise—to take online classes. Once a student completed this online skills evaluation and training, she would be able to take any online course at the university. A shared, standardized orientation would eliminate the need to orient students every time they registered for a class. Some students have multiple online training sessions each semester that instructors have created. These are of varying quality, depth, and content. In addition, this duplication of efforts is a waste of time and energy for everyone involved. Ensuring that students have the necessary start-up skills would help everyone.

The dean or director of online learning would also be responsible for assessment, both of individual classes and of online learning at the university in general. Online classes should have questions on student evaluations that reflect the qualities of successful online teaching. Students should be asked to comment on the ease of navigation and the organization of each course. Students should evaluate the level of communication and feedback they received, and they should be asked about how well they connected with other students in the class. Students should also evaluate the specific online teaching materials used. Although there is overlap with student evaluations of face-to-face courses, online classes *do* have special qualities that should be evaluated. At the level of the university, the dean or director of online learning would be responsible for evaluating the quality and success of online delivery overall. Preparing yearly internal reports, as well as materials for outside evaluation (such as the Higher Learning Commission), would also be expected.

Establishing central oversight for online offerings would also allow for planned curricular delivery, with courses working as a structured organism. Such planned scheduling is particularly important in the general education courses that all students must take. Larger institutions have employed groups of instructional designers to

3

ensure cross-curricular design. Smaller ones—our own included—have no such plan in place. Some departments regularly offer a rich array of online classes every semester, during J-Term, and in the summer. Other areas rarely offer any classes online. Students who want or need to take classes online have their progress toward graduation negatively affected by this lack of overarching planning. Departments that offer online courses to satisfy general education requirements are inundated with students and struggle to find seats to satisfy the demand, while departments with scant online offerings leave students who need online courses in the lurch. A planned rotation of online offerings would address the issues facing both students and departments.

A dean or director of online instruction could be the point person to oversee student support for all other functions—bill paying, book buying, registering, etc. Online students need access to the registrar, to the bursar's office, and to all other services without having to come to campus. There are few universities that do this well, and online students are usually thought of as second-class citizens if they are thought of at all.

ONLINE EDUCATION AS A CAMPUS-WIDE INITIATIVE

A second area of structure that needs to take online learning into account is our committee structure. Committees that work with academic and curricular questions should include a faculty member who teaches online. An online instructor needs to be at the table when decisions are being made that could impact online teaching. This representative would specifically advocate for online students and understand policies and issues through the perspective of teaching and learning online. For example, a campus policy on attendance looks very different in an online class than in a face-to-face one. The timing of being given access to the learning management system (LMS) is critical for online classes, but less important for a face-to-face class. University policies about student access to email also have a much greater impact on a student in an online class than a student who attends in person. It is easy to miss these kinds of differences without a voice to remind us.

Another key structural change campuses experiencing growth in their online offerings should make is an investment in an instructional designer or a Center for Teaching and Learning (CTL) focused on online learning. An instructional designer or the CTL helps create a shared vocabulary around online teaching. For example, students and instructors on my campus have many different assumptions about what "online" means. Some students expect to meet in a Zoom session with all their classmates and their instructor and carry on in the same way they would in a face-to-face class. Other students expect to never have contact with their classmates and to work at their own pace. Disappointment and misunderstandings about expectations are widespread when a campus has no shared vocabulary to describe how online learning will be structured and delivered.

Similarly, a campus instructional designer can help create a standard shell on the LMS so that online classes have a consistent look and organization. Online students say they waste time and effort figuring out how each instructor has set up a class. Having materials organized consistently means that it is easy for students taking multiple online classes to navigate any class site.

PROFESSIONAL DEVELOPMENT

Professional development of online instructors would also be housed in the CTL. Those new to teaching online could look to the CTL for basic best practices, design coaching, and reviews of their courses. Ongoing support and training in more advanced software, coupled with continual review of courses, would benefit experienced teachers. The CTL could help instructors experiment with new methods and refine older ones.

The campus CTL would also be the source for researched, data-driven policies to help students succeed in online classes. These best practices and policies could then be used across campus, ensuring that students know what is expected of them and how course policies work. Navigating multiple conflicting policies in different courses leaves students unsure of the rules that could affect them. Finally, the CTL would be the home base for innovation in course delivery models. Two such models are discussed later in this chapter.

The last structural revision needed to support online teaching would take place in student affairs. Currently, student affairs work assumes a face-to-face course delivery and an on-campus student experience. Support for students in online classes is often scarce. Although obvious needs like providing online tutoring support are starting to be met, every way we support students who are on campus should be reexamined. For example:

- What kind of library research support do we provide for online students?
- What kinds of social activities do we plan for them? Do we have any cohorts organized to support online students?
- How do we encourage online students to meet friends? What extracurriculars and clubs do we have for online students?
- What academic support might be needed specifically to support students working online?

Trying to modify existing tools built to serve face-to-face students is not enough. Student affairs must look at online students as a key population worthy of targeted programming.

The Upside of Change

Innovative delivery may be the most important development in online teaching that we are missing when we lack structures for long-term strategic planning. When institutions try to make online teaching walk lockstep with how face-to-face classes are delivered, they leave valuable options on the table. Online delivery opens the door for creative solutions to issues that our students struggle with. For example, the traditional 16-week semester is often too long for students with families and other serious outside obligations—the very population most likely to take online classes. Online classes could be offered in 4-week, 6-week, or 8-week sessions. Intensive work over a shorter time might serve those students better.

Another possibility is allowing online students to earn credits as they go. For example, a student would register for a series of 1-credit classes rather than the traditional 3-credit course. Once she completes the work for the first credit, she earns that credit and it goes on her transcript. If she successfully continues to the second credit, she will then earn that credit. However, if she is unsuccessful in the second credit, she will not lose the first credit she had already "banked." Students frequently complete a large portion of a class, only to fail at the end of the semester. The failure happens for many reasons, but most often it happens because the student did not complete the final project or take the final exam. All the work, progress, and learning that such a student *has* completed fails to show on her academic record. This is not only discouraging, but also expensive. If students earned credits as they progressed, some of their progress could be captured. This kind of delivery could be disruptive in a face-to-face class, but it would work well in an online environment. This is simply one example of how learning in an online environment could be tailored to our students' needs. The CTL and online instructors on any campus should meet to design innovations in online delivery that best support their students.

A robust support system with the right people in administration, on committees, in instructional design, and in student affairs could shape online learning to better serve our students in ways that we have not even begun to discuss. It is time to start those discussions.

FACULTY GO ONLINE

When our university went online in the Spring semester, 2020, the two of us had the advantage of years of online teaching experience. Even so, the pressures everyone faced were enormous in scale, both professionally and personally. Like everyone else, we were concerned about our families and friends, our elderly community, and the world at large. Our first instinct was to try to help our students stay safe, continue in school, and make something of the rest of the semester academically. Faculty at our institution who had never taught online faced far greater hurdles. It was, as the saying goes, "trial by fire." It no longer mattered if one wanted to teach online; the only thing to do was adapt.

It is nearly impossible to get by as an academic in the modern world without using some computer technology. Nonetheless, we were surprised at how unfamiliar some of our faculty were with technology and how resistant some were to moving fully online. Many of our faculty had only used our LMS to do the bare minimum requirements (post a syllabus and keep attendance), and a small few didn't even use the computer for that—and now, they were asked to go fully online. What many did was find a way to give lectures as they usually would, but from their home, and upload assessments. Luckily, we had a number of faculty with significant online experience who were able to help. Some of us offered open sessions for questions. Our IT and instructional designer offered significant help to those who needed it, and somehow, like the rest of the academic world, students continued to learn.

The dangers of COVID-19 aside, of course, we believed that this influx of new online learning would alter minds and hearts about the efficacy of online teaching and there would be an explosion of creative solutions and new approaches. In some cases, that did happen. After another year into the pandemic, though, we saw many instructors still plodding along, trying to teach in online spaces the same way they taught face-to-face. Moreover, in our estimation, the faculty at our university are some of the most talented and dedicated teachers we know. We were sympathetic to how highly successful face-to-face instructors would not want to leave their well-honed strategies behind. It was logical that in the face of so many changes, they would be even more reluctant to try new things. After all, they used best practices, wrote fantastic lectures, and delivered them convincingly and with passion: why not keep doing this in an online space?

Everyone was doing their best under difficult circumstances, but it led us to question how academics were, or were not, embracing online best practices. For some context, until last year neither of us had ever given a full-length lecture in an online class, even though we had already taught online for twenty years. When we started, the technology was frankly not good enough, even if one wanted to produce and upload a full-length lecture. In the case of Julie's history courses, her pedagogical intuition suggested that live online lectures wouldn't work either. She saw how long lectures could be difficult to listen to, even for those who appreciate them and enjoy the content. However, faculty insisted that online lectures were, in fact, working and seemed to feel that other options would not be as effective. Thus, Julie tried them. While putting a Latin American history course online for the time, she thought: "Maybe I have misjudged online lectures? Perhaps I needed to take my own advice, reflect on my bias and try something new?" Julie did try it, and it was an enormous mistake. It was impossible to force every student to have their camera on during live lectures, much less to have them participate. Even the well-intentioned participants started losing focus after 20 minutes, and Julie felt like she was droning. She teaches interesting material, and does it well, but she knew her online format was bad pedagogy, even though it was the same lecture for which she would get a great response in a face-to-face setting. This is not to say that students won't learn anything from an online lecture: many can and will. It is, however, fair to ask whether reproducing teaching approaches that work well in face-to-face classes is the best pedagogical answer to delivering content in online spaces.

Excellence in online teaching can come in many forms, but we believe there are some general tips that make for strong online teaching.

- Put yourself in your students' chairs. Imagine you are at the computer, taking a class. Try to conceptualize the space as they would. If you keep this viewpoint, it will help guide your choices for content delivery and assessments.
- Create an orientation packet specific to your course in addition to a traditional syllabus. This is particularly crucial is your institution does not have a general orientation to online learning. Don't assume that students know how learn online. Provide links to resources that discuss tips for successful online learning and get the class thinking about the digital space as unique and valuable.
- Make sure your student learning outcomes can be achieved in the online space. Just as you work back from an end goal in a face-to-face class, do the same for your online course. What are you trying to achieve, and what is the best way to get there? Additionally, keep an open mind to alternative media. You are not boxed in to only using a discussion forum or a file upload.
- Student attention spans are about 20-30 minutes. If a lecture is the best way to teach certain content, then try to make lectures that are about this length. In other words, choose your online content wisely.
- Use the tools you have at your disposal—don't reinvent the wheel! The class is still yours, but if there is a great podcast or short video on one of the topics you cover, then use it. A variety of material and media helps maintain student interest and engagement. It has the added benefit of offering content

in different ways to students who might learn better by listening or viewing images. As the instructor, you curate such material and contextualize it for your students.

- If you are going to use an additional app or software, make sure it is worth the time both you and your students will invest in learning how to use it. If it is difficult to use and you are only going to use it once, maybe it isn't the right choice. Connect any significant investment in software or other applications to a learning outcome so that students understand its importance.

- Be present. One of the hardest balancing acts is the use of your time as a faculty member. The grading can quickly become the only way you interact with students, which is not the best relationship builder. You might make a regular announcement on the weekly agenda or send an inspirational quote or a silly comic. If most students do well on a particular assignment, send a message praising their work.

- Check in often and elicit real feedback. For example, do a check every two or three weeks as part of a participation grade. Some sample questions are: 1) How do you feel the course is going? 2) How can you improve your study habits? 3) Is there anything I can do as the instructor to help you succeed in this class? Students appreciate the ability to be heard and to feel that you care about them as individuals. These check ins can head off major issues before they gain ground, and students often have excellent suggestions for improving the class as well. If you grade them as complete or incomplete, it does not consume too much time.

- Have high standards and demand good work, but also give grace to students and yourself. Sometimes a link won't work, an assignment date will be wrong, or a student's computer will actually crash—for real. Have a good technology policy for what happens if the whole system goes down or an individual student's computer crashes. Allow students one penalty-free mistake in the semester if they miss a due date or get confused.

Faculty new to online teaching might only try one or two of these suggestions at a time. The important thing is to frequently and thoughtfully reassess your strategies.

During COVID-19, once faculty grappled with the new technological demands, considered their fears surrounding them, and made decisions about content delivery and assessment techniques, the next looming question became how to ensure academic integrity in an online class. For most faculty, this concern came late in the semester, often only after academic dishonesty had occurred in their class. For those with experience teaching online, it is clear that cheating will occasionally happen and cannot always be 100% prevented. It is also clear that some of the techniques faculty employ might even inadvertently encourage poor academic behavior. Yet, there *are* strategies to limit cheating. Here some ideas for good course design elements that encourages students to do their own work online.

1. Write unique assignments that encourage individual work.

Sample 1: Rather than asking students to analyze the role that the fool plays in Shakespeare's play *King Lear*, ask them to compare the fool to a contemporary comedian and consider the subversive roles that comedy can play. The first assignment (analyze the role of the fool) is a classic, but it opens the doors for plagiarized and purchased papers. The second assignment—because it is more unique—is much less likely to produce academic dishonesty.

Sample 2: Rather than having students write an essay analyzing the decline of the British Empire, have them write from the perspective of someone living in the Empire. Again, the second assignment is unlikely to pave an easy path to purchasable papers, and thus will head off the temptation to cheat.

2. Avoid purely objective assessments that rely on matching, multiple choice, and fill-in-the-blanks, as these are notoriously easy to cheat on. Instead, ask students to apply knowledge of the content area.

Sample: Rather than having students in a geography class take a traditional map quiz, have them describe places in relationship to one another.

Sample: Rather than having students in a linguistics class take a quiz on phonological problems, have them design a made-up language that demonstrates a particular rule.

3. You have to regularly change up and refresh the assessments that you created, preferably completing a significant revision each semester. Avoid entirely using online assessments produced by others as well as exams and assessment provided by publishing companies; they are readily available for students.

4. If your university has anti-cheating software, carefully consider the pros and cons of using it. While such programs can be useful in ferreting out plagiarism, they can also create undue and counterproductive stress for students who are trying to follow the rules. In particular, test surveillance programs can be difficult for students who lack private space for test taking.

While cheating is a regular occurrence in online classes, it also occurs in face-to-face instruction. What is perhaps most concerning is the effect that cheating has on honest students who find themselves working much harder than others for worse grades. It is demoralizing, and over the course of a semester, repeatedly subjecting students to the temptation to easily cheat is simply wrong. Students should not have to think all the time about whether or not they want to, or should, cheat. The more they are tempted, the more likely it is that cheating will occur. Moreover, it is both exciting and rewarding to create unique assignments and good course design, which has the added bonus of staving off dishonesty.

Good course design is pivotal to effective online teaching and learning. Good intentions can never be a substitute for thoughtful pedagogy. As faculty continue to refine their online offerings, they should consider seeking mentorship from other faculty and campus resources such as instructional designers. They should also be wary of giving into the temptation to simply "put" a class online. Most importantly, reflect often your pedagogical choices and keep an open mind.

STUDENTS GO ONLINE IN RESPONSE TO THE PANDEMIC

When the pandemic started, faculty rushed to accommodate the needs of their institutions and their students, and the first half semester online was necessarily an ad hoc situation. The questions that needed immediate answers were largely about infrastructure and LMS training. Not all students had access to computers much less access to high-speed internet. At our institution, great strides were made to help students obtain access to the technology they needed, but worldwide, the need to learn remotely revealed widespread technological inequity. Now lacking high-speed internet was not just an inconvenience for students, it meant that they could not learn. While the digital divide is still great, the attention brought to the issue has led to increased funding for reliable internet and computer access. More colleges and universities are making computers part of student aid packages and many colleges also have wireless hotspots available.

Even as our university focused successfully on meeting the *hardware and software* technology needs of our students, there was huge influx of students and faculty who were novices at online *instruction and learning*. Even if students had done "online" learning in high school, the term has come to encompass so many types of instruction as to lose all real meaning. Just because a student can do *some* things online, doesn't mean that student is prepared to fully participate in a college-level online class. Meeting the challenges of this transition proved to be more complex than simply making the technology available. The following is a short list of topics that this massive transition to digital learning raised, followed by some ideas on how to improve how we handle them going forward.

Students are not really Tech Savvy

We are often told that our students know so much more than we do about being online. In one sense, this is true. They are aware of social media sites, how to post about their lives and hobbies in different ways, and how to use popular apps. While we grew up in a world where homes didn't have computers, they have been online all of their lives. And yet, we have had many students unable to upload an assignment, take a screenshot, or insert a hyperlink. These are all necessary skills in an online class. What this means is that faculty should build instructions into assignments when it calls for a particular digital skill, rather than assuming all their student come with computer competencies. Here are two samples of how to do this.

Sample One

Getting ready. This assignment serves as an effective orientation for students. At our institution, faculty quickly realized that everyone could use a good orientation to our LMS and to online learning generally. Many universities have general orientations for students and faculty, and that is a great first step. We would go a step further. Whatever skills you are going to require regularly of your students should be taught in the first week of class through your orientation. For example, we know that we are going to have students post in discussions forums, upload documents and images, and take quizzes. In our orientation packet, students complete the introduction post above that includes an avatar, photo, or other image that represents something about their identity. They also create a schedule for their course work and upload it as a word document. And finally, they take a quiz on the salient points of the syllabus. In the first few days they demonstrate that they can complete the technical submission processes the class demands.

Sample Two

Keep help close at hand. It is possible that students have never made or uploaded a video before. This assignment makes sure that all necessary instruction is included in the prompt. Students can click on the link to get help with making or uploading their video. Embedding these helpful links means that you can keep instructions in one place and not repeat them in every assignment. You might link back to a portion of your syllabus or to a special section created in the LMS. That way, students who are familiar with the skills needed can simply proceed, but those who are not ready can easily find the path forward. By making instructions accessible, faculty support student success.

There can never be too many ways or too many places to put instructions.

We know that students learn in different ways. They also seem to *see* directions in different ways. We have been teaching online for twenty years, and we are still amazed when students tell us that they can't find the directions to a given assignment. This amazes us because we put them in the syllabus, in the assignment box, on the assignment page when the box is opened, and in an email the week before the assignment is due. As an instructor, it would be easy to become disgruntled, even offended, when students still claim to be unable to find directions. But, students learn and see in different ways. We now also provide instructions through a recorded message that students can click on and on the course announcement page. The point is, put the directions in many different places and in different formats. It will save you time and reduce student frustration.

When Students get Frustrated, They Quit

We are often frustrated when students do not take the initiative to ask questions or persevere in looking for answers when they find that something is not immediately clear. It is important to remember that in an online class there more physical barriers between the faculty and the students, so students cannot simply come up after class and ask. And, they have to go through more steps in a digital space to get where they need to be to complete the work. Making the path from initial assignment to completion as smooth as possible is really important to student success. While faculty likely feel that they are always available and open to helping students, student perception might be that the instructor is intimidating, or they might tell themselves they are only ones having trouble and so they should just give up. Undoubtedly this happens in face-to-face classes as well, but there the faculty can more readily see the difficulty or frustration and address it immediately in real time. Students online may sit with their frustrations or sense of failure for days without the faculty knowing or sensing that there is a problem. Testing all aspects of a course from the student view to catch and address any missing or broken links or other problems is key. Reaching out right away to a student who misses an assignment is critical to reducing the time that the student experiences the kinds of frustration that leads to disengagement or even non-retention.

Online Time is Different than Face-To-Face Time

Time is indeed relative and shaped by individual perception. Structuring a face-to-face class is significantly easier than managing time online. This is the case for many reasons, but primarily because when people are occupying digital space, they use time differently. For the most part, academia schedules class time in 1-2 hour increments, with the occasional longer lab or accelerated course. Online attention spans are different. Think of the last time you were completing a task online. Did you think of the number of clicks it took to accomplish said task or think about how quickly you moved through screens, giving each only a cursory glance? Students utilize digital space very quickly. They scan social media sites, giving each entry perhaps a second or two and then move on to the next. They do not sit and read long articles, instead scanning headlines, skimming bulleted lists, and moving as quickly as possible through screen. We have noticed that even a two-hour movie is too long for students' attention spans online. As faculty, then we have two options. We could try to force students to conform to face-to-face time management, or we can meet them in the middle. We have had far more success with the latter option. We suggest that you try chunking assignments into half hour intervals. Use a series of sources in different media, rather than one longer piece so that students can complete an assignment a bit at a time. If you do have students read a longer portion or watch a longer video, give them ways to break it up throughout the week. We also found that coding each assignment to indicate how long it would take to complete helps students. Assigning a mix of shorter (under 10 minute) pieces with mid (10-20 minute) and longer (20-30 minute) assignments helps our students plan and use their time effectively.

Example

Give options when possible. When I assign a longer documentary, I break it up into 30-minute segments and give students the option of submitting handwritten notes. Structuring an assignment this way, gives students the option to leave the computer and occupy a more traditional space with pen and paper. Assigning just the first half of the film, allows students to focus for a shorter period of time. This also suits students who have active family and work lives and may need to complete homework in several shorter stints. Having the option of uploading photos or scans of notes also gives them a break from typing responses and activates different parts of the brain. In this case the format of the assignment submission is not important to the learning objective.

When Practical, Allow Students Different Options for Assignment Submissions

Maintaining student focus and engagement is also key to a successful online class. In the early days of online teaching there were not many options for assignments. Instructors could plan a very traditional discussion forum and students could submit word documents. Now, most LMSs have much more capacity for variety. Allowing students to submit photos of handwritten work, or letting them create a podcast instead of writing a paper offers solutions to many barriers to student success. Students often try to complete online courses by using only their phones and campus computers, particular students already struggling with structural inequities. One way to make things easier for them is to have some work that can be completed offline. For example, we have had great success with students submitting their hand-written notes on short readings. They can print at school or read on their phones, and then take notes on paper or on the reading itself and submit photos. We offer this option on almost every reading that we can and at least a third of students submit using this method. Offering creative options like a podcast or a video can engage those who either have more access or more interest in using other technologies. Either way, we can see that students have picked out the salient points of the text; the format of this assignment submission makes no difference.

IF YOU ARE TEACHING IN THE ONLINE FORMAT, USE THE INTERNET!

There is a great hesitancy on the part of many faculty members to encourage students to use the internet for research. They insist that the internet isn't the answer to everything. And, they are absolutely right. However, we cannot get over the idiosyncrasy of saying to a student, "I want you to take a fully online class, but go to the physical library to do all of your work." Not only does it not make sense, it will not actually happen. Moreover, without guidance, our students are not really that much better at using the library effectively. The hesitation to use online research also speaks of our unwillingness to embrace new modes of producing and accessing academic material. Some of this bias is understandable. The internet is full of bad information, sometimes willfully bad information. But that only makes it more necessary that we teach students to navigate it effectively. Our response shouldn't be, "Internet, bad! Books, good!" It should be, "let me show you how to find reliable information." In the avalanche of information that the average internet search brings up on page one, students need instruction in how to separate the wheat from the chaff. Assessing information for reliability is a critical skill for future generations. We would go so far as to say it is a civic moral duty to teach students to find reliable information online. It might be the greatest contribution good online education makes to society at large.

CONCLUSION

Online Education Can Be Good or Bad. It Is What We Make It

As we argued earlier, just as in the face-to-face environment, the online space is based on a relationship between the teacher and the students. It is about fostering the effective communication of ideas and the ability to assess student learning outcomes.

Chapter 2
Engaging Students Through Creative Assignments and Best Practices

Julie Tatlock
Mount Mary University, USA

Paula J. Reiter
Mount Mary University, USA

Stepanka C. Korytova-Magstadt
Mount Mary University, USA

ABSTRACT

This chapter offers several models teachers can use to better engage students in content through the use of creative assignments. It begins with the importance of effective online orientation and building student learning outcomes specific to online classes. That is followed by examples of how to use the traditional discussion forum in new ways to encourage true intellectual exchange. The chapter ends with a series of sample creative assignments that help students personalize and fully integrate complex content.

INTRODUCTION

As stated in the opening chapter, there is not only one way to create effective online spaces. This chapter models the ideas in the opening work and offers practical solutions to some of the issues raised therein. It is intended to be a resource and a place to start for those wishing to improve their online offerings.

DOI: 10.4018/978-1-6684-4055-1.ch002

Copyright © 2023, IGI Global. Copying or distributing in print or electronic forms without written permission of IGI Global is prohibited.

Creating an Effective Orientation Module (Julie C. Tatlock, PhD)

It is important to remember that while students have ample experience with social media online, they have far less skill doing the kinds of work required in a fully online course. In a fully asynchronous online class, it is essential to evaluate students' technological abilities and teach them what they need to successfully navigate the class. Even if your university benefits from an organized LMS orientation through an instructional design team, you still should invest the time to create an orientation specific to your class. While students might be used to a paper syllabus, I go with a fully integrated orientation module in my LMS. In my mind such a syllabus module forces students into the digital space right away.

ORIENTATION MODULE

Introductions and Discussion Forum

Humanize yourself as the faculty member. In a face-to-face class, you may want to ensure that student's respect your authority from the first moment, while in an online class, you might already seem quite distant to students. I suggest finding a way to make yourself feel less remote by using an introduction forum. Ask students to offer a unique representation of an aspect of their personality. It might be an avatar, a song, an animal they relate to, or an art piece they create. Also consider requiring that they choose a student learning outcome that most resonates with them. This assignment also ensures that can use the discussion forum from a technical standpoint. The faculty should be present in this opening but in a simple way. You might like a students' post or comment quickly on the outcome they chose. Make this initial assignment low stakes, perhaps even a simple complete/incomplete grade.

Student Learning Outcomes, Expectations, and Submitting a Work Calendar

As Student Learning Outcomes (SLOs) are our main goals for the course, I want to make sure students take some time to think about them. It is helpful to list each goal and connect that goal with a specific assessment. For example, one of my SLOs says that students will learn to use digital information in a sophisticated and academic way. In a chart, I connect this to where in the course this will happen. While the humanities generally shies away from emphasizing work skills, I do not. I think that our courses already prepare students for future employment and pointing it out simply makes it clear.

Students are also given the expectations for course engagement—what it really means to "show up" in an asynchronous class. I have moved away from the word, "participation," as it no longer conveys the way I want students to think about being a part of an online space. The digital world is now the metaphorical four walls of the classroom. They should visit it regularly, there should be different activities to engage them, and they should learn to treat it with respect. It is also quite true that if you do not assess a class item, many students won't complete it. Here again, using a complete/incomplete can be a useful tool. You may also consider using course engagement as extra credit. Perhaps if a student completes 75% of the supplemental offerings, they receive a significant bonus at the end of the course.

To get students thinking about online interactions, they are exposed to the idea of Netiquette. There are many online sources faculty can link to for this as it has been around a long time. I use the following set of statements:

When working online in a professional capacity, it is important to use formal communication. Here are some general guidelines:

- Treat everyone with respect.
- Use respectful language. While you will not always be doing formal academic writing, please avoid using colloquial language or language that might be offensive.
- Avoid hyperbole in your writing as it can be difficult to discern mood online.
- As people cannot see your body language or hear inflection, make sure you are explicit in your writing.
- Ask questions before assuming anything about another student's writing. If you feel something is offensive, ask for clarification or explanation. If you feel anything is inappropriate, contact your instructor write away.

A calendar of assignments is provided in this section. I also give list of assignment expectations and what they are worth to the overall course grade. Students are then required to submit a work calendar for the semester. The Assignment looks like this:

How much time do you think you will need to dedicate to your classes this term. Remember that online learning needs to spaced out. You should not try to complete all work in one sitting and you should take frequent breaks to walk, stretch, relax, etc. I would suggest at least three separate times for working on the week's material. Please present a calendar/plan for your work. Assume you will need at least three separate occasions of quality work time 1-2 hours each. You can present your plan anyway you like--screenshot, online calendar, photos of a planner book.

Students have actually thanked me for making them do this as it helps them conceptualize the space and time of their online classes in relations to the rest of their schedule. If time management issues begin, you can refer back to their initial calendar as a reference point for this conversation. Students also learn how to upload assignments to the LMS.

Campus-Related Statements and Student Services and the Syllabus Module Quiz

In the final orientation page, I list the required materials given by the university administration to include, such as mission and vision statements, and ADA requirements. But, I follow this with links and phone numbers to student support services, including the library, tutoring services, and counselling service. At the end of this module is a quiz on the orientation packet. I use a series of open-ended questions rather than multiple choice as it gives more opportunities to share concerns. I ask them, for example, what skills they bring to the table and what they may need to work on to be successful. I also ask if they have initial questions and concerns.

Learning Online

After all of this skill building and orientation, I have a module that asks students to take a look at a few links pertaining to what it means to learn online, the skills students need to cultivate to be effective, and general tips for success. Just as faculty need to think about the digital space as unique and design courses based on best practices, students should also be introduced to online learning in a deliberate way. It can help dispel myths about online classes, such as they are easier than face to face ones, and simply offer a way to discuss their successes and challenges from a shared understanding of what teaching and learning looks like in online spaces.

This type of online orientation rather than a traditional syllabus has the following attributes:

1. It gets students used to the online space as unique from the first day.
2. It engages students in the technology and ensures that can use what it is needed for success in the course. If you use other outside technology, you should include it here with an accompanying assessment as well. Remember that you should only use outside apps if they are used often.
3. You will find out right away if there are students who are having issues with technology, either because they aren't sure how to use it or that don't have the access they need to it.

4.   You can provide links to resources so that when issues arise later in the course, you can refer students back to various sections of the orientation to review.

5.   The quick, low-stakes assessments in the orientation build confidence and a relationship with the instructor in the first week.

STUDENT ENGAGEMENT ONLINE: RETHINKING THE TRADITIONAL DISCUSSION FORUM

When I first began teaching online over fifteen years ago, the discussion forum was the primary way of "engaging" students in the online space. Born out of a desire to maintain some sort of Socratic exchange, such forums seemed to preserve that which faculty hold so dear about face-to-face instruction, the free exchange of ideas in an academic environment. The instructor would write a prompt based on class resources and students would respond both to the prompt and to one another thus simulating a lively class discourse. In theory, that is a great idea. In practice, however, it usually fails at the main thing it is meant to achieve, true intellectual exchange. All too often, each response is virtually the same and when students respond to one another they usually write a simple statement of agreement. It is time to rethink how we use discussions in our online classes.

There are more ways now for students to communicate in online classes. Chat apps and video calls provide for real time exchanges and most LMS platforms allow for group spaces, where small collaborations can happen. And, yet, many still use the discussion forum to fulfill those functions as well as for working with course content. Student Learning outcomes thus become muddled. Faculty must first decide the purpose of the discussion forum and then use best practices to achieve that goal.

At the same time my frustration with the static and boring forums that I produced reach a peak, I was also thinking about ways to transform how and why students write in humanities courses. At my institution, humanities departments generally have small numbers of majors and primarily run classes for our core curriculum. These are students who will not major in my discipline and not write lengthy research papers in my field. They still need to learn how to research and write effectively, but in their future careers they will largely be writing digitally via email and presentations. I was no longer sure that a traditional term paper was achieving the outcomes I desired, particularly given the level of plagiarism in recent years. As these pedagogical strands came together, I began to think of the discussion forum as a focus for the changes I wanted to make.

MODEL 1: THE RESEARCH FORUM

Some of the key goals of a traditional research paper in the humanities are to:

1. Foster a student's ability to generate an original argument.
2. Teach students how to find and use reliable source material.
3. Model how a student can build an argument based on evidence in a specific content field.
4. Encourage good writing through critical thinking, reflection and revision.
5. Cite materials according to a given discipline's style.

These same goals can be achieved in the discussion forum setting. Rather than assigning one long research essay scaffolded throughout the semester, try building a research-based discussion forum series that **also** teaches the following digital skills:

1. Obtaining reliable source material online. Or, using online information in a sophisticated way.
2. Engaging a reader effectively in the digital environment.
3. Responding to others appropriately in a professional online space.

Sample Assignment

Throughout this course, students will work on a research-based discussion forum series on a topic related to course content. Please see the course calendar for relevant due dates:

Discussion Forum One

Initial Student Post

Find six reliable, academic sources online. (For instructions on finding good online sources, refer the orientation packet). These sources may be in any media, but must meet the standards established for reliability. You will write a post that provides an abstract for each source, including but not limited to, specific authorship and why the author is reliable on the topic, an assessment of bias, and a paragraph about how this source will help you research content and/or make an argument.

Response Post

Choose **two** students in the class (please start with students who do not yet have a response), and critique their source options adding two new reliable, academic sources that you find on their topic.

Summation

Review the replies to your own post and summarize where you fell you are at in your research, where you might be week, and how you can fill any gaps that exist in your source material.

Intermediary Assignment

Submit your notes on each source listed in your first discussion forum and any additional materials you have added based on your fellow students' critiques and your own further research.

Discussion Forum Two

Initial Student Post: Write a post that includes the main argument you will be making about your content based on the source material you have reviewed. Explain how each source will support your view and write a draft of your opening remarks. Your post should have a minimum of 1000 words.

Response Post

Choose **two different students** and critique their argument. You must offer meaningful and specific points of agreement and of constructive criticism. Your response posts should have a minimum of 300 words.

Summation

Offer a reflection on your work thus far that includes comments referring to your fellow students' critiques.

Discussion Forum Three

Initial Student Post: Prepare a post (in traditional written form, a podcast, or creative presentation) that effectively teaches your fellow students about your topic.

Requirements

- must make use of at least four of the sources you found in your research
- must make an argument and convey content effectively
- must be professionally presented regardless of chosen media
- must be cited according to MLA or Chicago style

Response Post

Write a reflection on how effectively the student conveyed their content. While this is an opinion piece, please offer constructive criticism based on what you have learned about online writing over the course of this class.

Summary: Each student will write a final summary reflecting on their experience of this project. What did you find enjoyable? What skills did you build throughout the assignments? How would change the assignment for future students? What advice would you give future students?

MODEL TWO: THE CREATIVE POST

Another option to engage students that might work better in freshman and sophomore courses is the creative post. Have the students take on a character and write from that perspective, have them write a poem or letter to someone based on content, or find a way to have them connect the content they have learned with something expected. Not only will this help them personalize and retain material, it also helps everyone avoid dealing with issues of plagiarism. It might be easy, for example, to cut and paste an answer about Hamlet's style of leadership, but it would be harder to find something to use in an advice letter from Hamlet to Macbeth. The first two samples might be used in a survey course with first or second-year students. the idea is for students to make new connections using course content to demonstrate analysis and writing. The third sample might be used in an upper level course with more requirements for source work and critical analysis.

Sample Assignment One

This assignment is from an Early American history course and asks students to work with the very earliest of human societies

For your first discussion forum, you will be writing a letter to your descendants. You should choose a character from one of the civilizations we have covered so far and write a letter telling future generations about your life. You might tell them what a day would be like for you, what you believe to be great about your civilization, what your civilization's struggles are. You may be as creative as you wish, but you must stay true to the civilization and character you choose. You should also consult two additional online sources. These sources should be academic sources, i.e., museum web sites, sites hosted by universities or academics, government archival sources, etc. You will be graded on your sources as well as your post. Your post should be at least 600 words.

Sample Assignment Two

Travel Blog for the Ancient World Post

Come to My Empire!!!

For your second discussion forum, you will be writing a travel blog for your chosen Empire/Civilization. If you, as the Minister of Ancient Tourism, were trying to attract visitors, what you emphasize about your homeland. You could speak to the sites, the religion, the leadership, the goods that are available, etc. You should have two additional, **academic,** sources. Your initial post should be 600 words.

Like the last post, you should speak in character and from the time period.

You should respond to at least two other students. You should respond to one student as to why you would love to see their empire and one as to why you would never go there. You should include one additional source in each response. Each response should be 200 words.

Sample Assignment Three

Upper Level History Course on the British Empire

Throughout the semester you will be writing three discussion posts that follow a character in the British Empire. You will choose someone like, a poor single woman, a clergyman, a soldier, or a wealthy heiress. The first post will be written in character from the Early Modern Era, the second from a similar character in the nineteenth century, and the final post will consider the character in the era of decolonization. The posts will each be in the form of a letter to a relative.

Requirements:

- At least 1000 words per post
- Four quality, academic sources must be cited.
- Two primary sources should be used in each post
- You will be assessed on the period qualities of your piece.
- You should at least make the effort to bring creativity to your piece.

Creative Assignments in Literature (Dr. Paula Reiter)

Sample Assignment One

Project 2: Ephron's "What I Will Miss" and "What I Won't Miss"
   Due by 11:59 on Wednesday, June 22. Upload as a Word document in Canvas-Assignments.

"Sometimes I think that not having to worry about your hair anymore is the secret upside of death." Nora Ephron

   Nora Ephron (1941-2012), an award-winning screenwriter, journalist, and noted humorist, faced death with grace and wit. She made two lists: things she will miss and things she won't miss. First, read her piece, Then, for this project, I would like you to make the same two lists. (Warning: I have done this and it is much harder than it looks, so take your time to think about it, and have a box of tissues nearby.)

SAMPLES OF ONLINE BEST PRACTICES AND CREATIVE/INNOVATIVE ASSIGNMENTS (STEPANKA KORYTOVA-MAGSTADT, PH.D.)

I will list the following from the simplest ones to the more complicated ones.

1.   I give extra points for students attending my office hours during the first two weeks of classes. They are offered via Zoom. They are voluntary. I want to meet to the students live, and I also want them to know that I am not a robot and I offer clarification of all the assignments.
2.   The goal of my writing assignments to be authentic and practical. All the assignment have a link to "how to write..." and I also refer to the Purdue Writing Lab for further information. I explain why it is necessary to keep the word limit.

They are:
   a. A meaningful paragraph – eight sentences maximum
   i. A description of this assignment from the syllabus: **A Meaningful Paragraph**: Step 1: Decide the Topic of Your **Paragraph**. Step 2: Develop a Topic Sentence. Step 3: Demonstrate Your Point. Step 4: Give Your Paragraph Meaning. Step 5: Conclude. Step 6: Look Over and Proofread. The first "meaningful paragraph" will

be graded as follows: 5% for the draft + 5% for the rewrite. The length: at least 8 sentences.

3.   A letter to a friend – no more than three to four paragraphs.

a. Write a letter to a friend about an article on migration that you have read in the Guardian newspaper. State what the article is about, your reaction to the content of the article (did you detect any author's biases - what were they?) and why you think the content of the article is important enough for your friend to read it as well. 250 words (one page double spaced). Submit this assignment using Word or PDF format, in Canvas, by the due date and time identified.

4.   A reflection paper – up to 300 words. I state that I will read only the first 300 words.

a. **Reflection paper**: Start by **writing** a few sentences that are relevant to your main theme. Use these as a sort of summary of the rest of your notes. From there, jot down ideas and thoughts that relate to this theme. Remember, that the idea of a **reflection paper** is to present your own opinions, so keep this in mind while brainstorming. Length: 300 words maximum (only the first 300 words will be read), write the word count at the end of your paper.

5.   A newspaper article – up to 500 words. This assignment is only given after the class has read a number of newspaper articles. I assign this as the final paper. I used this assignment for an article on immigration.

i. *Many (not all) papers have a 500-word limit for staff-written stories, unless the subject calls for more. Understand, much longer than 500 words, and people skim or skip the story. In traditional (paper) newspapers, space = paper = money. Your newspaper article has to be no less 450 and no more than 500 words maximum.* End of the text from the course syllabus.

ii. Who are you going to interview? If you do not know anyone in your family and relatives who you think can be interviewed, look elsewhere: at this school, your friends, there are many ethnic and immigrant organizations in Milwaukee; their members would be happy to talk to you and tell you their story. You might be asked to change their name to protect their privacy, but that is OK. You may also consider interviewing your school mates, your teachers, I certainly will be honored if you chose me to be interviewed.

iii. I provide some sample immigrant stories.

6.   Finally, I like to ask students to reflect on assignments and the course; what could they have done differently in their final assignment, for example.

FINAL PROJECT FOR A SOCIOLOGY COURSE (STEPANKA KORYTOVA-MAGSTADT, PH.D.)

This project is suitable for any kind of community-based course or a service learning course where a shift of thinking about a global issue, and an action locally are expected from the students. At Mount Mary University the leadership believes that students should be involved in being the agents/advocates of a change on their campus and in their communities.

The idea came to me when I was asked to be the Director of Global Studies at Semester at Sea in Fall 2019. I think a student group collaboration is desirable in academic setting as it is a tool they will utilize in their professional life.

The learning outcome of this project is for the students to imagine that they are presenting their project in front of a donor who may or may support their project using the skills they have learnt in the course: discussion, reflection, focusing on a thesis statement etc.

Students are guided during this process by the instructor. In the first module I list the due dates of each assignment so the students may plan how they will proceed.

Each assignment is preceded by a **discussion** within each group on how they are going to proceed, what issue they are going to address, whose skills are useful for what part of the project etc. This discussion is either written or videotaped.

Here are the main assignments:

- **Pitching the Project**. Students may choose a "Call to Action", and NGO, and a Social Media. See the attached document
- **Storyboard/screenplay** for the project
- **A draft version of the video**
- **Video**. 3-4 minutes.

A comprehensive rubric for the final project is provided to the students at the beginning of the course (the rubric is result of collaboration with Courtenay Biser-Suarez and Shannon Rushe, Semester at Sea, Fall 2019, CSU).

If students need to I meet with them synchronously over Zoom.

I also provide a peer evaluation form for each of the member to fill in. The evaluations affect the grade of each of the students.

Sources for the course: assigned readings, media, and websites, for example: https://actionguide.localfutures.org/actors/community-groups

ENVIRONMENTALLY SUSTAINABLE COMMUNITIES

Video Project Meeting

Group _____ -

Names of Group Members:

Non-profit Call to Action Social Media Campaign

What is your idea/topic? What impact do you intend for it to have?

What aspects of the readings (in SOC 363 or in your other courses) are related to your idea?

What sources are you using (readings, personal interviews, etc.)?

Have you thought about which types of images/videos/interviews/etc. do you plan on using?

Evaluation (by the Instructor):

Pitch Presentation

Performance Level:

1. Needs Improvement: Students did not complete a pitch presentation or do not have a clear, agreed upon vision for their project.
2. Satisfactory: Students complete the pitch presentation on time. Students either do not have a clear vision or do not agree upon vision for their project.
3. Excellent: Students completed the pitch presentation on time. Pitch is thorough and group has a clear vision for their project.

Additional Notes/Feedback:

Video Project

Purpose Statement:

To identify a change in your values/attitudes/behaviors as a global citizen and a community organizer that can have an impact on your interaction with others and/or the environment and to create a well-researched, digestible piece of media to call others to action.

Learning Outcomes:

1. Recognize the opportunities to act as a global/local citizen with capacity to improve the health and welfare of others, and the sustainability of the Earth's systems.

2. Think ethically about global and local issues, inequalities, and your impact in the world and your community.
3. Critically analyze the history and diversity of your own community, home country and its role in the world.

Description:

In this group project you will demonstrate how successfully you recognized that an issue you encountered triggered a personal, affective response, to the point where an important change in attitude and subsequent behavior was incorporated into your value system and interactions. You will demonstrate these changes by creating a three- to four-minute (points will be deducted for going over time) video about your organization/ action group/advocacy group espousing a carefully thought out and researched action plan addressing one community concern leading to: an improvement of life(s), the health and welfare of others or sustainability of the Earth's systems. Your video should include a well thought out argument in support of your plan, incorporating your research, information from readings, and other relevant sources. You should also discuss how your own views have changed as a result of your experiences and learning in the project. In other words, you'll be describing both the research behind your ideas and the personal attitudes and values gained. A mobile phone or a camera is recommended to be used for this project.

Process:

Video Project (3 Components)

a. Read relevant passages from the readings provided by the instructor
b. Carry out literature searches and communicate effectively with others in your group by way of online discussions in Canvas.
c. Evaluate the credibility and relevance of sources
d. Look for further evidence, talk to as many individuals as possible. Record or take photos of your interactions and conversations with others that are relevant to your change in view/value/behavior/etc. Keep track of how your interactions with others or the environment have impacted your view/attitude/behavior/etc.
e. Your group will prepare a short 'pitch' of your idea and present it to the instructor via Zoom during your video project meetings. Your pitch should include information about the organization (social media campaign, call to action) that you plan to create and the type of impact you intend for it to have. Ideas about the video itself can be in the early stages at this point but the value/ attitude/behavior change should be clear.
f. Fill out a Peer Feedback rubric for your team members.

2. Screenplay/Storyboard & Peer Feedback
    a. Continue to find, read and evaluate relevant literature (course readings and additional sources) in discussions posts.).
    b. Evaluate, synthesize and integrate the collected information: your sources from the lectures, readings and field work
    c. Create a storyboard for the video project. Your story board should include the research you plan to include in the video, ideas about which videos, photos, interviews, images you plan to include in the video, and a rough script of what will be said in the video.
    d. Look for further evidence in your community, talk to as many individuals as possible. Record or take photos of your interactions and conversations with others that are relevant to your change in view/value/behavior/etc. Keep track of how your interactions with others or the environment have impacted your view/attitude/behavior/etc.
    e. Fill out a Peer Feedback rubric for your team members.
3. Final Product
    a. Act upon acquired knowledge, skills, and attitudes in global and local contexts by creating an organization, social media campaign or call to action. In the end be firmly committed to the value that you acquired through your research and through your planned actions.
    b. Create a 3-4 minute video (see technical details below) about your call to action, social media campaign or non-profit organization.

Table 1. Project Evaluation

Performance Level	Needs Improvement	Satisfactory	Excellent
Pitch Presentation	Students did not complete a pitch presentation or do not have a clear, agreed upon vision for their project.	Students complete the pitch presentation on time. Students either do no have a clear vision or do not agree upon vision for their project.	Students completed the pitch presentation on time. Pitch is thorough and group has a clear vision for their project.
Storyboard	Students did not complete a storyboard or storyboard did not match video.	Students completed the storyboard on time, but some items are not thoroughly described. Storyboard matches the video.	Students completed storyboard on time. Storyboard is thorough and matches the video.
Global/Local Citizen Concern	Students description of the action plan is incomplete and lack evidence from research, or is inappropriate for the chosen issue. Argument for needed action has no evidence from research and field interactions.	Students description of the action plan leaves out details or evidence from research. Students' argument for needed action has minimal evidence from research and field interactions.	Students give a thorough description of the researched action plan which addresses a global citizenship concern. Students' argument for needed action is clear and supported with evidence from research and field interactions.
Action Plan	Students plan for action is not clear and does not consider the potential consequences of their plan.	Students provide a plan for action but it lacks detail or does not include consideration of both positive and/or negative consequences of their plan.	Students provide well thought out plans and consider both positive and negative consequences of the implementation of their plan
Changes & Growth	Students do not include impressions, experiences or impact of interactions in port cities. Provide no examples of group change or future plans.	Students record/share impressions and experiences but do not focus on impact of interactions in community. Examples do not focus on group change or do not include future plans.	Students record/share impressions, experiences, and impact of interactions in community. Students provide examples of how they have changed by engaging in the project and share plans for future changes.
Documentation, References and Sources	There is no documentation or citing of sources.	Most of the elements taken from other sources are documented or referenced; however, some documentation may be inaccurate or missing.	All elements from other sources are accurately documented and/or referenced.
Video content and organization	The video lacks a central theme, clear point of view, and logical sequence of information. Much of the information is irrelevant to the overall message 0-2 points	Information is connected to a theme. Details are logical and information is relevant throughout most of the video.	Video includes a clear statement of purpose. Events and messages are presented in a logical order, with relevant information that supports the video's main idea.
Mechanics	The text and audio have 4 or more grammar or spelling errors. 0-2	The text and audio have 1-2 grammar or spelling errors.	The text and audio have no grammar or spelling errors
Production	Video is of poor quality and is unedited. There are no transitions added or transitions are used so frequently that they detract from the video. There are no graphics. 0-10	Video is edited. A variety of transitions are used and most transitions help tell the story. Most of video has good pacing and timing. Graphics are used appropriately. 11-15 points	Video is edited. Video runs smoothly from shot to shot. A variety of transitions are used to assist in communicating the main idea. Shots and scenes work well together. Graphics explain and reinforce key points in the video. 16-20 points
Total			
Project Grade			

Chapter 3

Social Justice Through Socratic Seminars:
Promoting Critical Engagement in a Virtual Learning Environment

Jessica A. Manzone
(iD) https://orcid.org/0000-0001-6291-894X
Northern Arizona University, USA

ABSTRACT

The need to critically engage learners whether the classroom space is traditional, hybrid, or virtual is one of the most pressing educational issues teachers face today. Engaging learners specifically in an online environment requires the examination of both the content being taught as well as the methods or pedagogical models used to deliver the content. This chapter highlights how both the content, and the delivery can be filtered in ways that are relevant to the learners, that value their home and community assets, and that provide them with tangible touch points to transfer classroom information into the real world to maximize student engagement. The core of this chapter focuses on the use of Socratic Seminars as a means of engaging learning through targeted and purposeful conversations around social justice issues. This chapter demonstrates how the original tenets of Socratic Seminar can be used to present content in a manner that leverages students' cultural and linguistic wealth, develops personal and social identities, and builds critical competencies and global awareness in all learners. Specific connections between justice oriented Socratic Seminar, anti-bias teaching frameworks, and online learning environments are made.

DOI: 10.4018/978-1-6684-4055-1.ch003

Copyright © 2023, IGI Global. Copying or distributing in print or electronic forms without written permission of IGI Global is prohibited.

INTRODUCTION

The Need to Critically Engage

Education in the 21st Century calls for students to *engage* – to think critically, to problem-solve, and to become contributing members of society that can adapt to a changing and globalized set of norms. The need to critically *engage* and to transfer learning from one situation to another has never been more apparent. The COVID-19 pandemic and subsequent quarantine has extended the need for remote learning to the equivalent (in many cases) to multiple school years and has forever altered the way that students *engage* in the classroom. "Nearly everything about teaching has changed for teachers over the last few months" (Lemov & Woolway, 2020, p. 2). The image of the "ideal classroom" that teachers had in their minds no longer exists. Their walls, painstakingly designed with bulletin boards, flexible seating arrangements constructed to promote conversation and collegiality, and carefully curated classroom libraries have been replaced with Zoom rooms, Web-Ex sessions, and Google Meetings. But that does not mean that the *ideals* of classroom teaching that educators value have been abandoned. Ideal classrooms are ones where people are *engaged*, where they share ideas, where they are valued, and where they are encouraged to contribute in ways that reflect their community and culture (Ladson-Billings, 2014). The question then becomes: How can we take the ideals of traditional classrooms and translate them into relevant and *engaging* virtual learning experiences?

One of the major struggles teachers faced (and continue to face) in the transition from in-person to remote learning is the building and sustaining of student *engagement* in an online environment (Ali & Herrera, 2020; Kurt, Atay, & Ozturk, 2021). According to Wu (2016), *how* educators structure a virtual learning environment impacts the degree to which students *engage* in the learning experience. Any framework or pedagogical model for remote learning should take into account the intersection between content delivery, assessment, and engagement (Green, 2020). Content focuses on the subject matter and the resources provided to meet both the needs of the learners and the objectives of the learning experience (Green, 2020). Assessment addresses the formative and summative opportunities students have to demonstrate knowledge. Finally, *engagement* is defined as the amount of energy students devote to the learning experience and to their overall sense of joy as a learner (Beymer & Thomson, 2015; Shan & Cheng, 2019). This chapter highlights how the inquiry pedagogy of Socratic Seminar, traditionally presented in-person in Humanities classrooms, can be effectively implemented in a virtual learning environment to generate student interest and sustain critical *engagement*.

According to Driggs and Brillante (2020), building a culture of *engagement* in an online classroom relies on employing instructional methods that are hands-on, active, and of value to the learners. Socratic Seminar has always been a pedagogical model of teaching focused on critical thinking and active *engagement* (Adler, 1982; Helterbran & Strahler, 2013). In the original work on Socratic Seminar conducted by Mortimer Alder in the *Paideia Proposal* (1982), he argued that any educational experience of value should expand one's understanding of critical ideas, values, and issues. Through questioning and active discussion, students evaluate concepts of substance, challenge previously held misconceptions, and generate interdisciplinary connections between topics and themes (Griswold, Shaw, & Munn, 2017). This chapter takes the original intent and outcomes of Socratic Seminar and reorients them to specifically examine issues and themes of social justice. When justice oriented themes serve as the nexus of a Socratic Seminar, they raise students' awareness of the intolerance and prejudice that continues to exist, and create the empathetic citizens necessary to address these issues. Social justice can be explored through Socratic Seminar in virtual classrooms through a lens of developing one's personal and social identities. The strategic integration of *Social Justice Standards: The Teaching Tolerance Anti-Bias Framework* (Teaching Tolerance, 2016) into Socratic Seminar is a critical step in promoting social justice in a virtual classroom. This chapter will describe how the original steps of Socratic Seminar intersect with the Anti-Bias Framework to create experiences that build critical *engagement* through social justice and action.

This chapter is written for faculty in the Humanities disciplines at any grade level or institution. Organized into three parts, the chapter (a) defines the original tenets of the Socratic Seminar model, (b) reorients the original model to view content through a lens of social justice and action, and (c) provides concrete recommendations for how teachers can implement justice oriented Socratic Seminars in a virtual learning environment. The author hopes this chapter stimulates teachers' creativity and confidence in translating a seminal inquiry pedagogy of the Humanities disciplines to an online classroom. The remainder of the chapter will explore how justice oriented Socratic Seminars:

- Can be used as a means of discussing issues of social justice
- Can be used as a means of building empathy and a culture of understanding among students in a virtual classroom
- Can leverage digital technologies to create equitable means of participation in a virtual classroom
- Can be used as a means of valuing the funds of knowledge and home pedagogies students bring to the digital classroom
- Can be used as a means of creating "agents of social change" in learners as a consequence of engaging in community action

BACKGROUND

This chapter presents a framework for implementing Socratic Seminar in a virtual learning environment. This framework is based on the concept that the original steps of Socratic Seminar can be reoriented through the lens of social justice to authentically promote critical *engagement* in a digital classroom. This section of the chapter briefly defines (a) the critical features of effective online environments, and (b) the original tenets of Socratic Seminar. The intersection of these areas provide the theoretical, conceptual, and pragmatic foundation for the framework described in this chapter.

Effective Online Environments

Technology and digital resources are forever changing the way that content is delivered by teachers and accessed by learners. An effective online classroom is achieved through the intersection of best-practice pedagogies, technological elements, and social context (Stieler-Hunt & Jones, 2015; Wang & Huang, 2017).

- *Pedagogical designs* for effective online instruction should provide many and varied opportunities for teacher, student, and peer interactions. Any pedagogical practice should promote globalization, active learning, and an open exchange of ideas. Pedagogy in a digital classroom should create authentic ways for students to engage in meaningful work that exposes them to the world beyond the textbook (Laur, 2019). These pedagogies can include virtual labs, embedded videos with quizzes and discussion questions, polling features, role-playing exercises, and interactive simulations.
- The *technological elements* or features available to teachers and students directly impacts the construction and effectiveness of an online classroom. Technology in a virtual learning environment encompasses both the tools used during the teaching of content and the "managerial tasks" of the learning experience (Keengwe & Kidd, 2010, p. 536). Managerial tasks refer to the technical components of the classroom experience. This includes how students enter the classroom, how they interact with others, how they obtain the necessary course materials, and how they demonstrate their learning. Any technological platform or Learning Management System (LMS) must be easy for both teachers and students to navigate, should interface with other popular platforms, and align with the developmental readiness of the learners (Wang & Huang, 2017). The technological elements of an online classroom should incorporate digital tools that honor the instructional purpose and objectives of the content. Tools should facilitate participation between students in

ways that promote equity and engagement. They should provide all students with an opportunity to "learn while doing" – to create, produce, evaluate, and access deeper learning experiences in a virtual classroom (Budhai & Skipwith, 2021, p. 5). Examples of such tools could include small group breakout rooms, chat pods, gallery view screens, interactive whiteboards, and application sharing features.

- Learning, whether in-person or virtual, takes place in a socio-cultural *context* (Wang & Huang, 2017). *Context* in an online classroom focuses on the characteristics of the learners and on the conditions that create communities of practice. Online educators must strive to create a safe and comfortable digital classroom where students feel valued and seen. They should cater to diverse learning preferences, encourage participation in many forms, and shift control of the thinking from the teacher to the student. For example, moving from a static discussion board where students individually type their response to a project-based learning activity where students engage in group brainstorming and collaboration. According to Angel (2018), online classrooms *contexts* should (a) provide students with space to highlight their personal and community identities, (b) nurture their curiosity through the art of questioning, (c) engage them in real world problem solving, and (d) develop their ability to think critically and creatively. Examples of socio-constructed online techniques could include jigsaw discussions, role playing, small group breakouts, hands-on experiments, and Socratic Seminars.

Tenets of Socratic Seminar

Socratic Seminar has been used as a model of teaching in the K-12 sector since 1937 (Schneider, 2013). In the 84 years since Socratic Seminar first became popular as a means of teaching and learning, numerous books (Adler, 1982; Copeland, 2005; Moeller & Moeller, 2002; Strong, 1996) have been written outlining both the conceptual rationale and practical how-to's of an effective seminar. Conceptually, Adler (1982), describes the purpose of Socratic Seminar as a method for promoting "collaborative, intellectual discussion facilitated by open-ended questions about a text" (p. 7). Socratic Seminars are rooted in the values of a democratic classroom, where student collaboration and critical thinking take precedent over lecture style instruction. Dialogue is at the core of Socratic Seminar, and becomes the vehicle for students to analyze, evaluate, and create their own meaning from the content (Gee, 2014). Dialogue within a Socratic Seminar is characterized by several key features and non-negotiable conceptual elements.

- *A dialogue is not a debate.* In a debate, students are asked to take sides as they defend a position on an issue or topic. The goal of a debate is to win. A dialogue, on the other hand, "aims to listen and understand" (Tannen, 1998, p. 5).
- *A dialogue does not end in a consensus.* Students do not need to come to an agreement at the end of a Socratic Seminar. The teacher does not take a vote at the conclusion of the dialogue to determine the most popular position. A dialogue is a place where multiple perspectives are welcomed and valued (Nikulin, 2006).
- *A dialogue promotes collaboration and the co-construction of knowledge.* Socratic Seminar provides an environment where all participants have something to contribute and something to learn from each other. The open exchange of ideas in a dialogue allows thoughts to be started, expanded, elaborated, and finished by different members of the group (Moffett, 1968). This creates an ebb and flow within a dialogue where learners are working together to synthesize previously constructed ideas and generate new ones.
- *A dialogue requires the ability and willingness to listen.* Listening in a dialogue is more than just politely waiting for your turn to speak. Active listening requires devoting energy and mental capacity to understanding the message the speaker is trying to convey (Bakhtin, 1986). To truly listen in a Socratic Seminar, students must listen both internally to their own thoughts, and work together with others to create meaning.

Pragmatically, Socratic Seminar is a pedagogical model of inquiry that promotes analysis, curiosity, and critical thinking (Katsara & Witte, 2019). Researchers and practitioners are in agreement about the purpose of a Socratic Seminar. However, variability exists in its implementation. Schneider (2013) goes so far as to argue that Socratic Seminar has no real agreed upon syntax or set of steps beyond "asking questions" (p. 632). Although the practice of Socratic Seminar in the classroom can take many and varied forms, the National Paideia Center (2003), outlines seven essential steps for implementation. These steps serve as the basis for the justice oriented Socratic Seminars described in the remainder of this chapter. Table 1 delineates each step of the Socratic Seminar method and provides a brief definition for each stage of the model.

Table 1. Steps and Definitions of the Socratic Seminar Method

Steps of Socratic Seminar	Description of the Steps
Selection of Text	This step involves the selection of a set of anchor materials (texts) aligned to the topic under study. These materials will serve as the basis for analysis and dialogue as students interpret and uncover big ideas and themes. Anchor materials for Socratic Seminar are not limited to just written documents. They can be anything where "ideas or values are embedded" (Ayres Paul & Tay, 2016, p. 106). This can include pictures, artwork, artifacts, songs, poems, testimony, scientific formulas, and mathematical equations.
Pre-Seminar	This step involves building background knowledge related to the content and themes in the anchor materials. Exposing students to the anchor materials before the seminar helps create equitable access and participation in the seminar. Students can work alone or with the teacher to unpack key themes in the anchor materials, develop an understanding of the context and perspectives of the content, and begin to form questions in their minds. The goal of this stage is for students to organize the information gleaned from the anchor materials and connect it with other disciplines and personal experiences (Davies & Sinclair, 2014).
Goal Setting	This stage of the process is about setting personal and community expectations. Community or group norms could include active listening, equitable opportunities to talk, and establishing trust and respect for peers (Helterbran & Strahler, 2013). Individual goals are set by the students themselves. Goals could reflect areas of personal strength or points of reflection. An example of an individual goal could include taking an academic risk during a seminar, challenging a currently held point of view, or listening carefully to the comments of others before responding.
Questions	Carefully constructed questions form the core of Socratic Seminars. Questions are not asked to determine a "right answer," but to stimulate dialogue and critical thinking. Typical Socratic Seminars are constructed around four types of questions: opening questions, core questions, follow-up questions, and closing questions. Opening questions are designed to get students thinking about the details and main ideas of the anchor materials. Core questions provide students with opportunities to explore the values and perspectives in the anchor materials. Follow-up questions ask students to dig deeper into an original question or line of thinking. Closing questions ask students to "personalize what was discussed," and apply themes from the anchor materials to their own lives (Mangrum, 2010, p. 42).
Facilitation	This step of the process is where students engage in the discourse and dialogue of the seminar. Students are typically seated facing each other in a circle. Teachers can also choose to have an inner and an outer circle in a technique known as a "fishbowl." Having students sit facing each other builds trust and community by visually representing the equity that exists among all seminar participants (Ayres Paul & Tay, 2016). The role of the teacher is that of a facilitator, posing the initial question, probing for deeper understanding, and engaging in the inquiry alongside the learners.
Assessment	This step of the process occurs after the discussion has come to a close. Students evaluate their experience in seminar against the community and individual goals created earlier in the learning experience. Students can keep track of their progress and strengths over multiple seminar experiences to develop a longitudinal trajectory of their thinking.
Post- Seminar	This step of the process provides students with opportunities to extend themes from the seminar into additional activities. Students can personally reflect on the connections between the anchor materials, the seminar's big ideas, and their lived experiences. Teachers can use the Socratic Seminar as a catalyst for other inquiry lessons such as project-based learning, role playing, and independent study. Extension activities resulting from Socratic Seminars provide students with a chance to synthesize and apply what they have learned. This type of generative thinking is necessary to build critical engagement in all learners (Katsara & Witte, 2019).

JUSTICE ORIENTED SOCRATIC SEMINARS

Teaching and learning are inextricably linked to the changing milieu of society and cannot remain neutral in regards to issues of social justice. *Social justice* is defined as the actions taken to treat all people with respect and dignity, while affirming and honoring the culture and groups with which people identify (Nieto & Bode, 2018). Authenticity is critical to the implementation of any justice oriented pedagogical practice (Paris, 2012). Justice oriented Socratic Seminars define authenticity as both equitable and consequential learning experiences. Equitable seminar experiences engage learners in thinking about the content in culturally relevant and rigorous ways (Calabrese Barton, Tan, & Birmingham, 2020). These experiences are designed to recognize and value the home pedagogies and funds of knowledge students bring to any learning experience (Wynter-Hoyte, Braden, Rodriguez, et al., 2019). Consequential seminar experiences are designed to shift the balance of power and authority in the classroom. They explore content in ways that challenge systemic notions of racism and White supremacy that continue to exist in public education (Birmingham, Calabrese Barton, Jones, et al., 2017). Justice oriented Socratic Seminars recognize that what happens politically, socially, and economically directly impacts how children learn and what they learn about. They develop critical *engagement* by raising students' awareness of local, national, and global issues, and encouraging learners to take action in solving them.

Critical *engagement* in justice oriented Socratic Seminars is contingent on how relevant and connected the seminar experience is with the lives, backgrounds, cultures, and communities of the students (Calabrese Barton, Tan, & Birmingham, 2020). Justice oriented Socratic Seminars recognize that issues of social justice exist in every discipline and context. Teachers must purposefully provide opportunities for students to explore issues of social justice within the Socratic Seminar topic in ways that develop their personal and social identities. In justice oriented seminars, students take ownership over their own thinking and participate in the dialogue in ways that reflect their prior knowledge and home assets. One way teachers can authentically create justice oriented Socratic Seminars is to connect aspects of the seminar experience to the domains of the Anti-Bias Framework Standards (Teaching Tolerance, 2016). Table 2 provides a brief definition for each of the four domains.

Justice oriented Socratic Seminars value students as people. They recognize that their prior knowledge and personal experiences are integral to building and sustaining critical *engagement* during a seminar dialogue (Davis & Schaeffer, 2019). According to Chesters (2012), the "lived experiences and funds of knowledge" students bring into a Socratic Seminar dialogue helps them unpack justice focused issues and relate to their classmates as well as the content on a personal level (p. 57). Teachers can create justice oriented Socratic Seminars in an authentic manner

Table 2. Domains and Definitions for Justice Oriented Classrooms

Anti-Bias Framework Domains	Definition
Identity	Identity is related to who someone is and the qualities that define them.
Diversity	Diversity is the practice of valuing and including people from a range of backgrounds and groups.
Justice	Justice is a recognition that power and privilege influence how people are treated and what they have access to.
Action	Action involves planning and carrying out initiatives that combat bias and injustices at any level: local, state, national, and global.

by making connections between the steps of Socratic Seminar and the domains of identity, diversity, justice, and action. These connections can occur in a myriad of ways and should be responsive to the social, emotional, and academic needs of the learners within a specific classroom. Figure 1 visually represents a sample of the connections that can be made. These connections form the basis for implementing authentic, justice oriented Socratic Seminars.

Learning experiences cannot remain neutral in regards to issues of social justice (Ladson-Billings, 2014; Paris, 2012). Educators are not just teachers of skills and essential concepts. They are the foundational facilitators of a social justice mindset. The integration of justice oriented Socratic Seminars into virtual learning environments creates experiences that build students capacity to respond to the current and future needs of society (Rubel, 2017). As learners co-construct their own experiences and formulate their own connections to the text, they recognize that their lived experiences matter and develop the agency necessary to solve problems on their own (Daniel & Zybina, 2019). Table 3 demonstrates how the original steps of Socratic Seminar can be funneled through a lens of social justice to build student capacity, agency, and critical *engagement* in a virtual classroom.

IMPLEMENTING VIRTUAL JUSTICE ORIENTED SOCRATIC SEMINARS

Transitioning the seminal Humanities practice of Socratic Seminar from an in-person to virtual classroom requires the strategic and purposeful use of technology. Key features in a Zoom, Web-Ex, or Google Meets platform can be leveraged to execute justice oriented Socratic Seminars in a digital environment in ways that promote critical *engagement* and create equitable access to content for all learners.

Figure 1. Connection the Steps of Socratic Seminar to the Anti-Bias Framework Domains

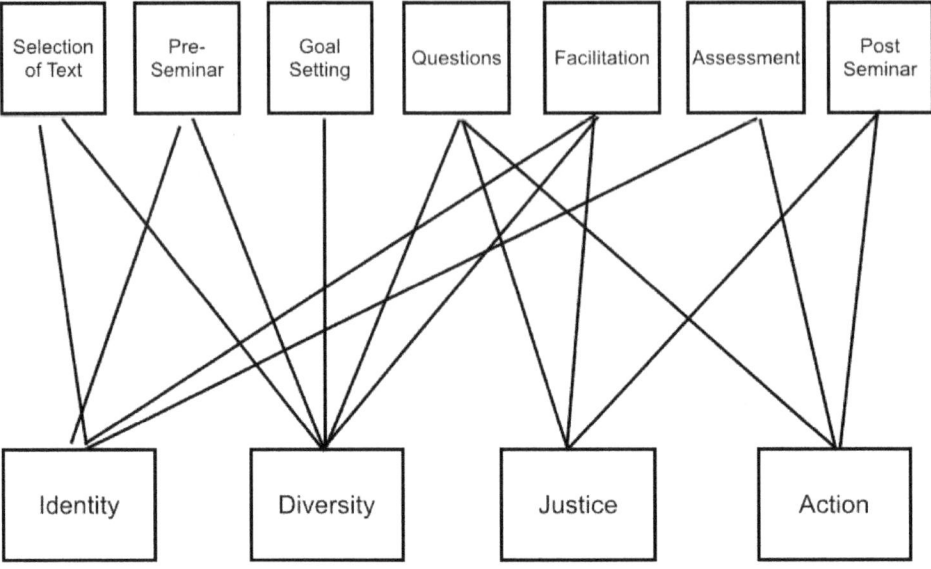

Steps of Socratic Seminar

Anti-Bias Framework Domains (Teaching for Tolerance, 2016)

Table 3. Reorienting the Steps of Socratic Seminar through a Justice Lens

Original Steps of Socratic Seminar	Reorienting Socratic Seminar through a Justice Lens
Selection of Text	In justice oriented Socratic Seminars, the anchor text and/or resources must specifically target aspects of diverse literature. Diverse literature refers not just to the diversity of the authors, but how the genre, characterization, and structure of the piece itself are reflective and relevant to the students in the classroom (Boyd, Casey, & Galda, 2015). Every piece of diverse literature conveys a dominant message. In justice oriented Socratic Seminars, the anchor text and/or resources must represent a range of messages, and specifically use those messages to promote social justice and action in any content or subject matter.
Pre-Seminar	In justice oriented Socratic Seminars, background knowledge is built that directly connects universal themes related to social justice and action with content or subject matter. These themes can include: power, systems, structure, conflict, oppression, and change. Social justice themes serve as reference points or touch-stones throughout the Socratic Seminar in ways that push students' personal boundaries, anchor the seminar experience to the lives of learners, and uncover areas of social action in any content or subject matter (Boyd, Casey, & Galda, 2015).
Goal Setting	This stage of a justice oriented Socratic Seminar is about setting goals for participation related to one's personal and social identity. Students are provided time prior to the start of a Socratic dialogue to share aspects of themselves as learners and as people that connect with themes from the anchor text and/or resources. They set goals and intentions that are interest-based and that leverage the prior knowledge and funds of knowledge they bring to the learning experience (Manzone & Peeples, 2021). Students can also use this "goal setting time" to build relationships and cultivate friendships that help lower their affective filter for participating in seminar dialogues.

continues on following page

Table 3. Continued

Original Steps of Socratic Seminar	Reorienting Socratic Seminar through a Justice Lens
Questions	Justice oriented Socratic Seminars employ the same strategies and question types as the original model. The major distinction is that the closing questions in a justice oriented seminar directly integrate (a) ideological positions from the diverse anchor text and resources, and (b) social justice themes from contemporary society. The integration of these elements into the dialogue questions allows for a greater transferability between disciplines and contexts. For example, students can take the ideological positions and social justice themes in any justice oriented seminar and connect them with a self-selected piece of text, image, or event.
Facilitation	This stage of a justice oriented Socratic Seminar is about recognizing and honoring individual differences. Teachers can facilitate the Socratic Seminar process using a myriad of authentic and inclusive scaffolds. Authentic scaffolds must value the racial, ethnic, socioeconomic, cultural, and linguistic diversity in response to the academic needs, interests, and abilities of the learners (Casserly, Tiernan, & Maguire, 2019). Scaffolds should also provide students with opportunities to (a) increase their motivation and participation in seminar dialogue, (b) make personal connections between the seminar and their own lives, and (c) equitably contribute to the dialogue.
Assessment	In this stage of justice oriented Socratic Seminars, students assess the new knowledge they gained from the class dialogue against previously held assumptions. Implicit learning exists in the nuances of a situation (Holroyd, 2015). The perceptions, stereotypes, and beliefs that unconsciously influence how we respond in Socratic Seminar can be exposed and analysed. As students assess their personal growth and possible discomfort in a justice oriented Socratic Seminar, they begin to question the status quo, develop a sense of empathy for others, and an urgency to address issues of inequity in their world.
Post- Seminar	This step in justice oriented Socratic Seminars is about influencing and impacting social change. Defined as "active citizenry" (Budhai & Skipwith, 2020, p, 17), students participate in experiences that make meaningful contributions to their families and communities. Community-oriented extension activities can take any form and serve as a way for learners to personalize the seminar experience. Students are provided time to find and pursue extensions from the themes in the seminar that align with their interests, aptitudes, and funds of knowledge. They create authentic products that benefit themselves and others.

Digitizing the Anchor Text(s) and Resources

Both in-person and virtual Socratic Seminars begin with the building of background knowledge. This is usually accomplished through the introduction of the topic and connection to an anchor text or image. In justice oriented Socratic Seminars, it is critical that the anchor text and/or resources be culturally sustaining (Gonzalez, Moll, & Amanti, 2005). When implementing Socratic Seminar in a virtual classroom, teachers can leverage the vast resources available on the internet as potential options to cultivate a repository justice oriented anchor materials. These resources should represent diverse perspectives and provide relevant context and meaning to the students by connecting to their community (Manzone & Peeples, 2021). Resources can include video, podcasts, posters, interviews, and other media as a way of altering the means and modalities of accessing the content in a virtual setting. Teachers can also use a variety of technologies to differentiate the resource set so that it is responsive to the academic, social, and cultural needs of the learners. Audio books, dictation software, virtual Post-it Notes, and collaborative software provide many and varied pathways for students to prepare for a virtual Socratic Seminar. The inclusion of leveled and varied resources "transports" an online classroom from a static experience reserved for some, to an interactive and inclusive one that responds to all learners (Budhai & Skipwith, 2021, p. 53). Table 4 provides a set of digital resources that teachers could use to select anchor texts and build background knowledge in culturally authentic ways. Reflection questions for teachers to cultivate their own repository of digital anchor resources for justice oriented Socratic Seminars are provided.

Table 4. Digital Resources and Questions to Anchor Justice Oriented Socratic Seminars

Potential Anchor Resources	Teacher Reflection Questions
● TED Talks ● Expert testimony or transcripts ● Synchronous interviews with community personnel ● Diverse picture books read aloud over YouTube ● Culturally authentic artwork and artifacts ● Virtual field trips to museums or historical sites ● Music – songs, lyrics, etc. ● News outlets – digital newspapers, magazines, etc. ● Journals and research studies	Do my anchor resources offer a range of diverse perspectives on the topic? Do my anchor resources give a voice to the perspectives of historically marginalized groups? Do my anchor resources offer access to the content for learners with different abilities, talents, and interests? Do my anchor resources give learners an opportunity to connect their home pedagogies to the content?

Gallery View

A major characteristic of justice oriented Socratic Seminars is the sense of community created during the whole group dialogue. In-person seminars maximize the collaborative spirit by arranging the physical classroom in a circle, with students sitting facing each other. The ability to connect with others via eye contact, proximity, facial expressions, and body language impacts the shared meaning created during the dialogue (Chesters, 2012). This effect can be more difficult, but not impossible to accomplish in a virtual classroom. Creating a virtual "circle" for Socratic Seminar begins by having participants select the Gallery View option in their Zoom, Google Meets, or Web-Ex platform. This feature allows all students to be visible at the same time and creates the equity of participation not offered by the Speaker View. In a technique known as "dissolving the screen" (Rugani & Grijalva, 2020, p. 37), students learn how to establish online connections with their peers and teachers. Students learn how to read the nuances of their classmates' body language and facial expressions. They openly acknowledge each other's contributions, value the collective work, and honor the person behind the computer screen. The Gallery View feature allows students to be "seen," literally and figuratively, in a virtual classroom. When this occurs, critical *engagement* and participation in an online environment is developed.

The ability to "dissolve the screen" and read the virtual room is a skill that can be taught and practiced in a digital environment. The use of theatre games such as charades, follow the leader, and tableaus help students develop an online presence and learn the skills necessary to participate in a virtual Socratic Seminar. As students follow non-verbal commands or guess actions in a game-like fashion, they begin to develop a receptivity for viewing facial expressions and body language online (Budhai & Skipwith, 2021). This aids in their ability to engage in a virtual Socratic Seminar that demands a nuanced approach to conversation and dialogue in a whole group setting. Table 5 provides a list of three theatre games that help build students' capacity for dissolving the screen and ultimately participating in virtual, justice oriented Socratic Seminars.

Table 5. Gallery View Games that Help Dissolve the Screen in Preparation for Socratic Seminar

Virtual Theatre Game	Brief Description	Dissolving the Screen Targets
Follow the Leader	The teacher or a student volunteer stands at the computer screen. They begin making movements that the rest of the class follows. The leader can vary the speed and frequency of the movements to help build attention and active participation in the rest of the group.	Recognizing non-verbal clues Taking turns Sustained attention
Charades	The teacher or a student volunteer acts out an action (flipping pancakes, walking the dog, etc.) with no words or sound effects. The rest of the group takes turns guessing what the action is using only the visual clues provided.	Abstract representation Open-ended thinking Inference and interpretation
Tableau	A tableau is a technique where students use their bodies to create a picture of important themes and concepts. The teacher gives the group a concept: winter, happiness, conflict, etc. Each student creates a position with their body that represents that concept at the same time. The teacher takes a screen-shot in the Gallery View of everyone's individual image. The class analyzes how the individual images work together to create a collective picture of the concept.	Synthesis of big ideas Creative thinking Collaboration and cooperation

The Chat Pod

The Chat Pod is a text-based feature of any LMS platform that creates unique opportunities for critical *engagement* and student participation. The Chat Pod allows students to *backchannel*, or to "engage in online conversations while others are talking" (Chisholm & Quillen, 2016, p. 88). Traditional seminars rely heavily on oral/verbal contributions to the dialogue. This format caters to and relies heavily on students who speak frequently and are comfortable sharing ideas openly with others. The integration of the Chat Pod provides a concurrent access point into the seminar dialogue for students who are more reluctant to speak out loud. Students can post their comments into the chat openly for the class to view, or can message the teacher privately. Alternative forms of participation help to challenge the "preexisting social dynamics" within a classroom that allow some voices to dominate (Walsh-Moorman, 2016, p. 72). The integration of the Chat Pod in a virtual Socratic Seminar helps create equity and access to the content for all learners. Through the Chat Pod, students can:

- Contribute to the dialogue via different modalities
- Build on the ideas of others in ways that are non-linear and iterative
- Scaffold their participation into Socratic Seminar in ways that are socially and developmentally appropriate
- Retrieve and revisit their thoughts later in the learning experience
- Form parallel threads of dialogue with a Socratic Seminar that encourage critical and creative thinking

The Chat Pod can also be used to translate the traditional "fishbowl" technique in Socratic Seminar to a virtual environment. In a traditional "fishbowl," the teacher divides the class into two groups. Half of the class organizes their chairs into an inner circle, and the remaining students sit behind them in an outer circle. In a virtual classroom, teachers cannot actually "move" students, but they can place them into partners. Person A in the partnership becomes part of the inner circle and contributes orally/verbally to the Socratic Seminar. Person B represents an outer circle of online "bloggers." Their role is to contribute to the Socratic Seminar via text in the Chat Pod. "Bloggers" can contribute to the Chat Pod on two levels: (a) they can synthesize the key ideas and themes arising from the inner circle dialogue, and (b) they can pose questions or connections that generate new lines of thinking on the original topic. While the dialogue is occurring in both the inner and outer circles, the teacher is monitoring the private messages in the Chat Pod. The teacher can post an "anonymous message" to the class on behalf of any student who is not yet ready to make an open contribution. The variance in participation type and disclosure builds the "democratizing power" of a virtual Socratic Seminar (Walsh-Moorman, 2016, p. 77). Table 6 provides a series of questions that can help guide the integration of the Chat Pod into a virtual Socratic Seminar.

Table 6. Activating the Chat Pod in a Virtual Socratic Seminar

Questions to Synthesize Inner Circle Dialogue in the Chat Pod	Questions to Aid "Bloggers" and "Chatters" in Chat Pod Posts	Questions for Teachers in Facilitating Private Messages in the Chat Pod
How can I use the Chat Pod to build on something said verbally in the inner circle during this seminar? What is something I heard in the inner circle dialogue that I agree with and can summarize in the Chat Pod? What is something I heard in the inner circle dialogue that I want to argue against? How can I use the Chat Pod to introduce a different perspective? What are the main ideas emerging in the dialogue at this point in the seminar? How can I connect one or more of those main ideas to something in my community?	What are the major takeaways so far in the dialogue? How can I summarize them in the Chat Pod? What social justice themes have emerged as a consequence of the dialogue? How can I highlight them in the Chat Pod? What trends in perspective are emerging as a result of the dialogue? How can I reinforce the dominant perspective or share an alternative in the Chat Pod? What impact has that dialogue had on me thus far? How can I share a personal reflection in the Chat Pod?	What do you want me to know that you know about this topic that you do not feel comfortable sharing openly? How is this seminar experience making you feel? What can I do to make you feel more comfortable in this learning experience? What has been said or posted during this seminar that resonates with you? How does this connection help you understand the themes in the topic? What is one word that you would like to contribute to this seminar dialogue? May I post this contribution anonymously on your behalf?

KEY RECOMMENDATIONS FOR JUSTICE-ORIENTED SOCRATIC SEMINARS

There is not one "right" way to implement justice oriented Socratic Seminars in a virtual classroom. The author proposes the following recommendations to aid in their implementation. Reflective questions to promote critical *engagement* for both teachers and students have been provided.

Recommendation One: Focus on Inclusion

At its core, inclusive education focuses on recognizing and accommodating the barriers that block participation and access for all students (Krischler, Powell, & Pit-Ten Cate, 2019). Inclusive learning environments extend the access to content so that every student's "potential for learning is achieved" (Casserly, Tiernan, & Maguire, 2019, p. 618). As children participate in justice oriented Socratic Seminars, they bring with them linguistic, social, and cultural capital from the home. Justice oriented seminars begin with the belief that each student has a voice, and a personal and community connection to the content. Honor these voices – create a "space of belonging" (Garcia & Delgado Bernal, 2021, p. 592) within a virtual classroom that leverages student assets and strengths. This space provides all learners with the opportunity to feel welcome, develop empathy for others, contribute to class conversations, and authentically analyze issues of justice through their own socio-political lens. When students know that Socratic Seminar is a place for them, they begin to build their own capacity for the transfer of knowledge and skills. The following questions can be used to reflect on the creation of inclusive, virtual learning environments through the implementation of justice oriented Socratic Seminars.

Table 7. Reflection Questions for Focusing on Inclusion

Teacher Reflection Questions	Student Reflection Questions
How am I using justice oriented seminars to challenge current systems of power and racism in my virtual classroom? To what degree did this justice seminar create space for all student voices and home connections? What have I learned about the life experiences of my students as a consequence of their participation in this justice seminar? How can I continue to use technology to create inclusive, virtual learning environments that promote justice and action?	To what degree am I giving space for others to talk and share during justice seminars? How did my participation in this justice seminar help me empathize with one or more of my classmates? How did I use this justice seminar to share a part of my individual and community identity with others? To what degree did I actively listen to others during this justice seminar? What aspects of this seminar either facilitated or hindered my ability to hear and respond to the perspectives of others?

Recommendation Two: Actively Seek out Talent

Justice oriented Socratic Seminars provide a unique opportunity to both uncover and sustain talent in all learners. Talent development is the deliberate and purposeful creation of experiences that highlight the strengths and assets students possess (Subotnik, Olszewski-Kubilius, & Worrell, 2021). The use of justice oriented Socratic Seminar as a means of talent-focused instruction provides all learners with a chance to demonstrate their interest and abilities in several ways. As students make personal connections to the themes and texts from the seminar, they enact those connections in ways that highlight their personal identity (Yosso, 2005). Justice oriented Socratic Seminars also provide students with opportunities to "dabble." Dabbling is when students engage with different materials and concepts to intellectually and creatively "poke around" (Hunt & Yoshida-Ehrmann, 2016, p. 166). Like a sandbox, students can play in new spaces without the fear of failure. This approach to Socratic Seminar provides students with opportunities to extend identified talents and to realize latent ones. The development and sustainability of talent through justice oriented seminars is about *potential*. The *potential* for all students to engage in ways that cater to their strengths. The potential for students to show what they know and can do in a culturally and linguistically authentic medium. The *potential* for students to be seen in an online space for their talents and interests, rather than their deficits. In justice oriented Socratic Seminars, teachers function like talent scouts to purposefully build opportunities to expose *potential* in all learners. The following questions can be used to help teachers and students seek out talent through virtual, justice oriented Socratic Seminars.

Table 8. Reflection Questions for Actively Seeking Talent

Teacher Reflection Questions	Student Reflection Questions
What is something I learned my students could do as a consequence of the seminar? What behaviors, talents, and interests were exhibited during the seminar that are not seen in the regular curricular experiences? How can I provide opportunities for students to replicate a talent exhibited during a seminar in other learning experiences? What extension opportunities could I create for students to further develop and sustain a talent uncovered during the seminar experience?	To what degree did this seminar allow me to show what I knew about the topic? What new interests do I have as a consequence of my participation in the seminar? How did I capitalize on a strength, interest, or talent in today's seminar experience? How can I continue to use my strengths and talents in future seminars?

Recommendation Three: Leverage Current Events

Building capacity in learners requires the development of thinkers who can *transfer* what they are learning in the classroom to real-world situations (Halpern, 1998). *Transfer* is defined as the degree to which students internalize and apply something taught in one situation to another (Gentner, Rattermann, & Forbus 1993). Justice oriented Socratic Seminars can leverage current events as a means of transferring knowledge, skills, and concepts. A current event is defined not only by its contemporary occurrence, but by its proximity to the lives of the learners. The integration of current events into virtual, justice oriented Socratic Seminars helps students personalize the learning experience. Current event connections can occur on multiple levels: local, state, national, and global. Each level provides students with a nuanced orientation to the relationship that exists between their lives, the content under study in seminar, and the larger factors that influence their communities (Schrank, 2020). Access points for integrating current events into virtual, justice oriented Socratic Seminars are described below:

- *Local* -- Local current events relate to the issues and important happenings in the students community. Students and their families are personally invested in these events and are directly impacted by their outcomes.
- *State* -- State-based current events deal with the issues pertinent to the state in which students reside. Different states have unique political, social, geographic, and economic influences that impact its residents. The analysis of state-wide issues provides learners with an orientation to how these factors affect the various communities, counties, and townships that make up their state.
- *National* -- National issues focus on the current events that impact all U.S. citizens. The analysis of national issues filters content through the various perspectives, influences, and trends that construct the large-scale landscape of this country.
- *Global* -- Global issues provide learners with a "big picture" approach to the study of any content or subject matter. Global issues impact all human beings, regardless of location or country. The integration of global issues into justice oriented Socratic Seminars highlights the generalizability and longevity of the theme and/or topic.

The overt integration of current events into justice oriented Socratic Seminar helps students build a capacity for critical consciousness required of future leaders (Ladson-Billings, 2014). The following questions can be used by teachers and students to reflect upon the integration of current events in justice oriented Socratic Seminars.

Table 9. Reflection Questions for Leveraging Current Events

Teacher Reflection Questions	Student Reflection Questions
To what degree did this justice oriented Socratic Seminar connect with the lives of my learners? To what degree did this seminar leverage an issue relevant to the lives of my learners? In what ways can I purposefully integrate current events to generate meaning and connections in a digital classroom? How does the integration of a current event impact the level of engagement during Socratic Seminar?	How did I make connections between the content of the Socratic Seminar and an issue in my own community? How did the connection to current events help me examine the content of the Socratic Seminar from different perspectives? What additional text or material did I connect to the seminar discussion? How did this connection highlight an aspect of my personal or community identity?

Recommendation Four: Promote Transformational Social Emotional Learning (TSEL)

Justice oriented Socratic Seminars facilitate social emotional learning by building empathy and community in a virtual environment. Contemporary definitions of social and emotional learning examine the development of empathy and community from a socially conscious, global perspective. Defined as Transformative Social Emotional Learning, empathy and community are built through the direct examination of social issues like power, prejudice, and discrimination (Jagers, Rivas-Drake, & Williams, 2019). As students examine these issues and universal themes, they begin to develop the ability to make responsible decisions. They learn to identify the context surrounding a problem of practice, evaluate and reflect on potential solutions, and reconcile their personal responsibility in promoting positive change in their community. Under this approach to social and emotional development, the focus shifts from personal conformity to community empowerment. Students engage in purposeful discussions centered around their life experiences and identities. They are provided time and direction to reflect on their own identities, while simultaneously examining those that differ in some way. These experiences help them develop the complex tools of social awareness that include perspective taking, respect for others, and appreciating diversity (Zinn, Bloodworth, Weissberg, et al., 2007). Finally, Transformative Social Emotional Learning experiences via justice oriented Socratic Seminars have the potential to inform students' "civil and political processes" (Rivas-Drake, Rosario-Ramos, McGovern, et al., 2021, p. 2). This model of teaching has the power to instill in students today the critical thinking skills necessary to make a lasting impact on society in the future.

Table 10. Reflection Questions for Promoting TSEL

Teacher Reflection Questions	Student Reflection Questions
To what degree did I use this Socratic Seminar to help students analyze the relationships they have with the world? To what degree did I bring supplementary materials into the Socratic Seminar to ensure representation? To what degree did this Socratic Seminar attend to the immediate and urgent needs of students, including experiences of trauma? How am I using Socratic Seminar as a pedagogical model to affirm the identities of my students and their communities?	To what degree did this Socratic Seminar support my understanding of social justice issues and the emotional toll they take on different groups of people? How did this Socratic Seminar provide me with an opportunity to use my voice to enact change in my community? How did my participation in this Socratic Seminar help me reflect on the collective well-being of others? To what degree did my participation in this Socratic Seminar help me identify solutions for personal and societal problems?

Recommendation Five: Extend into Service Learning

The use of justice oriented Socratic Seminars in the virtual classroom provides a natural bridge into authentic learning experiences in the real world. Authentic learning experiences are created when students are involved in tasks that are both cognitively *engaging* and relevant to their lives (Salmon, 2018). Authentic learning requires application. Learners can take the experiences they have in the virtual classroom and apply through Service Learning projects. Service learning is defined as experiences that connect the content in the classroom to real world activities that address the needs of people and community (Jacoby, 1999). Under this approach to experiential learning, students extend the themes found in justice oriented Socratic Seminar with community problems of practice. Students work in talent teams to research these issues, and design authentic products that offer solutions within their own sphere of influence. They then reflect on the outcomes of their Service Learning endeavour from various stakeholder perspectives (Center for Community Engaged Learning, 2020). According to Alexander and Murphy (2020), a "scarcity in critical thinking about civic engagement" exists in public education (p. 322). As students participate in Service Learning, they learn to break down barriers, challenge stereotypes, build relationships, and examine diverse perspectives. Extending justice oriented Socratic Seminar discussions into Service Learning projects pushes students beyond a superficial examination of social justice issues. As students solve problems in their own communities, they become more invested in the communities, see themselves as agents of change, and develop the ability to critically engage in civic responsibility.

Table 11. Reflection Questions for Extending into Service Learning

Teacher Reflection Questions	Student Reflection Questions
How did I use this Socratic Seminar to cultivate civic responsibility and social action in my learners? To what degree did I leverage community contacts as mentors in the service learning extension of this Socratic Seminar? How can I provide additional instructional time in my classroom for students to continue their service learning projects and passions? How can I provide an authentic opportunity in my virtual classroom for students to share their work and reflections?	To what degree did this Socratic Seminar uncover problems of practice in my community that I can work to solve? How did this Socratic Seminar provide me with opportunities to network with professionals and experts in my community? How can I continue to advocate and understand the community issues raised during this Socratic Seminar? How has the service learning extension to this Socratic Seminar uncovered or sustained a talent or passion?

CONCLUSION

The colloquial expression "experience is everything" aptly applies to the implementation of Socratic Seminar in the Humanities classroom. As a pedagogy, justice oriented Socratic Seminars provide opportunities for all learners to access content in culturally sustaining ways. In a virtual classroom, justice oriented Socratic Seminars:

- Create the experiences necessary for students to uncover and analyze the issues of social justice inherent in any topic or discipline
- Create experiences that directly thread the content under study in the classroom to contemporary problems of practice in the community
- Create experiences that individualized and personalized pathways for students to connect their home and community funds of knowledge to classroom content
- Create engaging experiences that target multiple modalities and aspects of technology
- Create experiences that transfer knowledge through the completion of meaningful work
- Create experience that leverage students cultural, linguistic, familial, and social capital
- Create experiences grounded in real-world applications

According to Yun and Shin (2021), the recognition of social justice issues within a Humanities classroom is not enough. It is in their practice and application via experiences that shift the balance of power in a classroom and generate lasting change. Virtual learning experiences and digital classrooms provide the perfect vehicle for practicing and applying justice oriented pedagogies. Instant access to information, the ability to travel in seconds to any part of the world, and the connections to mentors in the field are literally at students' fingertips. This causes the gap between the classroom and the community to disappear. When the community and the world at large become synonymous and interchangeable with the "school classroom," it creates the experiences necessary for the development of socially conscious thinkers. Ask yourself: *What would the world look like in 10 years if all learners had access to high-quality, justice-oriented Humanities curriculum?* The answer to this question is the rationale for implementing virtual, justice oriented Socratic Seminars, and the mission of every classroom teacher.

REFERENCES

Adler, M. J. (1982). *The Paideia Proposal*. Macmillan.

Alexander, A. S., & Murphy, E. R. (2020). "It started with this project": A mixed methods examination of a service learning project for preservice art educators. *Studies in Art Education*, *61*(4), 312–329. doi:10.1080/00393541.2020.1820833

Ali, T.T., & Herrera, M. (2020). *Distance learning during COVID-19: 7 equity considerations for schools and districts*. Southern Education Foundation.

Angel, S. L. (2018). If I would have learned this way! In A. K. Salmon (Ed.), *Authentic Teaching and Learning for PreK-Fifth Grade: Advice from Practitioners and Coaches* (pp. 32–49). Routledge. doi:10.4324/9781351211505-2

Ayres Paul, K., & Tay, J. (2016). Critical conversations about big ideas in art using Paideia seminars. *Gifted Child Today*, *39*(2), 105–113. doi:10.1177/1076217516628567

Bakhtin, M. M. (1986). *Speech genres and other late essays*. University of Texas Press.

Beymer, P. N., & Thomson, M. M. (2015). The effects of choice in the classroom: Is there too little or too much choice? *Support for Learning*, *30*(2), 105–120. doi:10.1111/1467-9604.12086

Birmingham, D., Calabrese Barton, A., Jones, J., McDaniel, A., Rogers, A., & Turner, C. (2017). "But the science we do here matters": Youth-authored cases of consequential learning. *Science Education*, *101*(5), 818–844. doi:10.1002ce.21293

Boyd, F. B., Casey, L. L., & Galda, L. (2015). Culturally diverse literature: Enriching variety in an era of Common Core State Standards. *The Reading Teacher*, *68*(5), 378–387. doi:10.1002/trtr.1326

Budhai, S. S., & Skipwith, K. B. (2021). *Best practices in engaging online learners through active and experiential learning strategies* (2nd ed.). Routledge. doi:10.4324/9781003140405

Calabrese Barton, A., Tan, E., & Birmingham, D. J. (2020). Rethinking high-leverage practices in justice-oriented ways. *Journal of Teacher Education*, *71*(4), 477–494. doi:10.1177/0022487119900209

Casserly, A. M., Tiernan, B., & Maguire, G. (2019). Primary teachers' perceptions of multi-grade classroom grouping practices to support inclusive education. *European Journal of Special Needs Education*, *34*(5), 617–631. doi:10.1080/08856257.2019.1580835

Center for Community Engaged Learning. (2020). Retrieved from https://communityengagedlearning.msu.edu/

Chesters, S. D. (2012). *The socratic classroom: Reflective thinking through collaborative inquiry*. Sense Publishing. doi:10.1007/978-94-6091-855-1

Chisholm, J. S., & Quillen, B. (2016). Digitizing the fishbowl: An approach to dialogic discussion. *English Journal*, *105*(3), 88–91.

Copeland, M. (2005). *Socratic circles*. Steinhouse.

Daniel, S. M., & Zybina, M. (2019). Resettled refugee teens' perspectives: Identifying a need to centralize youths "funds of strategies" in future efforts to enact culturally responsive pedagogy. *The Urban Review*, *51*(3), 345–368. doi:10.100711256-018-0484-7

Davies, M., & Sinclair, A. (2014). Socratic questioning in the Paideia method to encourage dialogical discussions. *Research Papers in Education*, *29*(1), 20–43. doi:10.1080/02671522.2012.742132

Davis, N., & Schaeffer, J. (2019). Troubling troubled waters in elementary science education: Politics, ethics, and black children's conceptions of water [justice] in the era of flint. *Cognition and Instruction*, *37*(3), 367–389. doi:10.1080/07370008.2019.1624548

Driggs, C., & Brillante, J. (2020). Culture of attention and engagement. In D. Lemov (Ed.), *Teaching in the Online Classroom: Surviving and Thriving in the New Normal* (pp. 57–80). Jossey-Bass.

Garcia, N. M., & Delgado Bernal, D. (2021). Remembering and revisiting pedagogies of the home. *American Educational Research Journal*, *58*(3), 567–601. doi:10.3102/0002831220954431

Gee, J. P. (2014). *An introduction to discourse analysis: Theory and method*. Routledge. doi:10.4324/9781315819679

Gentner, D., Rottermann, M. J., & Forbus, K. D. (1993). The roles of similarity intransfer: Separating retrievability from inferential soundness. *Cognitive Psychology*, *25*(4), 524–575. doi:10.1006/cogp.1993.1013 PMID:8243045

Gonzalez, N., Moll, L. C., & Amanti, C. (Eds.). (2005). *Funds of knowledge*. Routledge.

Green, T. (2020). Distance education in k-12: Guiding practice through a shared definition and framework. In J. P. Green (Ed.), *Thriving as an Online K-12 Educator* (pp. 1–16). Routledge. doi:10.4324/9781003127635-1

Griswold, J., Shaw, L., & Munn, M. (2017). Socratic seminar with data: A strategy to support student discourse and understanding. *The American Biology Teacher*, *79*(6), 492–495. doi:10.1525/abt.2017.79.6.492 PMID:29147033

Halpern, D. F. (1998). Teaching critical thinking for transfer across domains: Dispositions, skills, structure training, and metacognitive monitoring. *The American Psychologist*, *53*(4), 449–455. doi:10.1037/0003-066X.53.4.449 PMID:9572008

Helterbran, V. R., & Strahler, B. R. (2013). Children as global citizens: A socratic approach to teaching character. *Childhood Education*, *89*(5), 310–314. doi:10.108 0/00094056.2013.830902

Holroyd, J. (2015). Implicit bias, awareness and imperfect cognitions. *Consciousness and Cognition*, *33*, 511–523. doi:10.1016/j.concog.2014.08.024 PMID:25467778

Hunt, L., & Yoshida-Ehrmann, E. (2016). Linking schools of thought to schools of practice. *Gifted Child Today*, *39*(3), 164–172. doi:10.1177/1076217516644650

Jacoby, B. (1999). Partnerships for service learning. *New Directions for Student Services*, *87*, 18–35.

Jagers, R. J., Rivas-Drake, D., & Williams, B. (2019). Transformative social and emotional learning (SEL): Toward SEL in service of educational equity and excellence. *Educational Psychologist*, *54*(3), 162–184. doi:10.1080/00461520.2019.1623032

Katsara, O., & Witte, K. (2019). How to use Socratic questioning in order to promote adult's self-directed learning. *Studies in the Education of Adults*, *51*(1), 109–129. doi:10.1080/02660830.2018.1526446

Keengwe, J., & Kidd, T. T. (2010). Towards best-practices in online learning and teaching in higher education. *Journal of Online Learning and Teaching*, *6*(2), 533–539.

Krischler, M., Powell, J. J., & Pit-Ten Cate, I. M. (2019). What is meant by inclusion? On the effects of different definitions on attitudes towards inclusion education. *European Journal of Special Needs Education*, *34*(5), 632–648. doi:10.1080/088 56257.2019.1580837

Kurt, G., Atay, D., & Ozturk, H. A. (2021). Student engagement in K-12 online education during the pandemic: The case of Turkey. *Journal of Research on Technology in Education*. Advance online publication. doi:10.1080/15391523.2021.1920518

Ladson-Billings, G. (2014). Culturally relevant pedagogy 2.0: Aka the remix. *Harvard Educational Review*, *84*(1), 74–84. doi:10.17763/haer.84.1.p2rj131485484751

Laur, D. (2019). *Authentic project-based learning in grades 9-12: Standards-based strategies and scaffolding for success.* Routledge. doi:10.4324/9780429275258

Lemov, D., & Woolway, E. (2020). Remote teaching and the new normal. In D. Lemov (Ed.), *Teaching in the Online Classroom: Surviving and Thriving in the New Normal* (pp. 1–14). Jossey-Bass.

Mangrum, J. R. (2010). Sharing practices through socratic seminar. *Kappan, 91*(7), 40–43. doi:10.1177/003172171009100708

Manzone, J., & Peeples, R. (2021). Curated conversations: Transferring diverse literature to the K-12 classroom. In D. Hartsfield (Ed.), *Handbook of Research on Teaching Diverse Literature to Pre-Service Professionals* (pp. 257–275). IGI Global Publishing. doi:10.4018/978-1-7998-7375-4.ch013

Moeller, V. J., & Moeller, M. V. (2002). *Socratic seminars and literature circles for middle and high school English.* Eye on Education.

Moffett, J. (1968). *Teaching the universe of discourse.* Heinemann.

National Paideia Center. (2003). *The Paideia seminar: Active thinking through dialogue in the elementary grades.* Chapel Hill, NC: Author. www.paideia.org

Nieto, S., & Bode, P. (2018). Affirming diversity: The sociopolitical context for multicultural education (7th ed.). New York, NY: Pearson.

Nikulin, D. (2006). *On dialogue.* Lexington Books.

Paris, D. (2012). Culturally sustaining pedagogy: A needed change in stance, terminology, and practice. *Educational Researcher, 41*(3), 93–97. doi:10.3102/0013189X12441244

Rivas-Drake, D., Rosario-Ramos, E., McGovern, G., & Jagers, R. J. (2021). Rising up together: Spotlighting transformative SEL in practice with Latinx youth. CASEL: University of Michigan.

Rubel, L. (2017). Equity-directed instructional practices: Beyond the dominant perspective. *Journal of Urban Mathematics Education, 10*(2), 66–105.

Rugani, J., & Grijalva, K. (2020). Dissolve the Screen. In D. Lemov (Ed.), *Teaching in the Online Classroom: Surviving and Thriving in the New Normal* (pp. 36–56). Jossey-Bass.

Salmon, A. K. (2018). Frameworks that promote authentic learning. In A. K. Salmon (Ed.), *Authentic Teaching and Learning for PreK-Fifth Grade: Advice from Practitioners and Coaches* (pp. 1–31). Routledge. doi:10.4324/9781351211505-1

Schneider, J. (2013). Remembrance of things past: A history of the Socratic method in the United States. *Curriculum Inquiry, 43*(5), 613–640. doi:10.1111/curi.12030

Schrank, Z. (2020). Integrating the daily newspaper into the college classroom. *The Journal of Scholarship of Teaching and Learning, 20*(2), 122–126. doi:10.14434/josotl.v20i2.24386

Stieler-Hunt, C., & Jones, C. M. (2015). Educators who believe: Understanding the enthusiasm of teachers who use digital games in the classroom. *Research in Learning Technology, 23,* 1–14. doi:10.3402/rlt.v23.26155

Strong, M. (1996). *The habit of thought: From Socratic seminars to Socratic practice.* New View.

Subotnik, R. F., Olszewski-Kubilius, P., & Worrell, F. C. (2021). The talent development megamodel: A domain-specific conceptual framework based on the psychology of high performance. In R.J. Sternberg & D. Ambrose (Eds.), Conceptions of Giftedness and Talent (pp. 425-442). Palgrave Macmillan. doi:10.1007/978-3-030-56869-6_24

Tannen, D. (1998). *The argument culture: Moving from debate to dialogue.* Random House.

Teaching Tolerance. (2016). *Social justice standards: The teaching anti-bias framework.* Author.

Walsh-Moorman, B. (2016). The socratic seminar in the age of the common core: A search for text-dependent discourse. *English Journal, 105*(6), 72–77.

Wang, Q., & Huang, C. (2017). Pedagogical, social and technical designs of a blended synchronous learning environment. *British Journal of Educational Technology, 49*(3), 451–462. doi:10.1111/bjet.12558

Wu, Y. (2016). Factors impacting students' online learning experience in a learner-centered course. *Journal of Computer Assisted Learning, 32*(5), 416–429. doi:10.1111/jcal.12142

Wynter-Hoyte, K., Braden, E. G., Rodriguez, S., & Thornton, N. (2019). Disrupting the status quo: Exploring culturally relevant and sustaining pedagogies for young diverse learners. *Race, Ethnicity and Education, 22*(3), 428–447. doi:10.1080/13613324.2017.1382465

Yosso, T. (2005). Whose culture has capital? A critical race theory discussion of community cultural wealth. *Race, Ethnicity and Education, 8*(1), 69–91. doi:10.1080/1361332052000341006

Yun, S., & Shin, H. Y. (2021). Social justice-oriented activity models for young learners illiteracy development in a Korean language classroom. *NABE Journal of Research and Practice*, *11*(1-2), 13–21. doi:10.1080/26390043.2021.1950518

Zinn, J. E., Bloodworth, M. R., Weissberg, R. P., & Walberg, H. J. (2007). The scientific base linking social and emotional learning to school success. *Journal of Educational & Psychological Consultation*, *17*(2-3), 191–210. doi:10.1080/10474410701413145

Chapter 4
Tracing Bias in a World of Binary:
Instilling Anti-Racist Information Literacy Skills in Online Environments

Jennifer Kontny
Mount Mary University, USA

ABSTRACT

The chapter details how the first-year writing program at a small, highly diverse, private university in the Midwest responded to the pandemic and the social unrest of the time by engaging in a wholesale revision of the information literacy curriculum. The authors aimed to build a pedagogical framework that would acknowledge the power, influence, and lure of digitally but simultaneously would trace its complex biases. In sharing the curriculum that aims to recoup central critical questions—a more holistically imagined, digital curriculum designed to bolster anti-racist pedagogy—this chapter will answer the following questions: What does digital, anti-racist, and culturally responsive information literacy curriculum look like in this moment? and What kinds of methodologies for teaching information literacy might we follow to help make space for the continual evolution required when teaching through an anti-racist, culturally responsive lens?

DOI: 10.4018/978-1-6684-4055-1.ch004

Copyright © 2023, IGI Global. Copying or distributing in print or electronic forms without written permission of IGI Global is prohibited.

INTRODUCTION

Holistically Considered, Anti-Racist, And Online: New Directions for Devising Information Literacy Curriculum – An Introduction

Librarians and writing studies faculty have long acknowledged the need to devise more robust information literacy curriculum. Teaching "information literacy" has often meant guiding students though using technologies in order to gain access to particular kinds of information and cite sources in ways that align with convention (e.g. *How does one find a peer reviewed article? A government report? How does one cite an interview in APA format?*).

But such traditional approaches to teaching information literacy – those that have focused tightly around accessing and citing particular academic genres of information – have historically excluded broader, critical questions about information itself: considering what information is in the first place, how it circulates, how we critically evaluate it, and how we can position different kinds of information in our own research to have various kinds of social, cultural, and political effects. Moreover, our current approaches to information literacy often exclude questions of power, privilege, and access – how particular kinds of information are more likely to be represented and disseminated than others.

A more critical approach to information literacy insists on seeing our students not just as passive consumers of information, but as active agents who already circulate and produce information as members of the culture – most often by using digital platforms and tools within online environments. Notably, it is what has long been relegated to the margins of our higher ed information literacy curricula that our culture most needs. When we lament the poor information literacy skills of Americans, it is typically a critical understanding of information (and the technologies that produce and circulate such information) that we find most lacking. And currently, our American social landscape seems more riddled than ever with misinformation and conspiracy theories – theories often born, nurtured, and set loose to roam free in online environments.

Beyond addressing our missed opportunity to take a more critical, holistic approach to information literacy – one that is so very needed, this chapter details how the convergence of the global COVID-19 pandemic alongside the Black Lives Matter (BLM) movement created new priorities in developing better information literacy instruction that both occurred online and fostered space for students to critically analyze digital contexts. In short, we need information literacy curriculum that acknowledges the fundamental truth that technologist Marshall McLuhan declared decades ago: "the medium is the message" (McLuhan 1964).

McLuhan and whole bodies of scholarship across fields responding to his work point out that information is inextricable from the environments where it lives. To teach information literacy in robust, dynamic ways today – *and in socially responsible and just ways* – our students must understand how information is inherently linked to the networked technologies that produce and distribute it, and they must understand the inherent biases braided into the binary used to fashion those technologies.

The chapter details how our first-year writing program at a small, highly diverse, private university in the midwest responded to the pandemic and the social unrest of our time by engaging in a wholesale revision of our information literacy curriculum.

Our recent revisions set out to accomplish two goals: 1) to devise information literacy curriculum best suited for a digital context (that is, instruction that occurs online *and* instruction that asks students to critically examine online environments; and 2) to craft online information literacy curriculum for a highly diverse student population – curriculum that we could consider "anti-racist" in its own right. We wanted to build a pedagogical framework that would acknowledge the power, influence, and lure of digitally but simultaneously would trace its complex biases.

In sharing our curriculum that aims to recoup central critical questions – a more holistically imagined, digital curriculum designed to bolster anti-racist pedagogy – this chapter will answer the following questions: *What does digital, anti-racist and culturally responsive information literacy curriculum look like in this moment?* And: *What kinds of methodologies for teaching information literacy might we follow to help make space for the continual evolution required when teaching through an anti-racist, culturally responsive lens?*

Undoubtedly, teaching during the pandemic presented higher ed classrooms across the country with obstacle upon obstacle. And yet, the convergence of the pandemic with increased attention to social justice and inequality through the BLM movement demanded that we turn our attention toward the complexities of information and the politics and policies that surround it.

I argue that the digital, anti-racist approach to teaching information literacy that we devised in a relatively short timeframe was not simply yielded *in response to* our times, but *because of* our times. And yet, it's true that good information literacy curriculum is *always* evolving. Our work to holistically update and revise our program's approach to information will situate us to emerge on the other side of the pandemic as savvier guides for our students. As we all learn to more adeptly wade through the vastness of available information, we know that teaching information literacy today is truly riveting work. Social change is tightly bound not merely to how we *consume* or even *understand* information, but to our ability to be active participants in shaping and reshaping social, cultural, and political dialogues. In sum, our ability to posit "facts" and "truths" in the online environments that we inhabit is directly correlated with our ability to shape and reshape our collective reality, our collective future. It is this set of possibilities, the lessons that circulate in this orbit, that we are exploring with our students and to share with readers here.

What We Know: Obstacles to Better Information Literacy Curriculum

While writing studies contains a long lineage of sources documenting a need for more robust and relevant information literacy curriculum, this scholarship seems to catalogue a number of obstacles that often stand in the way of doing such work.

At the undergraduate level, information literacy instruction often resides at the intersection of campus libraries and writing programs – including both first-year writing programs and campus writing centers (Bronshteyn & Baladad 2006; Holliday & Fagerheim 2006; Deitering & Jameson 2008; Barratt et al. 2009; and Brady et al. 2009; Holliday & Rodgers 2013; Fielding et al. 2013). Perhaps it is information literacy's "joint" custody within the space of the university that has slowed progress in devising more timely, robust curriculum for our students. It takes a lot of work to thoroughly revise *any* curriculum, but when that curriculum is shared between and across multiple factions, the collaboration required to make major overhauls can pose obstacles to getting this work accomplished.

Despite the institutional challenges to devising more robust and relevant information literacy curriculum, scholars in both library science and writing studies have increasingly worked to collaborate in order to create current and responsive information literacy instruction, and much of this work has occurred during the past decade.

In "Perceptions of Students' Information Literacy Competencies, and a Call for a Collaborative Approach" Elizabeth Birmingham et al. (2008) argue that without a truly cooperative effort across writing programs, writing centers, and libraries, students won't gain much ground in feeling confident in their information literacy skills. Even when campus-wide collaboration is incited, writing center scholars have argued that campus writing centers often get left out of the loop when initiating such collaborations regarding information literacy (Clark 1995; Cannon & Jarson 2009; Zahua 2014). Further, campuses that have Writing Across the Curriculum programs, while offering many benefits in general, also experience unique challenges when attempting collaboration as those involved in teaching research writing may be spread across colleges or schools within the university, and may therefore find it challenging to work together, both logistically and/or politically (Sheridan 1992; Elmborg 2003).

Samson & Millett (2003) point out that, even in looking beyond institutional constituencies, the precarious roles of those who are responsible for teaching information literacy – often graduate students or adjunct faculty – make uniformity and consistency a challenge, even when broader collaborative dialogues are occurring within a university.

As if these challenges weren't enough, when considering digital – especially fully online – information literacy curriculum, the challenges of collaboration become even more tricky. Prior to the pandemic, not all writing instructors had taught online; not all writing and research tutors had tutored online. Hence, devising digital information literacy curriculum – curriculum that's not just *about* digital spaces, but *about digital spaces within digital spaces* – was impossibly complex, and often not considered as a central priority when designing program-wide curriculum.

In addition to challenges to collaboration posed by institutional infrastructure, institutional roles, the the limited knowledge of digital technology and culture among those teaching, good information literacy curriculum also poses its own inherent challenges. Technological advancements in our increasingly global, techno-capitalist world seem to be coming at lightening speed. Hence, while we *know* our traditional methods for approaching information literacy in our writing courses – taking students for a single, "one shot" library session (Artman et al. 2010; Watson et al. 2013), teaching paraphrasing or quotation (Bronshteyn & Baladad 2006) and, more broadly, teaching citation practice (Watson 2012) – simply aren't enough anymore, many of the constituents responsible for teaching these skills seem at a loss for how to move beyond these traditions and into something richer and more rewarding for students – something more beneficial to those participating in our digital culture at a moment when a more critical approach to information literacy is vitally needed, albeit constantly shifting in terms of what that might look like.

In sum, our methods for teaching information literacy have long been outpaced by our cultural contexts. And while we've known for at least over a decade that we need to work together to collaborate on something better, that something remained a bit unclear. For us, at my institution, the project of attempting something better was a murky shape in the distance – something that we knew we needed to do, but something that didn't seem urgent until the spring of 2020.

A Pedagogical Collision: The Fusing of Two Timely Scholarly Conversations

In March of 2020 professional development online conferences and seminars sprang up touting best practices in teaching writing online, but extremely little of that work specifically focused on teaching students to research and write in completely digital, online environments.

There was, thankfully, an existing foundation of work delving into information literacy and digitality to draw from as writing instructors attempted to teach students about researching and writing in such environments. And yet, while this material was largely *about* digital environments – it often assumed in-person contact with students for instructional time.

For example, while Sweeney (2012) argued that Wikipedia can be a fruitful site for students to learn about information, credibility, and citation online, much of the pedagogical discussion embedded in articles like these assumes that lessons about information online would be implemented in physical classrooms. Hence, while there were a number of smart, savvy observations within writing studies about the potential of online spaces for teaching information literacy, there was little research about how to teach information literacy *from a strictly digital environment.*

There was, however, also some scholarship on moments of fully online instruction in otherwise in-person or face-to-face courses. There was research documenting attempts to move instruction about information literacy online (McClure et al. 2015); articles about integrating information literacy within online communities (Burgoyne & Chuppa-Cornell 2015); and scholarship on holding what is sometimes referred to as the one-shot "library class" online (Ovadia 2010).

While these earlier attempts to imagine how information literacy curriculum could be taught with digitality in mind (whether by attending to digital spaces or by imagining how we could teach within them), many of these efforts did little to redress how we approached information literacy in the first place. That is, many of these online efforts stayed true to traditional information literacy pedagogies.

During the spring of 2020, as those scrambling to put together digital information literacy curriculum turned back to these conversations, many of us were were reminded of the work that awaited – an approach to information literacy that more centrally embraced not only critical thinking skills (Alfino et al. 2008), but also a view of students as active circulators and producers (Sweeney 2012). We needed an approach to information literacy that felt more relevant to our students, that harnessed the power of the ways they reviewed, used, and produced information in their everyday lives.

As if the spring of 2020 wasn't enough of a wake-up call on its own, within my institution – and I suspect many others – it was the historical collision of the pandemic (which invited those across writing studies to more fully embrace digitality) with the BLM movement (which reminded us of the ever-present bias of information and information technologies) that incited our realization that a broad-based revision to information literacy curriculum wasn't just a good idea, it was vital. The time was now.

By the summer of 2020, many educators seemed to be grappling with re-situating and reshaping various aspects of their pedagogy once again, this time with social justice as the driving value. While difficulties of online teaching in a pandemic didn't stop, many pedagogues turned their attention beyond the challenges of online teaching itself.

The BLM movement drew pedagogues' attention toward teaching writing in socially and linguistically just ways. While there was an ample foundation for culturally responsive writing instruction, significantly less had been written about how information literacy curriculum could be taught in ways closely aligned with the social and linguistic justice efforts that attempted to define anti-racist writing pedagogy.

The remainder of this chapter attempts to directly merge these scholarly efforts and fill in this gap. It answers the questions: *What does socially just and culturally responsive information literacy curriculum look like in this moment?; How can we build this curriculum online?;* and *What kinds of methodologies for teaching informational literacy might we follow to help make space for the kinds of revision and continual evolution that are required?*

The body of this chapter invites readers into a dialogue about how we can work together to update information literacy curriculum within digital environments for the good of our students, our universities, and – ultimately – our nation.

PRIORITIES AND DIRECTIONS IN ONLINE INFORMATION LITERACY INSTRUCTION – PULLING FORWARD FROM HERE

In the process of pulling together resources for a wholesale curricular revision, we knew we wanted to fuse the conversations happening around online or digital information literacy with those about social justice, and create a bank of materials from which to shape our own anti-racist, digital information literacy curriculum.

Although the conversations about online information literacy curriculum and socially just writing curriculum share moments of overlap, these conversations have often occurred discretely in the field of writing studies, and so I will discuss the main resources we pooled as such – two distinct conversations that we fused together in our curriculum. In the last section of this chapter, that fusion will be discussed further and our full syllabus will be appended.

In collaboration with our campus librarians, we first started our project by discussing the expectations and student learning outcomes (SLOs) of our program that pertained to information literacy. Unsurprisingly, we discovered that our program SLOs and, therefore, our assessment tools were aligned much more strongly with traditional approaches to information literacy, those that valued academic genres and white papers over many other forms of information. For example, our SLOs spoke of citation practice, citation convention, content development, and the ethics of citation, but all in ways that seemed aligned most tightly with the academic white paper. We seemed to be sending a message to students that there were "good" and "bad" sources; "accurate" and "inaccurate" information. And that bifurcated representation seemed, even to those of us who taught it, as reductive, problematic, and outdated.

Because our previous program SLOs were adapted from the American Association of Colleges and Universities (AAC&U) Rubric for Written Communication, we wanted to review other assessment tools that specifically focused on information literacy, and did so in ways that not only acknowledged but prioritized the wealth of digital culture that surrounds us. In doing so, we reviewed a large number of samples from educational organizations and institutions, including the AAC&U's rubric on information literacy. Certainly, there is no shortage of resources or research on information literacy. In fact, as Mike Caufield argues in his blog on open education and digital information literacy, perhaps the problem is that there is too much, and too many varied approaches that are applauded, but not fully understood.

In his blog *Hapgood* the post "Yes, Digital Literacy. But Which One?", Caufield argues that the acronym-based models often used to teach information literacy (RADCAB or CRAAP) are simply not enough. He acknowledges that the "inevitable calls for more information literacy [are sure to result in] inevitable waves of applause" (2016). And yet, he continues:

We do need more education to focus on information literacy, but we can't do it the way we have done it up to now. We need to come down from that Bloom's Taxonomy peak and teach students basic things about the web and the domains they evaluate so that they have some actual tools and knowledge to deal with larger questions effectively (2016).

What Caufield suggests here is that we need to start simpler, to slow down. His caution in the year 2016 perhaps resonates with us now, in a pandemic world, more than ever. But his point that we need to come down the from "Bloom's taxonomy peak" in our information literacy instruction is interesting, particularly if we think of the student learning outcomes (SLOs) that commonly crop up in writing programs. Verbs like "evaluate" and "analyze" – higher order skills – are often central. Caufield's point that sometimes teaching information literacy means starting from a more accessible place – teaching the basics of technology – was something we wanted to hold onto as we began our project.

In keeping Caufield's argument in mind, alongside considering our own programmatic needs, we found that the best "broad strokes" curricular tool to get us started was the Association for College and Research Libraries (ACRL) Framework for Information Literacy. The ACRL offers a full guide on the framework that is free to download, in addition to an online sandbox space where users can share and download .docx files of adapted ACRL frameworks composed by various programs. The sandbox space allows users to easily make and share adaptations to the ACRL

Information Literacy Framework, which was something those working on this project appreciated. We could see how this tool was used in other writing programs across American institutions, and even within some international universities.

To give a very brief overview, the ACRL framework has six basic "frames" which are: "Authority is Constructed and Contextual; Information Creation as a Process; Information has Value; Research as Inquiry; Scholarship as a Conversation; Searching as Strategic" (ACRL). In the official guide, each of these frames are thoroughly described, but what we liked best about them is that they acknowledge the need to start simply, as Caufield's research cautions. The guide to the ACRL framework explains how these skills might be gained, and acknowledges that this learning in non-linear.

From even a cursory glance at the ACRL framework, it is clear that the six frames, in and of themself, encourage a dynamic view of information. However, upon reviewing the language in the framework, and across various adapted samples posted by users at various academic institutions, it is clear that this framework was designed for users who are actively investigating information in its *many* forms and who are committed to the idea that information is inextricably bound to the digital contexts where it often lives today.

In one example ACRL framework adaptation located in the user sandbox, the framework spells out learning objectives for students. In the first category, "Authority is constructed and contextual," the framework considers students to be reaching the highest level of development when they realize, among other things, that students "recognize [sic] that authoritative content may be packaged formally or informally" and, additionally, that they "recognize [sic] that authority may include sources of all media types" ("UWC Libraries ACRL Framework Rubric"). These SLOs and how they are manifested in this particular example make a clear move away from viewing authority in staid ways, ways ignoring the complexity of digital culture. The language used in this adaptation assessment tool acknowledges that authority doesn't reside in particular forms, but in how those forms are situated and responded to within a context. There are countless other examples of how this framework makes space for recognizing the power of digital information – it is wholly and intentionally designed for information literacy curriculum that embraces the ways technology, information, and forming knowledge are deeply entwined with our networked world.

But the framework goes beyond this – it asks students not just to develop "knowledge practices" for each of the frames, but also "dispositions". This way of representing literacy draws our attention to the fact that literacy skills are embodied and rooted in practice and lived experiences. This approach to information literacy felt familiar to how canonical work in our field has approached other kinds of literacies (Gee 1989; Delpit 2006).

And in thinking back to one of the challenges of instilling better digital information literacy instruction – that instructors themselves felt at a loss – we found the guide and resources for the ACRL framework to be immensely helpful. By doing hours of professional development work with our writing instructors, we all felt as if our own understanding of information literacy was challenged and changed for the better because of the ACRL Framework guide. And perhaps by viewing literacy as sets of "practices" and "dispositions" we can resist the temptation to jump to the peak of Bloom's taxonomy when teaching information literacy. That is, by emphasizing that practices and dispositions are key to literacy, the ACRL Framework might legitimate pedagogical choices that emphasize slowly swimming out to the depths of networked spaces, rather that what Caufield argues that we tend to do now – ask students to dip their toe in and pull out complex and elaborate analyses without understanding the basics.

Further support for how this framework offers a deeper dive into technology all the while viewing literacy as something integrally connected to practices and dispositions can be found on the ACRL Information Literacy Framework's "Resources" tab, where pedagogues can post related curriculum. One example exercise asks students to consider the relationship memes have to research, another asks students to translate census data into an infographic. My favorite, "#ForYou: Algorithms & the Attention Economy", has students consider recommendation algorithms and how those shape our attention and identities online (Chisholm 2021). There are countless lesson plans, exercises, and assignments posted on this Resources page, each corresponding to one or more the ACRL frames, each taking quite a cutting-edge approach to asking students to consider today's technologies – both their startling possibility and potential and the way in which bias may be braided into their fabric.

While the ACRL framework was game-changing in setting our agenda for a more robust information literacy curriculum, it is not really a tool that helped us map out our curriculum in a week-to-week or class-to-class sense (although the "Resources" page gave us some exciting ideas). In one meeting, when we wondered about using the six frames as organizing principles on a syllabus, our instructional librarian reminded us that these frames were meant to be threaded through the curriculum, not to be explored discretely or distinctly.

We discussed and highlighted main components of the ACRL Framework that we wanted to piece into our revised curriculum, and as we did so we knew we needed an additional tool or structuring apparatus to frame these lessons. That's where the information cycle has come in.

The shift away from traditional one-shot (or two-shot, as was standard in our previous curriculum) library models and toward the information cycle has been central. The information cycle's main purpose is to help students visualize the circulation of information, pointing out the various merits and drawbacks or limitations of particular kinds of information. While there are many explanations of the information cycle circulating (a lot of university or research libraries have their own definitions or videos of this concept), in developing our curriculum we found the most useful resource to be the University of Illinois Libraries' infographic and paired video. This seemed to be the clearest and most efficient source for adapting to our own classrooms after testing several during our semester-long pilot.

The concept of the "information cycle" is valuable to students because not only does it visually portray that different kinds of information existing in the moment (e.g. a day after an event, a week after, weeks after, months after, and so on), but it gets readers to think about the relationship between those various informational sources. Both COVID-19 and the Black Lives Matter movement were both commonly discussed examples when we taught the information cycle in class. Students understand that what we know on Day 1 of an event is almost always different from what we know on Days 2 or 3 or 4 or 36. When piloting the Information Cycle with our students, our discussions landed on realizations that particular mediums can allow or constrain certain forms of information, knowledge, and reflection.

Perhaps most importantly, in using the Information Cycle as a tool to teach SLOs on the ACRL Framework, students begin to realize the necessity of using multiple sources, at multiple moments in time, across multiple genres and perspectives, and with varying purposes. In other words, by using the Information Cycle to teach information literacy, students often begin to be able to very clearly see one of the major frames of the ACRL – Scholarship as a Conversation.

A major omission on not only University of Illinois' representation of the Information Cycle, but the representations of many other libraries as well, is the idea that artistic production can be a kind of information. In our own curriculum we attempt to make significantly more space for visual, aural, tactile, and other kinds of artistic information in how we teach the information cycle. While I won't have time to get into this with much detail in this chapter, the sample syllabus points to a few specific exercises that draw students' attention to the way that information is visually represented (and how one can do that in anti-racist ways).

Despite this notable limitation, we – like many other institutions – have found enumerable benefits of teaching through the lens of the Information Cycle. Like the ACRL Framework, the Information Cycle doesn't just combat the idea that journalistic or social media sources, for example, aren't inherently "accurate" or "good" sources. The Information Cycle almost insists that we look at all kinds of information in the context of other information in order to better understand it. Information then becomes not something that's simply good or bad, but something that must be investigated, considered, weighed critically with the many dispositions suggested in the ACRL Framework.

Taken collectively, then, the ACRL rubric and the Information Cycle do something powerful when combined. They place digitality front and center. In an era where so many of our courses are happening online, this is certainly useful and timely. While Institutions will continue to offer research writing courses in a variety of modalities – "online", "hybrid", or "in person", what we have learned this past year in our own institutional context is that there are rich possibilities for holding information literacy curriculum, or aspects of that curriculum, in an online environment despite how a course is offered.

When we are teaching fully online, it's necessary to talk about the structure of a good online comment and how that contributes to academic conversation, or how algorithms are shaping our sense of community, or how social media posts are often all the information we have on important events in the minutes or hours, even, after they occur. But whether or not students are learning these things in online contexts, these are digital aspects of information literacy and composing that we should no longer ignore, that we can no longer ignore despite how a course is offered.

While, going forward, not every research writing course will be taught fully online, both the ACRL framework and the Information Cycle have been adapted within our program and they are here to stay. So too, then, will the understanding that online contexts and classes cannot be exceptional spaces where we acknowledge and consider research writing in a digital context. This, instead, should be the norm and the standard across all sections. And realizing this will also help us foster a greater degree of curricular continuity across sections of research writing despite what modality courses happen to be offered within.

Priorities and Directions for Anti-Racist, Online Information Literacy Instruction –Pulling Forward from There

While we found a significant bank of materials that would easily lend themselves to online adaptation, we found it much more challenging to gather materials that explicitly focused on doing anti-racist work through information literacy curriculum.

My field of origin within writing studies, rhetoric and composition, certainly has a history of acknowledging the ways that language instruction has historically been racist (Canagarajah 2010; Young 2010; Lippi-Green 2012; Condon & Young 2016; Lyiscott 2018; Inoue 2019; Baker Bell 2020). There has been attention to the ways that anti-blackness, in particular, has affected writing pedagogy (Smitherman; Lyiscott 2018; Baker Bell 2020) and writing assessment (Inoue & Poe 2012; Inoue 2019; Inoue 2019), and in the wake of the BLM movement and the murder of George Floyd, recent scholars have made significant headway in bringing these conversations onto the main stage of the field.

Yet, broadly speaking, while better information literacy is usually viewed as one way of redressing the racism ingrained in our culture, there has been significantly less work to explicitly tease out how critical race theories might inform information literacy instruction. Or, even when information literacy skills have been addressed in the workshops and professional development efforts that sprang up in response to the murder of George Floyd, it seems that anti-racist instruction is set alongside information literacy instruction rather than developed as integral to it.

While her work is certainly not stemming from writing studies, one text that's often brought into conversations about digital information literacy and anti-racism is the work of Saffiya Noble. Noble's book, *Algorithms of Oppression*, focuses on how technologies – Google, specifically – are racist and deeply biased. Noble reminds us that these technologies were, in fact, created by humans and therefore are no more forward thinking than humans who work in big tech industries (often white men). While Noble's work is often discussed when talking about anti-racism in writing studies, it's been difficult to locate curriculum that digs into her central arguments with complexity and nuance, adapting her work for an undergraduate student audience.

Despite the fact that there has been less attention to developing explicitly anti-racist information literacy curriculum within writing studies itself, University of Minnesota librarians Shanda Hunt and Amy Riegelman have developed a robust library guide from a library sciences perspective that our team found thoughtful and thorough as we revised our curriculum.

In the introduction, Hunt and Riegelman state that the guide was created after requests from faculty who were "looking to incorporate anti-racism into their research practices" (Hunt & Riegelman 2021). The authors go on to to qualify their project by stating:

Conducting research through an anti-racism lens is a long-term and ongoing process and must be considered as part of a complex system which oppresses people and groups in multifaceted ways (i.e., classism, ethnocentrism, capitalism, casteism, etc.). While some disciplines, mainly in the humanities and social sciences, have mitigated racism through a depth of understanding of critical race theory, others have not"

(Hunt & Riegelman "Guide for Anti-Racist Research", UMN Libraries).

While it is very brief, the definition of anti-racism in this guide acknowledges intersectionality. The brief definition, during our pilot of the curriculum, made room for interesting discussion in and of itself within our classrooms. Further, because Hunt and Riegelman acknowledge that different academic discourse communities are starting from different places on this journey, they provide a diverse set of examples and linked articles that might gain traction with students in various fields from medicine to linguistics or computer science. In other words, the guide encourages instructors teaching information literacy (often those housed in the humanities) to draw explicit bridges between more humanistic thinking and the thinking in applied, professional fields. Our team considered this an asset in our first-year writing program, and this resource, coupled with class exercises on the ACRL Information Literacy Framework Resources page, made for an excellent foundation for our revised curriculum.

The six webpages (or, what I'm calling "tenets" here) in the UMN Anti-Racist Library Guide are as follows: "Decenter whiteness in primary research; Decenter whiteness in secondary research; Acknowledge that data is not objective; Acknowledge that scholarly publishing is racist; Acknowledge that search algorithms are racist; Acknowledge that library cataloging systems are racist (Hunt & Riegelman, "Anti-Racist Library Guide", University of Minnesota). We have found the six tenets of the guide to be useful as a potential organizing principle for a course, especially when approaching those tenets through the lens of "tracing bias in a binary world".

These six tenets of antiracist research hook in nicely with the broader attempts to see information as inherently digital and dynamic mentioned in the previous section. In fact, we see clear overlap across learning outcomes on the ACRL Framework and the tenets above. For example, the third tenet states, "Acknowledge that data is not objective". This resonates perfectly with the ACRL idea that research and scholarship are situated, contextual, and that all kinds of information come from a particular vantage point.

What perhaps makes this guide most compelling for those hoping to do information literacy education in online contexts is that under each of the six tenets, Hunt and Riegelman have linked examples from our current culture, and such examples make for great links in fully online courses, whether in discussion boards or forums, or on digital discussion platforms like Slack. While the UMN library guide is not the only guide on anti-racist research, we have found it to be one of the better guides, especially with regard to the linked examples it provides. Boston University (BU) also has a Center for Anti-Racist Research. That webpage, while containing less linked examples, does provide some interesting statements about anti-racist research alongside useful resources for those interested, too. Namely, the BU page provides a link to national data project on COVID (Center for Anti-racist Research, Boston University).

Other schools, like San Jose State, have generously posted anti-racist research writing resources online, resources that are the result of working groups. One such resource, "Approaching Writing with an Antiracist Perspective" author Seher Vora writes, "Many stylebooks [sic], such as APA, MLA, Chicago, and the AP, only address writing about race by advising writers to avoid bias and stereotyping. Yet, they don't necessarily explain what falls under racist language and what does not." While Vora's critique is correct – style books that have long been the foundation for information literacy curriculum – namely, discussions of citation – do not adequately delve into the politics of what it means to write in anti-racist ways. And turning back to the ACRL Information Literacy Framework as well as the arguments of scholars like Noble, we know anti-racism research practice isn't limited to the language we use in our writing. Noble's research reminds us that anti-racist research must include considering how we find sources to begin with, what representations of research are more or less available, and how the technologies we use to engage in our research process are inherently working against our anti-racist goals. In other words, anti-racist research must extend far beyond the linguistic expression we use to frame our scholarship. Because bias is braided into the binary, the very means by which we engage in research, anti-racist research encompasses an intentional rejection of the systems and codes that keep racist notions circulating within our broader culture, and within the academy.

On whole, it is true that anti-racist thinking in general is an area that many across the academy are hoping to better develop, and we are seeing more resources daily. But there remain huge gaps in resources for teaching information literacy in explicitly anti-racist ways. And this is especially true when thinking about how we might teach information literacy in anti-racist ways online.

What we found as we worked on this project, was that the collision of social contexts: the pandemic with the social unrest surrounding the BLM protests, helped us see an important connection. Teaching online wasn't a constraint to teaching anti-racist information literacy curriculum. And teaching through an anti-racist lens wasn't more challenging online. Rather, these efforts buoyed one another. While these two initiatives remain relatively separate in the literature of writing studies, we found that pursuing the goals of either initiative was directly and deeply aligned with the other.

That is, as we shift away from viewing research in conventional and in unnecessarily bifurcated ways – as either "good" or "bad"; "accurate" or "inaccurate" based on the historical standards of the academic white paper, we are thereby shaking up what counts as information, knowledge, and even wisdom. In trying to critically situate all information within its broader context and to assess that critically, we are compelled to recognize broader and altogether different pathways to viewing information or forming knowledge. By contextualizing and potentially legitimating new kinds of information – often new genres as they emerge and exist online – we are often, too, inviting new voices to the table. While the race to move courses online followed by the urgent need to re-up our commitment to social justice felt, in the moments we experienced them, as incidental, the fusion of these two curricular efforts has been anything but.

What we have attempted to do is to mindfully create efforts to open up critical conversations about what information is and how it lives and breathes, especially in the worlds we inhabit online. And threaded through that are conscious attempts to understand that in the opening up of information, there are new kinds of biases, new issues to consider. But there are new possibilities, too. New affordances.

The challenge we set for ourselves in building the curriculum below was to forge these projects – to offer students a chance to recognize the many ways that bias slips under our collective radar in the seamless, shiny online interfaces and platforms that we all live among. Yet, we wanted our students to recognize and acknowledge such biases in critical ways that offered them a sense of how to use technology most effectively, how to participate in and re-shape such online spaces in ways that would mitigate their harm and maximize their potential for social change.

ANTI-RACIST INFORMATION LITERACY CURRICULUM ENACTED ONLINE

Notes on a Revision in Four Nodes

Before describing the four major nodes to building stronger anti-racist information literacy curriculum online, it's important to say a bit about the institutional context in which these revisions took place and how those factored into the redesign of our curriculum.

Our small, midwestern, liberal arts institution is both a Title III institution, meaning it serves students with high levels of financial need, and a Title IV-eligible institution, meaning it serves high number of students identifying as Hispanic or Latinx/Latino/a. Our institution, while not an HBCU, also serves a high number of students who identify as African-American. Around 60% of our student population from year to year identifies as "non-white".

Our institution is, at the undergraduate-level, a women's college and admits only students who identify as women. Additionally, many of our students identify as a first-generation college students.

Perhaps most relevant to the writing classroom, our university is exceptionally linguistically diverse, with many of our students speaking multiple languages, others considering themselves heritage speakers, and others yet who identify as bi-dialectal speakers.

According to our institution's NSSE survey data, we know our commuter students in particular work a relatively high number of hours per week and are often very involved in family caretaking.

Yet, despite the ways that institutions of higher learning have historically posed challenges for learners with high financial need, non-white learners, first-generation students, mothers or other caretakers, as well as many of the other secondary statuses our students occupy that I discussed above, our institution has been nationally recognized for graduating high percentages of students who occupy one or more of these subject positions.

Additionally, while the emergency decision to move writing courses online during the pandemic originally incited some of the revisions we made to our information literacy curriculum, on whole we have historically valued curricular accessibility and flexibility, which is a benefit often offered through online instruction – whether it be synchronous, asynchronous, or a blended approach.

For reasons of accessibility, then, creating online information literacy curriculum was something we were highly motivated to do in order to make this important curriculum the most accessible to our students. Not only would developing this portion of our curriculum online make it more accessible for students, as members of a first-year writing program we hoped the the online presence of the curriculum would eventually make it more exportable for staff and other faculty who could potentially build upon the information literacy skills students would learn in their writing courses.

Because of what we knew about our student demographic, our institution, and the nature of the project itself, we developed our curricular revision in four "nodes" so to speak, as enumerated below. These didn't necessarily happen discretely, but were efforts that we thought about, tracked, and reflected on as key pieces within our larger project.

1. *Collaboration as Key to Curricular Continuity – Building a Cross-Institutional Team*

From the outset, given the literature on the obstacles to designing better, more robust information literacy curriculum, we knew we wanted a team that spanned across areas and roles within our university. To accomplish this, while balancing time and fiscal constraints, we set up two meeting groups.

The primary meeting group, intended to draft original materials, held bi-weekly meetings. The secondary meeting group, intended to critique and significantly revise those materials, met monthly.

The primary team had representation from our campus library (the head librarian, humanities librarian, and a librarian with experience in instruction) along with representation from writing faculty (the Director of Composition and an Assistant Professor who teaches our central research writing course). Additionally, we included a faculty member from outside of English studies who often teaches writing intensive courses and heads up another area of general education curriculum that would eventually also touch on information literacy.

The secondary team represented folks from the writing program – all adjunct instructors teaching were invited to participate, and most did; professional writing tutors; and peer writing tutors. As the Director of the Writing Program, I served as the liaison between the groups, although on a number of occasions, members of the secondary group would join the primary group of us who were meeting biweekly, or vice-versa. Since many folks in the secondary team were not tenure-track or full-time staff, they were compensated for their participation through a Title III grant.

We were especially mindful, in creating both groups, to include folks who had varying levels of comfort and familiarity with digital literacy and/or information technology.

We began the project in spring, where we redesigned curriculum for the first writing course in our two-course sequence. In the summer, we actively revised these lessons, piloting them in select summer sections as well as during the subsequent fall semester. We are now going through the same process with the second course in our curriculum and hope to have permanently adopted changes across our writing program by Fall 2022.

While collaboration had countless benefits, probably the benefit we wanted to hold most closely in our sight lines was that of curricular continuity. Instead of the "one-shot" (or two- or three-shot) library session, which often feels a bit curricularly disjointed from classroom-level research writing curriculum, we wanted the information literacy work braided into our writing sequence seamlessly. Moreover, we wanted to ensure that this curriculum, once revised and through its pilot, could be accessed by other professors throughout the university should they wish to build upon it. Finally, we wanted representation from the writing program, the library, our tutoring center, and from other faculty so that students would experience recursion in developing these skills. Eventually, we are hoping to develop an information literacy certificate that students can gain across their degree programs to encourage even more consistency and further work with these skills. On whole, as campuses initiate projects to develop better information literacy curriculum, building a team collaboratively and with the structure and demographics of the university in mind, is key. This choice to work collaboratively was not simply a means to do the work – it was the work. Like reflective practice, collaboration was a key to the methodology of this project, and it will certainly be a central to the way we maintain and revise this curriculum moving forward.

2. *Anti-Racist Research in Online Environments – Tracing Bias in a World of Binary*

In our previous curriculum, as is fairly common with traditional approaches to information literacy, students are indirectly positioned to think about sources as either "accurate" or "inaccurate"; "academic" or "not academic"; "good sources" or "bad sources". We wanted, from the outset, to get students to think about sources more complexly, and in richer ways that transcended those reductive binaries. To do so, we designed what we are currently calling our "Tracing Bias in a World of Binary" curriculum – a curriculum that, instead of asking students to think about some sources as inherently biased and others less so, puts the emphasis on identifying and tracing bias in all information resources, and then putting those sources into dialogue within research conversations accordingly.

The main tools of developing this curriculum, all mentioned above, were used to sketch out the structure of the new information literacy curriculum, a curriculum that we planned to enact online and hoped to align with the other anti-racist work happening in the field.

To set broader curricular goals, compose assessment tools, and to think about language that bridged information and library sciences with writing studies, we used the ACRL rubric. Although the rubric was incredibly helpful in the initial phases of this work (especially among members of the primary group), this tool wasn't something heavily or directly used with students. Instead, in the foundational weeks of our entry-level course, students spent time learning the information cycle, and critically analyzing sources in terms of where they might be located on the Information Cycle.

After students were comfortable using the language of the Information Cycle, as well as finding and analyzing sources according to their situatedness in the cycle, we used the structure developed UMN Anti-racist Research Guide to get students to more deeply consider bias as it is inherently braided into research and research technologies. While we don't impose a "standard curriculum" on writing instructors in our program, a general calendar of the semester might look like this, and we have included an sample syllabus in the appendix:

Week 1 *What is information anyway?*
Week 2 *The information cycle*
Week 3 *The information cycle – what is "primary" research?*
Week 4 *Decentering whiteness and privilege in primary research*
Week 5 *The information cycle – what is "secondary" research?*
Week 6 *Decentering whiteness and privilege in secondary research*
Week 7 *Reflecting on our role in shaping information*
Week 8 *Acknowledging that data is not objective – the art of critical analysis*
Week 9 *Acknowledging that scholarly publishing is racist – critical analysis cont.*
Week 10 *Acknowledge that information technologies are racist and othering*

Week 11 *Acknowledging that search algorithms are racist and othering*
Week 12 *Acknowledge that information cataloging systems are racist othering*
Week 13 *Decentering whiteness and privilege through visuality and design*
Week 14 *Re-shaping and revising as part of anti-racist research and writing*
Week 15 *Reflecting on anti-racist response and anti-racist citation*
Week 16 *Responding to audiences in through an anti-racist lens*

Note that the schedule above begins with indirectly drawing from many of the student learning outcomes mentioned in the ACRL rubric. To accomplish these, it uses the lens of the Information Cycles, but heavily folds in the University of Minnesota Anti-Racist Library Guide. For example, in Week 3, students are asked to consider the Information Cycle, and with respect to that, consider both what is meant by "primary research" and a "primary source". When doing so, in class, students had an excellent conversation about how primary research was formalized, and therefore there was more gatekeeping as to who might consider themselves as "primary researcher"; however, a "primary source" could be almost anything. A person on the side of the road who takes a video of an instance of police brutality, an original idea, or response posted to social media. This sets students up to recognize sources as inherently linked to the contexts and conversations that they live within.

The initial week discussing primary research, primary sources, and the information cycle is followed up on in "Week 4: Decenter whiteness primary research". Here, students come to understand that decentering whiteness doesn't just mean writing in a particular voice or according to a particular set of politically correct conventions. Decentering whiteness is something anti-racist researchers must do across every part of the research process.

Certainly, there is so much else to say about the nuances of our curriculum, the primary resources we drew from in creating it: The ACRL framework (in broad strokes, and indirectly), the Information Cycle, and the UMN Antiracist Library Guide, are the core texts that bind sections within our writing program together.

While the sample syllabus provided gives one glimpse into the interplay of these pieces, we also heavily emphasized curricular flexibility so that different instructors could approach these conversations where they and their students felt most comfortable. Circling back to the first node, then, collaboration, we found that having a shared foundation and offering many opportunities for instructors to come together and share with one another – both synchronously and asynchronously online – really supported our transition into and through our pilot.

3.   *Diving into Digitality – Benefits of Teaching Information Literacy Online*

While each of the weeks in our curricular calendar above were designed as online modules, with an abundance of online resources and supportive platforms, we knew we needed to reap the benefits and richness of online spaces by making sure that we included flexibility in how these were implemented.

While all students – no matter their course format – were looking at sources in ways much more complex than those neatly catalogued in any given database, we knew that helping students discuss and analyze online texts in online environments would give rise to different conversational possibilities. That is, we wanted *every* student – despite the modality of their course – to learn about information literacy through inhabiting digital worlds together, reflecting on digital texts, and attempting to compose in online, networked spaces themselves (experimenting with blogging, websites, and other elements of visual composing).

What new skills arose from this? Students learned about hyperlinking, citing images, searching images, reverse searches, algorithms, searching and citing videos. They delved into following and citing commenting threads on news sources, tweets, snaps, Facebook stories, and text messages. The richness of how they saw these sources, because of the information cycle, became clear in their writing. In sections where it used to be difficult to pry students away from overly formal and often stiff language positioning academic white papers as the only valid ideas, students began to take up challenging questions with no easy solutions. The critical, inquiry-driven research some of our instructors had been chasing in their assignment sequences for years started happening more and, when it did, it seemed to occur more organically.

While using resources designed with online environments in mind might seem like a modest change, we've found that these tools have had a dramatic effect on how students see, read, and use sources in their work. For example, after a lesson introducing the information cycle, one writer, Marianna, revised her paper to cite a music video she'd heard while living in Mexico. This became the point of origin for her research. A paper that started out attempting to report on the illegal detention of children at the border turned into a paper about the history of separating children from their families in the U.S., and how those separations were framed by art and media of the time. Through citing that music video, Marianna was able to contextualize the issue of family separation in a personal, emotional, cultural, and historical ways for readers, and in doing so she was able to create broader links to other historical moments and communities. These conversations about family separation were easy to have in online contexts. Students used Wikipedia, library data bases, search-engine results to come up with paintings, songs, radio and television coverage of other instances of the nation removing children from their families of origin – during slavery, in internment camps, in the destruction of native American communities, in the foster care system – historically and today. While some of this would have been able to occur in an in-person classroom, the incessant movement between the student's research writing and the worlds of information online certainly helped shape this student's ideas, as well as the ideas of her colleagues.

4.   *Room for Reflection – From Metacognitive Reflective Writing to Curricular Evaluation & Revision*

Perhaps most importantly, alongside with the assignments on analyzing and creating anti-racist research in online environments, our revised curriculum provided ample opportunities for students to reflect on that work according to best practices.

In terms of meta-cognitive opportunities for reflection, students were asked to do two low-stakes exercises and given one "extra-credit" opportunity.

In Week 2 students were asked to complete an "Information Log" logging a two day period of where and how they received information (on what mediums or platforms). In Week 10, where students consider the ways that information technologies are racist and othering, they are asked to complete a technology inventory and technology de-cluttering exercise. This assignment was based off of a draft from writing studies scholar, Kristin Ravel, who, in her assignment "Decluttering Our Technology" encourages student to remove distracting apps, reminders, and subscriptions on their personal devices.

Both of these low-stakes reflective assignments are meant to help students create connections between theoretical and exemplary texts about technology and their own lived experiences using technology. And they do so, as Mike Caufield argues we all should, in ways that talk about this work simply and accessibly for our students.

These exercises were responded to with a lot of enthusiasm and, by having students complete them in solely online environments, they were able to easily attach links and screenshots, making the trends they discussed more visually observable. For example, in the technology de-cluttering exercise inspired by Ravel's assignment, students were able to post both before and after photos of their phone home screens demonstrating how much "clutter" was removed.

In addition, the low-stakes work in-class, students were also given an "extra-credit" opportunity to complete a "digital habit tracker and mood tracker" — students would set goals for themselves relating to their technology-use or behavior and then log their mood correspondingly. For example, one student said she wanted to take 1,000 steps in between every hour she spent gaming. She noticed that when she did this, she felt better and she found her focus improved, even if it was only her focus in the next hour of gaming. Another student said she wanted to avoid logging into our course Learning Management System after 8pm each night, and found that when she stuck to this, her anxiety decreased.

Beyond the classroom exercises and activities that linked theories and examples to students' own technology practices and behaviors, there were two formal writing assignments asking students to reflect on their own anti-racist, digital research writing.

In the first, during Week 7, students compose a paper on what kinds of practices they've come to associate as anti-racist in others' research, and how they have adopted those practices as research writers themselves. One student writer reflected, "While there is so much research that I don't see as anti-racist, or that furthers the vicious cycles of racism and other kinds of privilege. I think anti-racist research means that when we can't find sources that hold themselves to anti-racist standards, we know how to hold them [the researchers] accountable and respond. To ask good questions of that research. That's the starting point for me, anyway!" (Anonymous Student Sample, Mount Mary University, Fall 2021).

In the next formal reflective assignment, students are asked to talk about specific places in their own text that demonstrate or represent anti-racist research writing practices, specifically anti-racist response or citation practice. The focus here is on particular moments or decisions made in the text. That specificity, we've found, leads students into saying some complex things. One student who I mentioned earlier, Marianna, wrote about why she chose to begin her paper by citing lyrics and visual depictions from a music video:

I chose that video because while there was a lot of research done on family separations, many of those writers were white or not Spanish-speaking. They were removed from the issue. The music video was made by a Latina. There were people who looked like me acting in it. To talk to my Latin audience, I wanted to bring in something that was ours. To me, that's anti-racist citation. Being present in the list of names on the page"

(Anonymous Student Sample, Mount Mary University, Fall 2021).

Moments like these allowed students to hold onto all they have accomplished as anti-racist researchers and to understand that anti-racist research isn't about a wholesale political stance – and it's much more than simply using the most politically correct language – it's about how we see information to begin with, how we legitimate that or not, and how we respond to and validate information in ways that are equal and just.

Lastly, while students had a number of opportunities, ranging from low-stakes to formal to optional reflective assignments, they were also given the opportunity to reflect on quarterly self and class assessments, assessments that we also used within our contract-grading (Inoue 2019) model of assessment. On these assessments, we asked students about how things were going for them in class, in both specific and general ways – what they found complex, troubling, or useful. What they wanted to know more about.

While I won't get into the benefits here of a contract-grading model of writing assessment, it is this work alongside the other reflective work in our classes that we, as writing instructors, perhaps found most useful. What we know about both information literacy, digital culture, and anti-racism, is that the codes are always shifting, always changing. The solutions that work in one context, one moment, will demand a different approach in another. So while the chapter has presented what's worked well for us, we don't pose it as a uniform "code" that will work well everywhere. Hopefully by sharing our collaborative approach for arriving at anti-racist, digital curriculum – the way we attempted to trace the bias of binary, so to speak – readers have seen a glimpse into our process, understood the roles that both collaboration and reflection played in our methodology, as well as gained and understanding of the sources we drew from and where we landed. And it is through reflection in particular that, even though this chapter is written as demonstrating a landing of sorts, a fixed moment in time, we intend to keep working and revising toward these goals into our future.

IMAGINING A MORE LITERATE FUTURE – STEPS FORWARD AND CONCLUSION

While there is undoubtedly a lot of work to be done in shifting the landscape of information literacy instruction in American higher education, the challenging moment we are living within is one that can be enormously useful as campuses begin this work. Revising information literacy curriculum is a challenging task that deeply benefits from collaboration – a holistic and cross-disciplinary approach that both reflects and responds to the time we are living in.

While information has always been linked to the technologies that produce it and help to disseminate it (from the ink and quill, to the newspaper, radio, television, and the internet), our current approaches to teaching information literacy too often shut out the way information today is inextricably bound to networked, digital technology. And while all students should learn about how the information we consume and produce is bound to digital environments, increasing numbers of our students are learning about information literacy *in* completely digital environments. Our approaches must reflect this fact.

In our own program's journey designing curriculum for that helps students best interrogate the digital environments where information circulates, and where we are learning, undoubtedly, that we must confront the inherent racism braided into those spaces (in their architecture, content, and circulation). We have found that moving toward an information literacy curriculum that draws closer to digitality also meant it was possible to more easily embrace anti-racist ideas about information. Similarly, extending anti-racist pedagogy into the realm of information literacy reinforced our move to turn more intentionally in the direction of online curriculum. The revisions we discussed here, as well as those evidence in the appended syllabus, were composed with the intention of forging connections between anti-racist writing pedagogy and information literacy practice.

In sum, this chapter is one that has hoped to share with readers how we collaboratively arrived at richer and more rewarding destinations with our students. But ultimately, I want to invite those contemplating the place of information literacy in education to think about how their own information literacy curriculum, however research writing central or adjacent it might be, could benefit from a similar collaborative rethinking and – perhaps more importantly – a methodology of reflection and revision.

While we are sure to all arrive somewhere a bit different because of our campus' individualized needs, we know that what many campuses are doing now is often not meeting the needs of our students, our communities, or our broader society when it comes to teaching information literacy. In order to better guide students through the complexities of information, we need to do this work in spaces that feel real and relevant for students, and we need to do so in ways that echo the values we hope – as a class, a community, and a society – to uphold. We want our student to understand the biases threaded into the world of binary not so that they can avoid this world, see it as dangerous or false, but because we believe it's possible to do better. We know that each of our students will participate in complex ways in the worlds we inhabit online. By teaching them to ask better questions, and to communicate in savvier ways online, we believe – truly – that the work we are doing will help shape and reshape our collective future.

REFERENCES

Alfino, M., Pajer, M., Pierce, L., & O'Brien Jenks, K. (2008). Advancing Critical Thinking and Information Literacy Skills in First Year College Students. *College & Research Libraries*, *15*(1/2), 81–98.

Artman, M., Frisicaro-Pawlowski, E., & Monge, R. (2010). Not Just One Shot: Extending the Dialogue about Information Literacy in Composition Classes. *Composition Studies*, *38*(2), 93–109.

Baker-Bell, A. (2020). *Linguistic Justice: Black Language, Literacy, Identity, and Pedagogy*. Routledge. doi:10.4324/9781315147383

Barratt, C. C., Nielsen, K., Desmet, C., & Balthazor, R. (2009). Collaboration Is Key: Librarians and Composition Instructors Analyze Student Research and Writing. *Portal*, *9*(1), 37–56.

Birmingham, E., Chinwongs, L., Flaspohler, M. R., Hearn, C., Kvanvig, D., & Portmann, R. (2008). Perceptions of Students' Information Literacy Competencies, and a Call for a Collaborative Approach. *Communications in Information Literacy*, *2*(1), 6–24. doi:10.15760/comminfolit.2008.2.1.53

Boston University. (n.d.). *Center for Anti-Racist Research*. https://www.bu.edu/antiracism-center/

Brady, L., Singh-Corcoran, N., Dadisman, J. A., & Diamond, K. (2009). A Collaborative Approach to Information Literacy: First-Year Composition, Writing Center, and Library Partnerships at West Virginia University. *Composition Forum, 19*, 1-18.

Bronshteyn, K., & Baladad, R. (2006). Librarians as Writing Instructors: Using Paraphrasing Exercises to Teach Beginning Information Literacy Students. *Journal of Academic Librarianship*, *32*(5), 533–536. doi:10.1016/j.acalib.2006.05.010

Burgoyne, M. B., & Chuppa-Cornell, K. (2015). Beyond Embedded: Creating an Online-Learning Community Integrating Information Literacy and Composition Courses. *Journal of Academic Librarianship*, *41*(4), 416–421. doi:10.1016/j.acalib.2015.05.005

Canagarajah, S. (2011). Codemeshing in Academic Writing: Identifying Teachable Strategies of Translanguaging. *Modern Language Journal*, *95*(3), 401–417. doi:10.1111/j.1540-4781.2011.01207.x

Cannon, K., & Jarson, J. (2009). Information Literacy and Writing Tutor Training at a Liberal Arts College. *Communications in Information Literacy*, *3*(1), 45–57. doi:10.15760/comminfolit.2009.3.1.68

Caufield, M. (2016). Yes, Digital Literacy, but Which One? *Hapgood*. https://hapgood.us/2016/12/19/yes-digital-literacy-but-which-one/

Clark, I. (1995). Information Literacy and the Writing Center. *Computers and Composition*, *12*(2), 203–209. doi:10.1016/8755-4615(95)90008-X

Condon, F., & Young, V. A. (2016). *Performing Antiracist Pedagogy in Rhetoric, Writing, and Communication. Across the Disciplines Books*. The WAC Clearinghouse; University Press of Colorado.

Corbett, P. (2010). What about the 'Google Effect'? Improving the Library Research Habits of First-Year Composition Students. *Teaching English in the Two-Year College*, *37*(3), 265–277.

Deitering, A.-M., & Jameson, S. (2008). Step by Step through the Scholarly Conversation: A Collaborative Library/Writing Faculty Project to Embed Information Literacy and Promote Critical Thinking in First Year Composition at Oregon State University. *College & Undergraduate Libraries*, *15*(1/2), 57–79. doi:10.1080/10691310802176830

Delpit, L. (2006). The Politics of Teaching Literate Discourse. In *Other People's Children: Cultural Conflict in the Classroom*. New Press.

Elmborg, J. (2003). Information Literacy and Writing Across the Curriculum: Sharing the Vision. *RSR. Reference Services Review*, *31*(1), 68–80. doi:10.1108/00907320310460933

Fielding, J., Hans, J., Mabee, F., Tracy, K., Consalvo, A., & Craig, L. (2013). Integrated Information Literacy and Student Outcomes in Foundational First-Year Writing. *Journal of Assessment and Institutional Effectiveness*, *3*(2), 106–139. doi:10.5325/jasseinsteffe.3.2.0106

Framework for Information Literacy for Higher Education. (2016). Association of Research and College Libraries. https://www.ala.org/acrl/sites/ala.org.acrl/files/content/issues/infolit/framework1.pdf

Gee, J. P. (1989). Literacy, Discourse, and Linguistics: Introduction and What Is Literacy? *Journal of Education*, *171*(1), 5–25. doi:10.1177/002205748917100101

Holliday, W., & Fagerheim, B. (2006). Integrating Information Literacy With a Sequenced English Composition Curriculum. *Portal*, *6*(2), 169–184.

Holliday, W., & Rogers, J. (2013). Talking About Information Literacy: The Mediating Role of Discourse in a College Writing Classroom. *Portal*, *13*(3), 257–271. doi:10.1353/pla.2013.0025

Hunt, Shanda, & Riegelman. (2020). *Conducting research through an anti-racist lens*. University of Minnesota. https://libguides.umn.edu/antiracismlens

Inoue, A. B. (2019). Classroom Writing Assessment as an Antiracist Practice: Confronting White Supremacy in the Judgments of Language. *Pedagogy*, *19*(3), 373–404. doi:10.1215/15314200-7615366

Inoue, A. B. (2019). *Labor-Based Grading Contracts: Building Equity and Inclusion in the Compassionate Writing Classroom. In Perspectives on Writing. The WAC Clearinghouse.* University Press of Colorado.

Inoue, A. B., & Poe, M. (2012). Race and Writing Assessment. Academic Press.

Isbell, D., & Broaddus, D. (1995). Teaching Writing and Research as Inseparable: A Faculty-Librarian Teaching Team. *RSR. Reference Services Review*, *23*(4), 51–62. doi:10.1108/eb049264

Jacobs, H. L. M. (2008). Information Literacy and Reflective Pedagogical Praxis. *Journal of Academic Librarianship*, *34*(3), 256–262. doi:10.1016/j.acalib.2008.03.009

Jacobs, H. L. M., & Jacobs, D. (2009). Transforming the One-Shot Library Session into Pedagogical Collaboration: Information Literacy and the English Composition Class. *Reference and User Services Quarterly*, *49*(1), 72–82. doi:10.5860/rusq.49n1.72

Kautzman, A. M. (1996). Teaching Critical Thinking: The Alliance of Composition Studies and Research Instruction. *Reference Services Review*, *24*(3), 61–66. doi:10.1108/eb049289

Kennedy, C. (2005). Teaching Information Literacy to the Advanced Writing Class in Three Sessions. *Electronic Journal of Academic & Special Librarianship, 6*(1).

Kraemer, E. W., Lombardo, S. V., & Lepkowski, F. J. (2007). The Librarian, the Machine, or a Little of Both: A Comparative Study of Three Information Literacy Pedagogies at Oakland University. *College & Research Libraries*, *68*(4), 330–342. doi:10.5860/crl.68.4.330

Lyiscott, J. (2018). *Why English Class is Silencing Students of Color*. The Benjamin School.

McClure, R., Cooke, R., & Carlin, A. (2011). The Search for the Skunk Ape: Studying the Impact of an Online Information Literacy Tutorial on Student Writing. *Journal of Information Literacy*, *5*(2), 26–45. doi:10.11645/5.2.1638

McLuhan, M. (1964). *Understanding Media: The Extensions of Man*. Routledge.

Mounce, M. (2009). Academic Librarian and English Composition Instructor Collaboration: A Selective Annotated Bibliography 1998-2007. *Reference Services Review*, *37*(1), 44–53. doi:10.1108/00907320910934986

Nagelhout, E. (1999). Pre-Professional Practices in the Technical Writing Classroom. *Technical Communication Quarterly*, *8*(3), 285–299. doi:10.1080/10572259909364669

Noble, S. U. (2018). *Algorithms of oppression: How search engines reinforce racism.* New York University Press. doi:10.2307/j.ctt1pwt9w5

Norgaard, R., Arp, L., & Woodard, B. (2004). Writing information literacy in the classroom. *Reference and User Services Quarterly, 43*(3), 220–226.

O'Connor, L., Bowles-Terry, M., Davis, E., & Holliday, W. (2010). Writing Information Literacy: Revisited Application of Theory to Practice in the Classroom. *Reference and User Services Quarterly, 49*(3), 225–230. doi:10.5860/rusq.49n3.225

Ovadia, S. (2010). Writing as an Information Literacy Tool: Bringing Writing in the Disciplines to an Online Library Class. *Journal of Library Administration, 50*(7), 899–908. doi:10.1080/01930826.2010.488990

Palsson, F., & McDade, C. L. (2014). Factors Affecting the Successful Implementation of a Common Assignment for First-Year Composition Information Literacy. *College & Undergraduate Libraries, 21*(2), 193–209. doi:10.1080/10691316.2013.829375

Patterson, D. (2009). Information Literacy and Community College Students: Using New Approaches to Literacy Theory to Produce Equity. *The Library Quarterly, 79*(3), 343–361. doi:10.1086/599124

Ravel, K. (2021). Decluttering Our Technology [Sample Assignment]. Rockford University.

Rinto, E. E., & Cogbill-Seiders, E. I. (2015). Library Instruction and Themed Composition Courses: An Investigation of Factors that Impact Student Learning. *Journal of Academic Librarianship, 41*(2), 14–20. doi:10.1016/j.acalib.2014.11.010

Sabatino, L. (2014). Improving Writing Literacies through Digital Gaming Literacies: Facebook Gaming in the Composition Classroom. *Computers and Composition, 32,* 41–53. doi:10.1016/j.compcom.2014.04.005

Samson, S., & Millett, M. S. (2003). The Learning Environment: First-Year Students, Teaching Assistants, and Information Literacy. *Research Strategies, 19*(2), 84–98. doi:10.1016/j.resstr.2004.02.001

Sheridan, J. (1992). WAC and Libraries: A Look at the Literature. *Journal of Academic Librarianship, 18*(2), 90–94.

Smitherman, G. (1976). 'God Don't Never Change': Black English from a Black Perspective. *College English, 34*(6), 828–833. doi:10.2307/375044

Sult, L., & Mills, V. (2006). A blended method for integrating information literacy instruction into English composition classes. *RSR. Reference Services Review*, *34*(3), 368–388. doi:10.1108/00907320610685328

Sweeney, M. (2012). The Wikipedia Project: Changing Students from Consumers to Producers. *Teaching English in the Two-Year College*, *39*(3), 256–267.

University of Minnesota. (n.d.). https://libguides.umn.edu/antiracismlens

Vora, S. (2020). *Approaching Writing with an Antiracist Perspective*. Contributions by Writing Center Antiracism Working Group.

Watson, A. P. (2012). Still a Mixed Bag: A Study of First-Year Composition Students' Internet Citations at the University of Mississippi. *Reference Services Review*, *40*(1), 125–137. doi:10.1108/00907321211203685

Watson, S., Rex, C., Markgraf, J., Kishel, H., Jennings, E., & Hinnant, K. (2013). Revising the "One-Shot" through Lesson Study: Collaborating with Writing Faculty to Rebuild a Library Instruction Session. *College & Research Libraries*, *74*(4), 381–398. doi:10.5860/crl12-255

Young, V. A. (2010). Should Writers Use They Own English? *Iowa Journal of Cultural Studies*, *12*(1), 110–117. doi:10.17077/2168-569X.1095

Zahua, J. (2014). Peering Into the Writing Center: Information Literacy as a collaborative conversation. *Communications in Information Literacy*, *8*(1), 1. doi:10.15760/comminfolit.2014.8.1.160

Zoetewey, M. W., & Staggers, J. (2003). Beyond 'Current-Traditional' Design: Assessing Rhetoric in New Media. *Issues in Writing*, *13*(2), 133–157.

Chapter 5
Creating Community Through the Teaching of Multicultural Literature Online

DuEwa M. Frazier
Coppin State University, USA

ABSTRACT

Teaching an online multicultural literature course during the early stages of the COVID-19 pandemic from Fall 2020 to Spring 2021 created an opportunity to engage in reflection on instructional practices and student reactions to diverse literature selections. In an effort to understand how community was created and dialogue maintained between instructor and students, the author sought to reflect on strategies that encouraged critical thinking and ongoing sharing of individual student perspectives during the course. This chapter examines how an online multicultural literature course was created and facilitated for students during a time when college courses were delivered solely through online instruction. The chapter illustrates how the online multicultural literature course was developed with culturally responsive pedagogy in mind to generate online discussion, guide literary analysis, and develop student writing. In examining this process, the chapter highlights instructional strategies that can be utilized by faculty to create engaging online learning communities.

DOI: 10.4018/978-1-6684-4055-1.ch005

Copyright © 2023, IGI Global. Copying or distributing in print or electronic forms without written permission of IGI Global is prohibited.

INTRODUCTION

The COVID-19 pandemic caused college enrollment to shift from in person to online learning formats at higher percentages than seen in prior years. Higher education online student enrollment was at 72.8% by the Fall of 2020 (US Department of Education, 2020).

Online education provides a unique opportunity to create increased faculty to student communication due to its flexibility and accessibility in virtual space and time (Singh & Hurley, 2017). Teaching and revising the curriculum for a new online multicultural literature course during the pandemic, presented an opportunity and challenge to engage with students using technology and digital communications as a means to create community. The course was taught during Fall 2020 and Spring 2021, at a mid-size, suburban, private, 4-year university. According to Fleming (2021), courses focusing on multicultural literature in higher education emphasize the use of multiple perspectives to study an ethnic or cultural group. The course, while not focusing on one specific ethnic group, does seek to provide a survey of multicultural literature created by diverse literary voices, including a range of themes for analysis and discussion, particularly from authors students may not be familiar with.

The course, Multicultural Selections in American Literature is offered each semester to all undergraduate students, from freshmen to seniors. It is offered as an English and Humanities elective. Students can earn three undergraduate credits from the course. On average the course enrolls sixteen to eighteen per 8-week session in Fall, Spring, and Summer. But in the last year, the course has gained more popularity, as more students chose to enroll in online courses during the pandemic. Enrollment in the courses rose from an average of sixteen to eighteen students to up to twenty students per online section with a waitlist.

The course was created with culturally responsive instruction in mind, for a diverse cross section of undergraduate students focused on various majors of study. The course has appealed to students who need an additional humanities or English elective to graduate. Students from freshmen to senior level have enrolled in the course. Characteristics of the online multicultural literature course includes a survey of digital literature across the genres of poetry, speech, interviews with poets and prose writers, essays, memoir, and short fiction, written by Latinx, African American, Asian American, Middle Eastern American, and Native American authors. Topics and themes studied include: cultural duality, language and identity, memories, experiences of immigrants coming to America, jazz and blues in poetry, the *American Dream*, and social justice. Students are asked to share their openness to studying literature from diverse authors whose parents and cultural heritage are native to other countries yet who are American citizens. Tasks for the online multicultural literature course include writing literary analysis and reflection essays, quizzes, group tasks, and weekly online discussions.

The chapter discusses the author's reflections and communications with students while teaching the course during the beginning of the pandemic, from Fall 2020 to Spring 2021. The chapter offers the author's insights into developing and facilitating student learning in an online multicultural literature taught with culturally responsive texts in mind. Reflection on course assignments, online discussions, student comments and feedback, instructor feedback on student writing, and end of course survey responses are used to highlight the focus on creating community within the online course. Instruction in the online course conveys the author's goal to maintain student engagement while managing online curriculum content and making revisions along the way as needed.

BACKGROUND

Baldwin, Ching, and Friesen (2018) found that the development phase of an online course begins with the course designer creating student learning objectives, creating online lessons, and selecting online assessment tools. Research examining online course design and implementation of online curriculum has included an investigation of how instructors utilize discussion forums, wikis, and assessments to plan instruction (Baldwin et al., 2018). The literature on sustaining student engagement in online learning spaces reveals that there are a number of characteristics that make up a student-centered learning community. The definition of a distance community is one that has several essential elements including, but not limited to members having: shared purpose, interactivity, mutual support, a sense of belonging, trust and connectedness (Sadera et al., 2009). DiRamio and Wolverton (2006) noted that student collaborative learning and social activities is what makes for an engaging online community. A study conducted by Vesely et al. (2007) found that 85% of student participants believed their academic progress was linked to being a part of an online community that helped them to learn. Research conducted by Rovai (2002) concluded that categories that create an online learning community such as trust, and interaction can be measured by his Classroom Community Scale instrument. Assignments that incorporate peer feedback to contribute to creation of responses online, can help students foster a sense of community (Waycott et al., 2013).

Adams (2020) found that the use of instructional strategies that increase student autonomy and improve practice, help to develop and enrich the online learning community. Baran et al. (2011) and Martin and Bolliger (2018) assert that the online discussions encourage student participation and helps students share personal insights while also boosting engagement. Collaborative activities in the online learning space can encourage students who typically want to work alone, to engage in community with peers (Athens, 2018). Demmans Eppe et al. (2017) noted that instructor's active style in facilitating can impact how students participate in online learning communities. Research conducted by Liu et al. (2007) concluded that there is a meaningful relationship between students' perceptions of their online learning and their sense of belonging, activity, and satisfaction with their academic experiences in the online space.

Theoretical Frameworks

According to Samaras and Freese (2006), self-study for an instructor is a continual process where knowledge is produced, involves situated inquiry, and allows for various methodologies and theoretical perspectives to be used. Guided by personal inquiry and the position of practitioner, situated inquiry helped to create questions to enable the author to reflect and learn from instructional practices (Turner, 2010). Engaging in the process of questioning, challenge, and then discovery was at the root of the author's observation of gaps in knowledge for online teaching as well as successful strategies best used to create an engaged online community of learners. In consideration of multiple methods and frameworks, self-study researchers are in constant pursuit of examining their practices and taking action to practice what is learned (Samaras & Freese, 2006).

Lave and Wenger's (1991) community of practice includes participant engagement, an overlapping of relatable identities, supportive exchange of information, and sustained relationships that can be transformative for learners. Applying community of practice (1991) to the creation of a supportive online space where college learners can exchange ideas and learn from each other informs the author's approach to culturally responsive pedagogy. Culturally responsive pedagogy (Ladson-Billings,1995) provides that instruction creates an equal opportunity for students and acknowledges students' diversity, prior knowledge, learning styles, and experiences that contribute to the quality teaching and learning.

The author's development as an instructor and curriculum developer stems from belief in the philosophy of educational theorist, Vygotsky (1978), which places social and cultural learning at the center of learner development as collaboration takes place. This is the premise in which the author developed the online multicultural literature course and instructed students during Fall of 2020 and Spring of 2021. With the goal of collaborative learning and student engagement in mind, the author believed that an online learning space could provide as much of a supportive, knowledge sharing community as an in-person, traditional classroom space.

Data Collection

The author who is also the instructor of the course, and course developer observed and recorded student feedback from the course in Fall 2020 and Spring 2021, in addition to reviewing online student discussion responses and evaluations. Student discussion responses were reviewed from week 1 of the course in the Canvas evaluations module to compare to student responses by the end of the course within their final reflections and discussions. Short narrative excerpts from student feedback along with the author's reflective notes on the process of teaching and developing the online multicultural literature course were used to understand how an online cohesive community was created and how students were able to engage and remain productive in the course. Ethical precautions were made by the author in protecting the identity of students and by excluding the use of student written work samples to convey student participation in the online literature course.

Enrolled Students

Students enrolled in the course (Table 1) during the initial stages of the pandemic, shared their thoughts on studying multicultural literature, engaging with peers in an online format, and receiving feedback from the author/instructor. Enrolled students were freshman to senior level students of varying majors of study, who are pursuing bachelor's degrees.

Questions for Self-Study

The author reflected on the process of revising and instructing an online multicultural literature course during the pandemic, in order to self-study and improve upon instructional practices for students. Questions the author used for self-study as points of reflection on instructional practices and student experiences in the online multicultural literature course were:

- *What were the key strategies that made the online course an engaging learning community for students?*
- *How did students respond to the multicultural texts and varied themes?*
- *What can be improved in the online course for future students?*

Table 1. Sample of Enrolled Online Students in Fall 2020 and Spring 2021

Student	Semester Enrolled
1	Fall 2020
2	Spring 2021
3	Fall 2020
4	Fall 2020
5	Fall 2020
6	Spring 2021
7	Spring 2021
8	Spring 2021
9	Spring 2021
10	Spring 2021
11	Spring 2021
12	Fall 2020
13	Fall 2020
14	Fall 2020
15	Spring 2021

MAIN FOCUS OF THE CHAPTER

Early Stages of Online Course Development

At the beginning of course development in early December of 2018 the course was titled Minority Writers in American Literature. The author drafted a request for a course title change, from Minority to Multicultural Selections in American Literature. After developing and revising the curriculum for the course from December 2018 to August 2020, the author proposed to administration that the course name and description should represent a respect for diversity and inclusion of all students, as the author believed the word "minority" was not culturally responsive language to continue to use, particularly in the wake and aftermath of social justice issues before and during the pandemic that impacted higher education's approach to DEI (Diversity, Equity, and Inclusion). The author realized that the word "minority" carries a negative connotation and can be received as being demeaning to people of color. In the age where diversity, equity, and inclusion is a great consideration across educational institutions, it was beneficial to change the course name to a title that was culturally responsive. This change was approved by the department administration. The revision for course description also included the change from

Hispanic American authors to Latinx authors for greater inclusion of all voices of Latin heritage regardless of gender identity or countries of origin. It was important that offering a course with an inclusive title and description reflecting contemporary understanding of diversity and inclusion, would ideally have a positive influence on the decision for interested students seeking an elective to register for the online multicultural literature course.

By Fall 2020, the course title was officially changed to Multicultural Selections in American Literature in the course catalog. The main course textbook in ebook format was initially the notable memoir, *Between the World and Me* (2015) written by Ta-Nehisi Coates. The author later changed the main textbook for the online course, to an anthology of global literature titled, *Penguin Book of Migration Literature* (2019) edited by Dohra Ahmad. This anthology was selected for the myriad of diverse American authors included in the text, within the genres of poetry, short fiction, essay, and memoir. The anthology would also be fully accessible for students and linked within the course modules in ebook format. This was an exciting new curricular change that the author was eager to use for instruction to observe the impact on students' understanding of learning objectives and the multicultural texts as a whole. The author was also interested to find by the end of the course, how student feedback may have changed after curriculum revisions.

SURVEYING STUDENT OPENNESS TO MULTICULTURAL LITERATURE

The second of two week 1 online discussions in the course, asks students to share their openness or hesitance to study multicultural literature. The discussion also asks students to describe their experience, if any, with previous English or humanities courses with a similar focus. This question helps to reveal student perspectives and backgrounds in studying multicultural literature and completing online coursework. Their responses can convey previous knowledge and experience with multicultural literature, writing, reading, and their openness or lack thereof, to such an online course.

During week 1 of the course, the first online discussion asks students to share who they are, their identities, and explain their openness or hesitance to studying literature written by diverse American authors. Students discuss their identities as related to their families, communities, university, academic level, religion, gender, race/ethnicity, and sexual orientation. Kumi-Yeboah et al. (2020) reported on the importance of students sharing their identities and previous learning experiences within online learning communities, to discover the perspectives that each individual contributes, in order to form connections both inside and outside of the online environment.

Students expressed their prior experience with similar online or literature courses, their openness to studying new literature, and hesitance or openness to discuss themes that may pertain to themes on cultural diversity, social justice, bias, and diversity within the literature. The author appreciated the students' initial thoughts during their introductory discussion post, because it revealed the student's perspective on their first thoughts about immersing themselves in the content. Some students shared their experience as immigrants or students of color who have experienced bias or feeling judged for their ethnicity. This helped the author to understand how these diverse students may connect with the themes and personas within the literature, which would further broaden their ideas about identity and its many forms. Because the course explores themes, literary devices, native cultures, and migration experiences of people of color, students are encouraged to make connections to what they read and respond with their own analysis of the author's purpose and meaning.

Lawyer (2018) asserts that multicultural courses can serve as an initial introduction to diverse perspectives and social issues for many students. The diversity of writers we study, being those from African American, Caribbean, Asian, Middle Eastern, and Native American cultures and heritages, fosters a foundation of rich discussion, critical thinking, peer dialogue, collaboration, and understanding of diverse American voices that students have not previously been introduced to. Many of the students had read the work of Langston Hughes, but not Willie Perdomo, Claudia Rankine, or Marilyn Chin. Some students were familiar with Junot Diaz and Amy Tan, but not Sherman Alexie, Naomi Shihab Nye, or Gloria Anzaldua. Exploring the works of diverse American writers whose works may not have appeared in students' previous high school honors, AP English or introductory college literature curriculum was critical in considering how to best introduce the literature, key themes, and literary elements present in them. Understanding that the authors whose works we study may or may not mirror the identities of our students, offers an opportunity to provide culturally responsive texts while engaging students with themes and discussions that they can make personal or global connections to. The author hoped that students may place themselves in the writers' shoes or in the setting of the narrative, in order to envision worlds and identities different from their own. Therefore, creating a course that explores themes from social justice (in reflecting on current events and socially relevant news in our society), the act of leaving one's native home, jazz and blues in poetry, dreams, memories, cultural duality, and identity –student's prior knowledge, identities, prior biases, and empathy for others can connect with the curriculum in a meaningful way, toward creating community within this online multicultural literature course.

Students shared their thoughts on their own identities and perspectives on studying multicultural literature during week one online discussions in the course.

Student 1, who took the course in Fall 2020 opened up about her experience as an immigrant. Student 1 stated,

Being an immigrant can in fact be hard, and at times I feel that there is no equality.
There are many struggles that come from being an immigrant, such as discrimination
and racism, which is something I have faced quite often.

Similar to Student 1, Student 2, took the course in Spring 2021, shared a similar perspective on being from a diverse background and facing bias. She expressed, "Kelly Tsai's poem really spoke to me because in the poem it talks about value and how your value may be underestimated in the world. As a Latina woman in America I am consistently judged."

The choice students make on their own to select and enroll in the course, contributes to their motivation to study multicultural literature and engage in critical discussions surrounding the topics and literary elements present in the works. The majority of students expressed positive motivation for enrolling and being open to the diverse American author's works in the course. Students mostly expressed their openness to studying multicultural literature. However, there were some who discussed their hesitance and concerns about beginning the online multicultural literature course.

Student openness to explore the literature was conveyed as they discussed a willingness to understand different voices and opinions.

Student 7, expressed openness to the course in his week 1 discussion. Student 7 stated,

In relation to literature, and openness on discussing different voices. I am open to
discussing any subject that is brought up. I believe that everyone has the right to
voice their opinion or have a drive for what they want to have a voice on. That is
what makes us all American.

Similarly, Student 3, connected his cultural heritage to his primary interest in the multicultural online literature course. Student 3 expressed, "Being bi-cultural made me see life in a different way, which lead me to wanting to learn more and more about the world cultures."

Students who discussed the connection between the course and their careers, came to a further realization. Student 4 shared that the different themes studied in the course interested her. Student 4 stated, "Usually literature doesn't hold my attention, but because of the interesting themes I really enjoyed reading in the class." Student 11, stated that learning about diverse literature would help her have a better understanding of care for diverse patients in her career as a nurse. Student 11 expressed,

This is the first humanities course I have taken, so I'm excited to learn more as we go. As a nurse I have contact with patients from many different cultural backgrounds and in an effort to provide the best care I can, it's important to know and understand their point of views and practices. I want to learn so that I can be a more diverse nurse and continue to provide quality care.

Students expressed that their openness to explore the course content was accompanied by some hesitance. Student 5, shared some hesitancy about the course at the beginning. Student 5 stated, "I am open to discuss the perspectives of diverse voices in literature, however, I can be a bit hesitant on discussing certain things if I feel it, is a sensitive topic."

Similar to student 5, student 8, shared having an openness to the course, yet also expressed her belief that the writing of diverse authors would be analyzed differently depending on students' own cultural backgrounds. Student 8 discussed, "While I am open to discussing different perspectives, I am hesitant because the way I interpret a certain voice in literature is not the same way someone of a different cultural background would interpret that same writing or text."

On the other hand, student 6, discussed learning from other's points of view. He expressed, "Even if I disagree with certain points and aspects, it's a great way to learn and be able to understand how/why an individual thinks the way they do."

Student 2, shared some hesitancy in the course, regarding sensitivity toward cultures. Student 2 expressed,

I am a bit hesitant of expressing and discussing perspectives of multicultural voices in American literature (specifically with people I do not know personally), due to the fact people's culture(s) is/are a very sensitive and intricate topic at times (dependent on who you are speaking to).

On the other hand, Student 10, shared that her hesitancy to delve into the multicultural literature was due to a concern that she would have difficulty comprehending the meaning of the texts. Student 10 shared, "I think the biggest hesitation I have with this course is that I'm worried I won't understand or be able to grasp what the author is trying to convey through his/her works."

Students also discussed the belief that social justice as a component of studying multicultural literature in an online course was of particular interest. Student 9, expressed that her openness to study multicultural literature was connected to her interest in social justice. Student 9 expressed, "Because social justice is one of my passions, discussing the perspectives of diverse voices in literature is something that I am very open to."

While the majority of students in the Multicultural Selections in American Literature course shared their openness or hesitance in studying the selections, some discussed concerns that sensitive issues and topics may arise through the study of diverse authors in American literature.

Student Online Access and Navigation of Course Modules

The course is built for students to independently go through each module to locate and download course readings from digital texts and the ebook literature anthology. Students access pre-recorded weekly lectures filmed by the author in the multimedia room at the university (some lectures were recorded at the author's home during the height of the pandemic). The weekly lectures give an overview of the authors, themes and literary elements present, and assignments due for the week. The author's video lectures point students in the direction to find course materials in the Canvas modules. Lewis (2018) noted that the use of video where students and instructors can see each other in online environments encourages community. Connections in online courses are created with the use of video and audio that is aligned to course curriculum, that text alone cannot provide (Bickle & Rucker, 2018).

The video lecture presentations in the course also inform students of the cultural backgrounds of the diverse American authors, the weekly theme focus, and a description of the week's required readings and related assignments – short essays, quizzes, reflections, and discussions. Students have access to the literature anthology in ebook format and a reference manual to help them use MLA format. At the beginning of each week the author posts an announcement giving an overview of the theme focus, readings, and writing tasks for each week. Students are encouraged to ask questions and inform the instructor if they are having any technical difficulty that hinders their access to the readings or discussion forums in Canvas modules. When students have expressed that they cannot access or download the readings from RedShelf, the author refers students to IT support for troubleshooting. The author encourages students to ask questions if there is anything they are not clear about. Students were encouraged to send the author direct messages either via university email or Canvas message.

Instructor Feedback and Communication with Students

Communication between the author and students has been key for keeping students informed and for expressing concern for student well-being and productivity. The communication is digital yet is intended to engage students in the same way with instructor personal communication as if the course were in person. This is an important aspect of creating community within the online course. Upon reading and reviewing each student writing submission, the author offers students feedback in the online submission portal for the task, expressing areas of writing that are strong within their essays and areas of improvement. Leibold and Schwarz (2015) assert that feedback in online classes is a crucial form of academic intervention because it provides the opportunity to develop a relationship between instructor and student, improve student productivity, and promote learning. This includes feedback on: thesis statements, sentence and paragraph structure, use of MLA style, grammar, and analysis of the literature and themes.

Encouraging engagement for weekly online discussions means that the author also participates in the discussions. Instructor participation in the online discussions is important to create online community and course engagement (1): To model for students the appropriate tone and language style to use during discussions and (2) to validate student responses and ask questions to help students delve deeper into author purpose and text meanings. Singh and Hurley (2017) found that student autonomy is encouraged during online learning through course discussions and small group interactions. Students respond to discussion prompts each week that focus on literature selections.

The instructor replies to student discussion posts and asks questions to elicit student understanding of the literature. When students send emails to ask questions or submit writing tasks, the author responds within 24 hours or less. Monitoring student progress and identifying barriers to learning for students is crucial for professors to prevent student disengagement (Roddy et al., 2017). Consistent attention to students' academic needs in the online environment helps to create community and maintain participation.

Student writing assignments in the course include three short literary analysis essays on themes such as: cultural duality, identity, and language. When students submit their final essay, the author reads the essay with the rubric for grading in order to provide feedback on: thesis statement, grammar, organization of ideas, essay length and structure, citation and bibliography, and clear understanding of author's purpose and themes. The author first gives students points on what is working well within their essays, to validate students and support their writing progress. The author then focuses on giving feedback in "needs improvement" areas. Specific feedback that has been given to students on their essays includes:

- Well organized introduction that includes your main points of analysis and a clear thesis statement.
- Excellent textual evidence provided to support your analysis of the author's meaning.
- Very good use of in text documentation in (MLA style).

- Focus on going beyond summarizing the text to making specific points to analyze what the author says in order to support your thesis statement.
- Missing required bibliography (MLA Works Cited).

The instructor concludes the feedback with a note encouraging students to incorporate the feedback by improving upon the items that were highlighted for improvement. Feedback given to students is timely so that they are aware of their progress in the online course every step of the way. Because the online course is only 8-weeks in length, there is not a great deal of time in between submission from one weekly task to the next. Therefore, best practices for grading online and providing student feedback is to grade an item and turn it around within one week of submission with feedback.

Instructor participation in the required, weekly online discussions is paramount for building the trust and dialogue needed within the course that only the instructor can facilitate. The author found that students gave feedback that they had never taken an online course where the dialogue is so engaging because the instructor was involved, asking questions after student posts, and following up to provide comments to validate student's analysis and wonderings about a text. It is important that the instructor is present because some discussions can lend themselves to debate and disagreement from the perspectives that students are sharing on what they read. The author has on occasion come to the discussion to provide feedback in order to encourage students to maintain a positive and professional tone in the discussion forums even when there is a difference of viewpoint on text meanings, themes, or author's purpose.

The more experience an instructor has in teaching college courses, one may find that students rely more on receiving direct answers from the instructor about an assignment description or deadline for a task, rather than reviewing the syllabus or Canvas modules for such details. Therefore, incorporating the posting of weekly announcements for students which is sent to their emails and posted in modules, has been beneficial in providing reminders, tips, and validation for students. Each Monday morning, at the start of the new course week, the author posts an announcement to (1) inform students that they did a great job on the previous weeks' tasks and (2) to remind students of what is coming up in the new week and provide tips for writing or reading the materials. Students have remarked that the announcements are helpful, especially when they serve as reminders for student submission of assignments because students are juggling other courses and due dates. Since the instructor is unable to give the reminders and tips in person, the announcements serve as an additional tool of "presence" for the instructor in the course. The author has encouraged students to login to Canvas on a daily basis to check their "to do" list in the dashboard and participate in the discussions for the week. When students message the author due to confusion they may have about details in an essay tasks' guidelines, the author responds within the day the message is sent to provide clarity.

The authors we study in the course are American writers with diverse heritage and viewpoints presented in their works. To further engage students in the digital features of the online multicultural course and introduce students to some of the authors, the author arranged scheduled interviews with four of the authors who agreed to participate. The interviews are thirty minutes to one hour long featuring the authors discussing their works and inspirations for writing. Video interviews featured diverse writers such as Asian American poet and performer, Kelly Tsai, Caribbean American poet Roger Bonair Agard, Asian American poet, Marilyn Chin, Middle Eastern American poet, children's author, and Young People's Poet Laureate Naomi Shihab Nye, and Afro-Puerto Rican poet, children's writer, and New York State Poet Laureate, Willie Perdomo. The poets are all notable and award-winning writers whose works have been widely published and incorporated into college programs and multimedia. Introducing the students digitally to authors they may have not previously heard about or read, provides an added layer of understanding for students in the course. When they see the authors in the recorded interviews, and hear their voices, they can visualize their experiences and cultural perspectives that influence their writing.

Group Collaboration

Collaborative activity in online learning environments encourages the formation of community (Chatterjee & Correia, 2020). Lewis (2018) found that creating peer groups where classmates can collaborate and create presentations helps students release preconceived thoughts that group work online cannot be a positive learning experience. While many students thrive when participating in group tasks within an online course, others readily admit that they would rather work independently. In the sixth week of the course, students are to read three poems that feature jazz and blues themes and create a presentation for the class (posted in discussion) that conveys how the authors use the themes to reveal imagery and sensory description.

By week six students are more comfortable with one another in the online course because they have been responding to each other's discussion posts on a weekly basis and learning each other's digital "voices" and style of interacting in the community. The presentation created as a PowerPoint, has an aesthetic value for students to include culturally appropriate images that fit the themes in the works and show their overall understanding. Students have almost two weeks to work together and create the presentation. The assignment generally works well as students convene in Canvas group space to collaborate, share their ideas and contributions. The process breaks down and creates disconnect among students when one or more group members are absent from the beginning or become inactive during the collaboration.

While group collaboration is generally facilitated as an in-person task, group collaboration can help to break up the monotony of student singular expression online and help to exchange perspectives with individual peers and digitally within the class as a whole. Some students expressed that a group member could not be reached when inquiring about their contribution to a collaboration that required analysis of jazz and blues themes in poetry selections. There have been instances where out of four people in a group for this task, one or more did not respond to group messages or submitting their contribution by the deadline. The author responds to this problem by sending a message to the entire group to (1) ask if anyone needs help or clarification on the task and (2) if members wish to work independently or be switched to a different group. In a few cases, a student was alone in a group that may have been three or four members, yet due to a student's withdrawal from the course or lack of communication, one person is unfortunately left without a group to collaborate with. This is when it is important to give the remaining student a choice to either work alone or merge with another group to prevent losing the student altogether and to continue to foster an active online learning community.

Student Productivity, Feedback, and Online Engagement

Students who enroll in the online Multicultural Selections in American Literature course complete week-3 feedback survey. This survey gauges student understanding of course objectives, student communication and perception of the professor, and student online engagement including use of technology and course modules. Implementing student feedback contributes to building online learner engagement (Farmer, 2016). Throughout the course students write reflection essays to reflect on the literature, online discussions, interactions with peers, comprehension of themes, and writing requirements. It was important to create a group presentation project focused on poetry during the final weeks of the course. Martin and Bolliger (2018) assert that online instruction should include the opportunity for students to interact with peers in an effort to create meaningful learning. The author used student feedback and responses to assignments to provide insight into what is working well for students with online engagement, assignments, instruction, and course content, and what is not. Young (2006) found that in order for students not to feel isolated, a partnership between instructors and students should develop where communication and feedback drives learning and course activities.

Student feedback reveals their understanding and perceptions of multicultural literature, course writing tasks, peer engagement during group task and weekly discussions, and course learning objectives.

Student 11 gave valuable feedback about one of the course texts and her evolving understanding as a student writer. Student 11 expressed,

I think that having read Between the World and Me, has been one of the most eye-opening experiences in any class that I've had. I have gone back and re-read parts of the book, now that I have a better understanding of vernacular language and I feel that is what's going to make me a better writer.

Student 3 reflected that while he usually doesn't enjoy reading, he found subject matter that he liked during his semester in the online multicultural literature course. Student 3 noted,

The diverse topics and the diverse backgrounds in the writers choice gave me the opportunity to learn that no matter how different we are, we are still similar to each other more than we think. Reading is not a fun thing for me, but I learned that I like to read when the subject is right.

Student 10 wrote in a final reflection for the online course that the online discussions were the most engaging of any course she had participated in. Student 10 offered,

I am also appreciating the discussions of my fellow classmates; in courses prior to this one, the comments and discussions almost seemed forced, whereas this course they feel genuine and as though actual conversations are occurring; I find myself coming back to read and re-read responses and following up with others' comments.

Student feedback has been a necessary component for making adjustments or modifications to some task descriptions, due dates, and to overall understand how students respond to the online course curriculum. Student 12, gave feedback in a reflection essay about the course and instructor feedback. Student 12 shared, "This course has been a great bridge to help me shift my mindset back into more analytical, critical thinking and I'm deeply grateful for your guidance you have offered."

Student reflected on their writing progress during the online multicultural literature course. Student 13 reflected in a final paper about her writing. Student 13 expressed, "My writing has become more reliable in the idea that I now try to fully analyze and write to both sides of an argument which makes me as a writer more truthful and less biased."

Final reflections and discussions at the end of the course, found students sharing their reactions to having learned from the multicultural texts and peer discussions in the course. Student 14 reflected on the literature selections in her final discussion. Student 14 asserted,

Many of the stories were incredibly inspiring and changed my perspective on a lot of things. I also was excited to see the content each week because the selections were so capturing. I wish that I had taken a class like that in my earlier college classes.

Student 15 discussed his experience participating in the online discussions in the course. Student 15 shared,

Another interesting part of the course was the discussions. My discussions with my peers allowed me to develop opinions that are beyond my point of view. We all read the same materials; however, we sometimes have different opinions. Although I consider myself an open-minded person, sometimes it is hard to understand an opinion, especially, one that comes from more narrow thoughts of mind.

Table 2. Comparison of End of Course Student Evaluations

Fall 2020	Spring 2021
For an online course, it was well laid out and easy to understand. The instructor always gave clear instructions and feedback. This course was great online, I felt like I was learning in a very efficient way This instructor was fantastic. Instructions for the course are clear. Grading is fair and I appreciate the feedback Dr. Frazier gives. Professor Frazier was wonderful! I appreciate her dedication to ensure that there was a variety of voices/cultures/backgrounds being discussed in this course. Really enjoyed the course material and interacting with my peers. Not enough reading for a literature course, not enough assignments that apply the material. I liked the different types of assignments and felt there was plenty of time to complete them I enjoyed this course a lot. I gained a lot of insight from the classwork. I think this is a great class to open students' minds to new topics. There was some confusion in the modules overview with readings.	Loved the course and I am really interested in learning more. Dr. Frazier is amazing. Thanks for giving feedback it helped improve my writing skills throughout the course One of the great parts about Dr. Frazier were video lectures for each week. I found that to be a very smooth way to make the class professional but with a hint of personal touch. Multicultural literature in my opinion has a great potential to increase cultural awareness, cultural struggles, and lessen cultural appropriation. I really liked the way the course was laid out and how personal some of the assignments felt. Everything was manageable and linked back to the readings very well. I love the enthusiasm professor Frazier had when it came to her interviews with the authors and poets. I really enjoyed Dr. Frazier she was approachable and quick to respond when I had questions, she left nice comments on my assignments and helped me find room for improvement I would definitely take another class taught by her. I had a lot of interactions with classmates and could see everyone's opinions very quickly and easily. I really liked that each week had themes that allowed us to dive more clearly into the topics and formulate stronger opinions or perceptions about what we were reading.

Students shared their reactions and feedback to the course in their final discussions and reflections on the course. Student feedback on the literature, course sequencing, instruction provided by the instructor, online discussions, and within end of course evaluations, conveyed their experiences and outlook on the course (Table 2).

SOLUTIONS AND RECOMMENDATIONS

According to Richardson and Swan (2003), the benefit of taking an online course means that students are not locked into a physical location at one time, thus affording them freedom to communicate with instructors and peers, access course materials, and complete assignments from any place where the internet is fully available. However, students still report experiencing technology glitches, personal or academic challenges outside of the course that impact participation, difficulty understanding the use of MLA style, and preference to work alone versus in a team for the small group assignments. Dixson (2012) found that creating an interactive and unified online learning environment includes group work, assignments that connect to student learning objectives, and instructor feedback are necessary to facilitate a successful course.

Students who enroll in the literature course are informed that English Composition I and II courses are the basic prerequisites for enrolling in Multicultural Selections in American Literature. All students, whether enrolled for in person or online courses, are required to use Canvas. This is the platform used for student submissions, grading, communication, and tracking student attendance. Online courses, such as the multicultural literature course, have the entire curriculum for the course in modules, for student individual access.

This can present a challenge for students who are used to in person instruction and peer communication, and who have difficulty managing time within a virtual format. The online course format may give the perception that there is more time to complete assignments and participate in discussions, since the professor and class does not meet in person at set times. Distractions, whether virtual or in reality may surround students, causing the perception that a task can be put off to a later date, due to the independent and self-paced nature of the course within each week's module. Students may not understand until their first assignment deadline, that the published deadline for a task in Canvas means after that time, they will not be able to submit unless they reach out to the professor. One solution the author has used is to send weekly reminders to students informing them of deadlines in advance. Weekly check in messages are sent by the professor to students who have become inactive. The author informs students who show difficulty with writing that writing tutors are available on campus. Additionally, students are encouraged to utilize the

SmartThinking feature in Canvas modules to submit their paper drafts to an online tutor for feedback before the task is due.

Student retention in an online course can be a challenge. The course may begin with 18 – 20 students enrolled but by the second week enrollment may reduce to 15 – 17. The author regularly addressed student absence and lack of participation or assignment submission. While in a given semester only one to two students may present issues in attendance or task completion; the instructor addresses it from the beginning to try to prevent complete student inactivity and withdrawal. This was an item to address, particularly during the pandemic when students expressed experiencing heightened anxiety, stress related to personal, family, or academic needs, and illness or death of a family member while pursuing their studies. During the pandemic it was necessary to facilitate the online course with empathy in mind and address student needs pertaining to absence and lack of task submission on a case-by-case basis.

Being understanding toward students and open to work with them to submit their online assignments has been beneficial in building relationships and creating community in the online course. The author has experienced students reaching out who faced a personal emergency during the semester. During these times, the author granted accommodations such as extensions for assignments or exemption due to medical emergency. Students' attendance and participation in the online course may have lagged when they expressed that they had work schedule conflicts or family emergencies that arose. In cases when students informed the author that they would be absent for a period time, the author worked out a plan with the students in advance of due dates, for a deadline extension to submit the assignments.

The author sent check-in emails regularly to inquire about a student and their well-being if the author observed their lack of presence in the online course. Because Canvas tracks and records when students log in, it is easy for the instructor to identify attendance issues. Failure to complete online discussions or submit assigned essays, and quizzes by the deadline in Canvas were indications of student absence and lack of participation. It is reported by the end of the second week of the course if a student has not attended. Students who have missing and late assignments that have resulted in a failing grade by week 3 of the course, receive an early academic alert that is sent to their advisor. Many times, this academic alert helps students to get back on track and formulate a plan to participate consistently in the online course.

The online course curriculum focuses on diverse writers and their literary works. The works present themes related to immigration, pursuing the "American Dream," learning to live between two cultures, challenges in being bi-lingual (non-native English speakers), societal issues and problems related to equity and justice, and related topics. It is the students choice to enroll in the course, yet even though it is a self-selected course for the students, student comments and content in papers and discussions can reveal a bias and lack of empathy toward diverse authors and their writings. One example of this is when a student remarked in a final reflection regarding the course curriculum and instruction, that the course and its instructor "teaches reverse racism." The author responded to the student with understanding yet asserted that it is not racist to teach multicultural literature or to present the stories and perspectives of diverse authors according to their experiences and the experiences of people from their native lands and cultures. It was an eye-opening moment for both student and instructor, as the student revealed that they had little to no prior experience in a course that taught the literature of marginalized writers of color. Understanding that this is a new experience for many of the students, the author encouraged the student to continue to have an open mind and to send questions to the instructor anytime confusion arises while reading the literature. Support and encouragement for all learners is needed. Instructors of online communities can help shape student perceptions of course curriculum and also help students best navigate the technology.

FUTURE RESEARCH DIRECTIONS

Findings from this study were based on the instructional self-study of the author, and observation of responses of students enrolled in an online multicultural literature course during the initial period of the pandemic, Fall 2020 and Spring 2021. Therefore, the experiences as described in this chapter do not reflect those of all faculty at the university, or all students who have taken or will take an online course or this particular multicultural literature course at the university. Additionally, the author's reflection took place during an unusual time of uncertainty over the period of the early beginnings of the pandemic, within the specific time range of Fall 2020 and Spring 2021. Future research should include the perceptions and experiences of faculty who teach online humanities and literature courses, for both undergraduate and graduate students. Future research might include other online sections of a multicultural literature course taught by other instructors to learn about their successful instructional practices used to create a cohesive and engaging online learning community, and how student reactions may be similar or different. Finally, future research should also include a continued look at best online instructional practices that shape student writing and reading, student literary analysis, and student online engagement with peers. This research should include two-year colleges, urban colleges and universities, Hispanic Serving Institutions (HSIs), and Historically Black Colleges and Universities (HBCUs) where student demographics may differ and provide a range of rich instructor and student experiences.

CONCLUSION

The author learned the value of ongoing communication with students and providing students with case-by-case accommodations, while teaching an online literature course during the initial stages of the pandemic. Student feedback during online discussions and evaluations provided the instructor with input that allowed for periodic revisions in curriculum and course deadlines in order to best accommodate students' needs. Student's responses to being asked about their willingness to explore and actively participate in the online multicultural literature course, ranged from excited and motivated, to concerned and hesitant. Student responses within online discussions that expressed their motivation to study multicultural literature and the themes the texts presented, showed that students believe the course held both personal and academic value for their goals and career interests. Students who expressed hesitance to explore the diverse authors' works, shared that it was due to feeling that they may not entirely comprehend the texts meanings or that sensitive topics would create tension among the class during discussions. Students sincerely gave their feedback on their own writing progress, online discussions, engagement with peers, and guidance and feedback from the instructor.

Student feedback in reflections, online discussions, and evaluation surveys were important aspects of data used to make course improvements in consideration to optimize student learning in the online course. It was crucial for the author to make decisions based on student feedback. This included making changes to course text selections and revising course assignments to have more clarified alignment with course readings and learning outcomes.

Challenges that arose in the course such as student absence, student misperception or confusion about course focus or assignment guidelines, and group task interruption due to a group members' inactivity or absence, were found to have a number of solutions that the instructor could apply in order to create community within the online course. Student feedback, both positive and negative served as data for the author to make course revisions and understand how students absorbed the readings and achieved learning objectives as a whole. The author found that student enrollment increased with each semester that the online multicultural literature course was offered. Additionally, after each class session, the instructor took the opportunity to consult student evaluations to plan for course shell updates and curriculum revision that would benefit future students and instructors of the online course.

The value of the course has been determined by the successful completion that students have had from the initial period of the pandemic to the present. Reactions from students on their perceptions of the online multicultural literature and how they engaged as a community help to determine the quality and diversity of learning experiences. Overall, the instructor focused on using consistent online communication, timely feedback and grading, and practices that support student retention in the course rather than taking a more distant approach to student productivity. These strategies have resulted in more students enrolling in the course and providing positive feedback about what they learned and how they learned during the semester.

REFERENCES

Adams, K. (2020). Research to resource: Developing a sense of community in online learning environments. *National Association for Music Education*, *39*(2), 5–9. 10.1177%2F8755123320943985

Athens, W. (2018). Perceptions of the persistent: Engagement and learning community in underrepresented populations. *Online Learning*, *22*(2), 27–58. doi:10.24059/olj.v22i2.1368

Baldwin, S. J., Ching, Y.-H., & Friesen, N. (2018). Online course design and development among college and university instructors: An analysis using grounded theory. *Online Learning*, *22*(2), 157–171. doi:10.24059/olj.v22i2.1212

Baran, E., Correia, A. P., & Thompson, A. (2011). Transforming online teaching practice: Critical analysis of the literature on the roles and competencies of online teachers. *Distance Education*, *32*(3), 421–439. doi:10.1080/01587919.2011.610293

Bickle, M. C., & Rucker, R. (2018). Student-to-student interaction. *Quarterly Review of Distance Education*, *19*(1), 1–11.

Chatterjee, R., & Correia, A. (2020). Online students' attitudes toward collaborative learning and sense of community. *American Journal of Distance Education*, *34*(1), 53–68. doi:10.1080/08923647.2020.1703479

Demmans Epp, C., Phirangee, K., & Hewitt, J. (2017). Student actions and community in online courses: The roles played by course length and facilitation method. *Online Learning*, *21*(4), 53–77. doi:10.24059/olj.v21i4.1269

DiRamio, D., & Wolverton, M. (2006). Integrating learning communities and distance education: Possibility or pipedream? *Innovative Higher Education*, *31*(2), 99–113. doi:10.100710755-006-9011-y

Dixson, M. D. (2012). Creating effective student engagement in online courses: What do students find engaging? *The Journal of Scholarship of Teaching and Learning*, *10*(2), 1–13. https://scholarworks.iu.edu/journals/index.php/josotl/article/view/1744

Farmer, J. L., Leonard, A. E., Spearman, M., Quian, M., & Rosenblith, S. (2016). Picturing a classroom community: Student drawings as a pedagogical tool to assess features of community in the classroom. *Action in Teacher Education*, *38*(4), 299–314. doi:10.1080/01626620.2016.1226208

Fleming, J. (2021). *Teaching multicultural literature in the College classroom* (Publication No. 145) [Honors Thesis, Southeastern University]. Southeastern University. https://firescholars.seu.edu/honors/145

Kumi-Yeboah, A., Dogbey, J., Yuan, G., & Smith, P. (2020). Cultural diversity in online education: An exploration of instructors' perceptions and challenges. *Teachers College Record*, *122*(7), 1–46. doi:10.1177/016146812012200708

Ladson-Billings, G. (1995). Toward a theory of culturally relevant pedagogy. *American Educational Research Journal*, *32*(3), 465–491. doi:10.3102/00028312032003465

Lave, J., & Wenger, E. (1991). *Situated learning*. Cambridge University Press. doi:10.1017/CBO9780511815355

Lawyer, G. (2018). The dangers of separating social justice from multicultural education: Applications in higher education. *International Journal of Multicultural Education*, *20*(1), 86–101. Advance online publication. doi:10.18251/ijme.v20i1.1538

Leibold, N., & Schwarz, L. M. (2015). The art of giving online feedback. *The Journal of Effective Teaching*, *15*(1), 34–46. https://uncw.edu/jet/articles/vol15_1/leiboldabs.html

Lewis, K. A. (2018). A digital immigrant venture into teaching online: An autoethnographic account of a classroom teacher transformed. *Qualitative Report*, *23*(7), 1752–1772. doi:10.46743/2160-3715/2018.3036

Liu, X., Magjuka, R. J., Bonk, C. J., & Lee, S. (2007). Does a sense of community matter? An examination of participants' perceptions of building learning communities in online courses. *Quarterly Review of Distance Education*, *8*(1), 9–24.

Martin, F., & Bolliger, D. U. (2018). Engagement matters: Student perceptions on the importance of engagement strategies in the online learning environment. *Online Learning Journal*, *22*(1), 205–222. doi:10.24059/olj.v22i1.1092

Richardson, J. C., & Swan, K. (2003). Examining social presence in online courses in relation to student's perceived learning and satisfaction. *J. Asynchr. Learn.*, *7*(1), 68–88. doi:10.24059/olj.v7i1.1864

Roddy, C., Amiet, D. L., Chung, J., Holt, C., Shaw, L., McKenzie, S., Garivaldis, F., Lodge, J. M., & Mundy, M. E. (2017). Applying best practice online learning, teaching, and support to intensive online environments: An integrative review. *Frontiers in Education*, 2(59), 1–10. doi:10.3389/feduc.2017.00059

Rovai, A. P. (2002). Development of an instrument to measure classroom community. *The Internet and Higher Education*, 5(3), 197–211. doi:10.1016/S1096-7516(02)00102-1

Sadera, W., Robertson, J., Song, L., & Midon, M. (2009). The role of community in online learning success. *Journal of Online Learning and Teaching*, 5(2), 277–284. https://jolt.merlot.org/vol5no2/sadera_0609.pdf

Samaras, A. P., & Freese, A. R. (2006). *Self-study of teaching practices: Primer.* Peter Lang.

Singh, R. N., & Hurley, D. C. (2017). The effectiveness of teaching-learning process in online education as perceived by university faculty and instructional technology professionals. *Journal of Teaching and Learning with Technology*, 6(1), 65–75. doi:10.14434/jotlt.v6.n1.19528

Turner, S. A. (2010). Teaching research to teachers: A self-study of course design, student outcomes, and instructor learning. *The Journal of Scholarship of Teaching and Learning*, 10(2), 60–77. https://files.eric.ed.gov/fulltext/EJ890719.pdf

U.S. Department of Education. (2020). *Student enrollment.* https://nces.ed.gov/ipeds/TrendGenerator/app/build-table/2/42?rid=6&cid=85

Vesely, P., Bloom, L., & Sherlock, J. (2007). Key elements of building online community: Comparing faculty and student perceptions. *Journal of Online Learning and Teaching*, 3(3), 234–246. https://jolt.merlot.org/vol3no3/vesely.pdf

Vygotsky, L. (1978). *Mind in society: The development of higher psychological processes.* Harvard University Press.

Waycott, J., Sheard, J., Thompson, C., & Clerehan, R. (2013). Making students' work visible on the social web: A blessing or a curse? *Computers & Education*, 68, 86–95. doi:10.1016/j.compedu.2013.04.026

Young, S. (2006). Student views of effective online teaching in higher education. *American Journal of Distance Education*, 20(2), 65–77. doi:10.120715389286ajde2002_2

KEY TERMS AND DEFINITIONS

Canvas: Online learning platform that houses online course management tools and curriculum for student and instructor navigation.

Community of Practice: Process of social learning within members of a group who meet and communicate regularly and have a shared interest for what they do and how they learn.

Culturally Responsive Pedagogy: Student-centered approach to teaching that focuses on instruction that is culturally sensitive, respects and responds to the prior knowledge, experiences, and diversity of identities and cultures that students bring with them into the learning community.

DEI: Diversity, equity, and inclusion. Efforts in higher education to make inclusive and equitable learning environments a priority.

Humanities: Branches of knowledge and academic subjects concerned with culture, history, language, literature, religion, art, philosophy, writing, and anthropology.

Modules: Online pages containing curriculum organized for students to review and complete tasks; linked online forums that connect to one another and make up an online course.

Multicultural Literature: Literature (poetry, prose, and nonfiction text) written by authors of diverse heritage, presenting themes related to language, culture, and identity.

Online Learning Community: Members who share in learning and collaboration online.

Practice: The *how, what, and why* of an instructor's focus on facilitating student learning and developing curriculum for the classroom.

Self-Study: Reflection on one's research, pedagogy, and individual process in teaching and learning.

Chapter 6
Digital Literacy for Adult Education Beyond Borders:
Developing Learners' Intercultural Sensitivity Using Game–Based Learning

Hany Zaky

https://orcid.org/0000-0003-0342-8814
Kean University, USA

ABSTRACT

Game-based learning is a powerful instructional method to build students' sense of community and cultural awareness. Educators view game-based learning as one of effective pedagogy and learning principles. Therefore, integrating technology in the teaching process is an influential tool that spurs learners' academic achievements and awareness of the learning goals. Understanding intercultural sensitivity in digital classrooms needs the individuals' awareness of subjective and objective cultural dimensions to deepen this integration. Due to the current varieties of offered educational games, educators need to know each game's background, context, and the proper pedagogical approach. The chapter focuses on the impact of technological advancements on building learners' intercultural sensitivity using game-based learning, as an adult classroom instructional technique, toward a more humanistic approach. It proposes the educational approaches to designing, managing, and using games for learning development assurance.

DOI: 10.4018/978-1-6684-4055-1.ch006

Copyright © 2023, IGI Global. Copying or distributing in print or electronic forms without written permission of IGI Global is prohibited.

INTRODUCTION

The recent technological advancements have caused tremendous changes across all academic disciplines' dimensions. The technological innovations brought a noticeable difference in connecting the global educational environment setting and addressing nearly all social-related aspects (Smith, 2009). Educators, though, look for ways to integrate technology into their instruction focusing on real-world problems to provide their students with authentic learning experiences. Using the available technological tools successfully in classrooms depends on educators' capacities to make meaningful, relevant experiences that grapple with higher thinking orders. Teachers' professional associations developed several standards to propose the technological skills needed to secure a successful education. However, research on how higher education educators integrate technology into their instruction remains uncharted (Porter et al., 2014; Turugare & Rudhumbu, 2020).

Technology integration is an educational concept addressing the instructional practices that promote content deliverance (Koruyan, 2016). It includes technology-based instruction, such as e-learning, distance learning, online learning, and information and communication technologies (ICT). Researchers, however, use these concepts interchangeably. Each includes different software, hardware, and technical information. Thence, technology integration is "comprises the incorporation of technology resources and technology-based practices into the daily routines, work, and management of schools" (NCES, 2002, p. 75). However, the integration quality depends on educators' awareness of the available technology and delivery methods.

To enhance the quality of the delivered Education, the institutions should adopt computer-based technologies such as online learning formats and social media applications. However, the integration process could be driven by several factors (U.S. Department of Education, 2017; Faudler, 2011). These factors encompass institutional, technical support, time, technophobia, professional development, and learners' cultural backgrounds (Brown, 2016; Martirosyan et al., 2017; Zaky, 2022). With the development of computers and online technology, educators recently brought game-based learning to transform learning potential by securing a different context. It is a practical instructional approach for more online collaboration and socially interactive learning. It is built upon the constructivist approach and the research conducted by Kolb, 1984 (De Freitas & Neumann, 2009). To this point, game designers need to consider the various learning mechanics: Game, learning, and assessment (Plass et al., 2013) for solid design outcomes. Understanding these mechanics leads to a more alignment between the instructional objectives, the used games, and the humanistic approach.

Games posit at the heart of human communication, fostering societal engagement, cultural awareness, and learning motivation (Bozkurt & Durak, 2018). The educational games are structured learning experiences, including related constructive feedback. The feedback is shared instantaneously regarding the gaming design, the instructional procedures, and the shared learning goals. Providing feedback is the core of influential game design (Jarvis & de Freitas, 2009; Shute, 2008). Learners play a central role in the feedback design and deliverance procedures. The designed feedback should reflect learners' context, culture, and educational needs. Therefore, educators should be guided by whether game-based learning activities are a proper selection for the course scope and sequence (Protopsaltis et al., 2010). To this end, the game-based medium strengthens learners' cognitive and social competencies if the appropriate feedback is provided.

Technology integration depends on the educators' technology proficiency (Brown, 2016; Fathema et al., 2015; Kaminski & Bolliger, 2012). Research revealed that educators' behavior toward technology drives the incorporation process in the delivered instruction (Brown, 2016; Kim et al., 2013; Zaky, 2021). The effective integration of game-based practice in classroom instruction depends on the technology acceptance in the learning environment, and the received technical support (Fathema et al., 2015; Wickersham & McElhany, 2010).

The chapter proposed the importance of technology integration in teaching and learning. It highlights the impact of integrating game-based learning on students' cognitive learning capacities. It also explores technology integration in the adult learning environment, Game-based learning, cultural sensitivity, and the proper type of feedback in a digitalized environment. Given the above exposure, this chapter answers the following questions:

1-   To what extent could integrating technology in classroom instruction increase students' cultural sensitivity?
2-   Is there a relationship between game-based learning and students' learning capacities?
3-   What is the impact of the provided feedback on students' self-regulation?
4-   How can games be used more effectively to facilitate professional learning**?**
5-   What is the impact of classroom culture on game-based learning practice effectiveness?

TECHNOLOGY AND TEACHING

Technology Literacy is one of the 21st-century skills. Gay (2019) proposed that workers' technology illiteracy is one of the employers' concerns. Technology literacy is considered the main factor in social advancement and employability (Kaminski & Bolliger, 2012). It includes the learners' capacities to use technology to improve working productivity and performance (U.S. Department of Education, 1996). This learning ability is an indicator of job readiness in the 21st century. It is imperative to equip learners with the technological skills to compete in the global economy with all its progressive changes (Cheng et al., 2018). To this end, higher education institutions capitalize upon shaping technology-savvy mindsets to participate actively in community development. Therefore, technology integration in Higher Education becomes necessary for a more progressive society (Smith, 2009).

Higher education institutions are expected to modify their offered curricula to develop learners' technology literacy for learning enhancement (Smith, 2009; Yilmaz et al., 2020). Modern technologies secure golden opportunities to build students' technological Literacy (Brill & Galloway, 2007). More recently, learners have had access to computer-based classroom technologies (Schindler et al., 2017). Consequently, educators are motivated to integrate technology into their instruction to form an authentic learning environment (Sturgeon, 2011; Zaky, 2021). Research reveals that faculty members change their instruction based on the available technologies and students' readiness to integrate these technological tools (Yilmaz et al., 2020). Thence, the available technologies and students' learning desires motivate faculty members to differentiate instruction to meet those students' needs and societal progress.

INSTRUCTIONAL PROCEDURES

Modern classroom learning and teaching environments encompass an intricate relation between technology, learning, and instruction. Educators disregard the alignment between technological resources, content, instruction, and learning outcomes (Okojie et al., 2006). Nonetheless, the core of this alignment process is understanding the specific pedagogical principles related to technology in the available instructional setting. Okojie et al. (2006) defined technology integration as integral to lesson preparation and instruction. It requires teachers to use the available technological tools such as software applications and electronic media. Technology integration helps develop educators' critical thinking skills and students' intellectual capacities. Using technology secures the opportunities to examine and explore all the factors influencing learning and teaching progress. Thence the failure to realize the importance of technology integration degrades the quality of technology-based learning education.

The technological and pedagogical content knowledge (TPACK) addresses the factors impacting the technology integration into the delivered instruction. Scherer et al. (2021) proposed that teachers' readiness to integrate technology during the COVID pandemic could be low, inconsistent, or high, driven by culture and prior technology experience. The integration process's sign is the direct use of technological resources such as software, applications, communication devices, online platforms, and electronic media. To this end, the integration process shapes the delivered instructions to develop learners' cognitive capacities in an authentic learning environment. that could be created by gaming and simulation.

Game-Based Learning

The pervasiveness of games in education changed from being a source of entertainment to a learning catalyst. Game-based learning was developed rapidly as an instructional tool. Many young and adult learners become obsessed with gaming, such as Pong, Minecraft, and Space Invaders. More recently, Modern P.C has involved multiplayer games, such as "World of Warcraft," which attracted 1.5 million players worldwide (November 2009), and Minecraft, where students could come to the learning environment with various leveraged skills from their social interactions. Additionally, the gaming opportunities on Facebook unprecedentedly developed social gaming. The pervasiveness of social games in the USA has encouraged educators and trainers to integrate the available applications into schools, colleges, universities, and professional development units. Thence using gaming technologies in learning and training settings raises different questions such as "How can educators and trainers properly use gaming technologies to engage learners?", "How can the used games motivate learners to master the offered content?", "What are the strengths of using gaming technologies in education and training?" and "How can educators and trainers better design educational games?", To address all of these questions, educators need to be thoroughly aware of students' needs and learning objectives to integrate the game-based learning into the delivered instruction effectively.

Games and Learning Experience

Learning requires a cognitive activity as learners select relevant information and organize it into coherent structures (Mayer & Johnson, 2010). To facilitate the learning flow experience, Kiili (2005) proposed a model to connect the gameplay with experiential learning. Her design cycle brought Kolb's four experiential learning phases into the gaming process: Concrete experience, reflective observation, abstract conceptualization, and feedback or active experimentation. Then, the learning cycle shows how reflection translates knowledge into tangible concepts. The process is the guide to constructive feedback or active investigation of the new experience. Thence, learners could realize the importance of acquiring the concept, skills, and attitudes. Kiili's gaming design illustrates the main stages of the design process. The model addresses the importance of considering the various flow antecedents such as the skills challenges, clear goals, detailed feedback, a sense of control, playability, gamefulness, and focused attention (See Figure 1). Considering this model directs educators' attention to the differences between the gaming experiences in a formal context and informal ones outside the school setting. Therefore, it is vital to consider the pedagogical exploitation of the games in classrooms.

Figure 1. Experimental Gaming Model (Kiili 2005, p. 18)

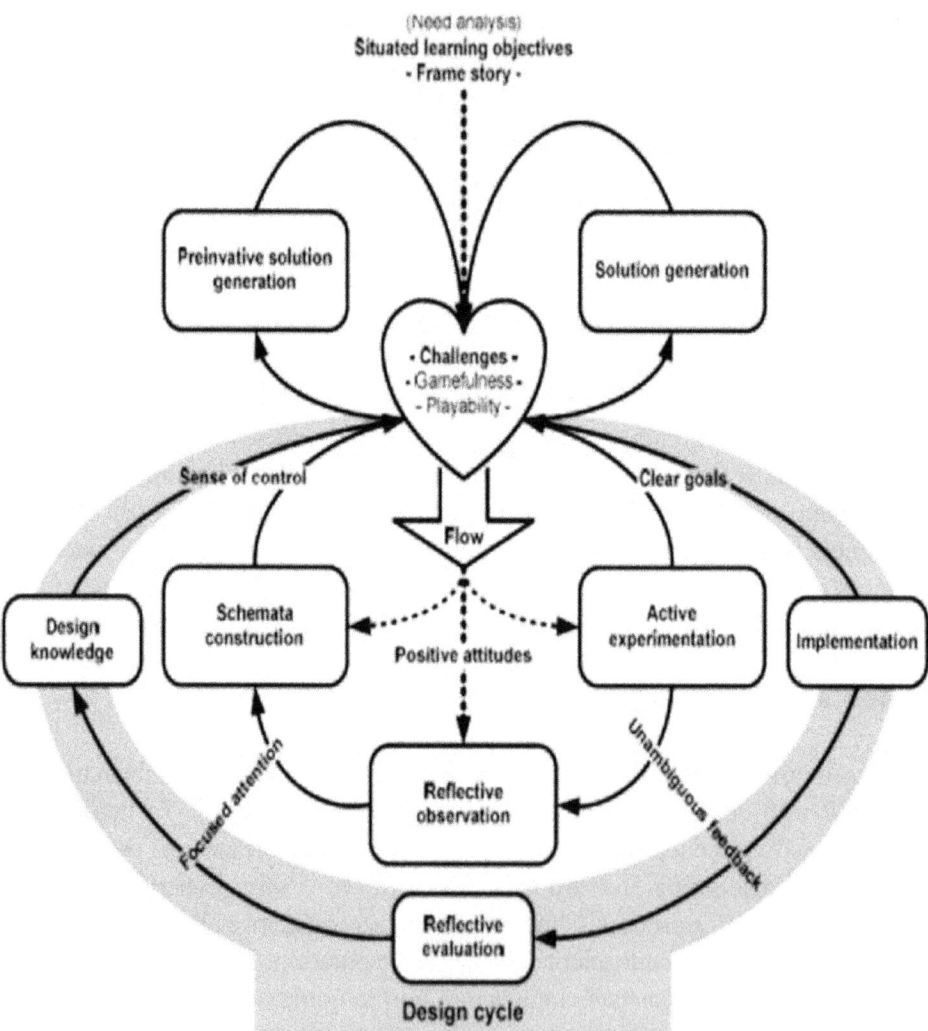

Games and Assessment for Learning

To assure the effectiveness of the game-based learning experience, educators need to increase the awareness of using immediate feedback. Players could progress and advance based on the feedback that guides their gaming promotion in the educational setting. Therefore the teaching and learning challenges lie in assessing the proper knowledge and skills. Shut (2013) labeled the process of collecting data regarding players' progress as "Stealth Assessment." Later Shut defined it as an evidence-based process through which educators could integrate their created assessment criteria into learning environments. The designed assessment provides educators with golden opportunities to collect lots of data about their student's academic competencies (Ash, 2012).

The body of research highlights the importance of providing learners with choice, feedback, and accommodation across the designed games. Therefore, educators need to use proper criteria and knowledge to form new students' gaming opportunities. Students increase their conceptual understanding and enhance their problem-solving skills and creativity by learning through designing. The current software secures the opportunities to facilitate students' interactions in the design process. This approach helps learners deepen their concepts and learning skills (Prensky, 2008). Thence, assessment for learning is deemed a cornerstone of successfully implementing game-based learning tasks.

Digital Games and Instruction

COVID-19 pandemic accelerated the digital transformation around the world. The flexibility and accessibility of technology in classrooms created a new learning environment. The sociocultural nature of the used learning digital networks and management systems directed educators to explore various humanistic approaches to foster their students' engagements in learning. Building the instructional process upon game-based learning transforms learning constructs from knowledge and information to lived experiences and apprenticeships. This paradigm shift with the instructional procedures enhances learning personalization. Similarly, game-based learning could be an effective teaching tool to capitalize on social learning opportunities (De Freitas & Conole, 2010). Therefore, teachers need to develop and deepen the conceptual work to effectively implement game-based learning in their learning environment. This teaching and learning approach is built around learners' brought experiences. Learning experiences, however, can encapsulate the shared learning elements and be linear in representing students' lived experiences (Kolb, 1984; De Freitas & Neumann, 2009). To this point, educators provide students with a personalized learning experience.

Games-based learning provides students with various scopes for learning in different contexts. The broadband availability secured new opportunities for more online social interactive learning (De Freitas and Neumann, 2009). Kolb (1984) proposed the role of "Learning experience," which is built upon two primary considerations: First, the role of social interaction; Second, the role of learning design. These two learning areas address two challenges. First, the tools educators could use to design and support the offered learning opportunities for group learning. Second, the used procedures to facilitate the experience-based learning scenarios. Mayes and De Freitas (2007) reported that using simulation in classrooms provides learners with the opportunities to deepen their learning skills. To this end, educators could shape their teaching environment to enhance learners' social and cognitive skills.

The use of simulation enhances innovative learning techniques. Researchers stressed the effectiveness of using empirical evidence for more game-based learning efficacy. However, the simulation provided learners with multimodal approaches to deepen their learning (Griffiths & Guile, 1999; Jarvis & De Freitas, 2009). Additionally, motivation, engagement, and empowering learners throughout the progressive shared feedback accelerate the learning transfer (Kato et al., 2008). Therefore, game-based learning cogently involves students in the learning process and activates their prior knowledge. However, embedding game-based learning into the traditional teaching environment could raise some challenges: First, the role of social interaction; and second, the learning design analysis in games regarding the editing and user-generated content (Protopsaltis et al., 2010). Thence, impeding simulation as a game-based learning approach secures the learning tools to overcome the arisen challenges in the traditional teaching environment.

The inter-relation between gaming and learning is complex. The learning process resembles gaming, as engagement and motivation enhance a more exploratory approach (Oliver & Pelletier, 2004). Learning, as an activity, constructs an immersive, engaging, and leading experience to ease the data collection significantly. The multisensory interaction within the game-based learning experience replicates the lived experiences and empowers the learning and teaching tools. De Freitas and Neumann (2009) framed the design process based on correlating the world inside the game and reality. However, a choreographic-created frame challenges an educational setting since educators should consider the games technologies and learning process (De Freitas & Conole, 2010; Anastasiadis et al., 2018). Additionally, the design process should be guided by the curricular structures, information dissemination, and teacher-students relation. Consequently, educators could transform deep and tacit structures of pedagogy and curriculum by developing, testing, and implementing new modified learning values and qualities such as judgment.

Bloom's Taxonomy of Educational Objectives

Educators need to consider Bloom's Taxonomy within the design process based on the games' instructional approaches' features. Researchers, though, describe games as tools to design engaging learning experiences, ideological contexts for interaction, and space for developing a highly complex social network (Squire, 2006; Young, Schrader & Zheng, 2006; Steinkuehler, 2006; Schrader, Lawless & McCreery, 2009). Using taxonomy, therefore, facilitates learning by fostering players' cognitive, behavioral and sociocultural engagement. Various factors shape Game-based learning effectiveness. These factors are pertinent to the theoretical foundation- cognitive, affective behavioral, and sociocultural.

Educators foster the integration of games in their instruction to motivate students to engage in the learning process (Gee, 2005; Gulikers & Bastiaens, 2004; Witeck et al., 2021). One of the steps to increase educators understanding of games is value realization. Bloom's Taxonomy generally increases teachers' awareness of the different educational games' genres. Consequently, developing a game taxonomy enhances educators' understanding of the game's content, structure, and affordances (Yang & Wang, 2008). The curriculum could be developed "backward." To this point, educators could select the games based on their educational objectives (Huang & Cappel, 2005; Steinkuehler, 2004). To this end, shaping the taxonomy of educational games becomes valuable in the teaching process to motivate learners and achieve the designated instructional objectives.

Selecting an appropriate game to achieve the instructional objectives is a complex process. However, Bloom's Taxonomy provides educators with the criteria enhancing the reasoning with that selection. It describes the related cognitive skills that learners could develop through the various gaming stages (Bloom,1956). A better understanding of this complexity helps educational researchers, game designers, and educators to embrace games in curriculum and instruction in various disciplines. Bloom described three domains of educational objectives: Cognitive, Affective, and Psychomotor. Most educational games, though, are built upon these three learning domains: Psychomotor is engaged with digital games. Cognitive development is fostered with all types of educational games as educators could teach the required knowledge through engaging exposure to the content within a given discipline. Educators could facilitate the learning process by stressing the Affective, Cognitive, Social, and behavioral aspects of the used learning games (Mayer & Johnson, 2010). In the same vein, the learners' engagement with the game constructs those learners' mental models toward more efficient communication (Gagne & Briggs, 1974; Mayer, 2005, 2014).

Gamification enables social support among the gaming participants. This support takes various forms: Synchronously through chats and Asynchrounsously through discussion forums (Laine & Lindberg, 2020; Vanduhe et al., 2020). For example, with role-playing games, learners could acquire rote knowledge, comprehend the used concepts, and evaluate them to implement and synthesize them in various situations (See Table 1). Therefore, designers and researchers should consider the learners' cognitive processing and how the learning mechanism should be designed to keep learners' engagement to facilitate the planned learning outcomes. To this end, developing an educational game is goal-driven activity (See Table 1; Figure 2).

Figure 2. Integrated Design Framework of Game-based and Playful Learning (Adapted from Mayer and Johnson, 2010)

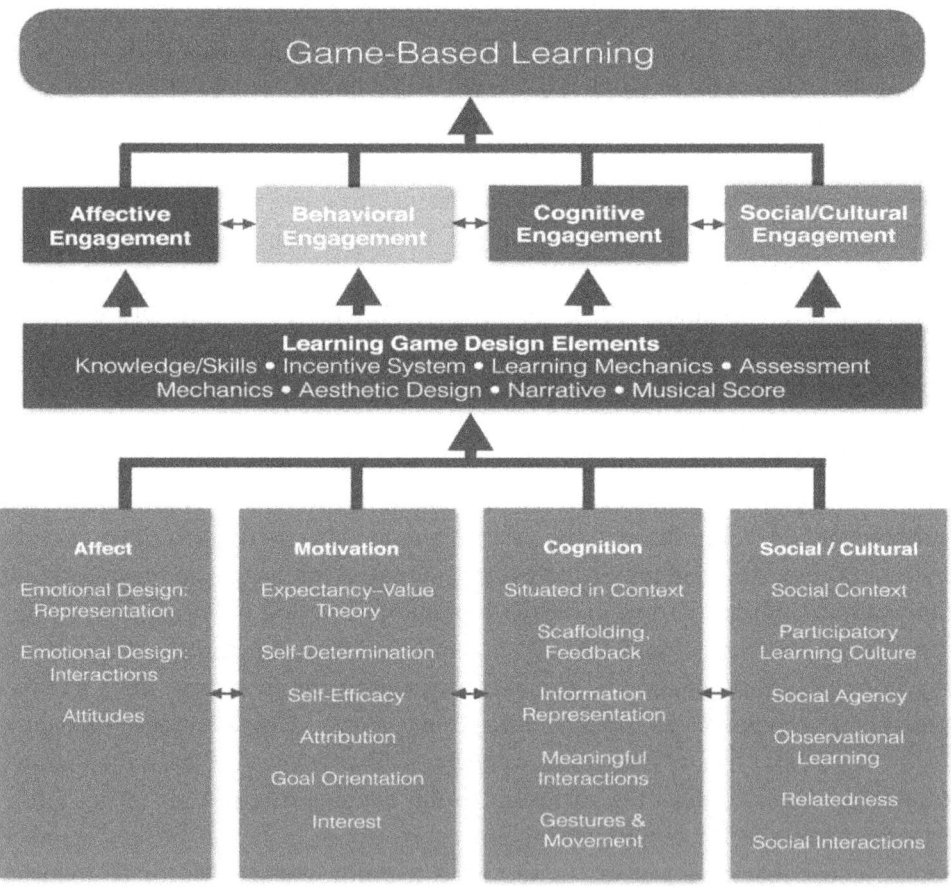

Table 1. The Taxonomy of Educational Game (Adapted from O'Brien, 2010)

Game Genre	Linear	Competitive	Strategic	Role-playing
Bloom's	Application	Synthesis	Evaluation	
Educational	Comprehension	Comprehension	Analysis	Synthesis
Objectives	Knowledge	Knowledge	Application	Analysis
	Psychomotor	Psychomotor	Comprehension	Application
			Knowledge	Comprehension
			Psychomotor	Knowledge
				Psychomotor

Games and Professional Learning

Games could be used to facilitate professional learning and training. Two sets of theories guide this facilitation process: A diegetic model and a Transactional Learning model. For the diegetic model, educators focus on learning upon experiences rather than shared content and curricula. Therefore, through rehearsal and roleplay, learners can build and develop knowledge during playtime (Bekoff & Byers, 1998; Edelman, 1992). Educators, from their side, should consider play-based learning as a teaching approach to conduct more scaffolding in classrooms to keep students engaged and interested in the offered learning experience (Vygotsky, 1978; Nelson & Erlandson, 2008). De Freitas and Oliver (2006) proposed a framework built upon several studies with educators and learners. The framework includes four dimensions: The context, learners, the game representation, and the used pedagogies. The game context is crucial as it activates the learners' background knowledge and makes the learning relatable. Furthermore, the representational dimension of the learning necessitates the game shared world or roleplay (See Figure 3).

On the other hand, the Transactional Learning model is used to understand the complexity of using game-based learning. The model explains the dynamic movement of subjects to objects via specific tools. Engestrom (1999) developed this model to include the social and cultural aspects: "Cultural-Historical Activity Theory"- CHAT (See Figure 4). This model was developed by Barton, McKellar, and Maharg (2007) (See Figure 5). In their model, Barton, McKellar, and Maharg (2007) suggested that learners move from the subject to the object through a mediational tool. The practice within this model refers to the reality of professional transactions to personal understanding that students need to change. The rules are those of the practice community with the resources and given guidelines. The community, though, is the transactional learning experience. The learners' identification of this process is the critical element of personal identity construction toward mastering the learning experience. To this point, learners learn the influence of enacting codes and ethics in their professional practice by constructing individual identity.

The transactional model gives learners insights into examining their beliefs as game participants. It involves gaming and simulation, including seven critical traits: Active learning, authentic transactions, progressive reflection, process learning, professional Assessment, and ethical standards. The model, therefore, secures a blueprint to guide the teaching and Assessment of CHAT. It also supports diegetic learning through social interaction and active learning tactics. Accordingly, learning design provides learners with the scaffolding opportunities to accelerate and deepen their learning experiences through activities, roleplays, and rehearsals.

Figure 3. De Freitas and Oliver's (2006) Designed Model

Figure 4.

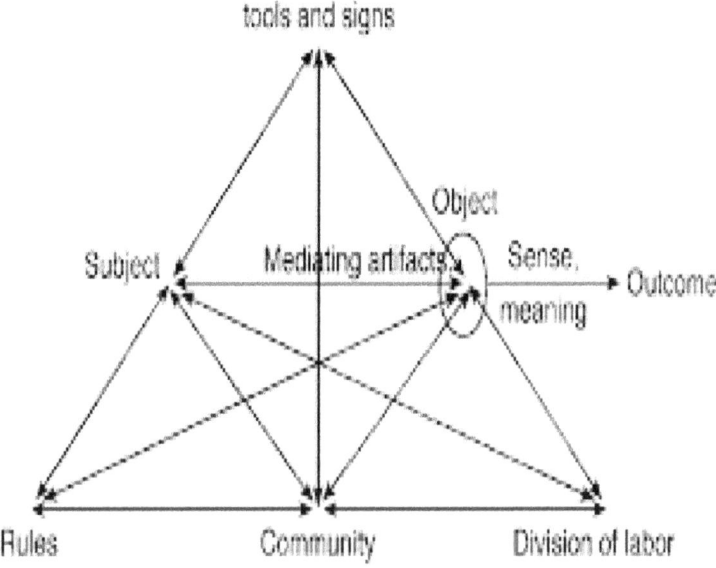

Figure 5.

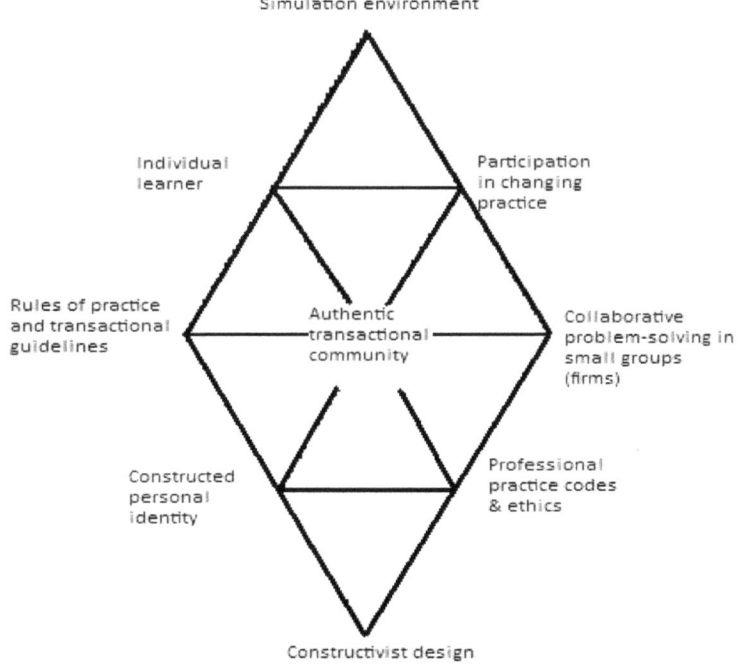

FEEDBACK AND GAME-BASED LEARNING

Feedback is one of the most influential factors in-game designs. Jarvis and De Freitas (2009) proposed that provided feedback is the central consideration in the practical design process. The constructive provided feedback drives the learning transfer. Accordingly, De Freitas and Oliver (2005) suggested a four-dimensional framework that could provide educators with the tools to guide the feedback design. The four dimensions: Learners, designers, context, and representational medium, effectively navigate the provided feedback. De Freitas and Neumann (2009) reported that Kolb's experiential model is the theoretical framework for shaping a robust feedback process. The effectiveness of feedback depends on the motivation tactic in the used educational medium (Gobet et al., 2004). Understanding the dynamic of providing effective feedback helps educators and game designers to consider the motivational character, the experimentation practice, the retention rate, the reflective observation, and the used concepts (Figure 6). To this point, feedback and motivation are two crucial factors of influential game design.

Figure 6.

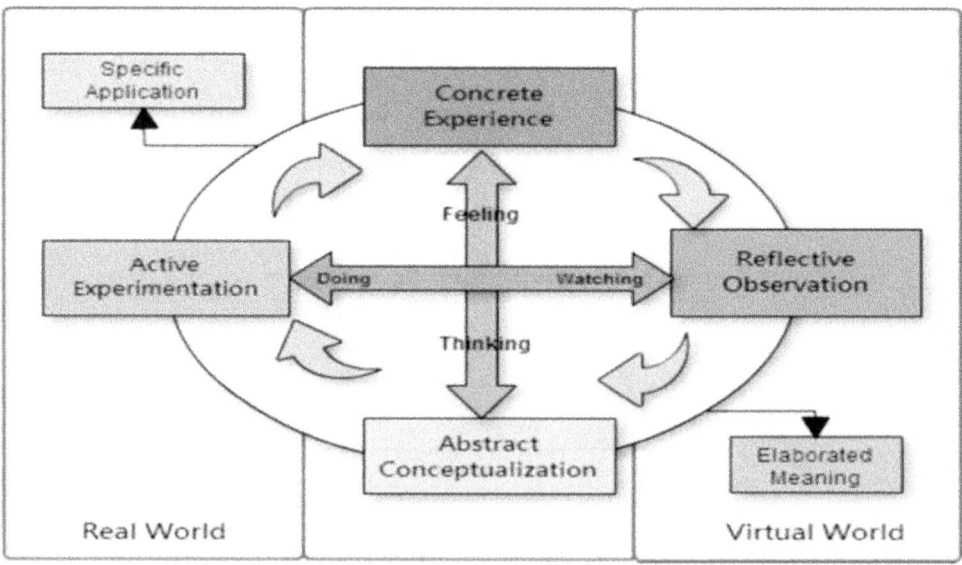

Motivation relates to several social and cognitive constructs. Reynold (2002) classified motivation into intrinsic or self-motivation. Intrinsic motivation is an internal drive to complete a task. At the same time, extrinsic motivation is formulated through interaction with others. Educators use extrinsic motivation to foster the scaffolding process within the educational environment (Şimşek & Barto, 2006). The intrinsic motivation reward mechanism benefits the agent-based reinforcement learning approach. Therefore the instructional designer should consider the innate motivational characteristics of a game-based process. The feedback type drives these motivational traits.

Feedback and Time

Shut (2008) examined the feedback frequency on the learning transference. The feedback timing is an ongoing argument among game designers. Alternatively, delaying feedback could prove an optimal gaming paradigm as it would not disrupt the flow experience. Accordingly, frequent feedback should be conveyed rather than sticking to instant or delayed feedback. Effective feedback should be evaluative, interpretative, supportive, probing, and understanding practice (Roger, 1951; Warburton, 2008). Shute (2008) reported that effective feedback should include verification elements in terms of evaluation and elaboration covering higher-level tasks (See Figure 7). To this end, the frequent feedback should be adjusted in terms of time and content for more learning efficacy.

Structured and systematic feedback has a positive impact on learning transference. Systematically designed feedback positively affects learners' motivation; therefore, feedback should be orchestrated in a structured environment as creating learning games (Shute, 2008; Betts, 2021). Educators, therefore, need to consider the learners' capacities to align their feedback to those learners' needs. However, effective, increasing feedback requires increasing technical development, ranging from simple performance related-variables to sophisticated artificial intelligence. Thence feedback could be shaped by learners' self-reflection, individual real-world experience, and technological artificial, driven systems for effective autonomous feedback.

Feedback is the central consideration in pedagogy. Educators need to consider the level of the delivered support outside the game. Recognizing if the game needs a principal feedback mechanism for learners is essential. The kind of feedback, either supportive or probing using technology, provides learners with the tools to receive rapid and accurate evaluatory feedback based on actions and behaviors. Learners, though, are essential catalysts in the formulation and deliverance of feedback. Educators need to consider the various characteristics of feedback: Types, content, format, and frequency. Rogers' research provides a strong foundation of different underlying paradigms considering the type of instructors, technology, and learners.

Figure 7. A Four-dimensional Approach to the Consideration of the Feedback Process

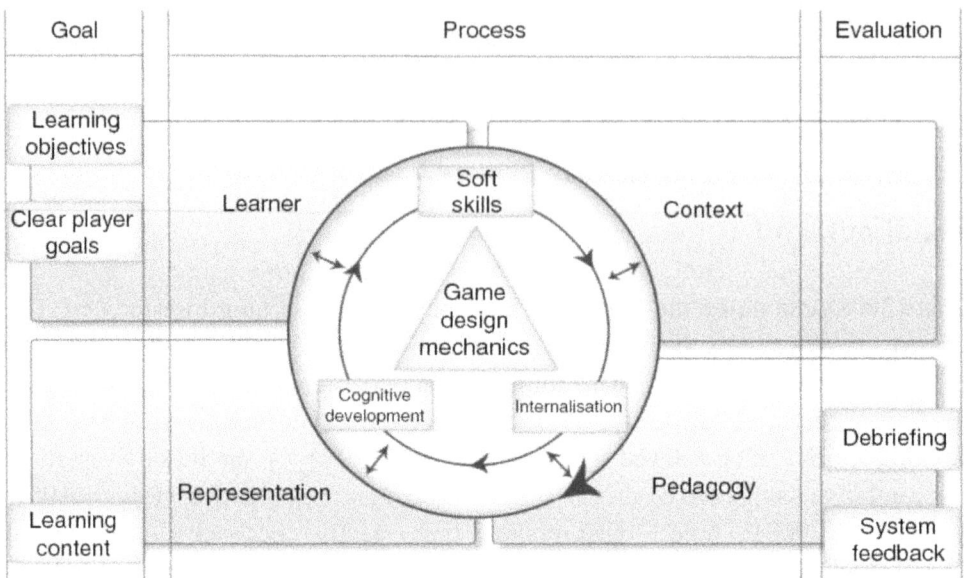

INTERCULTURAL SENSITIVITY AND GAME-BASED LEARNING

Intercultural Sensitivity

The language used to provide the feedback could promote intercultural dialogues to foster students' cultural sensitivity. However, it is beneficial for educators to be aware that intercultural sensitivity, intercultural communicative competence (ICC), cross-cultural Adaptation, and transcultural communication have been used interchangeably in the literature (Sinicrope et al., 2007). As a result, there are a lot of models that attempt to describe these various intricacies. Spitzberg and Changnon (2009) have categorized these models into five primary types: Co-orientational, developmental, compositional, causal, and adaptational. One of the most famous recently used models is the DAMS. Bennett's (1993) developmental model of intercultural sensitivity (DMIS) outlines the relationship between the individual's worldview (ethnocentric) and the culturally aware worldview (ethno-relative). Cultural awareness helps inform the conceptualization of the Game-based learning described in this article. The DMIS includes three ethnocentric stages: Denial, defense, and minimization of cultural differences, and three ethno-relative stages: Acceptance, Adaptation, and integration of cultural differences (See Figure 8).

Figure 8. Bennetts's DMIS' Model

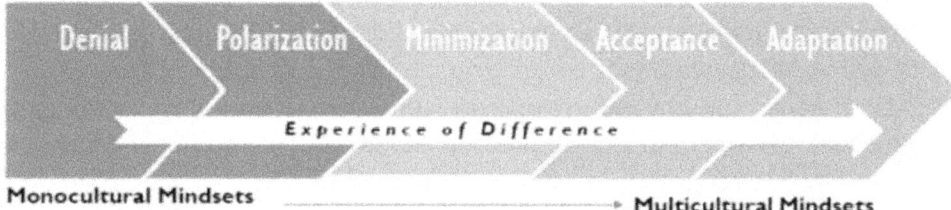

During the denial stage, one perceives the authentic culture as his/her own, and there is an unawareness of other cultures. In the defense stage, only one culture (one's own) is viable, and there is the idea of "us" and "them." In the minimization stage, one's cultural features are considered universal; one expects similar behavior from others and may even insist on correcting others' behavior to match their own. In the acceptance stage, one understands that one's own culture is just one among many others and accepts cultural differences, although not necessarily agreeing. In the adaptation stage, one's worldview expands, and empathy toward others' cultures is expressed. In the last step, integration, different cultural worldviews are included in one's own, with none being central. Ultimately, intercultural reflections aim to avoid stereotypes and individual "labels" and expand worldviews (Bennett & Bennett, 2004).

Intercultural Sensitivity and Game-Based Learning

Critical incidents are particularly helpful in clarifying misunderstandings between people from different cultural backgrounds. Critical incidents use "situations in which there is a cross-cultural adaptation or misunderstanding, problem, or conflict arising from cultural differences between interacting parties" as a preamble to develop intercultural awareness (Fowler & Blohm, 2004, p. 58). The expected outcome of using critical incidents in intercultural training is to "increase participants' understanding of their cultural and personal attitudes and beliefs as well as those of others" (Fowler & Blohm, 2004, p. 58).

Games and game-based learning are powerful tools for improving motivation and learning outcomes in various important humanities areas such as education, health, and social work. Critical Literacy, though, requires students to express their ideologies, beliefs, values, cultures, and identities openly. Identity in language has been a significant dimension in discussions of language and culture in the past decade (Cummins, 2001; Norton, 2013; Norton & Toohey, 2011). Negotiating identities can be particularly beneficial in multicultural classrooms where students can voice and expand on beliefs, values, and issues from a cultural standpoint. Digital Literacy, though, does not only include the knowledge of using computers, mobile phones, and other digital tools but also includes a social dimension that involves people's relationships, interactions, and "social identities" (Jones & Hafner, 2021).

Digital Literacy can promote active participation by community members, ranging from the local classroom to a larger one that crosses geographical boundaries (via social media). For example, video and movie projects have been gaining popularity in language learning as innovative ways to promote digital Literacy among language learners (Ron Darvin & Bonny Norton, 2014; Lotherington & Jenson, 2011; Toohey, Dagenais & Schulze, 2012). Toohey et al. (2012) have suggested that, through digital Literacy, language learners can develop critical reflections and higher levels of Literacy, as the use of "linguistic, cultural, material, visual, and gestural sources" is needed to deliver the message to an intended audience (p. 86). Learners' game experiences could add more valuable class discussions. How learners interact with the shared game-based learning activities shapes their insights regarding the various raised concepts in the learning environment. Therefore, educators need to ensure students' full awareness of the symbols, icons, and images used in the game design. This understanding is interpreted into players' engagement with the shared texts. Playing Statecraft X is an example through which students continuously interpret the provided information, symbols, and images based on critical reasoning, cultural inputs, and thinking skills (See Figure 9).

Figure 9. Statecraft X running on iPhone: Symbols, numners. And icons <http://cheeyamsan.info/NIEprojects?SCX/SCX2.htm>

Gender

Gender difference is an essential factor driving game-based learning in classrooms. Digital media, though, plays an influential role in shaping, understanding, and exploring gendered identities (Valkenburg et al., 2005). Consequently, the digital game's environment could create a new space to create new learning settings and shape learners' identities to align with the learning objectives. The body of research reports a gender difference in using video games: Men are more likely to play more than women (Terlecki et al., 2011). They are more engaged than women in achievement games (Williams et al., 2009; Lowrie & Jorgensen, 2011). Nevertheless, the gender role could be driven by the used digital technologies.

Digital technologies actively shape educational reforms in various parts of the world. Game-based learning, though, posits the core of using technologies. Therefore, researchers such as Bourdieu extensively researched games' role in enhancing learning. He suggested a robust framework for profoundly understanding the gaming impact on learning and learners. The raised framework includes three primary constructs: Habitus, field, and capital. Bourdieu stressed the linkage between the three constructs. For example, the field could shape the capital and habitus, including cultural inputs (See Figure 10). Thence, it is essential to consider the three constructs throughout the entire learning experience of gaming.

Figure 10. Theoretical Frameowkr (Adpated from Bourdieu, 1983)

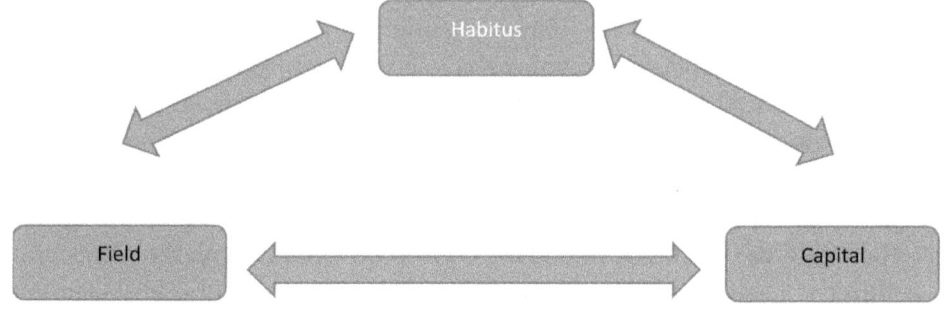

Game-based learning is a relatively new learning strategy that is progressively refined and developed. It offers a unique learning environment to increase social and psychological engagement in the learning process. Therefore, game designers must consider the new market and learning environments changes. Digital games could bring various learning opportunities to students from different backgrounds and learning capacities (Devlin-Scherer & Sardone 2010; Johnson 2011; Owston 2012). Therefore, the new digital games generation gives players the context to shape their collaboration and problem-solving. To this end, game-based learning capitalize upon pro-social behaviors driven by technology, gender, and culture (Ferguson and Garza, 2011; Kahne et al., 2009).

BEST PRACTICES

Educators seek games that could encourage, educate and promote their practice. Many games, therefore, claim to meet the educational criteria for being effective learning tools. Educators should seek out games with a narrow focus and define reasonable and achievable goals regarding learners' capacities and offered content. They should also choose the tested game and provide outcomes assessment and usability analysis, for example, the use of video games in teaching Literacy based on various attested game-based learning to foster students' Literacy skills (DeLoura & Metz, 2013; Clark et al., 2013) (See Table 2). Educators could scaffold students to learn the games' key constructs and patterns to deepen their understanding of the design process (Campe et al., 2013; Campe, Werner & Denner, 2012; Webb & Rossen, 2013). Games include specifically delivered worldviews that enable cultural practices and norms to appear within educational usability. For example, MMORPG and Minecraft introduce various worldviews shaped by culture, reasoning, and creativity. The gaming-raised views encourage players to value the learning environment and shape their cultural awareness. To this end, educators need to be guided by some rigorous rules to integrate gaming practice into their instructions.

Integrating the instructional learning goals and game objectives should center the designer's work. Referencing the mentioned research in this article, some essential principles help with the smooth integration of the two learning objectives to secure the gaming design efficiency use in educational settings:

- Backward design: Game designers need to be familiar with the Curriculum objectives and assessment methods before starting the game-based learning design.
- Engagement process: Sharing the games' learning objectives fosters learners' engagement to achieve the units' instructional objectives.
- Learning activities and games: Game designers need to impede the learning activities within the gaming and should consider these activities modifications based on the learners' needs.

- Gaming challenges: The gaming challenges should be guided by the designated learning objectives, the learning content, and the assessment and evaluation approach. Additionally, the provided feedback should be built upon various challenges to guide and motivate the learners.

Table 2. The Relationship Between Video Games and Literacy

Relationship between Video games and Literacy	Example
1. The pedagogical use of literacy games to improve reading, writing, and speaking skills	- A teacher uses Reader Rabbit to attempt to improve reading scores.
2. The pedagogical use of non-literary games to improve reading, writing, and speaking skills	-A teacher uses *The Sims* (2000) to have students write non-fiction
3. Studying the existing use of non-literary games to explore literacy practices of users	-An educator or researcher studies writing abilities and/or changes over time of *World of Warcraft* players.
4. Studying video game use and design as literate practices.	-Researchers and educators explore tutorial gameplay within *Lego Star Wars: The Video Game* (2005) to negotiate existing novice and expert practices.

MMORPG and Minecraft

Educators could use an existing game for educational practice. This use brings fun experiences and learners' previous achievements to the educational environment. Minecraft is a sandbox game providing players with the material and tools to construct their premises. During the day, they accumulate materials to build; however, the night is for rest. At night, enemies attack the players, so they need to create protective structures ahead of time. The game raises challenges humans could encounter in a natural environment, such as diverse cultural and original backgrounds. Thus many aspects of architectural construction could be related to many scientific fields. Thence, players should grapple with the fundamentals of physics and architecture. However, learners could educate themselves to use economic principles to demand goods and resources. Educators, therefore, use this game to introduce various engineering and science concepts (Short, 2012; West & Bleiberg, 2013). Educators have many resources at minecraftedu.com, including a wiki to help teachers and players answer questions and develop innovative ways to use the game. Minecraft encourages modding, in which players can modify the game by accessing the game source code and coming up with their content (Soflano, 2011). Bayliss (2021) reported that when players have the capacity for modding, they could practice artificial intelligence coding agents of the game. In the same vein, Piaget proposed that learners look for similarities and differences between the received information and prior knowledge to foster the assimilation process of this new information into the existing cognitive structure (Chie et al., 1983; Yi-Shiuan Chou et al., 2021). Therefore, Minecraft could be an effective tool to teach intercultural elements and scientific concepts.

Writing *Pal*

It is an intelligent- tutoring system directed by Arizona State University. The system develops learners' literacy skills, specifically writing competencies. It includes videos introducing students to the various writing modes with accompanied strategies to facilitate the writing learning process. Students could engage in multiple writing puzzles and competitions to practice the learned literacy tactics. The program also provides students with some related game-based strategies of rhetorical skills. The included essay tools provide automatic feedback and mechanical assessment. For example, one of the designed games, Adventurer's Loot, helps students practice paraphrasing techniques, word choice, and identifying the run-on sentence (Roscoe, Brandon, Snow, & McNamara, 2013). Students are motivated if they answer correctly, whereas a monster appears if they get the wrong response. Roscoe et al. (2013) reported that Writing Pal helps students accumulate a more significant number of new writing strategies besides a high level of gaming enjoyment. To this end, researchers examined many games and simulations to gauge their appropriateness in educational settings (See Table 3).

CONCLUSION

This chapter has reviewed the current use and integration of game-based learning in an educational setting. It has also analyzed the foundation of educational gamification. The use of game-based learning has shown to be effective for more students' motivation and a high sense of belonging. Educators could spur classroom motivation, engagement, adaptivity, simulation, collaboration, and data collection by integrating game-based learning into their classroom instructional processes. However, the real challenge is to increase the acceptance of games as educational tools to foster learning (New Media Consortium, 2012). The proliferation of games provides learners various gaming genres to secure the differentiated instruction environment. However, game-based learning should be guided by good pedagogy, sound learning principles, and social context awareness (Perrotta et al., 2013).

Table 3. Educators Gaming Sources

Games	3rd World Farmer-Angry Birds- Big Seed- FoldIt -Extrasolar-EyeWire-Minecraft-Motion Math games- Newton's Playground-Plague.Inc- Rube Works: The Official Rube Goldberg Invention Game-Save the Seas-Sid's Science Fair-World of Balance (http://smurf.sfsu.edu/~debugger/wb/)-Wuzzit Trouble
Simulations	Book Worm (https://www.nintendo.com/games/detail/PPPdYw-fw9kLv55iYhT5Llgo6XxFQRGQ) Grand Theft Auto (http://www.rockstargames.com/grandtheftauto/) Mentira (http://www.mentira.org/) Playtime Theatre (https://itunes.apple.com/us/app/playtime-theater/id411289693?mt=8) SimCity (https://www.facebook.com/SimCity) Smarty Ants (http://www.smartyants.com/) Storybook Workshop (https://www.nintendo.com/games/detail/8P8tfzT9FHjnkyhfreEvpn nKpxtngOvO) World of Warcraft (http://us.battle.net/wow/en/) Writing Pal (http://129.219.222.66/Publish/projectsitewpal.html)
Gaming Websites	MinecraftEdu: Bringing Minecraft to the Classroom (http://Minecraftedu.com) Educade (http://Educade.org) Common Sense Media (http://www.commonsensemedia.org

Formal pedagogical structures are the tools for understanding and reviewing games in classrooms. Games, though, need to be designed to create an active use of the attributes of the form. Consequently, learners become aware of the gaming interrelationships (Gee 2007). Game-based learning offers a different type of learning by securing a multimodel virtual world. This new learning model provides unique learning opportunities that the content-driven curriculum pedagogy could not offer. It increased the understanding level through the procedural rhetoric formed by the players' choices, actions, and lived experiences (De Castell 2011). Game designers should consider identity, relationships, and players' investments to strengthen learning (Chee 2011). For example, Statecraft X views to experience and observation as the center of the learning process. Creating new worlds in games enables learners to integrate thinking, technology, and social interactions (Shaffer et al., 2005; Chee, 2011).

Educators could reframe the learning process with game-based learning to be perspective, community-oriented, and contextual-driven focus. With this focus in mind, identity would be the center of learners' performance that could be figured out through narrative feedback. Consequently, the narrative background of the game is a crucial factor in directing the communicative and collaborative aspects of the game (Roth 2010; Perrotta et al. 2013; ErstadSefton-Green 2013). To this end, Game-based learning provides educators with the golden opportunities to improve classroom engagement, accelerate the learning process, and contextualize the learning opportunities. However, this game-based learning integration needs a comprehensive organization of the used games in terms of their applicability to the educational environment.

REFERENCES

Anastasiadis, L., Lampropoulos, G., & Siakas, K. (2018). Digital Game-based Learning and Serious Games in Education. *International Journal of Advances in Scientific Research and Engineering, 4*(12), 139–144. doi:10.31695/IJASRE.2018.33016

Anderson, L. W., & Krathwohl, D. R. (Eds.). (2001). A taxonomy for learning, teaching and Assessing: A Revision of Bloom's Taxonomy of Educational Objectives: Complete Ed. New York: Longman.

Artino, A. (2008). *A brief analysis of research on problem-based learning.* Retrieved April 12, 2009, from http://eric. ed.gov/ERICWebPortal/contentdelivery/servlet/ERICServlet?accno=ED501593

Ash, K. (2012). Attention, videogames, and the retention economies of affective amplification. *Theory, Culture & Society, 29*(6), 3–26. doi:10.1177/0263276412438595

Baek, Y. K. (2008). What hinders teachers in using computers and video games in the Classroom? Exploring factors inhibiting the uptake of computer and video games. *Cyberpsychology & Behavior, 11*(6), 665–671. doi:10.1089/cpb.2008.0127 PMID:19006464

Barton, K., McKellar, P., & Maharg, P. (2007). Authentic fictions: Simulation, professionalism And legal learning. *Clinical Law Review*, *14*, 143–193.

Bayliss, J. D. (2012). *Teaching game A.I. through* Minecraft *mods*. Paper presented at the Games Innovation Conference (IGIC), 2012 IEEE International.

Bekoff, M., & Byers, J. A. (1998). *Animal Play: Evolutionary, Comparative and Ecological Perspectives*. Cambridge University Press. doi:10.1017/CBO9780511608575

Bennett & Milton. J. (2004). From Ethnocentrism to Ethnorelativism. In Toward Multiculturalism. Newton, MA: Intercultural Resource Corporation.

Bennett & Milton J. (1993). Towards a Developmental Model of Intercultural Sensitivity. In R. Michael Paige (Ed.), *Education for the Intercultural Experience* (pp. 21–71). Intercultural Press.

Betts, A., Thai, K. P., & Gunderia, S. (2021). Personalized Mastery Learning Ecosystems: Using Bloom's Four Objects of Change to Drive Learning in Adaptive Instructional Systems. In R. A. Sottilare & J. Schwarz (Eds.), Lecture Notes in Computer Science: Vol. 12792. *Adaptive Instructional Systems. Design and Evaluation. HCII 2021*. Springer. doi:10.1007/978-3-030-77857-6_3

Bloom, B., & Krathwohl, D. R. (1956). *Taxonomy of educational objectives: the classification of educational goals by a Committee of College and University Examiners. Handbook 1: Cognitive Domain*. Longmans, Green.

Bourdieu, P. (1981). Structures, strategies, and the habitus. In C. C. Lemert (Ed.), *French sociology: Rupture and renewal since 1968* (pp. 86–96). Columbia University Press.

Bourdieu, P. (1983). The forms of capital. In J. G. Richardson (Ed.), *Handbook of theory and research for the sociology of Education* (pp. 241–258). Greenwood.

Bozkurt, A., & Durak, G. (2018). A systematic review of gamification research: In pursuit of homo Ludens. *International Journal of Game-Based Learning*, *8*(3), 15–33. doi:10.4018/IJGBL.2018070102

Brill, J. M. & Galloway, C. (2007). Perils and promises: University instructors' integration of technology in classroom-based instruction. *British Journal of Educational Technology, 38*(1), 95–105. .1467-8535.2006.00601.x doi:10.1111/j

Brown, M. G. (2016). Blended instructional practice: A review of the empirical literature on instructors' adoption and use of online tools in face-to-face teaching. *Internet and Higher Education, 38*, 1–10. 1.iheduc.2016.05.001 doi:0.1016/j

Campe, S., Denner, J., & Werner, L. (2013). Intentional computing: Getting the results you want from game programming classes. *Journal for Computing Teachers*. Retrieved on September 8, 2013 from http:// www.iste.org/store/product?ID=2850

Campe, S., Werner, L., & Denner, J. (2012). Game programming with *Alice:* A series of graduated challenges. In P. Phillips (Ed.), *Special Issue Computer Science K-8: Building a Strong Foundation*. Computer ScienceTeachers Association.

Chee, Y. S. (2011). Learning as *becoming* through performance, play, and dialog: A game-based learning model with the game Legends of Alkhimia. *Digital Culture & Education, 3*(2), 98–122.

Cheng, W.-L., Dohrmann, T., Kerlin, M., Law, J., & Ramaswamy, S. (2018). *Creating an effective workforce system for the new economy*. Retrieved from https:// www. mckin sey. com/ indus tries/ public- sector/ ourinsig hts/ creating- an- effective-workforce- system- for- the- new- Economy

Chia, L. S., Khang, G. N., & Wah, L. K. (1983). A Piagetian-Based Programme for Learning "Elements and Symbols,". *Singapore Journal of Education, 5*(1), 20–24. doi:10.1080/02188798308548539

Chou, Y.-S., Hou, H.-T., Chang, K.-E., & Su, C.-L. (2021). Designing cognitive-based game mechanisms for mobile educational games to promote cognitive thinking: An analysis of flow state and game-based learning behavioral patterns. *Interactive Learning Environments*. Advance online publication. doi:10.1080/10494820.202 1.1926287

Clark, D., Tanner-Smith, E., Killingsworth, S., & Bellamy, S. (2013). Digital games for learning: A systematic review and meta-analysis (executive summary). Academic Press.

Cummins, J. (2001). *Negotiating identities: Education for empowerment in a diverse society* (2nd ed.). California Association for Bilingual Education.

Darvin, R., & Norton, B. (2014). Social Class, Identity, and Migrant Students. *Journal of Language, Identity, and Education, 13*(2), 111–117. doi:10.1080/1534 8458.2014.901823

De Castell, S. (2011). Ludic epistemology: What game-based learning can teach curriculum studies. *Journal of the Canadian Association for Curriculum Studies, 8*(2), 19–27.

De Freitas, S., & Conole, G. (2010). The influence of pervasive and integrative tools on learners' experiences and expectations of study. In R. Sharpe, H. Beetham, & S. de Freitas (Eds.), *Rethinking Learning in the Digital Age*. Routledge.

De Freitas, S., & Jarvis, S. (2007). Serious Games – Engaging Training Solutions: A research and development project for supporting training needs. *British Journal of Educational Technology*, *38*(3), 523–525. doi:10.1111/j.1467-8535.2007.00716.x

De Freitas, S., & Jarvis, S. (2009). Towards a development approach to serious games. Games-based learning advancements for multisensory human-computer interfaces. IGI Global.

De Freitas, S., & Neumann, T. (2009). The use of 'exploratory learning' for supporting immersive learning in virtual environments. *Computers & Education*, *52*(2), 343–352. doi:10.1016/j.compedu.2008.09.010

De Freitas, S., & Oliver, M. (2006). How can exploratory learning with games and simulations within the curriculum be most effectively evaluated? *Computers & Education*, *46*(Special Issue), 249–264. doi:10.1016/j.compedu.2005.11.007

DeLoura, M., & Metz, E. (2013). *Games win big in education grants competition*. Retrieved August 18, 2013, from https://www.ed.gov/blog/2013/05/games-win-big-in-education-grants-competition/

Devlin-Scherer, R., & Sardone, N. B. (2010). Digital simulation games for social studies classrooms. *The Clearing House: A Journal of Educational Strategies, Issues and Ideas*, *83*(4), 138–144. doi:10.1080/00098651003774836

Edelman, G. (1992). *Bright Air and Brilliant Fire: On the Matter of the Mind*. Basic Books.

Engeström, Y. (1999). Activity theory and individual and social transformation. In Y. Engeström, R. Miettinen, & R.-L. Punamaki (Eds.), *Perspectives on Activity Theory* (pp. 19–38). Cambridge University Press. doi:10.1017/CBO9780511812774.003

Erstad, O., & Sefton-Green, J. (2013). Digital disconnect? The 'digital learner' and the school. In O. Erstad & J. Sefton-Green (Eds.), *identity, community, and learning live in the digital age* (pp. 87–106). Cambridge University Press. doi:10.3726/978-1-4539-1019-1

Fathema, N., Shannon, D., & Ross, M. (2015). Expanding the technology acceptance model (TAM) to examine faculty use of learning management systems in higher education institutions. *Journal of Online Learning and Teaching*, *11*(2), 210–232.

Faudler, T. R. (2011). *Technology integration: A research-based professional development program* [Unpublished master's thesis]. Mount Vernon Nazarene University.

Ferguson, C. J., & Garza, A. (2011). Call of (civic) duty: Action games and civic behavior in a large sample of youth. *Computers in Human Behavior, 27*(2), 770–775. doi:10.1016/j.chb.2010.10.026

Fowler, S., & Blohm, J. (2004). An analysis of methods for intercultural training. In *Handbook of intercultural training* (pp. 37-84). SAGE Publications, Inc. https://www.doi.org/10.4135/9781452231129.n3

Gagne, R. M., & Briggs, L. J. (1974). *Principles of instructional design.* Holt, Rinehart, and Winston, Inc.

Gay, A. (2019). *How digital Literacy affects the modern workforce.* Retrieved from https://the blog. Adobe. com/ how- digit al- literacy- affects- the- modern- workforce/

Gee, J. P. (2005). Learning by design: Good video games as learning machines. *E-learning, 2*(1), 5–16. doi:10.2304/elea.2005.2.1.5

Gee, J. P. (2007). *What video games have to teach us about learning and Literacy* (Revised edition). Palgrave Macmillan.

Gobet, F., De Voogt, A., & Retschitzki, J. (2004). *Moves in Mind: The Psychology of Board Games.* Psychology Press. doi:10.4324/9780203503638

Griffiths, T., & Guile, D. (1999). Pedagogy in work-based contexts. In O. Mortimore (Ed.), *Understanding Pedagogy, and Its Impact on Learning.* Paul Chapman Publishing. doi:10.4135/9781446219454.n8

Hammer, M. R., Bennett, M. J., & Wiseman, R. (2003). Measuring Intercultural Sensitivity: The Intercultural Development Inventory. *International Journal of Intercultural Relations, 27*(4), 421–443. doi:10.1016/S0147-1767(03)00032-4

Huang, Z. Y., & Cappel, J. J. (2005). Assessment of a web-based learning game in an information systems course. *Journal of Computer Information Systems, 45*(4), 42–49.

Jarvis, S. & De Freitas, S. (2009). *Evaluation of an Immersive Learning Programme to support.* Academic Press.

Johnson, G. M. (2011). Internet activities and developmental predictors: Gender differences among digital natives. *Journal of Interactive Online Learning, 10*(2), 64–76.

Jone, R., & Hafner, A. (2021). *Understanding Digital Literacy*. Routledge. doi:10.4324/9781003177647

Kahne, J., Middaugh, E., & Evans, C. (2009). *The civic potential of video games*. Massachusetts Institute of Technology Press. doi:10.7551/mitpress/8518.001.0001

Kambutu, J. (2016). Cultural Immersion Program Prepares Educators for Globalization Social Justice Teaching. In L. Nganga & J. Kambutu (Eds.), *Social Justice Education, Globalization, and Teacher Education* (pp. 271–290). Information Age Publishing, Inc.

Kaminski, K., & Bolliger, D. (2012). Technology, learning, and the Classroom: Longitudinal evaluation of a faculty development model. *Journal of Faculty Development, 26*(1), 13–17.

Kato, P. M., Cole, S. W., Bradlyn, A. S., & Pollock, B. H. (2008). A video game improves behavioral outcomes in adolescents and young adults with cancer: A randomized trial. *Pediatrics, 122*(2), 305–317. doi:10.1542/peds.2007-3134 PMID:18676516

Keynote address, multimodality, and learning conference. (2010). London Institute of Education. Retrieved from https://sites.google.com/a/lkl.ac.uk/cmr/conference-july-2010/keynote-Suzanne-de-castells- Jennifer-Jenson

Kiili, K. (2005). Digital game-based learning: Towards an experiential gaming model. *The Internet and Higher Education, 8*(1), 13–24. doi:10.1016/j.iheduc.2004.12.001

Kim, A., & Lai, V. (2012). Rapid interactions between lexical-semantic and word form analysis during word recognition in context: Evidence from ERPs. *Journal of Cognitive Neuroscience, 24*(5), 1104–1112. doi:10.1162/jocn_a_00148 PMID:21981670

Kim, C., Kim, M. K., Lee, C., Spector, J. M.. & DeMeester, K. (2013). Teacher beliefs and technology integration. *Teaching and Teacher Education, 29*, 76–85. .Tate.2012.08.005 doi:10.1016/j

Kolb, D. A. (1984). *Experiential learning*. Prentice-Hall.

Koruyan, K. (2016). *The influence of technology-enhanced task design on the development of language learner autonomy and motivation in an Anatolian high school; A case study*. The Open University.

Kutner, L. A., Olson, C. K., Warner, D. E., & Hertzog, S. M. (2008). Parents' and sons' perspectives on video game play - a qualitative study. *Journal of Adolescent Research, 23*(1), 76–96. doi:10.1177/0743558407310721

Laine & Lindberg, (2020). Designing engaging games for education: A systematic literature review on game motivators and design principles. *IEEE Transactions on Learning Technologies, 13*(4), 804-821. doi:10.1109/TLT.2020.3018503

Lotherington, H., & Jenson, J. (2011). Teaching Multimodal and Digital Literacy in L2 Settings: New Literacies, New Basics, New Pedagogies. *Annual Review of Applied Linguistics, 31*, 226–246. doi:10.1017/S0267190511000110

Maharg, P. (2007). *Transforming Legal Education. Learning and Teaching the Law in the Early Twenty-first Century.* Ashgate Publishing.

Martens, R. L., Gulikers, J., & Bastiaens, T. (2004). The impact of intrinsic motivation on e-learning in authentic computer tasks. *Journal of Computer Assisted Learning, 20*(5), 368–376. doi:10.1111/j.1365-2729.2004.00096.x

Martirosyan, N. M., Kennon, J. L., Saxon, D. P., Edmonson, S. L. & Skidmore, S. T. (2017). Instructional technology practices in developmental education in Texas. *Journal of College Reading and Learning, 47*(1), 3–25. 1. 2016. 12188 06 doi:0.1080/10790195

Mayer, R. E. (2014). *Computer games for learning. An evidence-based approach.* MIT Press. doi:10.7551/mitpress/9427.001.0001

Mayer, R. E., & Johnson, C. I. (2010). Adding instructional features that promote learning in a game-like environment. *Journal of Educational Computing Research, 101*(3), 621–629. doi:10.2190/EC.42.3.a

Mayes, T., & De Freitas, S. (2007). Learning and e-Learning: the role of theory. In H. Beetham & R. Sharpe (Eds.), *Rethinking Pedagogy in the Digital Age.* Routledge.

Nelson, B. C., & Erlandson, B. E. (2008). Managing cognitive load in educational multi-user virtual environments: Reflection on design in practice. *Educational Technology Research and Development, 56*(5–6), 619–641. doi:10.100711423-007-9082-1

New Media Consortium. (2012). *NMC Horizon Report 2012 K-12 Edition.* http://www.nmc.org/ publications/2012-horizon-report-k12

Norton, B. (2013). *Identity and Language Learning: Extending the Conversation.* Multilingual Matters. doi:10.21832/9781783090563

Norton, B., & Toohey, K. (2011). Identity, language learning, and social change. *Language Teaching, 44*(4), 412–446. doi:10.1017/S0261444811000309

O'Brien, D. (2010). *Gaming for Classroom-Based Learning: Digital Role Playing as a Motivator of Study*. IGI Global.

Okojie, M. C., Olinzock, A. A., & Okojie-Boulder, T. C. (2006). The pedagogy of technology integration. *The Journal of Technology Studies, 32*(2), 66–71.

Oliver, M., & Pelletier, C. (2004). *Activity theory and learning from digital games: implications for game design. Paper presented at Digital Generations: Children*, Young People and New Media.

Owston, R. D. (2012). Computer games and the quest to find their affordances for learning. *Educational Researcher, 41*(3), 105–106. doi:10.3102/0013189X12439231

Owston, R. D. (2012). Computer games and the quest to find their affordances for learning. *Educational Researcher, 41*(3), 105–106. doi:10.3102/0013189x12439231

Perrotta, C., Featherstone, G., Aston, H., & Houghton, E. (2013). *Games-based learning: Latest evidence and future directions*. NFER.

Plass, J. L., Homer, B. D., Kinzer, C. K., Chang, Y. K., Frye, J., Kaczetow, W., Isbister, K., & Perlin, K. (2013). Metrics in simulations and games for learning. In M. S. El-Nasr, A. Drachen, & A. Canossa (Eds.), *Game Analytics: Maximizing the value of player data* (pp. 297–729). Springer.

Porter, W. W., Graham, C. R., Spring, K. A., & Welch, K. R. (2014). Blended learning in Higher Education: Institutional adoption and implementation. *Computers & Education, 75*, 185–195. 10. 1016/j. Compe du. 2014. 02. 011 doi:https://doi.org/

Prensky, M. (2008). Students as designers and creators of educational computer games: Who else? *British Journal of Educational Technology, 39*(6), 1004–1019.

Protopsaltis, A., Panzoli, D., Dunwell, I., & De Freitas, S. (2010). Re-purposing Serious Games in Health Care Education. *The 12th Mediterranean Conference on Medical and Biological Engineering and Computing – MEDICON 2010.*

Reynolds, J., Caley, L., & Mason, R. (2002). *How Do People Learn?* Chartered Institute of Personnel Development.

Richey, A., & Leena, H. (2016). Contesting Institutional Epistemologies of Diversity: The Shift to Global/Local Framework in Teacher Education. In L. Nganga & J. Kambutu (Eds.), *Social Justice Education, Globalization, and Teacher Education* (pp. 55–72). Information Age Publishing, Inc.

Rogers, C. (1951). *Client-centered Therapy: Its Current Practice, Implications, and Theory*. Constable.

Roscoe, R., Russell, B., Snow, E., & McNamara, D. (2013). Game-based writing strategy practice with the *Writing Pal*. In K. E. Pytash & R. E. Ferdig (Eds.), *Exploring Technology for Writing and Writing Instruction*. IGIGlobal.

Roth, W. (2010). *Language, learning, context: Talking the talk*. Routledge.

Schindler, L., Burkholder, J., Morad, A., & Marsh, C. (2017). Computer-based technology and student engagement: A critical review of the literature. *International Journal of Educational Technology in Higher Education, 14*(25), 1–28.

Schrader, P. G., Lawless, K. A., & McCreery, M. (2009). Intertextuality in massively multiplayer online games. In R. E. Ferdig (Ed.), *Handbook of Research on Effective Electronic Gaming in Education* (Vol. 3, pp. 791–807). Information Science Reference.

Short, D. (2012). Teaching scientific concepts using a virtual world—*Minecraft*. *Teaching Science, 58*(3), 55–58.

Shute, V. J. (2008). Focus on formative feedback. *Review of Educational Research, 78*(1), 153–189.

Shute, V. J. (2013). *Stealth assessment: Measuring and supporting learning in video games*. MIT Press.

Şimşek, Ö., & Barto, A. (2006). An intrinsic reward mechanism for efficient exploration. *Proceedings of the 23rd International Conference on Machine Learning, 148*, 833–40.

Sinicrope, C., Norris, J., & Watanabe, Y. (2007). *Understanding and assessing intercultural competence: A summary of theory, research, and practice* (Technical report for the Foreign Language Program Evaluation Project). SLS Papers. http://hdl.handle.net/10125/40689

Smith, D. G. (2009). *Diversity's promise for higher education: Making it work*. Johns Hopkins University.

Smith, G., Li, M., & Drobisz, J., Park, K. D., & Smith, S. (2013). Play games or study? Computer games in eBooks to learn English vocabulary. *Computers & Education, 69*, 274–286.

Soflano, M. (2011). *Modding in serious games: Teaching Structured Query Language (SQL) using Neverwinter*. Academic Press.

Squire, K. (2006). From content to context: Videogames as designed experience. *Educational Researcher, 35*(8), 19–29. doi:10.3102/0013189X035008019

Steinkuehler, C., & Williams, D. (2006). Where everybody knows your (screen) name: Online games as third places. *Journal of Computer-Mediated Communication*, *11*(4), 26. doi:10.1111/j.1083- 6101.2006.00300.x

Sturgeon, C. (2011). *Faculty perceptions of the factors enabling and facilitating their integration of instructional technology in teaching* [Doctoral dissertation]. University of Tennessee.

Terlecki, M., Brown, J., Harner-Steciw, L., Irvin-Hannum, J., Marchetto-Ryan, N., Ruhl, L., & Wiggins, J. (2011). Sex differences and similarities in video game experience, preferences, and self-efficacy: Implications for the gaming industry. *Current Psychology (New Brunswick, N.J.)*, *30*(1), 22–33. doi:10.100712144-010-9095-5

Toohey, K., Dagenais, D., & Schulze, E. (2012). Second Language Learners Making Video in Three Contexts. *Language and Literature*, *14*(2), 75–96. https://doi.org/10.20360/G2S59R

Training, T. (n.d.). *Proceedings of the 1st IEEE International Conference in Games and Virtual Worlds for Serious Applications*. IEEE Computer Society.

Turugare, M., & Rudhumbu, N. (2020). Integrating technology in teaching and learning in universities in Lesotho: Opportunities and challenges. *Education and Information Technologies, 25*, 3593–3612. 10. 1007/ s10639- 019- 10093-3 doi:https://doi.org/

U.S. Department of Education. (1996). *Getting America's students ready for the 21st century: Meeting the technology literacy challenge*. Author.

U.S. Department of Education. (2017). *Reimagining the role of technology in Education: 2017 national education technology plan update*. Retrieved from https://tech. ed. gov/ files/ 2017/ 01/ NETP17. Pdf

U.S. Department of Education. (2017). *Reimagining the role of technology in Education: 2017 national education technology plan update*. Retrieved from https://tech. ed. gov/ files/ 2017/ 01/ NETP17. pdf

Valkenburg, P., Schouten, A., & Peter, J. (2005). Adolescents' identity experiments on the Internet. *New Media & Society*, *7*(3), 383–402. doi:10.1177/1461444805052282

Vanduhe. (2020). Continuance intentions to use gamification for training in higher education: Integrating the technology acceptance model (TAM), social motivation, and task technology fit (TTF). *IEEE, 8*, 21473 21484. doi:10.1109/ACCESS.2020.2966179

Vygotsky, L. (1978). *Mind in Society: The Development of Higher-Order Psychological Processes*. Harvard University Press.

Warburton, S. (2008). Defining a framework for teaching practices inside immersive virtual environments: The tension between control and pedagogical approach. *Proceedings of RELIVE '08 Conference*.

Webb, H., & Rosson, M. B. (2013, March). Using scaffolded examples to teach computational thinking concepts. In *Proceedings of the 44th ACM technical symposium on Computer science education* (pp. 95-100). ACM.

West, D., & Bleiberg, J. (2013). Education technology success stories. *Issues in Governance Studies*. http:// www.insidepolitics.org/brookingsreports/education_technology_success_stories.pdf

Wickersham, L., & McElhany, J. (2010). Bridging the divide: Reconciling administrator and faculty concerns regarding online Education. *Quarterly Review of Distance Education*, *11*(1), 1–12.

Williams, D., Consalvo, M., Caplan, S., & Yee, N. (2009). Looking for gender: Gender roles and behaviors among online gamers. *Journal of Communication*, *59*(4), 700–725.

Witeck, G. R., Alves, A. C., & Bernardo, M. H. S. (2021). Bloom Taxonomy, Serious Games and Lean Learning: What Do These Topics Have in Common? In D. J. Powell, E. Alfnes, M. D. Q. Holmemo, & E. Reke (Eds.), Learning in the Digital Era. ELEC 2021. IFIP Advances in Information and Communication Technology (Vol. 610). Springer. https://doi.org/10.1007/978-3-030-92934-3_31.

Yang, H., & Wang, C. (2008). Product placement of computer games in cyberspace. *Cyberpsychology & Behavior*, *11*(4), 399–404. doi:10.1089/cpb.2007.0099

Yilmaz, Y., Lal, S., Tong, X. C., Howard, M., Bal, S., Bayer, I., Monteiro, S., Chan, T. & M. (2020). Technology-enhanced faculty development: Future trends and possibilities for health sciences education. *Medical Science Education, 30*, 1787–1796. 10. 1007/ s40670- 020- 01100-1 doi:https://doi.org/

Young, M., Schrader, P., & Zheng, D. P. (2006). MMOGs as Learning environments: an ecological journey into Quest Atlantis and the Sims Online. *Innovate, 2*(4). Retrieved March 20, 2006, https://www.innovateonline.info/index. php?view=article&id=66

Zaky, H. (2021). Self-Regulation and Adult Learners: Investigating the Factors Enhancing Deliberate Practice in Composition Classes. *International Journal of Curriculum Development and Learning Measurement*, 2(2), 45–60. https://doi. org/10.4018/IJCDLM.2021070104

Zaky, H. (2022). Emotional Intelligence and Professional Development: The Impact of Affective Competence on Teacher Performance. In A. El-Amin (Ed.), Implementing Diversity, Equity, Inclusion, and Belonging in Educational Management Practices (pp. 174–202). IGI Global. https://doi.org/10.4018/978-1-6684-4803-8.ch009.

Chapter 7
The Sisterhood of Schooling, Teaching, and Education

Jennifer Schneider
Community College of Philadelphia, USA

ABSTRACT

The term "sisterhood" evokes a wide range of interpretations and responses, both positive and negative. Popular culture defines the term in a variety of ways, largely dependent upon and unique to context, authorship, and audience. In Race, Class, and Gender: Prospects for an All-Inclusive Sisterhood (1994), Dill takes on the complicated concept of sisterhood from a critical perspective. In many ways, online teaching is its own complicated sisterhood grappling with challenges similar to those Dill addresses. Dill raises questions that are not unlike the persistent question of how to better attract, retain, and support educators. The chapter explores both the questions as well as associated strategies to further support educators in online environments.

The term sisterhood evokes a wide range of interpretations and responses, both positive and negative. Popular culture defines the term in a variety of ways, largely dependent upon and unique to context, authorship, and audience. In a piece for *Harper's Bazaar*, Cash Carraway (2019) writes that "[e]veryone's version of the sisterhood is personal to them" (para. 6). Irrespective of the definition, the term is both personal and rarely (if ever) neutral. Sisterhoods have long been associated with a wide variety of concerns, rivalries, and persistent ambivalence (Chang, 2013). At the same time, the term is also associated (especially in popular media) with a range of positive, powerful, and hopeful associations, such as shared interests, affinity, and solidarity (Reinitz, 2019). Like most everything associated with modern feminism

DOI: 10.4018/978-1-6684-4055-1.ch007

Copyright © 2023, IGI Global. Copying or distributing in print or electronic forms without written permission of IGI Global is prohibited.

(and current day life), however, the term, its meaning, and its connotations are *complicated* (Luckhurst, 2016).

In *Race, Class, and Gender: Prospects for an All-Inclusive Sisterhood*, Dill (1994) takes on the complicated concept of sisterhood from a critical perspective and argues:

for the abandonment of the concept of sisterhood as a global construct based on unexamined assumptions about our similarities, and ... [substitutes] a more pluralistic approach that recognizes and accepts the objective differences between women. Such an approach requires that we concentrate our political energies on building coalitions around particular issues of shared interest. Through joint work on specific issues, we come to a better understanding of one another's needs and perceptions and begin to overcome some of the suspicions and mistrust that continue to haunt us. (p. 53)

Addressing the complexity and often controversy associated with the concept of sisterhood, Dill shares strategies (described as political but capable of broader applications) for working towards a "more inclusive women's movement" (p. 42). While Dill's writing focuses on sisterhoods in a more traditional (and feminist) sense, the suggested strategies prompt analogies and offer ideas for building more inclusive environments in a wide variety of similar contexts, including online education (a realm also subject to suspicions and mistrust) (Schultz, 2019).

In many ways, online teaching is its own complicated sisterhood grappling with challenges similar to those Dill addresses. Current data shows that despite increasing diversity in our classrooms, teachers remain predominantly White and female (Loewus, 2017). However, educators across generations, subjects, and disciplines share common experiences and student interactions. My own conversations and work mentoring peer online faculty of widely different racial, gender, class, religious, and other characteristics are dominated by reflections on similar experiences and an affinity for working with adult, online students. Educators also share feelings of alienation, struggle, and limited efficacy (Pugh & Zhao, 2003). My conversations with peers are also often dominated by reflections on the challenges associated with increasing class sizes, remote work, and hard to reach students. Limited decision-making influence and lower pay also present as commonly shared conditions and concerns in educational contexts (Ingersoll, May, & Consortium for Policy Research in Education, 2011). The shared experiences are both taxing and binding. These shared experiences also yield persistent questions that focus on improving educator retention and support.

Dill raises questions that are not unlike the persistent question of how to better attract, retain, and support educators and asks:

[W]hat can we do to upgrade the status of domestic labor for all women, to facilitate the adjustment and productivity of immigrant women, and to insure that those who choose to engage in paid private household work do so because it represents a potentially interesting, viable, and economically rewarding option for them? (p. 53)

Similar questions present time and time again in educational conferences, research studies, and news reports (Directorate for Education, Education and Training Policy Division, 2011). Seeking to address the former question, Dill cites Fox-Genovese's two conceptualizations of sisterhood (one, the bourgeois individualistic, where "women have been treated as unique" and the other, the politics of personal experience, which "views sisterhood as an element of the feminist movement") as both limited (and limiting) but writes that "[t]hese two notions of sisterhood, as expressed in the current women's movement, offer some insights into the alienation many Black women have expressed in the movement itself" (p. 43). The two notions offer insights into the alienation teachers (female and otherwise) have expressed in peer to peer conversations, popular media, and educational literature, as well.

Alienation has long been a topic of concern for teachers (Pugh & Zhao, 2003). Students (though not a focus in this essay) also experience alienation (Mann, 2001). Alienation concerns (and related evaluation of trends in composition and experiences of the teaching profession and sisterhoods therein) prompt questions reminiscent of those raised by bell hooks when studying the interactions between work and liberating forces (Dill, 1994). Despite the prevalence and the persistence of the challenge, alienation is not (or need not be) inevitable (among sisterhoods, teaching population, or student groups).

Carol Gilligan's (2003) work prompts and promotes similar questions regarding the dangers of narrow references, a focus on differences, and associated silencing of distinct voices. Gilligan's work also suggests a way forward, beyond alienation, silencing, and division. Fite and Ross-Gordon (2013) write that Gilligan's writing "leads us to question the narrow reference to masculine or feminine because doing so encourages division and alienation when [Gilligan] suggests that what we should be seeking is a more universal desire for love and freedom" (p. 59). Similarly, inclusive and supportive "sisterhoods" (broadly defined) are, I believe (and in the manner Dill suggests), also possible, if the contributing factors (societal, systemic, and human) are both embraced and addressed. This possibility is something I think about often in my own work in online learning spaces and online learning interactions.

Seeman (1959) describes factors that lead to alienation, including feelings of powerlessness and isolation. Dill writes that "the experiences of racial oppression made Black women strongly aware of their group identity and consequently more suspicious of women who, initially at least, defined much of their feminism in personal and individualistic terms" (p. 43). In educational contexts (and in my own work with teams of remote adjunct faculty), similar perspectives are seen. Colleagues often voice challenges associated with isolation, policy disconnect and value (especially in light of increasing class sizes, enhanced expectations regarding classroom documentation, and more frequent course reviews), and suspicions about long-term job security. Dill too references the low social value placed on educators, quoting an interviewee who notes "When I came out of school, the black man naturally had very chances of doing certain things…. In my home … [t]he best you could do was be a school teacher" (p. 49).

In terms of next steps and hopes for future progress, Dill's emphasis on the importance of group identity and "a collective movement toward liberation" are critical in both realms (pp. 43, 44). Just as Dill asks, in response to questions such as "[w]here do Black women fit into the current analytical frameworks for race and class and gender and class? … How might these frameworks be revised if they took full account of black women's position in the home, family, and marketplace at various historical moments?", questions of where Black and White women (and analogously adjunct and full time faculty) fit into current analytical frameworks explored in educational contexts might approach the question from a revised and a more comprehensive framework, as well (p. 47).

Dill further suggests strategies including reminders that "this work cannot exist in a vacuum" and that "the problems of education must be addressed as structural ones" (p. 54). In my own work, building "coalitions of shared interest" might involve additional opportunities for remote faculty to contribute to policy, meet informally (even if virtually) as a group to explore discipline-specific trends, and to discuss curriculum and instructional challenges. Additional strategies, grounded in research on alienation, might include work to build trust, community, and recognition opportunities (responding, as well and in part, to Wergin's (2001) work on what motivates faculty). In sum, in whatever context sisterhood is evaluated, these characteristics are necessary components of a united, rather than increasingly divergent, path forward. As Dill (1994) notes, most of all, the challenges necessitate an emphasis on inclusion coupled with focused analytical precision.

More than anything, I think, the sisterhood depends on continued discussion of these important issues. As hooks and McKinnon (1996) note, "it is very difficult to imagine concretely how we will actualize feminist thinking and practice without examples" (p. 823). Perhaps next steps rest, most critically and crucially, within ourselves and acting upon intentional efforts to share the personal stories, examples, and experiences (good and bad) that make up the complicated worlds, communities, and sisterhoods (whether face to face, virtual, or a uniquely personal blend) in which we live, love, and learn.

REFERENCES

Carraway, C. (2019). *So, what does sisterhood really mean.* Retrieved from https://www.harpersbazaar.com/uk/culture/a26751347/cash-carraway-sisterhood-meaning-and-comment/

Chang, A. W. (2013). Psyche's sisters: ambivalence of sisterhood in twentieth-century Irish women's short stories. *Estudios Irlandeses - Journal of Irish Studies,* (8), 1. Retrieved from https://search-ebscohost-com.ezproxy.snhu.edu/login.aspx?direct=true&db=edsglr&AN=edsgcl.336176159&site=eds-live&scope=site

Dill, B. T. (1994). Race, class, and gender: Prospects for an all-inclusive sisterhood. In L. Stone (Ed.), *The education feminism reader.* Routledge. doi:10.1515/9783110978919.401

Directorate for Education, Education and Training Policy Division. (2011). *Teachers matter: Attracting, developing and retaining effective teachers, pointers for policy development.* Retrieved from https://www.oecd.org/education/school/48627229.pdf)

Fite, K. E., & Ross-Fordon, J. M. (2013). Carol Gilligan: Critical Voice of Feminist Thought. In J. D. Kirylo (Ed.), *A critical pedagogy of resistance: 34 pedagogues we need to know* (pp. 57–59). Sense Publ. doi:10.1007/978-94-6209-374-4_15

Gilligan, C. (2003). *In a different voice. [electronic resource] : psychological theory and women's development.* Harvard University Press. Retrieved from https://search-ebscohost-com.ezproxy.snhu.edu/login.aspx?direct=true&db=cat04477a&AN=snhu.b1545291&site=eds-live&scope=site

hooks, b., & McKinnon, T. (1996). Sisterhood: Beyond Public and Private. *Signs, 21*(4), 814-829. Retrieved from https://search-ebscohost-com.ezproxy.snhu.edu/login.aspx?direct=true&db=edsjsr&AN=edsjsr.3175025&site=eds-live&scope=site

Ingersoll, R. M., May, H., & Consortium for Policy Research in Education. (2011). *Recruitment, Retention and the Minority Teacher Shortage.* CPRE Research Report # RR-69. Consortium for Policy Research in Education. Retrieved from https://search-ebscohost-com.ezproxy.snhu.edu/login.aspx?direct=true&db=eric&AN=ED526355&site=eds-live&scope=site

Loewus, L. (2017). *The Nation's Teaching Force Is Still Mostly White and Female.* Retrieved from https://www.edweek.org/ew/articles/2017/08/15/the-nations-teaching-force-is-still-mostly.html

Luckhurst, P. (2016). Reclaiming the biscuit; Crafting in the name of feminism, vagina-themed baking and safe spaces in the kitchen -- being a modern woman has never been such a complicated balancing act. Phoebe Luckhurst unpicks the new rules of the sisterhood. *The London Evening Standard*. Retrieved from https://search-ebscohost-com.ezproxy.snhu.edu/login.aspx?direct=true&db=edsbig&AN=edsbig.A465132119&site=eds-live&scope=site

Mann, S. J. (2001). Alternative Perspectives on the Student Experience: Alienation and Engagement. *Studies in Higher Education, 26*(1), 7–19. https://search-ebscohost-com.ezproxy.snhu.edu/login.aspx?direct=true&db=eric&AN=EJ628164&site=eds-live&scope=site

Pugh, K. J., & Zhao, Y. (2003). Stories of teacher alienation: A look at the unintended consequences of efforts to empower teachers. *Teaching and Teacher Education, 19*(2), 187. https://doi-org.ezproxy.snhu.edu/10.1016/S0742-051X(02)00103-8

Reinitz, J. (2019, April 11). Sisterhood program building positive bonds. *Waterloo-Cedar Falls Courier*. Retrieved from https://search-ebscohost-com.ezproxy.snhu.edu/login.aspx?direct=true&db=nfh&AN=2W61417354456&site=eds-live&scope=site

Schultz, K. (2019). *There is rampant distrust in education. Here's how to fix that*. Retrieved from https://www.edweek.org/ew/articles/2019/06/20/there-is-rampant-distrust-in-education-heres.html

Seeman, M. (1959). On the Meaning of Alienation. *American Sociological Review, 24*(6), 783–791. https://doi-org.ezproxy.snhu.edu/10.2307/2088565

Wergin, J. F. (2001). Beyond Carrots and Sticks: What Really Motivates Faculty. *Liberal Education, 87*(1), 50–53.

Chapter 8

Remote Literacy Interventions With Children During COVID–19:
Understanding the Access, Use, and Effect Factors in the Indian Context

Pradeep Mishra
Research Monitoring and Evaluation, Room to Read, India

Jannat Fatima Farooqui
Research Monitoring and Evaluation, Room to Read, India

ABSTRACT

The outbreak of COVID-19 pandemic resulted in large-scale educational disruptions for school-going children around the world. India was among the worst hit, as multiple lockdowns put a sizeable percentage of Indian children, out of school which resulted in accumulated learning gaps, particularly for children coming from marginalized socio-economic backgrounds. To confront this learning crisis and curricular deficits, Room to Read India, a global organization working towards a world free of illiteracy and gender inequality, adopted multiple remote literacy interventions to reach out to children from vulnerable families. The study recommends that a blended hybrid mode of education, incorporating both online and offline mediums of learning, is significant in bridging the digital divide for marginalized children, who do not have adequate access or knowledge about digital resources. It was inferred that successful digital learning for children cannot take place in isolation and a dynamic partnership between teachers and parents is essential to reach out to vulnerable children.

DOI: 10.4018/978-1-6684-4055-1.ch008

Copyright © 2023, IGI Global. Copying or distributing in print or electronic forms without written permission of IGI Global is prohibited.

INTRODUCTION

As the COVID-19 pandemic spread across the globe, a majority of countries undertook strict precautionary measures to curb the spread of the virus, including widespread shutting down of socio-economic and educational activities (Anderson et al., 2020). This resulted in large-scale literacy and learning disruptions for school-going children around the world (Kaffenberger, 2021). Countries such as India, which were among the worst hit by the virus, witnessed a long-term lockdown of many months together (Khlaif & Salha, 2020; Mishra, 2020).

Following the closure of schools, a sizeable Indian children population were kept away from educational institutions, resulting in widened and accumulated learning gaps, particularly for children coming from marginalized socio-economic backgrounds (Jena, 2020; World Economic Forum, 2020). Primary class children have been the most severely afflicted in India, with over 143 million (UNESCO, 2020).

The learning crisis and curricular deficits were acute for children of vulnerable families who did not have adequate access or knowledge about digital resources (Mishra, 2020). As unemployment was rampant, parents from low-income families did not even have enough resources for two square meals a day and children's uninterrupted education was last on priority list (Khanna & Kareem, 2021). Even if online-classes were accessed at home, preference was usually given to the boy child, leaving the girl child to be primarily engaged in household chores and child-care. It was also reported that there was a rise in cases of girl-child marriage, school dropouts and child-abuse.

In these unprecedented times of worldwide learning crises, many governmental and non-governmental international organizations, working in the field of child-education, sought to re-invent and re-design their interventions (Jena, 2020). Room to Read (RTR), a global organization focusing on literacy and gender equality in education for millions of children in third-world countries, also adapted its on-field programs as a COVID19 response strategy.

Room to Read's Literacy Intervention During Covid19

It has been researched that the school closures can result in hindrances in routine patterns of studying and can produce substantial long-term learning gaps (World Bank, 2020; Kuhfeld et al., 2020). As a result, children miss out on acquiring foundational literacy skills and lag behind their age-appropriate learning level (Beatty and Pritchett, 2015). Along with unprecedented learning gaps, there are very real possibilities of children dropping out, getting involved in activities of child-labor to support thier family income and never returning back to education, once school reopen (UNESCO et al., 2020).

RTR first launched its work in India in 2003 and since then India has gone on to becoming largest country of organisational operation. In its initial stages, the Literacy Program of RTR was limited to providing critical support by establishing libraries through the country. As part of a strategic planning process, RTR made reading and writing skills acquisition a global priority, based on the understanding that children can only benefit from a school library in meaningful ways if they have the skills to read. This led to the evolution of a comprehensive Literacy Program that focused on both reading habits and reading skills of children in primary school. Through its Literacy Program, RTR collaborates with local governments, schools, communities and families to ensure they understand the importance of literacy and how they can play a role in enabling children to achieve their full potential

During COVID-19, RTR adapted its Literacy Program in a manner that ensured continued learning for marginalized children across various states of India. To support children in the absence of school during lockdown, RTR conceptualized its systematic remote literacy intervention which involved research and development of digital educational materials (e.g. read-aloud videos, flip books, worksheets etc.) and their dissemination on diverse virtual and physical platforms like WhatsApp, government portals, telephone, radio, television and hard copies of worksheet. Additionally, children were also mentored through the interactive voice response (IVR) calls. Self-learning and awareness kits were designed to assist children and parents in making 'home' a learning space. Following the implementation its literacy intervention, RTR conducted a one-time dipstick study to assess the awareness, use and effect of programmatic input amongst different stakeholders in operational areas.

RESEARCH RATIONALE AND OBJECTIVES

Assessing access and utility of pivot education activities amongst stakeholders becomes significant to evaluate their on-field effectiveness, challenges and highlight possible areas of improvement (Waters, 2011). Dipstick studies, conducted at regular programmatic intervals, can be applied to facilitate need assessment of the target group, gain insight on process delivery of the program as well as determine the extent to which the education activity has met its intended aims (Metcalfe et al., 2008). Systematic assessment of pivot activities enables those involved to learn more about, not only what works, but how and why it works and even understand about how pivot outcomes may differ according to contextual realities of stakeholders (Waters, 2011).

A third-party evaluation study was conducted by RTR to gauge the effectiveness and stakeholder response to its Literacy Program initiatives during COVID-19, based on three research questions:

- What is the **level of awareness** about pivot literacy activities taken up by RTR during COVID19, amongst stakeholders?
- What is the **level of access** to learning material circulated by RTR through different channels amongst program stakeholders?
- What is the **level of utility** and programmatic effect of RTR's literacy intervention based on feedback from stakeholders?

As a response to school closures, during lockdown, RTR developed digital educational materials (e.g. read-aloud videos, flip books, worksheets) and disseminated these materials on diverse virtual and physical platforms like WhatsApp, government portals, telephone, radio, television and hard copies of worksheet. Additionally, a large repertoire of story books of different genre was made available to children through the interactive voice response (IVR) calls.

In the present paper, a systematic study of these RTR literacy pivot activities has been presented on parameters of access, utility and effect amongst different program stakeholders including children, teachers and government officials. This research paper aims to illustrate, discuss and critically analyse stakeholder response to literacy interventions, taken up by RTR during COVID19, which will be instrumental in guiding future remote educational interventions.

METHODOLOGY

Research Sample

Participants for the large-scale empirical dipstick study were sampled across nine Indian union territories/states of Chhattisgarh, Delhi, Karnataka, Madhya Pradesh, Maharashtra, Rajasthan, Telangana, Uttar Pradesh, and Uttarakhand. Using purposive stratified sampling methods, the sample was proportionately distributed across the operational project states based on the total population of each RTR's stakeholder group.

Adhering to COVID19 travel restrictions since a telephonic interview was to be conducted, a contact detail repository of stakeholders was developed. Out of the total stakeholders that were contacted, there was an average of 60% respondents from whom consent was received and interview conducted. Some of the reasons for not being able to establish contact with stakeholders were restriction of incoming calls due to network issues, number being out of service, call disconnections and refusal to participate in the study. In the end, as represented in Table 1, data was collected from a total of 2670 participants *(N=2670),* including parents, children (Grade 1 – 5), teachers and government officials.

Table 1. Sample Size Distribution

Stakeholder	Sample Size
Parents	1546
Children	787
Teachers	287
Government Officials	50
Total Sample Size	**2670**

Methods and Tools of Data Collection and Analysis

Data collection tool was prepared to understand access, utility and effect of RTR's literacy interventions like RTR's Radio Program, Literacy Cloud, Read Aloud Videos, Worksheets and Interactive Voice Response (IVR) calls. The tool was then coded and translated in local Indian languages. A team of data-collectors were selected and oriented on how to telephonically use the tool in four day training programme across four operational Indian states where Literacy Program was implemented, including Uttar Pradesh, Maharashtra, Telangana and Karnataka. Tool validation was conducted through pilot or trial calling in local languages, based on which performance data collectors were rated and assessed. Pilot calling was used as a small feasibility trial designed to test various aspects of the methods planned for the larger, more rigorous, confirmatory investigation (Lowe, 2019). Data collectors were screened during pilot or trial calling and the best performing ones were picked for final data collection processes.

Data was collected through semi-structured telephonic interviews and was collated via an app-based survey platform developed in Survey CTO. Since the study involved children participants, adequate mandates of parental consent and data confidentiality were adhered during the data collection process. After receiving consent, 100% of the calls were recorded for data accessibility and quality checks. Once data was collected, it was tabulated in statistical software package of SPSS, which was used to conduct inferential, descriptive, and cross-tab analysis.

DATA FINDINGS AND INTERPRETATIONS

Stakeholder Awareness: Literacy Intervention Activities

Data findings highlight disparate levels stakeholder response in terms of awareness, access and utility of RTR's literacy intervention activities taken up during COVID19.

As represented in Figure 1, around 60% parents, 99% teachers and 100% government officials were aware about RTR and its program activities.

It has been further presented that awareness levels amongst parents were highest in the states of Karnataka followed by Chhattisgarh and Rajasthan. These findings further provide significant insight into strategies and challenges related to implementation of different remote educational interventions disseminated through digital mediums. A few reasons that were reported by parent stakeholders for not being aware about RTR interventions were inaccessibility to smart devices, internet connectivity issues, not using phones for educational purposes and limited time to invest in their children's learning activities.

Figure 1. Overall Stakeholder Awareness about RTR and Program Activities

State	% of Parents
Chhattisgarh	50%
Delhi	17%
Karnataka	73%
Madhya Pradesh	26%
Maharashtra	37%
Rajasthan	40%
Telangana	35%
Uttar Pradesh	30%
Uttarakhand	15%

Parents: 60% Teachers: 99% Government Officials: 100%

Radio Programs

The RTR Literacy Programme developed radio and television programmes for children and parents to help provide them a comprehensive experience of language and literacy development. 24 radio episodes and 16 television episodes have been developed in Hindi, Marathi, Telugu and Kannada languages consisting of interesting stories, poems, tongue twisters, phonological- phonics and orality games, fun fact information and activities including exploration of thought and observations. While the radio episodes were aired through All India Radio *Aakashwani,* the television episodes were broadcasted on *Doordarshan Prasar Bharti* and other regional television channels.

Stakeholder Awareness and Usage: Radio Programs

One part of stakeholder interview included questionnaire items which gauged multiple stakeholder response to Radio Programs of RTR. Out of the total parent stakeholder groups who were aware of Radio Program, 25% of them stated that their children listened to radio episodes broadcasted by RTR during COVID19.

Further, 19% of these parents reported that regular and repeated listening to Radio Programs, particularly during times of school closures, lead to certain positive changes in their child's behaviour. These behavioural changes included improved interest in studying at home, increased duration of time spent in studying, enhanced reading habits, productive time engagement and through entertainment through radio episodes.

As has been illustrated in Figure 2, when children stakeholder's response to access, utility and effect of Radio Programs was assessed, it was understood that out of the children who listened radio episodes broadcasted by RTR, 38% of them remembered the content of the Radio program broadcasted in the previous week. There were 94% children who self-reported that they liked the Radio Program in terms of being fun and educational. Lastly, 99% children participants said that they would like to listen Radio Program by RTR in future, even after their school re-opened.

Figure 2. Children Response to Utility of Radio Program

Read Aloud Videos

With children having no physical access to books and learning material, the RTR team converted stories from their existing titles into 236 read aloud digital videos that could be used by children and their parents. Developed in a variety of languages including Hindi, Kannada, Marathi and Telugu, the videos also had discussion questions for parents and children at the end, to allow children to engage with the story and understand it in depth. These videos feature some of RTR's best titles and were shared with parents, teachers and government officials through WhatsApp messages for easy accessibility.

Stakeholder Awareness and Usage: Read Aloud Videos

Stakeholder response to read aloud videos circulated by RTR to enhance learning activities during COVID19 showed that a majority percentage of parents had access to internet and received the learning material through WhatsApp. However, only 38% of these parent stakeholders reported that they took out the time to open, watch and discuss the Read Aloud Videos at home with their children. When parents, who did educationally engage with their children, were asked about whether their children were able to understand the stories that were narrated through read aloud videos, 61% of them reported that the stories were coherent and children were able to able to understand the complete story. The rest of 38% of children stakeholders had partial story comprehension circulated through read-aloud videos.

These results were further reinforced by a majority of children stakeholders, who self-reported that they found stories to be relatable and interesting and they watched the videos till the end. Also, when teachers and government officials were asked about the use of read aloud videos, more than 80% of them reported that the E-Learning material can be easily used by parents for their children's home-learning.

Figure 3. Usage and Effect of Read Aloud Videos by Children Stakeholders

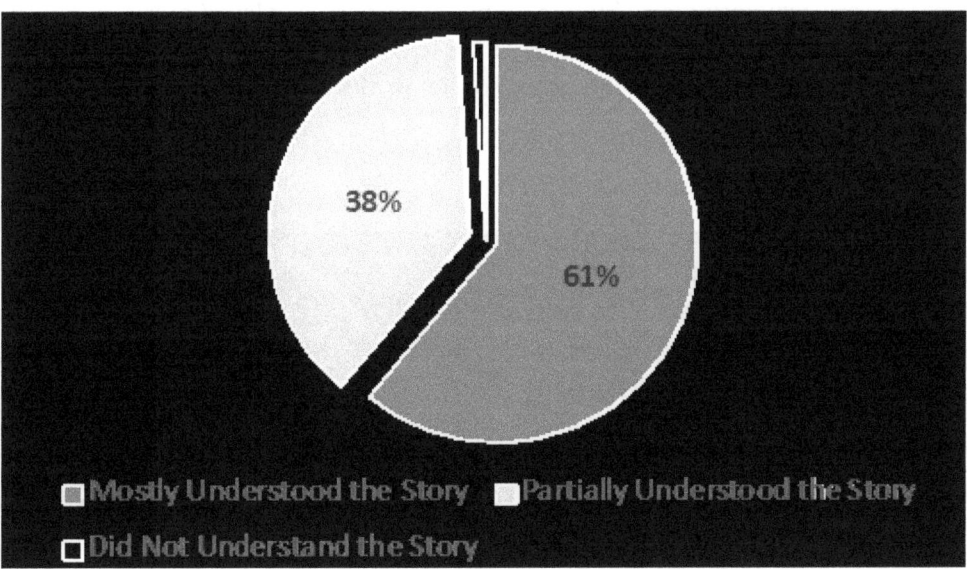

Worksheets

With children being stuck at home during the pandemic, it was important that children continue their lessons to ensure that there is no gap in their learning. The RTR team thus developed weekly worksheets in four languages, including Hindi, Marathi, Telugu and Kannada for children from Grade 1-5. These worksheets were circulated among 255000 (approx.) children, parents and teachers through online and offline channels every month. The worksheets included multiple activities like orality, reading & listening comprehension, independent writing, stories and poems, problem solving, observations and vocabulary development to provide a comprehensive literacy experience to children.

Stakeholder Access and Usage: Worksheets

Worksheet were the only educational material that were circulated to stakeholders through both online and offline mediums on monthly basis. Figure 4 illustrates that out of the total parents who received worksheets, 34% percent received hard-copies through physical dissemination, 39% percent reported to receive soft-copies through virtual mediums like WhatsApp and 27% percent parents received worksheets from both mediums. A majority of more than 88% parents reported that they shared these worksheets with their children. When a deeper knowledge assessment was conducted, out of the children who had access to these worksheets, only around 41% self-reported to remembered the content of the worksheet activities.

Figure 4. Parental Access to Worksheets

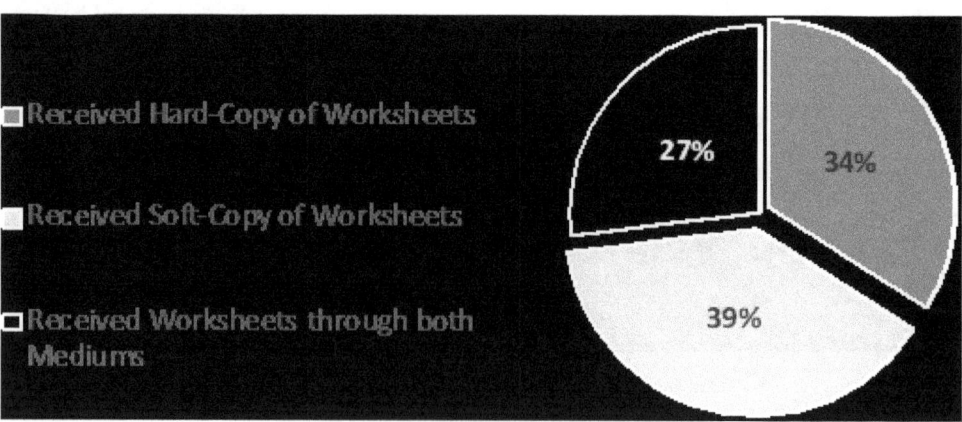

While understanding how useful worksheets were for children, as represented in Figure 5, it became a significant point of assessment to analyse usage of the same material through two kinds of platforms. It was observed that, on one hand, higher percentage of children who received hard copy of worksheets were able to fully complete the worksheet and found the worksheet to be a useful educational resource material. On the other hand, higher percentage using soft copy of worksheet showed enthusiasm and proactiveness to do worksheet activities and did not require encouragement or assistance to complete the worksheet.

Figure 5. Utility of two different Mediums of Worksheets by Children Stakeholders

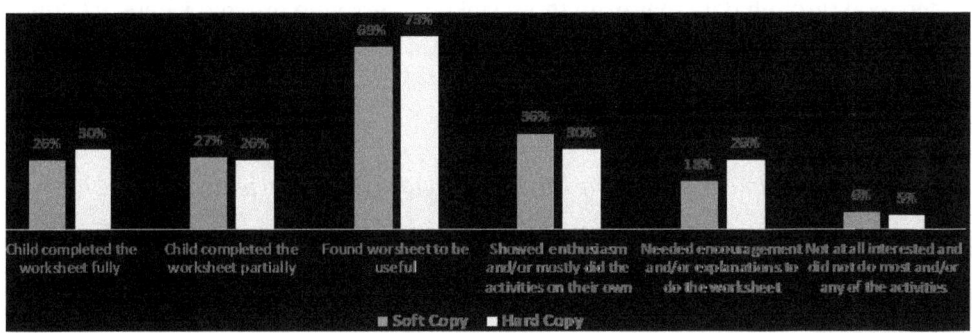

Literacy Cloud

During the pandemic, Room to Read has been uniquely positioned to bring the joy of reading to children in their homes as they find themselves displaced from their classrooms and libraries. To engage parents and educators in meaningful distance educational interventions, RTR attempted extend access and usage of Literacy Cloud to the most remote and marginalized children in India. Literacy Cloud, an online learning platform, hosts easy-to-access online books, which have been especially developed by children's authors and illustrators around the world for children in primary school. The books are available to download for offline use. Literacy Cloud also hosts professional development videos for educators and children's book creators on topics ranging from building a habit of reading to what makes a great children's book. These globally diverse books created by local authors and illustrators from around the world help children develop empathy and understanding for experiences and cultures beyond their own.

Stakeholder Awareness and Usage: Literacy Cloud

As stakeholder response to access and utility of literacy cloud was assessed, it was derived that out of the total parents who were aware about this educational resource, an average of only 61% logged into the online portal and read stories with their children. Parents reported that they were easily able to read the stories and their children found the plot, characters and context of the stories to be interesting and relatable.

As represented in Figure 6, a state-wise analysis revealed that the highest percentage of parental population using literacy cloud to read stories to their children came from the states of Karnataka, Rajasthan and Uttarakhand. Further, it was also understood through data that from those stakeholders who utilized Literacy Cloud, 78% parents, 84% teachers and 12% government officials passed on the link of the resource to others in the community.

Figure 6. Parent Stakeholder Using Literacy Cloud to Read Stories with their Children

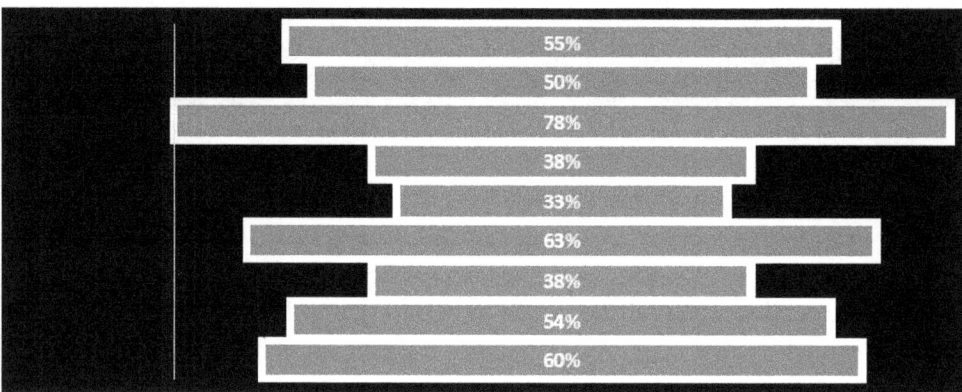

Interactive Voice Calls (IVR)

The Room to Read team put in place an easy to access story-telling mechanism for children. The toll-free IVR service ensured that children could dial in from their parent's phones at any point of time to hear stories developed by the RTR team. This ensured that while children enjoyed the stories, it also kept them engaged with learning resources. Till November 2020, a total of 4,82,193 calls were received from children across the country

Stakeholder Usage: Interactive Voice Calls

IVR calls, a one of its kind digital learning intervention initiated by RTR, is an automated phone system technology that allows incoming callers to access educational resources via a voice response system of pre-recorded stories. For this particular project activity, sampling of participants could be done only from stakeholders who had dialed into the IVR calling system. Hence, a repository of callers was collated from project sites and 500 callers were randomly chosen from the list. Out of these, consent and contact were processed only with 440 callers, with whom semi-structured interviews were conducted about awareness of IVR number, frequency of calls and feedback of children related to this call.

Figure 7 reflects that when parents or children were asked about from where they had received the IVR toll-free number, a majority of 46% reported that they got from school-based sources. Other sources of information dissemination were through other parents, community members, RTR field staff and educational awareness campaigns run by RTR in their locality. Further, it was observed that for more than half of the callers, preferred frequency of calling was around 2-3 days in one week. Lastly, a significant percentage of children not only reported that they not only found the story played through IVR calls to be interesting and engaging, but also that they would continue to dial in even after their school re-open in post-COVID times.

Figure 7. Usage and Effect of IVR Calls on Children Stakeholders

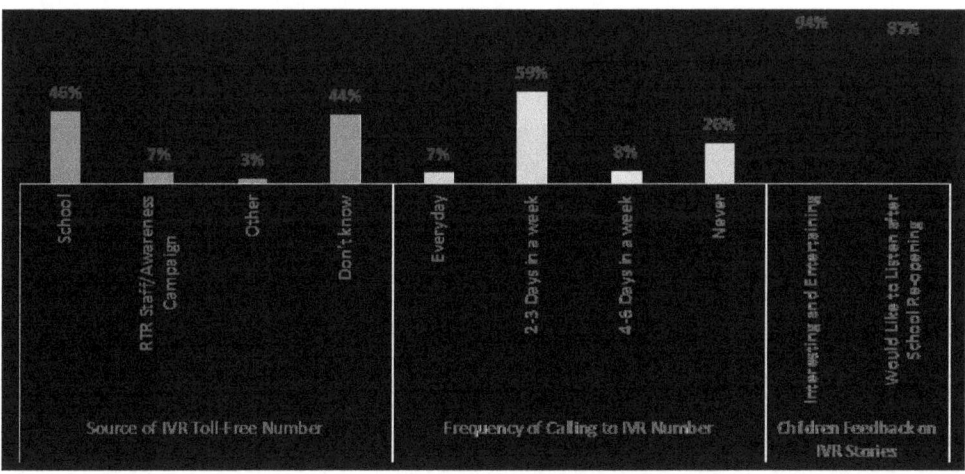

DISCUSSION AND RECOMMENDATIONS

While, on one hand, COVID19 did result in global school-based learning disruptions. However, on the other hand, the pandemic also paved way for multiple new opportunities of introducing and imbibing digital learning platforms (Guangul et al., 2020). During the last year, RTR continued to engage virtually with children of different grades, class, gender and regions with age-appropriated digital curriculum. This paper analysed the access, usage and effectiveness of different literacy interventions taken up by RTR during school closures.

Gaps between Access and Utility of Educational Resources

An underlying trend that was observed in the findings of the present study was that there was a distinct gap between access and utility of different digital educational resources disseminated by RTR. There were 83% parents who had access to smart devices and internet facility. Also, while a noteworthy number of parents were aware about digital learning resources circulated by RTR. However, as represented in Figure 8, but when it came to utilizing these resources, the percentage was much lower.

Out of the total parents who were aware about broadcasting of RTR Radio Programme, only 25% confirmed that their children regularly listened to radio episodes. Further, from sample size of 1546 parent participants in the study, 38% (i.e. 591) parents reported that they have watched and listened to Read Aloud Videos shared by RTR.

Figure 8. Level of Stakeholder Utility of Digital Learning Interventions by RTR

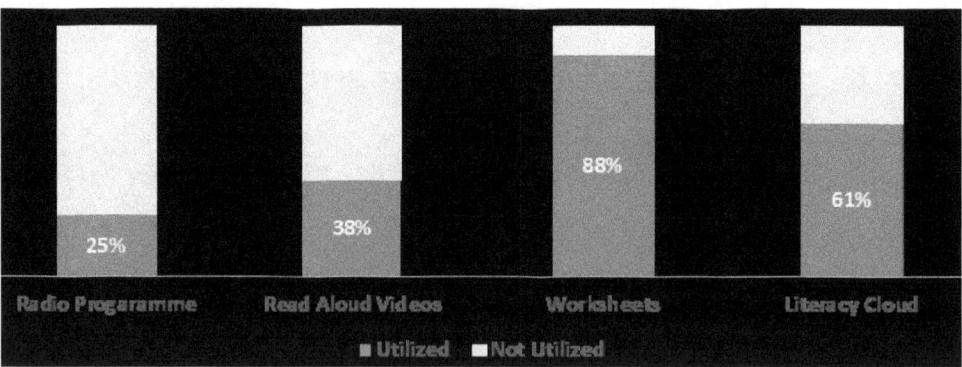

Data findings show that out of the total parents who received hardcopy or soft copy worksheets from RTR, a majority of 88% parents shared and discussed these worksheets with their children. Lastly, out of parents who visited Literacy Cloud, 61% of them discussed stories from the online portal with their children. Results of this study show that there is a need to systematically sensitize and train parent, teacher and community stakeholders on how and why to use educational resources.

Success of Hybrid Learning Mediums

Digital learning platforms have opened up opportunities for engaging with out-of-school girls and boys, even after the pandemic is over, by designing and scaling remote learning programs using appropriate technology. However, it cannot be overlooked that marginalized children, particularly girls, have limited access to technology (Khanna & Kareem, 2021). It has been researched that while flexibility and convenience of online classes make them an attractive option, but network connectivity issues in rural areas makes it a challenge for children to make use of online learning initiatives (Muthuprasad, et al., 2021). Hence, in developing countries like India, where a majority of the school-going children live in villages and have limited digital resources, it becomes significant to bring learners to a combined online and offline virtual learning space (Cahapay, 2020).

As RTR re-strategized its literacy interventions, it was realised that a blended mode, incorporating both online and offline mediums of learning, is essential during and after COVID-19, especially for the most vulnerable children population. As has been represented in this paper, worksheets were an educational resource that children stakeholders received through both physical and virtual channels. It was observed that there were positive implications of using both hard and soft copies of worksheets.

An analysis of stakeholder response to worksheets revealed that children were more enthusiastic to receive and read soft-copies of worksheets, disseminated through online mediums like WhatsApp. Approximately 36% of parents said that their children engaged independently with soft-copies of worksheets. But hard-copy worksheets were more likely to be used and fully completed by children. Around 73% of parents reported that they found hard-copy worksheets to be more practically useful. Consequently, through empirical evidence, it was understood that educational interventions are best designed and deployed through a hybrid model, particularly while working with low-income and rural families.

Strengthening Eco-Systems Around Digital Learning: Teachers and Parents

Ecological theory conceptualizes child development processes through relationships between mutually dependent and reciprocal systems working around a child (Bronfenbrenner, 1979). The approach theorizes learning to be directly and indirectly influenced by interactions between child's maturing biology, immediate environment, and societal landscape. If interactions between these systems are imbalanced and unhealthy, they can result in adverse effects in the learning levels of a child (Ryan, 2001). Digital learning also cannot take place in isolation and requires dynamic interactions between home and school systems, which evolve according to differential contextual realities like COVID-19.

Teacher Training in Technology

Teachers in India, who have been used to traditional chalk-talk teaching method for a long time, were compelled to shift to the online mode for education during the pandemic (Lederman, 2020). Many teachers in rural India had not used a computer and there was attached sense of anxiety in using technology for teaching-learning purposes (Khanna & Kareem, 2021).

This study puts forward how teachers played a significant role in introducing digital mediums of learning to children. Results showed that around 46% parents received information about educational initiatives of RTR like IVR calls from school teachers. Hence, a need is inferred to orient, train and provide technical support to teachers so that digital learning can be successfully penetrated from teachers to children.

Parental Involvement in Digital Learning

In India, majority of low-income parents are illiterate or semi-literate, have underpaid hourly jobs and earn minimum wages. Parents with limited educational, financial and technical resources lacked motivation and confidence to become a part of their child's academic journey (Sharma & Sharma, 1996). At the same time many Indian children, especially in tribal and rural areas, are first generation learners. Parents and children from marginalised context lacked support to navigate the educational materials shared through online mode.

However, with the advent of physical distancing measures and emergency remote teaching, 'home' was reconceptualized as a learning space (Cahapay, 2020). The imperative need of parental involvement in digital learning processes cannot be denied. In this study as well, parents were an important part of the intervention, from whom valuable information about access and utility of e-learning materials was derived.

Results of this study showed that out of the total parents who were aware about Literacy Cloud, 61% parents read stories from the online portal with their children and 78% parents shared the link of the Cloud with other parents. Parental workshops can be held for 'hard to reach' vulnerable group of parents, wherein they can be enabled with low-cost and practical parenting methods (Kendall et al., 2008) through which they can assist their children during digital learning processes at home.

The sudden closure of schools due to COVID-19, has halted the learning process of children. Room to Read team considering the ground reality, has developed several online digital content to address the learning needs of the children. At the same time, Room to Read team realised that children from marginalised background and remote geography are likely to be worst affected due limited access to resources and opportunities. This study, hence, proposes mutual strengthening and empowerment of teacher and parent eco-systems around a child for holistic and sustainable digital learning experiences.

CONCLUSION

While the COVID-19 pandemic raged through the world, economies, businesses, lives and livelihoods came to a standstill. As the world grappled to address the health crisis, schools across the globe shut down, forcing children and teachers to adopt digital technologies, almost overnight, and to adapt to the changing scenario (Moldavan et al., 2021). In countries like India, while the shift to e-learning was swift for many, several others were left behind in the race (Mishra, 2020). With regional and socio-economic disparities in access to digital learning, the transition was not smooth or in some cases, even possible for children and educators (Hussain, 2020). There existed spatial and infrastructural inequities which further deepened the digital divide for many low-income children, particularly for girls living in remote and rural areas (Mishra, 2020). These included having no or only one device at home to attend online classes which was reserved for the boy child, poor network connectivity issues, low comprehension in virtual learning, limited parental guidance in studies and being busy in household chores to take out time for educational activities.

It has been reported that approximately 320 million learners in India have been adversely affected by the pandemic (World Economic Forum, 2020). Room to Read's Literacy Program has worked in close collaboration with children, teachers, schools, local communities and government officials to help inculcate in children the love for reading and become fluent, engaged and independent readers. During COVID-19 pandemic, the Literacy Program amended and adapted its project activities to ensure that marginalized children did not lose touch with language and books and continued to practice their literacy and learning skills, while being at home.

The present study, conducted across a large sample of more than 2670 participants including children, parents, teachers and government officials revealed stakeholder levels of awareness, access and utility of RTR's literacy activities. Statistical frequency analysis of each literacy intervention helped to gain empirical insight into learnings and limitations related to on-field implementation of remote educational activities.

Findings of the study reveal that there exists unprecedented positive potential of digital learning as it helps to realise the potential of each child to adapt to new methods of learning. However, as gaps were observed between access and usage of digital resources, it can be inferred that there lies both challenges and opportunities for a successful interface of education and technology (Guangul et al., 2020). The aim should be to ensure equal, contextual, adequate access to remote digital learning for child coming from low socio-economic backgrounds (Mishra, 2020; Khanna & Kareem, 2021).

The study recommends that a blended hybrid mode of education, incorporating both online and offline mediums of learning, is significant in bridging the digital divide for the most marginalized children population. It was also suggested that successful digital learning for children cannot take place in isolation and a dynamic partnership between teachers and parents is essential to reach out to vulnerable children.

REFERENCES

Anderson, R. M., Heesterbeek, H., Klinkenberg, D., & Hollingsworth, T. D. (2020). How will country-based mitigation measures influence the course of the COVID-19 epidemic? *Lancet*, *395*(10228), 931–934. doi:10.1016/S0140-6736(20)30567-5 PMID:32164834

Bronfenbrenner, U. (1979). *The Ecology of Human Development*. Harvard University Press.

Cahapay, M. B. (2020). A Reconceptualization of Learning Space as Schools Reopen amid and after COVID-19 Pandemic. *Asian Journal of Distance Education*, *15*(1), 269–276.

Guangul, F. M., Suhail, A. H., Khalit, M. I., & Khidhir, B. A. (2020). Challenges of remote assessment in higher education in the context of COVID-19: A case study of Middle East College. *Educational Assessment, Evaluation and Accountability*, *32*(4), 519–535. doi:10.100711092-020-09340-w PMID:33101539

Hussain, T. (2020). *Education and COVID-19 in Nigeria: Tackling the digital divide*. SOAS Blog.

Jena, P. K. (2020). Impact of pandemic COVID-19 on education in India. *International Journal of Current Research*, 12.

Kaffenberger, M. (2021). Modelling the long-run learning impact of the Covid-19 learning shock: Actions to (more than) mitigate loss. *International Journal of Educational Development*, *81*, 102326. doi:10.1016/j.ijedudev.2020.102326 PMID:33716394

Kendall, S., Straw, S., Jones, M., Springate, I., & Grayson, H. (2008). Narrowing the Gap in Outcomes for Vulnerable Groups: A Review of the Research Evidence. National Foundation for Educational Research.

Khanna, R., & Kareem, J. (2021). Creating inclusive spaces in virtual classroom sessions during the COVID pandemic: An exploratory study of primary class teachers in India. *International Journal of Educational Research Open*, *2*, 100038. doi:10.1016/j.ijedro.2021.100038

Khlaif, Z. N., & Salha, S. (2020). The unanticipated educational challenges of developing countries in Covid-19 crisis: A brief report. *Interdisciplinary Journal of Virtual Learning in Medical Sciences*, *11*(2), 130–134.

Kuhfeld, M., Soland, J., Tarasawa, B., Johnson, A., Ruzek, E., & Liu, J. (2020). Projecting the potential impact of COVID-19 school closures on academic achievement. *Educational Researcher*, *49*(8), 549–565. doi:10.3102/0013189X20965918

Lederman, D. (2020). Will shift to remote teaching be boon or bane for online learning. Inside Higher Ed.

Lowe, N. K. (2019). What is a pilot study? *Journal of Obstetric, Gynecologic, and Neonatal Nursing*, *48*(2), 117–118. doi:10.1016/j.jogn.2019.01.005 PMID:30731050

Metcalfe, S. A., Aitken, M., & Gaff, C. L. (2008). The importance of program evaluation: How can it be applied to diverse genetics education settings? *Journal of Genetic Counseling*, *17*(2), 170–179. doi:10.100710897-007-9138-8 PMID:18247108

Mishra, S. V. (2020). *COVID-19, online teaching, and deepening digital divide in India*. Academic Press.

Moldavan, A. M., Capraro, R. M., & Capraro, M. M. (2021). Navigating (and disrupting) the digital divide: Urban teachers' perspectives on secondary mathematics instruction during COVID-19. *The Urban Review*, 1–26. PMID:34276100

Muthuprasad, T., Aiswarya, S., Aditya, K. S., & Jha, G. K. (2021). Children' perception and preference for online education in India during COVID-19 pandemic. *Social Sciences & Humanities Open*, *3*(1), 100101. doi:10.1016/j.ssaho.2020.100101 PMID:34173507

Pritchett, L., & Beatty, A. (2015). Slow down, you're going too fast: Matching curricula to child skill levels. *International Journal of Educational Development*, *40*, 276–288. doi:10.1016/j.ijedudev.2014.11.013

Ryan, D. P. J. (2001). *Bronfenbrenner's ecological systems theory.* Retrieved from http://www.floridahealth.gov/AlternateSites/CMSKids/providers/early_steps/training/documents/ bronfenbrenners_ecological.pdf

Sharma, R. N., & Sharma, R. K. (1996). *History of education in India.* Atlantic Publishers & Distributors.

UNESCO. (2020). *COVID-19 educational disruption and response.* UNESCO.

Waters, K. R. (2011). The importance of program evaluation: A case study. *Journal of Human Services*, *31*(1), 83–93.

World Bank. (2020). *The COVID-19 Pandemic: Shocks to Education and Policy Responses.* Author.

World Economic Forum. (2020). *How COVID-19 deepens the digital education divide in India.* Author.

Chapter 9
Educational Transformation Project's Remote Group Work (ETPRGW)

Antoine Toni Trad
https://orcid.org/0000-0002-4199-6970
IBISTM, France

ABSTRACT

This chapter proposes an educational transformation project (ETP), remote group work (RGW), to support students' group work in the context of online teaching and learning. An ETP assisted by RGW (ETPRGW) uses critical success factors and areas, natural programming language environment, and a dynamic decision-making system, which can be used to improve the organization's online learning capabilities. ETPRGW supports all phases of an ETP, and its concept is based on existing standards, methodologies, local specificities, and traditional educational practices. Complex educational topics, like information and communication systems (ICS) need particular RGW requirements that force educational organizations (simply entity) to integrate agile collaboration products, educational patterns, educational best practices, and educational services' management. An RGW approach forces the used transformation framework and the related set of existing modules to synchronize all types of transformation activities, like the integration of an automated coordination of RGW activities.

DOI: 10.4018/978-1-6684-4055-1.ch009

Copyright © 2023, IGI Global. Copying or distributing in print or electronic forms without written permission of IGI Global is prohibited.

INTRODUCTION

The ETP staff (or simply the *Staff*) set of skills, is a crucial issue in ETPRGW, such a *Staff* must capable of managing and execution various types of online education operations. The ETPRGW concept is based on: 1) An adapted version of Enterprise Architecture (EA); 2) An Applied Mathematical Model for RGW (AHMMRGW) (Trad, & Kalpić, 2014, 2020a); 3) Atomic services and architecture for ETP platforms (Trad, 2015a, 2015b); 4) Educational patterns and other types of patterns (Trad, & Kalpić, 2022a, 2022b); 5) The cloud and online platforms; and 6) Agile Project Management (APM) (Spencer, 2016). In this chapter the author tries to prove that the ETPRGW can transform the *Entity* and that it can be support its RGW activities; and added to that, that it can be modelled by using the AHMM4RGW. The AHMMRGW is based on Critical Success Areas (CSA), Critical Success Factors (CSF) and on a unique mixed research method (Trad & Kalpić, 2017a). The ETPRGW is supported by a Decision-Making System for RGW (DMSRGW), Knowledge Management System for RGW (KMSRGW) and an adapted version of an agile EA methodology (Blackburn, & Rosen, 1993). The author uses a Proof of Concept (PoC) that incorporates the following Applied Case Studies: 1) The insurance domain (Jonkers, Band, & Quartel, 2012a), that is used for pure ICS topics. The ETP is supported by a transformation framework that: Manages all ETP's phases and Estimates ETP's risks of failure; and 2) A set of online education ACSs. The ETP initial phase identifies its main interfaces, phases, main activities, and the optimal *Staff's* profiles and skills. ETP's main challenge is the transformation of its Monolithic Educational System (MES) into an agile and fully automated online educational system. A ETPRGW capable *Staff* must support the ETP's Implementation and Maintenance Phases (EIMP) that needs integrated agile EA methodologies, DMSRGW, KMSRGW, and implementation skills. The author's works have localized a major gap in transformation projects, which is related to failures that are mainly due to Architect of Adaptive Business Information System (AofABIS). Unfortunately, transformation projects are managed by accountants which is the main reason for failures. The ETPRGW requires a *Staff* with agile cross-functional (polymathic) set of skills, which can support topics like Humanities.

ETPRGW CROSS-FUNCTIONAL SET OF SKILLS

ETPRGW supports the transformation of MES's ICS and to exploit avant-garde online technologies to finalize the ETP. The ETPRGW needs to interface standard methodologies, like The Open Group's Architecture Framework's (TOGAF) and Schools Interoperability Framework (SIF). SIF is an eXtensible Mark-up Language

(XML) specification for data sharing among *Entities* (Service Architecture, 2022). This chapter shows that the ETPRGW needs holistic cross-functional capabilities. As shown in Figure 1, the ETPRGW can be used by the research *Framework* that is based on the Research and Development *Project* (RDP) that is based on the Architecture Development Method (ADM) (The Open Group, 2011a). The ETPRGW needs to be assisted by the DMSRGW and KMSRGW to solve various types of ETPRGW problems. The author's Transformation Research Architecture Development framework (*TRADf*, or simply the *Framework*) interactions include the following components: 1) ICS online technologies; 2) DMSRGW; 3) KMSRGW; 4) ETPRGW; and 5) RDP.

Figure 1. The relation between the ETPGRW and the RDP

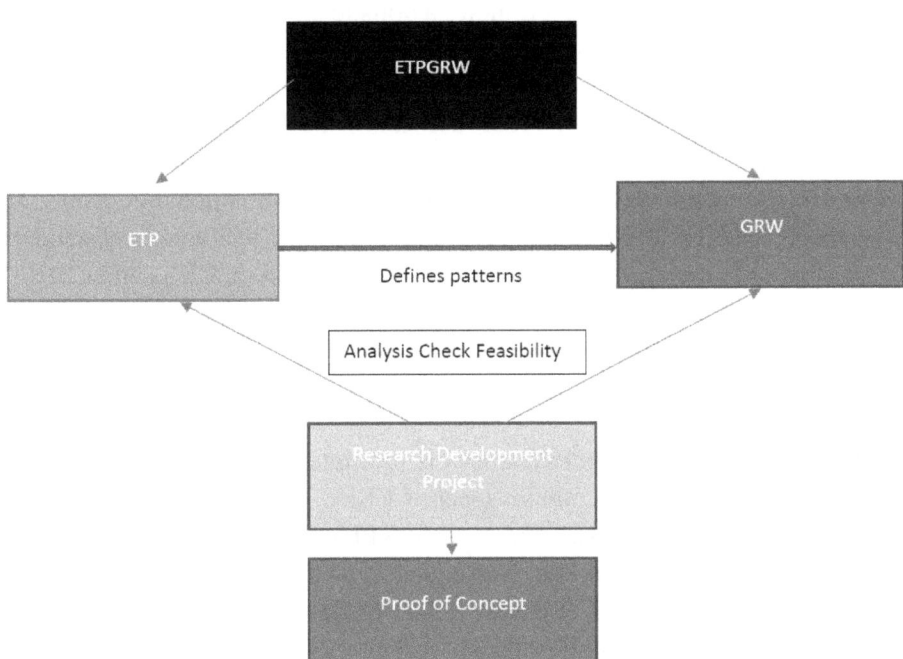

THE RESEARCH DEVELOPMENT PROJECT

The Researched Literature Review and the Research Gap

ETP's complexities and high failure rates are related to the EIMP, which need the right ETP skills and a framework. The ETP recommends the usage of AHMMRGW-based Heuristics Decision Tree (HDT), for decision making. This chapter's Research Question (RQ) is: "Which ETP characteristics to support the RGW?" In the context of online learning. This chapter is based on the author's *Framework* and related works: The Business Transformation Project's Holistic Agile Management (Trad, & Kalpić, 2022c); 2) Transformation Projects and Virtual Military Strategy (Trad, 2022a); and many others. This RDP acknowledges an important knowledge gap.

The Knowledge Gap

This RDP's knowledge gap was acknowledged because the existing literature on transformation projects' failure rates, online education, and RGW related methodologies. This RDP inspects the ETPRGW, which is mainly based on existing online education, organizational, and technology standards, and is enforced with RGW related findings. This RDP promotes a holistic unbundling process, the usage of RGW, and online education strategies in various domains, like Humanities. Where Humanities have a subjective, critical-thinking or opinion-based approach; and that can be enforced by the RGW. This RDP uses a holistic agile concept combines: 1) RGW topics; 2) AHMMRGW and HDT based decision making; 3) Educational patterns; 4) Organizational engineering; 5) It offers a cross-functional-concept; 7) EA which support the ETP; 8) Integrating standard online and technological standards; and 7) ETPRGW's integration and success metrics, based on CSAs and CSFs.

Review and Check of the Critical Success Factors/Critical Success Areas

As already mentioned, the author's framework promotes RGW based transformation concepts that use CSAs that contains a set of CSFs, where a CSF is a set of Key Performance Indicators (KPI), where each KPI corresponds to a single ETP requirement and/or an item that can be an educational requirement that has a column in each evaluation table (Putri, & Yusof, 2009; Peterson, 2011). *Project* starts with the first phase called the feasibility phase, that checks the basic CSFs (in the form of DMSRGW tables), to check if the ETP's objectives can be reached and delivers a success or failure values. Based on the literature review process and, the CSFs are used and evaluated by using the following rules: 1) RGW-related references must be credible and are estimated by the author, DMSRGW and follow a defined framework's classification process; 2) ETP's iterations are the result of measured CSFs; 3) EA's modelling language capacities; 4) The RGW-based ADM is mature and can be used to manage the EIMP; 5) The RGW-based ADM manages the framework's iterations and CSFs tuning; and 6) If the aggregations of all the *Project's* CSA/CSF tables are positive and exceed the defined minimum, the *Project* continues to its PoC, which uses RGW ACSs.

RGW's ACSs

The PoC uses an RGW-related ACSs, combined to cover various aspects and the central one is Open Group's which represents the possibilities to implement an ETP ICS. The used ACSs are suitable because they integrate cross-functional domains, in an online platform. ETPRGW CSFs are measurable by the HDT weighting concept that is roughly estimated in the 1st iteration and then tuned through ADM's iterations. In each iteration, the ETPRGW evolution is verified by using the DMSRGW; where CSFs are essential to support ADM's cycles (Felfel, Ayadi, & Masmoudi, 2017). These ACSs are:

- Educational institutions in Australia have tended to organize *flexible delivery* as a panacea for encountered problems in education in the 1990s. There are various justifications for the rise to prominence in online educational and training environments. It is considered that the main response to mass education and the need to integrate diverse student groups, another possibility of *on-the-job training*, or *lifelong learning*. A proposed possibility also was that emerging educational theories concerning teaching and learning, particularly those who support constructivist approaches should be privileged. This ACS is related to University's approach to offering postgraduate using online courses. The Faculty of online courses were restructured with a focus on the communication capabilities of online education, operating in a text-based environment. The *Staff* has accepted to adopt online delivery which brought different levels of expertise that suggested the need for an RGW culture, but they expressed concern over losing control of what they perceived to be their academic roles. At no point in this study have our respondents suggested that online education is inappropriate for higher education and complex topics like ICS (Postle, 2003).
- Actual complex ICS environments pose challenges for traditional higher education in universities, which want to apply ETP to become capable of delivering online courses for ICS topics. Online learning was accepted in professional organizations, like the government, high-tech segments… This ACS presents an investigation designed to explore advantages and disadvantages of online learning. Seventeen students from one master course participated in this investigation. The results proved that the best advantage of online learning courses was *flexibility* from the student's point of view. The resulting implications of this research recommended to the university to

expand its ICS infrastructure to support an ever-increasing student enrollment for online learning course. This ACS recommends the implementation and use of an ADM based conceptual model for online learning (Sagheb-Tehrani, 2009).

The Use of the Architecture Development Method in the ETP

This RDP focuses on RQ's feasibility and on delivering RGW integration patterns and it also presents the influence of EIMP activities. In the current age of distributed web/online system, Artificial Intelligence (AI), knowledge, online education, and technology, the author's *Framework* offers the HDT to support the solving process of ETPRGW related problems (Markides, 2011), where the DMSRGW offers a set of ETPRGW solution types in the form of patterns and recommendations. The *Framework* synchronizes ETP with ADM activities, especially in the business architecture phase, as shown in Figure 2; where in this chapter business is related to online education. ETPRGW activities are based on the AHMM4RGW.

Figure 2. ADM's phases (The Open Group, 2011a, 2011b)

The AHMM4RGW

The Basics

CSFs define the initial nodes that are identified as vital for successful targets to be reached and maintained and is the AHMMRGW's basic element which is needed for the ETP's capabilities. The ETPRGW uses a CSF/CSA/KPI based AHMMRGW, which is a proprietary model. The AHMMRGW nomenclature is presented in Figure 3. AHMMRGW's application *Domain* is online education and the RGW, as shown in Figure 3:

Figure 3. The applied mathematical model's nomenclature (Trad, & Kalpić, 2020a)

Basic Mathematical Model's (BMM) Nomenclature

Iteration	= An integer variable *"i"* that denotes a *Project/ADM iteration*	
microRequirement	= (maps to) KPI	(B1)
CSF	= Σ KPI	(B2)
Requirement	= (maps to) CSF = ∪ microRequirement	(B3)
CSA	= Σ CSF	(B4)
microMapping microArtefact/Req	= microArtefact + (maps to) microRequirement	(B5)
microKnowledgeArtefact	= ∪ knowledgeItem(s)	(B6)
neuron	= action->data + microKnowledgeArtefact	(B7)
microArtefact / neural network	= ∪ neurons	(B8)
microArtefactScenario	= ∪ microartefact	(B9)
AI/Decision Making	= ∪ microArtefactScenario	(B10)
microEntity	= ∪ microArtefact	(B11)
Entity or Enterprise	= ∪ microEntity	(B12)
EnityIntelligence	= ∪ AI/Decision Making	(B13)
BMM(*Iteration*) as an instance	= EnityIntelligence(*Iteration*)	(B14)

The Generic AHMM's Formulation

AHMM	= ∪ ADMs + BMMs	(B15)

AHMM's Application and Instantiation for ETPGRW

Domain	= ETPGRW	(B16)
AHMM4(*Domain*)	= ∪ ADMs + BMMs(*Domain*)	(B17)

- The symbol $\sum$ indicates summation of weightings/ratings, denoting the relative importance of the set members selected as relevant. Weightings as integers ranging in ascending importance from 1 to 10.
- The symbol U indicates sets union.
- The AHMMRGW defines the ETP as a model, using CSFs weightings and ratings.
- The selected corresponding weightings to CSF ϵ {1 ... 10} are integer values.
- The selected corresponding ratings to CSF ϵ {0.00% ... 100.00%} are floating point percentage values.
- A weighting is defined for each ETPRGW CSF, and a rating for each KPI.
- The AHMMRGW applied a research mixed model, which is mainly a qualitative concept which uses specific quantitative method.

A Quantitative-Qualitative Research Mixed Model

An ETPRGW problem, RQ, or CSF, are examined/analysed/solved in iterations relating breadth and depth, using AHMMRGW's HDT, which is specialized for known or unknown problems, which creates ETP's learning process. The initial set of problems and their corresponding CSFs are set in the ETP's preliminary phase or initial iteration(s). Then, the *Framework qualitative research module* inputs data sets, which consist(s) of sets of numbers and/or rules, that are collected from channels generated by using designed/structured and approved/validated statistically processed data object collection modules. Just analysing data is a partial, limited static solution, or a limited insight. There is a need for a dynamic proactive qualitative heuristic method like the proposed HDT algorithm. There is also a need to control the activities and behaviour of persons (and groups), which are an important part of the *Entity's* internals and to proactively detect any probable violations to the defined AHMMRGW constraints. Action Research (AR) is an optimal method for Professors and researchers, academic administrative *Staff...* Especially, AR is helpful in education and can be defined as the process of online learning and to improve the quality of the educative process. AR provides the *Staff* with valuable knowledge and technics on how to improve educational practices or resolve ETP problems. AR uses a systematic process, is participatory, and offers multiple, beneficial opportunities for Professors. These opportunities include facilitating the professional development of Professors, increasing teacher empowerment, and bridging the gap between research and practice (Hine, 2013). Possible violations can be modelled to deliver controlled access to *Entity's* internals through political backup, informational services, assigned roles, responsibilities & credentials, and defined standards; and to support ETP's unique applied transformation model.

The Applied Educational Transformation Mathematical Model

The AHMMRGW for ETPRGW has a composite structure that can be viewed as follows: 1) The static view; 2) The dynamic or behavioural view; and 3) As the skeleton of the *Framework* that uses Microartefacts' scenarios. The AHMMRGW can be modelled after the following formula for Business Transformation Mathematical Model (*BTMM*) that abstracts the ETP:

$$AHMMRGW = Weigthing_1 * AHMMRGW\_Qualitative + Weigthing_2 * AHMMRGW\_Quantitative \text{ (B18)}.$$

$$AHMMRGW = \sum AHMMRGW \text{ for an enterprise architecture's instance (B19)}.$$

$$BTMM = \sum AHMMRGW \text{ instances (B20)}.$$

The objective function of the *BTMM*'s formula can be optimized by using constraints and with extra variables that need to be tuned using the AHMMRGW. The variable for maximization or minimization can be, for example, the *Entity's* success, costs, or another CSF. For ETPRGW's PoC the success will be the main and only constraint and success is quantified as a binary 0 or 1, where the objective function will be to minimize the risk for BTMM. The BTMM is a combination of *Entities* methodologies and AHMMRGW that integrates the *Entity's* organisational concept(s) and the ICS. The AHMMRGW is a part and is the skeleton of the *Framework* that uses Microartefacts' scenarios to support ETPRGW requests (Kim & Lennon, 2017). The ETPRGW components interface the DMSRGW and KMSRGW, to evaluate, manage and map CSFs for ETPRGW's selection activities; if the aggregation of all the *Entity's* CSA/CSF tables exceeds the defined minimum, the *Entities* continues to its second part of the PoC. The initialization phase generates the ETPRGW types of RGW problems to be analysed. The AHMMRGW is a part of the *Framework* to support the application domain's requests (Agievich, 2014). Where the focused application domain is online education and HRW.

THE APPLICATION DOMAIN

Using CSAs and CSFs in Online Education Platforms

The ETPRGW uses CSAs and CSFs in various aspects like in *Entity's* domain specific collaborations and other cross-sector collaborations. These CSFs were identified in the literature review phase and then used further in the RDP (Thune, 2011). As already mentioned, the application domain is RGW, which includes many *Entity*'s resources, online educational cross-functional fields, features, and products, like the Minimum Viable Product (MVP).

Minimum Viable Product for the ETP

To support an online education for the *Entity's* agile aspects and internal resources, there is a need for swift and reactive activities related to change. Implementing various types of EA artifacts, like patterns and Building Blocks (BB), which can define all possible online educational scenarios, problems, and solutions. The located solutions correspond to all assembled requirements. At the ETP's initial phase, all the requirements might not be all specified. To achieve that, the MVP concept is in development of the minimal solution. So, the value of ETPRGW is to support the *Entities* in the EIMP, where the Development Sprints are precisely planned, with the notion of highest-value online educational services, which are implemented first. As the EIMP applies the burn-down phases, the *Staff* identifies the first implemented solution. Therefore, ETPRGW supports all MVP's requirements/requests, which is not encompassing all requirements, but it will move to patterns through a transitional state(s) towards a target EA blueprints (Spencer, 2016). For an RGW of an ETP and all its online ICS, there is a need for a Scaled Agile Framework (SAFe), which can support the GRW.

The Scaled Agile Framework

As shown in Figure 4, the main ETP'S complexities are not only related to the transformation process, but in using APM frameworks, tools and ready to implement infrastructure models (like the Cloud) that have be precisely designed and coordinated. Nowadays, *Entities* need to make very changes at which the MES structures, and methodologies, which were built previously, cannot keep follow such a high frequency rate. The ETPRGW recommends to ignore the existing archaic knowledge base, and to reintroduce a new ICS that runs in parallel with the MES. Such a transformed ICS is to be managed by a SAFe, which includes seven core competencies (Kersten, 2021).

The Core Competencies of ETP's Organizational Agility

Modern ICSs are based mainly online software systems; and need to incorporate an advanced state of Online Educational Agility (OEA), means that the whole *Entity*, and not only its ICS teams/department(s) must be engaged in continually and proactively delivering innovative online educational solutions faster than others and ensure high quality. OEA needs technical agility and a stakeholders' level commitment to support end-online educational sites, which is ETPRGW's main strategic requirement. The OEA requires all *Entity Staff* to use online lean and agile practices. Using SAFe, as shown in Figure 5, supports the integration by applying the Development and Operations (DevOps) into a its ICS. DevOps supports the *Entity's* online activities with a high level of quality (Kersten, 2021).

As shown in Figure 6, to manage the ETP, the *Entity* needs a *Staff* with OEA Leadership (OEAL) skills and an adequate OEA team.

Figure 4. The main evolution phases (Kersten, 2021)

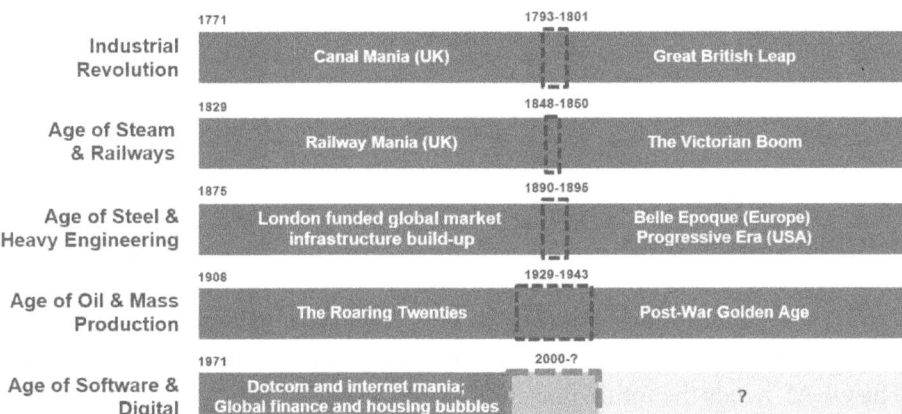

Figure 5. The relation between the speed of ETP and stability (Kersten, 2021)

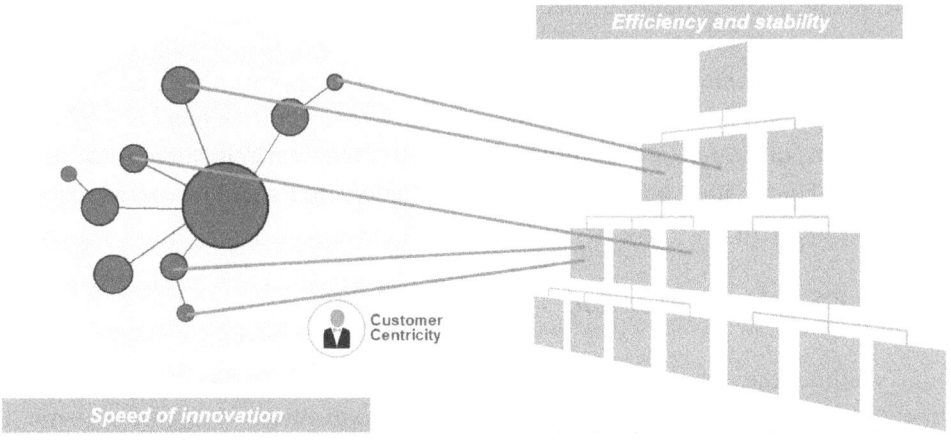

Figure 6. The seven core activities to support the ETP (Kersten, 2021)

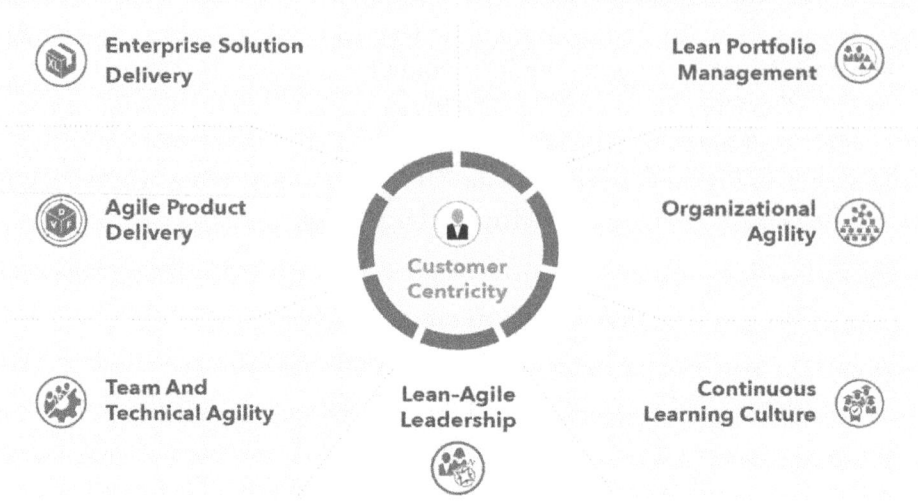

Lean-Agile Leadership

The *Staff* is responsible for the adoption, success, and ongoing improvement of lean-agile transformation iterations and the skills to integrate or build an online educational ICS. The OEAL needs the following set of skills (Kersten, 2021): 1) Drive the ETP and operational activities by enforcing agile *Staff*. 2) The *Staff* technical agility competency describe the needed critical skills; 3) To ensure OEA, *Entities* must increase their ability to deliver innovative online educational services; 4) OEA based services delivery is students' centric; 5) ETPs require innovation, experimentation, and knowledge from various domains; 6) Obsolete MES concepts to services portfolio management are obsolete; 7) The lack of organizational agility means that *Entities* cannot respond to online teaching challenges and new opportunities; 8) To thrive in the actual competitive online education's ecosystem, *Entities* must use ETPs to transform into automated online structures for continuous learning, for non-technical domains like Humanities; and 9) Complex online education's ecosystems need *RGW and OEA to be scaled*.

Scaling OEA Management

Today's online education's ecosystems and their ICSs are very dynamic, where this dynamicity demands from *Entitles* to deliver online education's software systems at faster pace and to be more tolerable to ever changing students' requirements during the EIMP. OEA based online software development is an iterative and incremental concept for online software development, which has emerged as an alternative to MES' concepts to address next challenges; and proposes the following (Stojanov, 2015): 1) Among the different agile methods is SAFe and its main focus is to highlight the roles, activities and EA artefacts that are necessary to scale OEA to online educational ecosystems; 2) Agile development originated from the success of Toyota and its production system. This lean production system is based on preserving value while minimizing work; 3) The Portfolio Level, as higher level of abstraction, is required for voluminous *Entities* which have many educational teams; and 4) The OEA needs to balance the online services portfolio on relevant levels by defining and managing educational and academic strategic objectives, which run across value streams. Such operations are to be supported by a *Framework and a competent Staff*.

The Author's Framework and the Staff

The *Staff* must have knowledge in RGW concepts, which is based a very of the ADM, SAFe, OEA, online educational services, and academic online teaching processes. The use of RGW processes will enhance the management of educational and academic activities. ETPRGW's specific characteristics require a special educational curriculum for the *Staff* and students. *Staffs* need to have the ability to deeply understand *Entity's* unique RGW and OEA paradigms, and to swiftly identify online educational plans. The *Staffs'* coordinator must have the described qualities and at least some education in organizational engineering, online systems, and ICS. The *Staff* needs to be supported by a *Framework*, that interfaces the ADM and SAFe to establish *Entity's* Online Educational Patterns (OEP). OEPs' structure the *Entity* and its critical EIMP; by executing the following tasks: 1) Unbundling through new online educational services, 2) the use of the ADM; and 3) Finding and aligning the needed Return on Experience (ROE).

Needed ROE and Using OEPs

The RDP is also based on literature review and ROE sources, which presented *Entities* with serious problems and having high rates of failure when using online educational systems. That is why they want to pursue this RDP and contribute to this complex problem and the main difficulty lies in the duration of the ETP that take many years to be finalized. ROE is mainly based on the *Entity's* learning process and the use of OEPs. The OEP's the instantiation or active BBs that support online educational service; these OEPs are designed using modelling languages to construct basic templates which can be reused. OEPs have the possibility to be translated them into XML and then to be used later in the *Entity's* ICS and platform. The possibility of using OEPs depends on the existence of the selected pattern language that permits the synthetic and visual expression of the patterns' constructs. An OEP is the abstract artefact of a solution and draws its origin of an insight of the instance concrete ETP problems, which the *Staff* has the responsibility to solve. Common pattern languages define a set of generic constructs and resources summarizing the fundaments of OEPs, mainly specifying the problem characteristics to be solved, then offering the solution(s) and eventually providing best online education practices and other useful references. OEPs and related generic pattern languages add the specification of online educational resources, scenarios and materials which are needed for the implementation an online education course. Professors are willing to try credible pedagogical strategies in their classes which allow their students to apprehend the course and to be successful. Nowadays students lack time, so there is a need for a specific and precise step-by-step guideline that they can use or adopt to their own understanding process. The OEPs offer a large set of patterns and provide an environment to assist the Professor in developing and deploying a successful and engaging online educational service with a robust didactical educational foundation. The use of the OEP based ETPRGW provides Professors with a methodology which that can be used to delivers a set of optimal scenarios and recommendations; where Professors can add and modify the content in real-time. The OEP offers various levels of representation from a detailed one (having a set of criteria for each online activity), to a higher-level approach (sequencing of online activities). So, the Professors can switch levels to manipulate the online services artefacts. At the *Entity's* level, it is recommended to develop, maintain, and support courses using the minimal number of EOPs and efforts. OEPs can be related using XML based relations, descriptions and then use them in the *Entity's* ICS (Botturi, & Belfer, 2014). The ETP offers a set of OEP and generic patterns needed for relating different academic environments which are needed for the *Entity*. The OEP are specialized for the creation online classes and research labs. Instead of using traditional teaching technics in a real classroom and moving to online educational services, the most important CSF is to do is to use OEPs for building the online learning system, and this achieved by linking various online services, building new technics for learning, and creating links to the students. The OEPs used to link students, assistants and Professors who can have the impression to be physically and mentally distant when they participate in the online class remotely. OEP must the impression that the online class is a visual remote communication tool, where students are listeners who are following remotely. OEP tries to make online classes attractive and interactive by, attracting and keeping the students glued to the session, which helps them to keep concentrated and to focus from daily/weekly educational activities to the online class wherever they are. Even though students and Professors are distant, binding the feeling of presence, will make students have the impression that they are taking the class in a real classroom. Creating online opportunities for interaction between students makes students come together and they can deepen their learning. To apply OEP correctly the following ETP activities: Using EA for online learning, Virtual environment integration, Asynchronous agile interaction, Enabling a DevOps support, Inviting capacities, Sharing ream world feelings like excitement, Emphasize students' reactions, Encourage switching on the cameras, Voices management & quality, Casual talk style, Conversation starter concept, … (Hayashi, Shibata, Inoue, Adachi, & Iba, 2022). The developed sets of OEPs supports the *Entity's* Cloud.

The OEP based Educational Cloud

Because of major technical ICS problems like security, availability, unreliable access, and the lack of support, can damage online educational platforms and such issues, prevent *Entities* to sign off on a Cloud for online learning platform. The Cloud based online learning platform offers the following advantages that (Pappas, 2022): 1) Simplifying the setup and maintain processes; 2) Is cost efficient, because it is the cheapest online-based learning platform; 3) Improves *Staff* retention, because the access to online learning materials and skill development resources are important for them; 4) Increases Staff productivity and quality work, because it ensures the synchronization of online processes and resources. It also supports students informed and that they have in depth understanding of educational policies and procedures; 5) Supports seamless collaboration in the distributed environment, the online platform enables the access the online training materials remotely and offers the support they need instantaneously. Localizing online learning courses, the students from different cultural background can communicate; 6) It scalability permits growth as the *Entity* evolves training needs; 7) Cloud based learning platforms are not dependable, and their ICS resources can be exchanged; 8) It offers mobile training to students, because they can be anywhere and they can login via their mobile phones, or access moment-of-need learning information; 9) No need for internal ICS support, because Cloud based solutions have ICS service personnel who can address these issues; and 10) Cloud based learning platforms are robust and safe, because they have a variety of safety measures, from data encryption to SSL. Many types OEPs can be used but there are some critical ones, like the students collaboration pattern.

Students Collaboration Pattern

In domains related to education in ICS topics, Professors need to integrate challenge-based and team-based collaboration projects to enhance online learning and prepare students for future professions. The successful use of online team-based projects structures is related to the students' ability to work in virtual teams. To achieve such a collaborative work. Where each team develops its own pattern of teamwork; by applying affinity propagation algorithm that is mainly based on patterns of collaborative behavior. Actions of groups should be categorized as different contribution types, like planning, coordination, input, deletion, or updates on project activities. Sequences of actions are dedicated to groups using specialized patterns of collaborative work. This pattern supports Professors to identify teams that need support in their teamwork; that enhances communication and organization. Collaborative online learning is superior to traditional learning because it promotes students' engagement and learning. Collaborative online learning assignments can include three or more students to work interdependently towards the completion of project's common goal. There are major differences in the perception of collaborative work and needed skills between engineering/ICS and business students, and these differences need specialized approaches in the development of an online education curriculum. Engineering/ICS education faces major challenges because students don't see the importance of these skills for their profession. The evident benefits of team-based and holistic/cross-functional projects, shows the difficulties in ICS related design and implementation teamwork tasks. Such team-work significantly slows down the diffusion of team-based educational activities. The adoption of innovative methodologies in ICS education is due to Professors' lack of concrete experience in the real world. ICS courses to include collaborative practices; and some Professors are discouraged by not meeting the expected online learning outcomes. An ETP recommends the transition from an iterative method which requires adjustment on the part of students and Professors. Virtual teams are defined as workgroups which are structured to complete project goals; and student teams, in the context of collaborative assignments, usually have 3 to 7 members. ICS student projects need an OEA approach in which highly frequent communication between all members is needed; this how they create their specific interactive OEP. They experience their limits and capabilities; and thus, initiating a specific OEP of interaction. Each virtual team member can modify his way of problem-solving concept that is optimal for the teamwork which that includes task allocations, time management, design, and implementation activities. Interaction OEPs contains: context data, working, data and, support data; used to support the DMS4RGW. Challenge-based online education provides a context for problem-solving and is self-regulated teamwork which provides to student teams with a set of project problems. In challenge-based learning, Professors participate as project managers or tech-leads, where they provide recommendations and monitor the project's progress. Professors must continuously improve teaching concepts as tasks progress. Challenge-based education, students work on a concrete case study, in which they trace their project tasks (Pisonia, Gijlersc, Nguyend, & Chene, 2021). The complex activity of interconnecting the

Entity's online and traditional educational processing nodes, is extremely complex, and in general it causes major resistance from the *Staff* and students. But to avoid such scenario(s) the use an RGW based ADM can be applied.

ARCHITECTURE DEVELOPMENT METHOD AND AGILE MANAGEMENT

The ADM is a generic method and recommends a set of phases and iterations to develop the ETP; it designs parts of the online system's interfaces, with other *Entity's* components. The ETPRGW must be capable of defining the set of ETP requirements and use the RGW to synchronize ADM phases.

ADM Phases

The ADM manages the online development process, and in this section the author present main ADM's phases and *Entity's* interactions: 1) The preliminary phase selects the relevant ETPRGW CSFs and interactions; 2) The architecture vision and domain/educational architecture; 3) ICS' architecture; 4) Online technologies integration; and 4) OEP requirements management and tests. For ETPRGW, OEP's integration is important.

OEP Architecture, Modelling and Integration

The ETP uses the *Framework* (with TOAGF's and SAFe's support) to apply technology and academic standards that delivers added value and robustness to *Entities*. In order to move towards an OEP based ICS, all related domains must be also synchronized. The ETPRGW must be capable to aligning: 1) OEP's vision; 2) OEP's principles; and 3) Standards management to support OEPs. OEPs' implementations can be used to automate the *Entity's* online educational services and to rationalize the *Entity's* activities and enables them to communicate with external academic partners. The implementation of ETPRGW is done by training of the *Staff*, who should have the minimal experience in these domains. To support an RGW based OEP, CSFs are needed, to ensure the rationalization of the *Entity's* ICS platform nodes and to enable Cloud enabled online services' communication. For various *Entities* that must be transformed using ETPRGW, the infrastructure is a crucial CSF, to link its ICS to partners and students. The ETP implements performance CSFs to monitor its progress. All these RGW activities there is a need for defining the Unit of Work (UoW) as a BB.

Unit of Work as the ETP's Building Block

The *Framework's* Microartefact granularity for the ETP is a complex task (Kim, & Lennon, 2017). The ETP uses the *1:1* mapping and classification concept, which supports that its online resources map to online services. The EA ADM to supports ETPRGW's activities, which use Microartefacts bundles in the form of UoW, that facilitates the integration of various web or online technologies and standards. The *Staff* must have skills to manage RGW based ETP; where mapping concepts can be used to integrate various types of standards like TOGAF, SAFe, Unified Modelling Language (UML)… The *Entity's* online education strategy provides the context for large-scale, high-impact end system for decisions making, priority setting, and control mechanisms (Lankhorst, 2016). ETPRGW, must consider all long-term aspects of the *Entity's security* concept, controls, and strategies.

Entity Security Strategies

Figure 7. Types of economic risks (Kiseleva, Karmanov, Korotkov, Kuznetsov, & Gasparian, 2018)

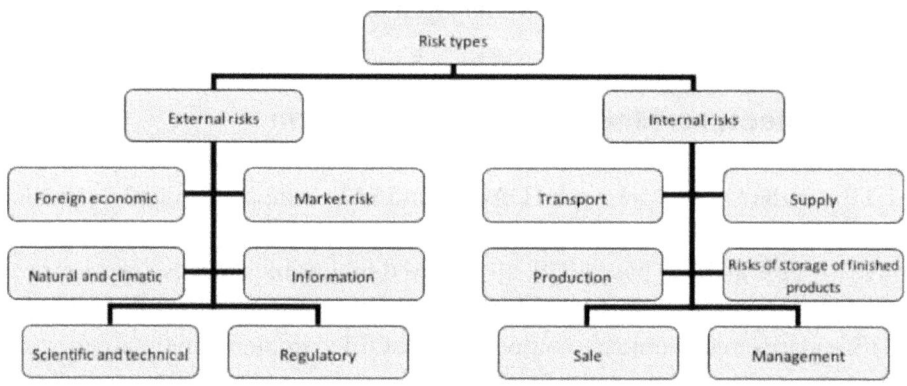

Entities face a set of barriers and difficult scenarios, which need the RGW of *Entity's* Online Educational Security Risks (EOESR), using a specialized component to support their activities. As shown in Figure 7, the EOESR may include CSFs related to reputation, routine Secured Development Operations (SecDevOps) procedures, legal and human resources management, financials, the risk of failure of internal controls systems and Entity wide governance. EOESR RGW system's key principles are: 1) Principle of online services integration using a systemic and holistic approach; 2) Principle of continuity using a set of online service procedures; 3) Integration of

SecDevOps; 4) Blocking manipulation and cheating; 5) Real-time tracing; and 6) Principle of validity based on CSFs and quality qualification procedures (Kiseleva, Karmanov, Korotkov, Kuznetsov, & Gasparian, 2018). ETP requests are intercepting the *Entity's* decision making and knowledge management systems.

DECISION MAKING AND KNOWLEDGE MANAGEMENT SYSTEMS

A Highly Complex Process

ETPRGW is supported by DMSRGW and KMSRGW systems, which deliver sets of possible solutions to identified types of ETP problems. The optimal solution(s) proposes transformational changes and minimizes transformation risks. The DMSRGW and KMSRGW systems' integration solves possible ETP problem types, due to complex HDT processing evaluation processes. Which implies that RGW related risk(s) is one of the important pre-requisites to ensure the success of the ETP (Hussain, Dillon, Chang & Hussain, 2010). The first is to transform the legacy knowledge management system.

The Knowledge Management System

The ETPRGW must be capable of managing online Educational Knowledge Items (oEKI); where oEKIs and Microartefact scripts are responsible for the manipulation of intelligence, and they control various online educational knowledge services. The KMSRGW supports the *Entity's* underlying mechanics to manage oEKI Microartefacts. The *Staff* is responsible for designing extraction of oEKIs using holistic systemic approach (Daellenbach & McNickle, 2005). The *Framework* interfaces the KMSRGW to enable an efficient oEKI search process. The KMSRGW manages various types of educational information related to *Entities,* which helps the ETPRGW activities. The ETP interfaces the KMSRGW/oEKI, where sets of CSFs are stored. KMSRGW's strategy is included in ETPRGW's roadmap that includes also the DMSRGW.

The Decision-Making System

The DMSRGW which is supported by the AHMMRGW formalism, uses a holistic approach for delivering a set of ETPRGW recommendations in form of ETP enhancements. The ETPRGW interfaces the DMSRGW, in which various RGW solution templates are stored; these solutions are selected, enhanced, and tuned, using selected CSF sets, then this process is orchestrated by the AHMMRGW's HDT, used to select the optimal ETPRGW set of actions. All the discovered actions and knowledge form the HDT based learning process. The HDT is a form of Deep Learning in the domain of AI. RGW oriented *Entities* have today, efficient environments to support DMSRGW; like the ones shown in Figure 8 (Scaled Agile, 2022): 1) *The alignment* with the ETP strategy which ensures that DMSRGW pursue beneficial educational results; 2) *Student centricity* is critical for ensuring that an AI initiative can solve an educational problem type. Explicitly defining the customer problem is an important step and hugely benefits from applying *Design Thinking to AI capabilities*; 3) *Continuous exploration* supports AI-enabled solution(s); where solution development contains a high degree of uncertainty; and 4) *Empirical milestones* directs the EIMP to achieve successful AI-based solutions; which can be used to support ETPHGRW's main blocks.

Figure 8. The decision-making framework enabled by SAFe (Scaled Agile, 2022)

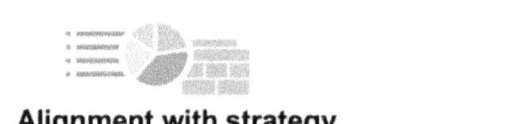

1. Alignment with strategy

2. Customer centricity

AI Decision-Making Framework

3. Continuous exploration

4. Empirical milestones

System Demos

THE ETPHGRW'S MAIN BLOCKS

GRW's Granularity

For traditional and online classes, the small group concept is optimal, but the issues are related to the type of small group granularity and to find the optimal size. Granularity depends on the original size of the class, the available period, the physical features of the classroom infrastructure, and the nature of the virtual team's task. And some of small team's granularity types are (Burke, 2022):

- Buzz groups, which has any class size, time frame of 3-10 minutes, the setting has no limitations. Its main purpose is to generate ideas/answers, re-stimulate student interests, gauge student understanding. This type of group involve students concerned in short, informal discussions. The best discussions are those in which students make judgments regarding the relative merits, relevance, or usefulness of an aspect of the course.
- *Think-pair-share* which has any class size, time frame of 5-10 minutes, the setting has no limitations. Its main purpose is to: generate ideas, increase students' confidence in their answers, encourage broad participation in decision sessions. This strategy has the following steps: 1) Students think individually about a task; 2) Then they pair up to discuss and compare their concepts; and 3) They share their ideas in a large class discussion. Think-pair-sharing forces students to propose an initial solution(s) to the task(s).
- *Circle of Voices* which has any class size, time frame of 10-20 minutes, the setting is moveable chairs preferable. Its main purpose is to: generate ideas, develop listening skills, have all students participate, equalize online learning environment. This group method involves students taking turns to speak in circles of four or five students. This student group concept supports creative evolution.
- *Rotating trios* which has a class size of 15-30 students, time frame of 15-30 minutes, the setting is a fair bit of space, moveable seating helpful. Its main purpose is to: introduce students to other team members and generate concepts/ideas. This strategy involves students discussing issues with many of their fellow classmates in turn.
- *Snowball groups/pyramids* which has a class size of 12-50 students, time frame of 15-30 minutes, the setting is moveable seating required. Its main purpose is to: To generate well-designed concepts, narrow a subject, develop decision-making skills. This method involves: students to work autonomously, then in pairs, then in fours, and in the group. In this group type, one selected student representative reports the group's project status and conclusions.

- *Jigsaw* which has a class size of 10-50 students, time frame of 20 or more minutes, the setting is: moveable seating required, a large space is recommended. Its main purpose is to: Learn concepts in-depth, develop virtual teamwork, and includes cases where students teaching students. This group's strategy involves students becoming experts on a specific project topic, then transferring their expertise to other group members. Jigsaw avoids unnecessary plenary sessions, because the most information is shared in small groups. This method can be expanded by having students develop expertise about their subtopics.

- *Fishbowl* which has a class size of 10-50 students, time frame of 15 or more minutes, the setting is: Moveable seating with and a lot of space. Its main purpose is to: Observe group interactions, provide real world concepts, and provide analysis activities. This method involves one group observing another group. If group members are not concentrated because their task is not challenging.

- *Virtual learning teams* which has a class has any size, any time frame, the setting is: Has no limitations. Its main purpose is to: Enforce relationships between students, and to increase their confidence. This type of group, students are divided into groups of four students, because each foursome can be subdivided into pairs, depending on the project's activity. Students get to know a small number of their classmates well over the course of the term and may come to see their teammates as study partners even outside the classroom. Student GRW activities need multimedia support.

Multimedia Support for the GRW

Multimedia interactive Web-based video collaboration environments have enormous transformative capacities for video-enhanced online education and for research activities. The *Entity* has to implement a platform to support video online collaborations. For that there is a need to identify the needed Online Collaboration Patterns (OCPs) to be in video-based practices. OCPs support interaction using collaboration technologies. Online learning, interaction, and GRW practices are influenced by contributions involving close analyses of video and audio recordings from conversation analysis, sociolinguistic studies of classroom discourse, anthropological and ethnographic inquiries of learning in formal and informal settings, and studies of socially significant nonverbal behaviors such as *body language* or kinesics gesture, and gaze patterns. This orientation to understanding learning in situ has led researchers to search for environments allowing for the capture of the complexity of real projects learning situations, where multiple simultaneous *channels* of interaction are potentially relevant to achieving a deeper understanding of learning behavior.

There can be considerable value in collecting and considering video of the user experience in the design process [30], but the logistics of incorporating this video into a design team's workflow can be tricky. (Pea, & Lindgren, 2008). The types of groups support GRW creative design activities.

GRW's Design Activities and Creativity

Design creativity is a crucial CSF in design-oriented online education, and frequently also a crucial competency during ICS professional activities. GRW and individual work are heavily used in online education. Many research studies have signaled the advantages of applying GRW in online design education, cultivating collaborative design abilities and enforcing sought-after employability knowledge and skills. Although the benefits of GRW in online design activities and online education are recognized, there are few studies which show evidence that GRW outperforms individual work in the field of creative design activities in ICS online education constellations. ICS Professors employ both GRW and individual work to complement each other in design courses. Creativity is the basis of human intelligence and is a significant CSF in design for ETP problem-solving, innovation initiatives, and it is related to educational performances. It is defined as *the process by which something so judged*, *the production of novel, useful products*, and *the ability to imagine or invent something new of value*. Creativity is often associated with designing concepts and even if ICS creativity is considered a valuable characteristic in science, ICS/technology, engineering and mathematics (or STEM) disciplines, and it is often associated with STEM education. There is a need for creative engineers and scientists, where creativity has to be enforced in the current STEM education curriculum. Complex ETP problems, frequent changes in ICS/technologies, and societal changes, needed new aggregate solutions, which need new type of didactical approaches. The research of new solutions for solving complex problems needs creativity; and teaching creativity in STEM education is significant for fostering STEM graduates with the abilities and skills to solve emerging problems and create innovative services. The use of a cognitive support method to support students in creative undertakings especially in design of STEM. Creativity is one of the top five competencies needed for professional industrial design and especially ICS related. GRW are the two main learning strategies used in *Entities* and has a universal approach in higher education topics. The RGW can form students' autonomy and independent thinking, characteristics that are lacked in global companies. RGW promotes virtual work groups and ensures: To access more information, stimulate creativity, follow project's interactive communication, better performance, and enforce generic and specialized skills. Companies are seeking engineers with advanced RGW skills, capable of designing creativity (Han, Park, Hua, & Childs, 2021).

Design Creativity in Education

Creativity in design, or design creativity, is a significant element for the development of innovative products and services. It is essential part of the conceptual design phase where feasible design artefacts are created. RGW is a common virtual teaching strategy in online education, and it is asserted that students need RGW experience prior to their professional activities. The main benefits include that it fosters students' abilities and skills in communication, DMS4RGW, RGW based management, interpersonal dynamics, critical reflection, self-study, and social interactions. These essential skills and abilities are not discipline-specific but are transferable that benefits lifelong online learning. Students perform better in RGW and use resources effectively. RGW based design education, supports students in experiencing and understanding collaborative analysis design processes, which needs virtual design practice. Virtual design activities need RGW to solve complex design topics and problems. An *Entity* has to be apply an effective RGW in virtual design assignments. Creativity has a significant role in practical design and can applicable in all phases of the virtual design process, including the central detailed design phase. Individual students are more creative and perform better in RGW especially in interactive brainstorming activities. Virtual creativity development environments can used in design classes that can involve the following activities: Brainstorming, C-Sketch, Lateral Thinking, Method 6-3-5, Mind Mapping, Six Thinking Hats, PMI, Strength, Weakness, Opportunity and Threat (SWOT), UML, ADM, ... Creativity development environments can used for mass collaboration and education (Cress, Moskaliuk, & Jeong, 2016).

OEP Based RGW

RGW skills are essential for ICS engineers and should be is included in the *Entity's* curricula, to support students in acquiring virtual team technics and skills. During RGW activities, problems happen, due to a set of conditions, like unstable group constellations or lack of instructor's guidance. Students have to find strategies for solving these RGW problems. OEPs offer a way of supporting students by providing problem-solving strategies, which in general have to be tested. OEP can be applied in an interdisciplinary ICS engineering projects. GRW forms the main part in ICS engineering education.; the ACM/IEEE CS Curriculum Guide 2013, explicitly includes GRW/teamwork, communication, time management, and problem-solving skills as part of the *software engineering and social issues* and *professional practice knowledge.* These skills are often included in curricula of students' GRW projects, ranging from small to larger ones. Reports on what makes projects manageable and successful include CSFs like, essential Professor's guidance. But important Professor guidance needs time and can lead to that the Professor solves their problems. Where Professors' role is to support students to be able to acquire skills autonomously. That is achieved using OEPs for communicating known collaboration scenarios, to impact positively on the acceptance of RGW. This is especially valid for collaboration OEPs based on experience acquired from other groups. That delivers tacit and relevant knowledge of the elaborated practices. The GRW based project needs the DMSHGRW to solve GRW related problems. The OEP offers a process pattern to address collaboration recurrent type of problems; which includes: The areas of communication, coordination, and motivation. OEPs offer design of knowledge that originated from an architecture model, like the BB. In the beginning of the 1990's patterns were introduced in ICS in the form of software design patterns by the Gang of Four. Various types of patterns have been used in online education. One of the important OEP work is the *Pedagogical Patterns Project,* a substantial collection of OEPs addressing various areas of ICS online education. There are also OEPs focusing on students' perspective on online learning. Student collaboration patterns support common solutions to problems that occur in student GRW based projects. OEPs' main goal is to support students solve common problems. OEPs are based on the experience of other GRW based projects executed in workshops. An OEP include a set of goals, possible professional practices, and generic competencies. A list of possible OEPs are: 1) Clearing questions; 2) Sharing explications; 3) Define a clear list of tasks of each team member; 4) Offer KMS4HGRW to support knowledge requests; 5) Centralize APM; 6) Follow the ETP; 7) Mediate conflicts; 8) Keep a high level of motivation; 9) Start as soon as possible; 10) Routinely the requirements fulfillment; and 11) Assign tasks correctly. This chapter's section refers to an external student project, which was an interdisciplinary ICS/software engineering project at Radboud University Nijmegen; which included third year undergraduate students of the ICS and AI curricula. There were nine groups of six students each, a total of 54 students; where each group had different ICS and AI project. These projects architecture and the requirements tasks were developed by other student groups from other courses. The resulting ICS and AI solutions were delivered to external real-life Clients. GRW collaboration, like participating in GRW activities and achieving project's results in a collective manner, was a strategic educational goal. At the project's initiation the used collaboration OEPs were presented to the students and templates were provided to apply these OPEs. The students were continuously informed virtual collaboration was a strategic educational goal and that the its an important element of their final written exam. When necessary, the Professor referred to the collaboration OEPs and how can they be applied; that was done using specific didatics. This section is considered an ACS and used in the PoC (Koppe, van Eekeleny, & Hoppenbrouwersz, 2015).

IMPROVE DIDACTICS

Online education especially in ICS topics as a subdiscipline of pedagogy, addresses the large impact of ICS in the business eco-system through its intersection with: Philosophy, business, AI, data processing, psychology, linguistics, natural sciences, and mathematics. In comparison with other types of education, ICS education is a new discipline. Its evolution started in the 1940s, and ICS didactics focuses on the implementation of online teaching resources for the apprehension of ICS education and the further development of complex concepts ETPRGW usage and integration, and other related topics like ETP, RGW, where presented and the next section presents the PoC.

THE PROOF OF CONCEPT

The already mentioned ACSs have an MES, based on a mainframe, various types of archaic education services, end students' service department. The main goal is to show how ETPRGW can support the move to online education, with the application educational portfolio rationalization scenario.

Online Services Portfolio Rationalization Scenario, ICS Unification and CSFs

he PoC will try to select the needed set of ETPRGW pool of CSFs to satisfy ETP's requirements. The used ACSs have generic *Entities* strategic management goals as shown in Figure 9, which can be considered as the base sets of CSAs and CSFs. The ETPRGW's needed actions in ADM phases, are: 1) In EA's Phase A or the Architecture Vision phase, to setup a global online services roadmap; 2) In Phase B, it needs to setup *Entity's* target architecture and the set of online educational requirements definition(s); 3) In Phase C or the Gap Analysis phase, there is a need for modelling a target online educational application landscape; 4) Phase D or the Target Technology Architecture and Gap Analysis phase needs the final *Entity's* online educational infrastructure design; 5) In Phases E and F, (verifies the EIMP), Implementation and Migration Planning, one needs to define the transition architecture, proposing possible intermediate situation, and evaluate ETP's status. This PoC focuses on ETP's capabilities to support the PoC's execution process.

Figure 9. Transformation goals (Jonkers, Band & Quartel, 2012)

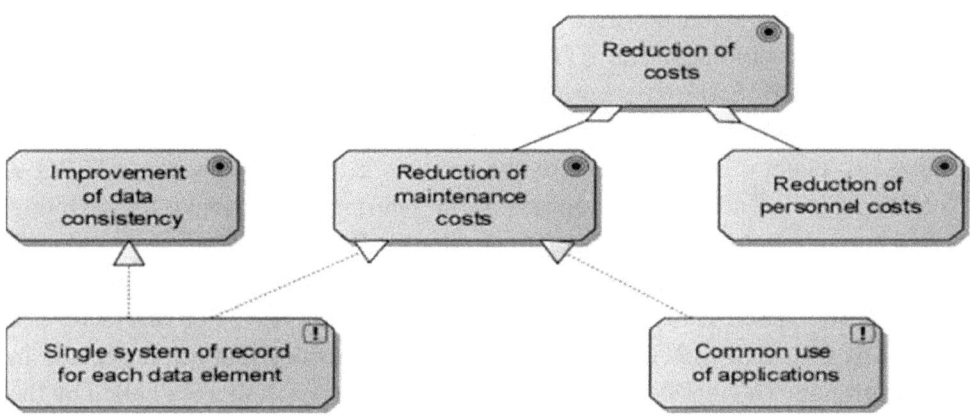

PoC's Execution

The PoC is implemented using the *Framework* and is based on the AHMMRGW's instance. The ETPRGW interfaces the DMSRGW that uses the selected sets of CSFs which are presented and evaluated in Table 1.

Table 1. The ETPRGW RDP's outcome is 8.40

CSA Category of CSFs/KPIs	Transformation Capability	Average Result
The RDP's Integration	Usable-Mature ▾	From 1 to 10. 9.0
The Methodology/ADM usage	Transformable-Possible-Mature ▾	From 1 to 10. 9.0
DMSRGW and KMSRGW	Transformable-Possible-Complex ▾	From 1 to 10. 8.00
RGW, OEP, OEA, OEL Concepts	Transformable-Possible-Complex ▾	From 1 to 10. 8.00
The ETPHGRW's Integration	Implementable-Complex ▾	From 1 to 10. 8.00

Evaluate First Phase

The ETPRGW-required skills have mappings to specific *Entities* online education resources like CSFs and the used microartefacts are designed using EA, SAFe, and RGW methodologies. The ETPRGW also defines relationships between the RGW (managed by SAFe) main artefacts like the original set of online educational requirements and OEP microartefacts. The PoC was implemented using the *Framework* client's interface, where the starting activity is to setup ETPRGW CSAs and CSFs. Once the development setup interface is activated, the scripting interface was launched to implement the needed OEP Microartefacts to process the defined CSAs. After starting the *Framework's* client, the sets of CSFs were selected and linked to a specific node of the HDT and the pool of OEP Microartefacts. The scripts link the AHMMRGW instance to the set of actions that are processed in the background. The AHMMRGW-based HDT uses services that are called by the DMSRGW actions. The ETPRGW instance and its related CSFs, RGW actions, were setup to be used; then the scripts were launched. This chapter's decision table and its result conclude the PoC's first initial phase, as illustrated in Table 1, which shows clearly that the ETPRGW can be used in *Projects*. ETPRGW is not an independent component and is bonded to all the *Project's* overall OEP, OEA, and RGW concepts. The *Framework* and hence the AHMMRGW's main constraint to implement the ETPRGW is that CSAs for simple *Entities* components, having an average result below 8.5 will be ignored. In the case of the current CSF evaluation an average result below 7.5 will be ignored. This work's conclusion with the result of 8.40 implies that ETPRGW's integration is feasible for all types of ETPs, but their enormous complexity is integrating the ETPRGW in *Entities*, where the initial phase should try to integrate the RGW and there is need to follow the recommendations.

CONCLUSION AND RECOMMENDATIONS

In this work the focus is on the ETPRGW which tries to transform *Entities*. There has been a lot developed and written on transforming traditional education and RGW, but the author proposes to verify OEP, OEA and OEL capacities. The complexity relies mainly due to silos concepts and the *Staff*'s lack of knowledge in RGW and the non-existence of adequate OEP and SAFe integration for such online initiatives. This RDP proposes a set of recommendations on how to proceed with ETPs where the RGW attempts a virtual teamwork approach. The usage of the ETPRGW considers that the ICS is a platform used to glue the various online education services of an *Entity*. There is a lot of resources on online education, but the author propose to inspect RGW to improve online education didactics. The resulting recommendations are offered to help *Staff* deliver optimal online services and RGW technics. ETPRGW's related recommendations, and the *Framework*, round up the approach needed for dynamic online educational environments, and the roadmap for integrating a coordinated ETPRGW with: OPEs, OEA, EA, RGW, SAFe... The most important recommendation that was generated by the previous research phases was that the business transformation manager must be an AofABIS, which can applied to the *Staff*. The recommendations for the ETPRGW are based on the processing of CSFs which resulted from the literature review and surveys' outputs; these inputs were fed in the HDT. In this chapter, the focus is on the ETPRGW's capabilities, coordination, and RGW's effect. These characteristics and prerequisites are needed to holistically manage the design of online services. The RDP tries to define the optimal ETPRGW, which should be capable to synchronize various types of ETP activities. There has been a lot developed and written on enabling success in *Entities*, but the author proposes to verify why such initiatives fail in the EIMP. Because of the low score, 8.4, Table 1 shows that ETPRGW's integration is possible, but difficult. The resultant recommendations are:

- As ETPRGW was established, the PoC checked its feasibility, and it replaces traditional education project technics.
- The EIMP is the major cause for failure, therefore there is a need for the optimal RGW concept.
- The *Staff* must be an OEP, OEA and RGW experts, who can implement tested blueprints.
- The literature review proved the existence of a knowledge gap between the traditional environments and online ones.
- An evolutionary HDT supported by the RDP is used to create the initial ETPRGW concept.
- The RDP proposes a concrete *Framework* on how to support RGW.
- Traditional education environments can hardly cope with complexity of heterogeneous educational systems.
- The PoC proved the research feasibility and delivered the recommendations on how to integrate the ETPRGW.
- ETPRGW coordinates OEPs integration to deliver architectural blueprints, patterns, and BBs.
- ETPRGW, uses an RGW like SAFe, to coordinate all ETP's activities.
- ETPRGW is optimal for Humanities curriculum because it promotes subjective, critical-thinking, and opinion-based concepts.

The *Framework* supports the *Entities* by using the ETPRGW and delivers a set of managerial recommendations.

REFERENCES

Agievich, V. (2014). *Mathematical model and multi-criteria analysis of designing large-scale enterprise roadmap* [PhD thesis].

Blackburn, R., & Rosen, B. (1993). Total quality and human resources management: lessons learned from Baldrige Award-winning companies. *Academy of Management Perspectives, 7*(3).

Botturi, L., & Belfer, K. (2014). *Pedagogical patterns for online learning.* ResearchGate.

Burke, J. (2022). *Group Work in the Classroom: Types of Small Groups.* Centre for Teaching Excellence, University of Waterloo. https://uwaterloo.ca/centre-for-teaching-excellence/

Cress, U., Moskaliuk, J., & Jeong, H. (2016). *Mass Collaboration and Education. Computer-Supported Collaborative Learning Series* (Vol. 16). CULS.

Felfel, H., Ayadi, O., & Masmoudi, F. (2017). Pareto Optimal Solution Selection for a Multi-Site Supply Chain Planning Problem Using the VIKOR and TOPSIS Methods. *International Journal of Service Science, Management, Engineering, and Technology.* . doi:10.4018/IJSSMET.2017070102

Han, J., Park, D., Hua, M., & Childs, P. (2021). Is group work beneficial for producing creative designs in STEM design education? *International Journal of Technology and Design Education.* Advance online publication. doi:10.100710798-021-09709-y

Hayashi, K., Shibata, S., Inoue, E., Adachi, S., & Iba, T. (2022). Online Education Patterns, Part 1: Patterns for Linking Separate Worlds. *EuroPLoP'21: 26th European Conference on Pattern Languages of Programs, 1*–16. 10.1145/3489449.3490003

Hine, G. S. C. (2013). The importance of action research in teacher education programs. In *Design, develop, evaluate: The core of the learning. environment. Proceedings of the 22nd Annual Teaching Learning Forum.* Murdoch University. http://ctl.curtin.edu.au/professional_development/conferences/tlf/tlf2013/refereed/hine.html

Hussain, O., Dillon, Th., Chang, E., & Hussain, F. (2010). Transactional risk-based decision making system in e-business interactions. *International Journal of Comput Syst Sci & Eng, 2010*(1), 15–28.

Jonkers, H., Band, I., & Quartel, D. (2012a). *ArchiSurance Case Study*. The Open Group.

Kersten, M. (2021). *Introducing SAFe® 5*. Your Operating System for Business Agility. Scaled Agile Inc.

Kim, J., & Lennon, Sh. (2017). *Descriptive Content Analysis on E-Service Research. International Journal of Service Science, Management, Engineering, and Technology*. doi:10.4018/IJSSMET.2017010102

Kiseleva, I., Karmanov, M., Korotkov, A., Kuznetsov, V., & Gasparian, M. (2018). Risk management in business: Concept, types, evaluation criteria. *Revista ESPACIOS*, *798*, 1015.

Koppe, Ch., van Eekeleny, M., & Hoppenbrouwersz, S. (2015). Improving Student Group Work with Collaboration. Patterns: A Case Study. In *2015 IEEE/ACM 37th IEEE International Conference on Software Engineering*. IEEE. https://ieeexplore.ieee.org/document/7202977

Lankhorst, M. (2016). *Enterprise Architecture and Agile Development: Opposites Attract? Agile EA with TOGAF 9.1*. BizzDesign. https://bizzdesign.com/blog/enterprise-architecture-and-agile-development-opposites-attract/

Markides, C. (2011, March). Crossing the Chasm: How to Convert Relevant Research Into Managerially Useful Research. *The Journal of Applied Behavioral Science*, *47*(1), 121–134. doi:10.1177/0021886310388162

Pappas, C. (2022). *Cloud Based e-Learning Platforms: 10 Advantages eLearning Professionals Need To Know*. Docebo. https://www.docebo.com/learning-network/blog/cloud-based-elearning-platforms/

Pea, R., & Lindgren, R. (2008). Video Collaboratories for Research and Education: An Analysis of Collaboration Design Patterns. IEEE Transactions on Learning Technologies, 1(4).

Pisonia, G., Gijlersc, H., Ha Nguyend, T., & Chene, H. (2021). Collaboration patterns in students' teams working on business cases. *CEUR Workshop Proceedings*.

Postle, G. (2003). Online Teaching and Learning in Higher Education: A Case Study. Department of Education, Science and Training. University of Southern Queensland.

Putri, N., & Yusof, S. M. (2009). Critical success factors for implementing quality engineering tools and techniques in malaysian's and indonesian's automotive industries: An Exploratory Study. *Journal Proceedings of the International MultiConference of Engineers and Computer Scientists.*, *2*, 18–20.

Sagheb-Tehrani, M. (2009). The Results of Online Teaching: A Case Study. *ISEDJ, 7*(42). http://isedj.org/7/42/

Scaled Agile. (2022). *Succeeding with AI in SAFe*. Scaled Agile, Inc. https://www.scaledagileframework.com/succeeding-with-ai-in-safe/

Service Architecture. (2022). *Education XML*. Service Architecture. https://www.service-architecture.com/articles/xml/education-xml.html

Spencer, M. (2016). *Agile EA – the MVP – enterprise architect-Building the Business Value Chain…* https://enterprisearchitect.wordpress.com/2016/04/11/agile-ea-the-mvp/1/2

Stojanov, I. (2015). *Scaling agile using scaled agile framework [Master's thesis]*. Eindhoven University of Technology.

The Open Group. (2011a). *Architecture Development Method*. The Open Group. https://pubs.opengroup.org/architecture/togaf9-doc/arch/chap05.html

The Open Group. (2011b). *TOGAF 9.1*. The Open Group.

Thune, T. (2011). Success Factors in Higher Education–Industry Collaboration: A case study of collaboration in the engineering field. *Tertiary Education and Management, 17*(1), 31–50. doi:10.1080/13583883.2011.552627

Trad, A. (2015a). *A Transformation Framework Proposal for Managers in Business Innovation and Business Transformation Projects-Intelligent aBB architecture*. Centeris.

Trad, A. (2015b). *A Transformation Framework Proposal for Managers in Business Innovation and Business Transformation Projects-An ICS's atomic architecture vision*. Centeris.

Trad, A. (2022a). Transformation Projects and Virtual Military Strategy. *CBER 2022*.

Trad, A., & Kalpić, D. (2014). The Selection and Training Framework for Managers in Business Innovation and Transformation Projects-An applied mathematics hyper-heuristics model. *Proceedings of the 2014 International Conference on Mathematical Methods, Mathematical Models and Simulation in Science and Engineering (MMSSE 2014)*.

Trad, A., & Kalpić, D. (2017a). *An Intelligent Neural Networks Micro Artefact Patterns' Based Enterprise Architecture Model*. IGI-Global.

Trad, A., & Kalpić, D. (2022a). Business Transformation Projects based on a Holistic Enterprise Architecture Pattern (HEAP)-The Basics. IGI.

Trad, A., & Kalpić, D. (2022b). Business Transformation Projects based on a Holistic Enterprise Architecture Pattern (HEAP)-The Implementation. IGI.

Trad, A. & Kalpić, D. (2022c). Business Transformation Project's Holistic Agile Management (BTPHAM). *CBER 2022*.

Chapter 10
Humanities in the Age of Blockchain Technology and Web 3.0

Zingisa Nkosinkulu

 https://orcid.org/0000-0003-3092-7352
Tshwane University of Technology, South Africa

ABSTRACT

Although there has been a call for the transformation of the world from the Eurocentric paradigms to a decolonised and decentralised world, the role of technology is still embedded and continues to be at the centre of everything in society. Over the past few years, particularly from 2019 to 2022, since the discovery of the COVID-19 pandemic, the technological interdependency intensified by moving contact spaces to online platforms, private resources to open resources, including the pedagogical space. Despite advances in technology and pedagogy and their relation to education, and the focus on the local and global, the new internet and teaching and learning including its policy still lack serious engagement with blockchain technology and the metaverse, as well as how to effectively utilise it. This chapter address this gap by using Howard Gardner's theory of 'multiple intelligences' to consider the role of blockchain technology and the metaverse as new options for the facilitation of open-ended teaching and learning that has emerged in the age of Web 3.0.

DOI: 10.4018/978-1-6684-4055-1.ch010

Copyright © 2023, IGI Global. Copying or distributing in print or electronic forms without written permission of IGI Global is prohibited.

SURFING THE WAY

It is here where the question of blockchain technology and Web 3.0 are explored concerning the scholarship field of the humanities and thus looking at its potential contribution to teaching and learning cannot be left un-entertained. The wave of Web3.0, its technological development, and solutions should be entertained by the humanities because of the tools and freedom it could offer. At the center of this progress what should also be positioned is the question of access to knowledge which most of the time is presented from a Eurocentric perspective. The Eurocentric perspective is based on distortion, exclusion, and whitewashing of most non-European knowledge systems. Knowledge systems are important for the development of human beings so they can develop the world they are living and operating in. A human being cannot grow without benefiting from the knowledge system of the parents that they have gathered from their culture, experience, and social existence. To think about blockchain technologies and Web 3.0 concerning the humanities is about a decolonized access and production to knowledge that is normally shared under colonial restrictions which are centered around European standards. This is important to grapple with how knowledge systems are restricted, in what is called coloniality of knowledge, to stand the test of colonial boundaries in that they are representations of unexplored knowledge which is left on the periphery of the humanities.

To argue for the inclusion of blockchain technology in academia is not something new. To argue for consideration of blockchain technologies and Web 3.0 to the humanities specifically is to argue for access, originality of knowledge, recognition of location, convenience, and pluriversal knowledge in the humanities. The technology that comes with blockchain, the apparatus that is new and yet untrustworthy, but necessarily needed yet frowned upon, brings to the table convenient ways in which knowledge can be excavated, shared, verified, stored, and utilized. This implies, in an innovative sense, exploring ways of connecting, recording, and licensing knowledge in the humanities that cannot be excluded from benefiting from the solutions that the new technology has to offer. This does not suggest the inclusion of untested technology for the sake of trends, but to explore different options that the modern/colonial world did not offer for the humanities, especially the ones that challenge the Eurocentric/Westernized paradigms. The Eurocentric/Westernized paradigm is the one that closes out the non-Eurocentric indigenous knowledge systems, in the Eurocentric humanities taught in a westernized setting that polices knowledge. This policing of knowledge went as far as arresting indigenous traditional knowledge to present it from a limited perspective and absent technology. The absence of technology means limited ways in which teaching, and learning can be conducted.

It is from this position that the new technology can be embraced as another option that has the potential to decentralize how knowledge is produced, shared, validated, and recorded. In a way, it can be argued that the new technology is for laymen. This is based on its fundamental principle of being open and free. It is open to be used by everyone without even having to be downloaded and installed by the end-user. Some open internet sources and resources allow the end-user to become a developer by being able to be rearranging the applications, documents, and content for remixing and distribution only for teaching and learning. The new technology might not be for everyone, but its solution can offer ways of making learning friendly and convenient for everyone. However, the development of blockchain technology and Web 3.0 is not only for teaching and learning but for other business ventures, gaming, art investment, and a variety of other things. Strategic involvement of blockchain technology and Web 3.0 does not mean things will be open and easy, still devices that can connect to the internet with specks that can allow installation of certain programs will be required. This is where blockchain technology and Web 3.0 comes in. This chapter explores this role by first, framing the theoretical perspective of decolonization and decentralization. Secondly, by briefly mapping the development of the humanities. Thirdly, by moving towards the benefits and solutions offered by blockchain and metaverse for the humanities in the Global South specifically, and human sciences in the world generally.

DECOLONISING AND DECENTRALISING THOUGHTS

This chapter applies a decolonial epistemic perspective and Howard Gardner's conception of 'Multiple Intelligence' as theoretical interventions to foreground blockchain technology and Web 3.0 as teaching and learning solutions in the humanities. It stands to answer the question: what role does Gardener's theory of Multiple Intelligence play in implementing humanities curriculum and decentralized education? The decolonial epistemic perspective is a theoretical framework and movement that comes from the periphery of modernity, it represents the voices of those who have been colonized by challenging the colonial paradigm and imperialism that positions Europe in the center of modernity. "Decolonization is the horizon of thinking and being that originated as a response to the capitalist and communist imperial design" (Mignolo 2011: xiii). A decolonial perspective is relevant for accounting for the understanding of the limits Eurocentric paradigm and the coloniality of knowledge influenced by the way knowledge is collected, licensed, and shared. Knowledge is shared from European intelligence in ways that bury non-European perspectives and knowledge systems, positioning them under certain colonial categories of inferior knowledge in contrast to superior knowledge which is Eurocentric. Technology and access are also something that is influenced by "global coloniality" (Ndlovu-Gatsheni 2013), coloniality of power, and modernity/coloniality. Technology and access to the internet is a different experience between the global south and global north, the periphery, and the center as shaped by the global colonial systems of modernity/coloniality. A decolonial perspective is instrumental to the dismantling of the colonial epistemological boundaries and its pedagogical limits to be open to different forms of intelligence as sources of legitimate knowledge. The decolonial perspective is interconnected, similar, and opposite to decentralization as depicted by Mignolo in his definition of decoloniality.

"...the anchor of decolonial epistemologies shall be "I am where I think" and better yet "I am where I do and think," as they become synonymous. What that means is not that you "think where you are," which is common sense, but that you constitute yourself ("I am") in the place you think. And that place is not, in my argument, a room or office at the library, but the "place" that has been configured by the colonial matrix of power" (Mignolo 2011: xvi).

The conception of decentralized intelligence is what is central to blockchain and Web 3.0 as such situating it concerning Howard Gardner's 'multiple intelligence' seems to be relevant for this chapter. Gardner (1983: 179-180) argues that "human beings have particular intelligences because of informational contents that exist in the world—numerical information, spatial information, information about other people." At the center of being a human being in precolonial and postcolonial times has been the need to know and share knowledge with other human beings of different cultures. The definition of knowledge and access to information, knowledge, or data is among many things in a modern/colonial world a politicized and centralized Eurocentric/ westernized affair. This shaping of information is connected to the coloniality of knowledge which is grounded on Rene Descartes 'cogito ergo sum' popular known as 'I think, therefore, I am' (Descartes (2004) [1637]). Descartes's theory of 'I think, therefore I am' became a foundation of western epistemology and Eurocentric colonial expansion, it privileged thinking overseeing, sensing, doing, experiencing, smelling, and being there. Leaning more toward Dascartes' idea privileged Western thinking and Eurocentric intelligence based on the coloniality of being, knowledge, and power. By definition "coloniality of knowledge denotes a complex process of development of global imperial technologies of subjugation taking the form of translating and re-writing other cultures, other knowledges, and other ways of being, and presuming commensurability through Western rationality" (Ndlovu-Gatsheni 2013:33). Coloniality of power refers to the colonial systems that are designed to enable Western rational through various tools and methods, political ideologies and academic fields that disabled non-European rational fostering coloniality of being.

The colonial gap between the global south and global north, center, and periphery are fostered through westernized intelligence and technology. Therefore, Western rationality creates students who are "white inside and black out side. They are physically located on the continent but epistemologically situated in Europe and America. They read and understand Africa from a European perspective. The cultural transformation of higher education is meant to change the character of institutions of higher education that continue to exist" (Ndlovu-Gatsheni 2013). The theory of multiple intelligence by Gardner can be a good extension to go beyond the limits of Western rationality or colonial/westernized intelligence that universalizes Eurocentric intelligence through education, laws, policies, and pop culture. Western rationality acknowledges and universalize only one form of intelligence, European/Eurocentric intelligence thus Gardner's theory of multiple intelligence becomes instrumental to this chapter. Listed below is a diagram that shows the differences between the so-called traditional view of intelligence and Gardner's conception of Multiple Intelligence.

Table 1.

Traditional view of "Intelligence"	"Multiple Intelligence" Theory
Intelligence can be measured by short-answer tests: Stanford-Binet Intelligence Quotient Wechsler Intelligence Scale for Children (WISCIV) Woodcock Johnson test of Cognitive Ability Scholastic Aptitude Test	Assessment of an individual's multiple intelligences can foster learning and problem-solving styles. Short answer tests are not used because they do not measure disciplinary mastery or deep understanding. They only measure rote memorization skills and one's ability to do well on short answer tests. Some states have developed tests that value process over the final answer, such as PAM (Performance Assessment in Math) and PAL (Performance Assessment in Language)
People are born with a fixed amount of intelligence.	Human beings have all intelligences, but each person has a unique combination or profile.
Intelligence level does not change over a lifetime.	We can all improve each of the intelligences, though some people will improve more readily in one intelligence area than in others.
Intelligence consists of ability in logic and language.	There are many more types of intelligence which reflect different ways of interacting with the world
In traditional practice, teachers teach the same material to everyone.	M.I. pedagogy implies that teachers teach and assess differently based on individual intellectual strengths and weaknesses.
Teachers teach a topic or "subject."	Teachers structure learning activities around an issue or question and connect subjects. Teachers develop strategies that allow for students to demonstrate multiple ways of understanding and value their uniqueness.

There have been many explorations of theories linked to intelligence and learning based on visual learning, auditory learning, and kinesthetic or tactile learning. Given 30 years of research and reflection, Gardner can summarize the pedagogical implications of Multiple Intelligence theory, also called elevator speech. He argues that educators who believe in the relevance of Multiple Intelligence theory need to individualize and pluralize. By individualizing Gardner means that educators should know as much as possible about the intelligence profile of each student they work with. Educators should also teach and assess students in a way that emphasizes their competencies whenever possible. By pluralization, Gardner means that educators must decide which themes, concepts, or ideas are most important and present them in different ways. By pluralization, the educator achieves two important goals. More students are reached when a topic is taught in multiple ways.

In addition, multiple modes of transmission convey what it means to understand something. For Gardener having a thorough understanding of a topic usually allows us to think about it in many ways, using multiple intellects. Understanding (by teachers or students) or learning can be limited when confined to one method of conceptualization and presentation. Within Gardner's theory of Multiple Intelligence, the process of learning is understood as something that should be aware and cater to different forms and levels of intelligence. Without intelligence, there is no possibility of learning because learning requires a level of intelligence to be potentially present. Through intelligence or consciousness, one can learn through "verbal-linguistic intelligence", "logical-mathematical", "spatial-visual intelligence", "bodily-kinesthetic intelligence", "musical intelligences", "interpersonal intelligence", "intrapersonal", "naturalist intelligence" and in addition, "existential intelligence" (Tapping into Multiple Intelligence 2004). This is where it is shown how the traditional view of intelligence imposes limits that are challenged by Gardner's perspective that offers an open room for intelligence that is beyond the limits of the Eurocentric humanities. Theory can go beyond conceptual limits and socio-political epistemological confinements; it allows re-writing the explanations of lived experiences that are inseparable from the project of critical transformation. Therefore, "decoloniality enters claiming its legitimacy to sit at the table when global futures are being discussed. For that reason, the first decolonial step is delinking from coloniality and not looking for alternative modernities but for alternatives to modernity" (Mignolo 2011: xxviii). The decolonial epistemic perspective introduces a new agenda for the humanities, to be open to alternatives of different definitions of alternative intelligence. Within Gardner's multiple intelligence, the traditional learning trajectory is understood from different forms of knowledge systems that can be expressed and were previously disadvantaged inferior knowledge. At the education level, contemporary recognition of technology can be recognized as a triumph over the global traditional view of intelligence. At another level, the combination of human intelligence and technology introduces Artificial Intelligence. It is at the border lines of Artificial Intelligence and education that blockchain technology and Web 3.0 could be open to accommodate different forms and levels of intelligence during learning that facilitate decentralization of knowledge, decentralization of being, and decentralization of power.

THE DEVELOPMENT OF THE HUMANITIES

This section offers a brief trajectory, genealogy, and the horizon of the development of the humanities and structural conditions of learning in the Global South to get a better view of the technological change which now influences teaching and learning. The problem with teaching current humanities is whether humanities have been westernized that its teaching and learning "would be a form of colonizing instead of decolonial practice" (Gordon 2018: 19). This literature review explores the development of the humanities through exploring and contextualizing recent epistemological developments. Since the publications by the Indian linguist Panini from 500 B.C.E, the Italian humanist Lorenzo Valla in the 15th century, the humanist Joseph Scaliger in the 17th century, Jacob Grimm and Franz Bopp a German linguist, and Gerard Genette a French literary theorist in the 21st century, humanities have been a definition and feature of academic disciplines that deal with the human, human creation, and human condition (Bod 2022). Although much is written on the biographical history of science that deals with the life and inventions of a particular person, whether as the science of exclusion and dehumanization that finds its way to the ways teaching and learning are conducted can be rarely compared to the scholarship of the history of the humanities. Of course, the list of the humanists goes beyond the listed names of the genealogy of the definition of the humanities to contemporary contributions as mentioned by Bod (2022:178).

This has resulted in a set of broad-ranging books, such as Rens Bod's A New History of the Humanities: The Search for Principles and Patterns from Antiquity to the Present (2013), James Turner's Philology: The Forgotten Origins of the Modern Humanities (2014), Eric Adler's The Battle of the Classics: How a Nineteenth-Century Debate Can Save the Humanities Today (2020), Paul Reiter and Chad Wellmon's Permanent Crisis: The Humanities in a Disenchanted Age (2021), and Christopher Celenza's The Italian Renaissance and the Origins of the Modern Humanities: An Intellectual History, 1400–1800 (2021).

The humanities, qua human sciences, were often ignored and only used as a step to justify and solidify scientific discoveries that were impossible without humanist interventions. This is not to say that there weren't those who wrestled with humanist questions, when it came to reflection on human inventions and discoveries, there was no appropriate place than science. Humanistic reflections on human inventions, including those in the history of art, literature, and linguistics were not uncommon. By humanistic reflection, I mean "the expressions of the human mind" (Bod 2022:180) and lived experiences. Currently, the humanities standard of teaching and learning has a strong growing link to technological solutions under the radar of the Fifth-generation wireless (5G). Of course, this is gradually being embraced by others (teachers or students) while it is being suspected by others. The fear comes from the technological gap between those who are technologically friendly and those who are not. To be technologically friendly means to be open to technology even at the basic level. Most standard technological tools, apps, and software have almost a universal language and interfaces that allow users of different countries to able to personally customize and use them. The basic level means being able to perform simple things like turning on and off a computer, using Microsoft Office, Outlook, and other software or apps that are provided by the institution for their staff. However, most academic staff that is expected to conduct teaching are specialists in their respective fields that they are teaching and as such, they are not computer experts. Most academic staff members acquired basic knowledge of computer and internet use on their own during their years of learning as students and very few took extra classes on computer and internet literacy. This can be one of the reasons that discourage most academics from embracing and fully integrating technology into their teaching experience. On the other hand, most students are very familiar with today's technology and how to use it. To be technologically unfriendly is to be illiterate by choice or not by choice, it is to be unfamiliar with the current trends of new apps and technology or be intimidated and overwhelmed by technology. On the other hand, individuals who are responsible for curriculum developing and teaching embrace the benefits of the "technological turn". They constantly enroll in workshops that develop and update their skills to be able to stay in tune with the current developments in technology and the internet.

"These are exciting times for the humanities. The impressive corpus of knowledge that the humanities have discovered, created, and cultivated over many centuries is available for the benefit of more people than ever and evolving rap-idly. Fresh perspectives open up as digital tools enable researchers to explore questions that not long ago were beyond their reach and even their imagination. Novel fields of research deal with phenomena emerging in a globalizing culture, enabling us to make sense of how new media affect our lives. Cross-fertilization between disciplines leads to

newly developed methods and results, such as the complex chemical analysis of the materials of ancient artworks, yielding data that were unavailable to both artists and their publics at the time of production, or neuroscientific experiments shedding new light on our capacity for producing and appreciating music (Bod et al., 2016:1).

Humanities have been identified as an important key field of study which enables reflection and development of human discoveries. Therefore, what the humanities embody are the lived experiences and reflections which entail the knowledge about the culture and social life of the people. At the epistemological level of the humanities, the aim is to decentralize the Eurocentric westernizing colonial code in the humanities that is being currently taught and maintained at the universities.

"The "code" has been preserved in the security box since the Renaissance. Diverse knowledge has been generated from that secret code in six European modern or imperial languages: Italian, Spanish, Portuguese, French, German, and English. One may discern a hierarchy within modern European languages when it comes to epistemology. Certainly, theology was grounded in Latin and translated to vernaculars, while romance language enjoyed a certain respectability in terms of knowledge making. However, after the Enlightenment, French was the romance language that led the second modernity, while German, and more recently English, have come to be language that preserves and hides the code" (Mignolo 2011: xii).

The humanities are no exception to the influences of the colonial code that Mignolo describes. The problem of the colonial code is what the "coloniality of being" contends with, and so are the humanities—that is, the knowledge and power are victims of this code. Through teaching and learning relation the colonial side of the code is realized and emphasized. Therefore, the transformation of the humanities is not only at the epistemological level, but also an ontological stance in its broader sense—say, the rethinking of learning content and methods of teaching. The way humanities have developed under the colonial rule of western modernity is the very same reason that opens room for an interrogation that has to do with the way the human sciences are being taught and practiced. It will be interesting to think about the humanities concerning the following questions. What is transformation and decoloniality in the context of online learning and Open Distance e-Learning in the humanities and decolonization of education? What is education if it is to be understood from the position of blockchain technology and metaverse, content, and access? It is important to think about these questions because the humanities are part of education, what influences education can influence the education of the humanities?

"In English, the term "Education" has been derived from two Latin words, Educare (Educere) and Educatum. Educare means to train or mould. It again means to bring up or to lead out or to draw out, propulsion from inward to outward. The term Educare or Educere mainly indicates development of the latent faculties of the child [or person]. But the child [or person] does not know these possibilities. It is the educator or teacher who can know these and take appropriate methods to develop those powers" (Kumar and Ahmad). It is fundamentally important to define the role of blockchain technology and metaverse to education of the humanities, the standard of education, the reason for education, the position of Africa in education and the importance of education towards African renaissance.

It is important to look at how blockchain technology and metaverse can shape education is used or can be used as a tool for the liberation of the humanities. Henrik Clarke argues that "anything that touches your life must be an instrument of your liberation or you must throw it into the trashcan of history". The new technology of Web3.0 has strong potential to be an instrument of liberation for the humanities specifically and for education specifically. For instance, South African education and curriculum do not speak to the teacher's experiences let alone of the students and the community they come from. South African Education and Curriculum need to speak to the framework of the African renaissance otherwise it will keep the African student trapped yet again in the web of colonial technologies. The current education and curriculum of the humanities need to be decolonized and decentralized, from the classroom, the intervals, university, digital platforms, and study materials to the extra activities.

First, we need to understand the teacher or lecture, the student, the family, and the society we are located in. We must see where all these people meet, when how, and why. Therefore, we must study the meaning, purpose, and contribution of blockchain technology and metaverse to the experience of education. We must look at the evolution of technology, we must look at what the humanities are not doing but should be doing. We must look if our education systems have changed after apartheid in the case of South Africa or if coloniality is over in the case of the global world. It will also be important to look at the purpose of education during apartheid and post-apartheid. Look at structures of schools, universities, prisons, and hospitals (psycho wards where intelligence is believed to be absent). The Surrealism art movement believed people with mental illness are the most intelligent. We must look if we have good teachers that are well supported by their communities, states, and their families. Currently, we invest less in our teachers, and eventually, we are paying more in the long run by having a dysfunctional society and a westernize world view. Amid this, every time the African scholar seek education of themselves that is outside of the westernized context it is always frowned upon and called names as a way of discouraging this self-seeking education in the westernized humanities.

It is everyone's dream or their birthright to have access to good education and it is all societies' dream to see their children and people leave in a better society. Unfortunately, before we embark on any journey that requires looking back to go forward does not allow us to look beyond our past historical factors. Although the kind of education our curriculum provides looks beyond some historical factors and turns a blind eye to other humanities. It, therefore, tells the story of the colonial victor while it omits the voice and the presence of the victimized, that is, the colonized people who are very far from technological stability and the center of the humanities. Education is a process of acquiring knowledge and skills sharing while referencing heritage, culture, and tradition. It also includes political and economic influences, decoloniality of being, decoloniality of knowledge, and decoloniality of power for the humanities through blockchain technology and metaverse.

TEACHING TOWARD THE METAVERSE

Blockchain technology and metaverse are here to provide transformation to a lot of things. But first, what is transformation? "In an organization context, a process of profound and radical change that orients an organization in a new direction and takes it to an entirely different level of effectiveness. Unlike 'turnaround (which implies incremental progress on the same plane) transformation implies a basic change of character and little or no resemblance with the past configuration or structure" (Business dictionary Online). Transformation is not decolonization in the sense that transformation as defined above only involves a process of changing something while still located within that thing or situation. Transformation becomes a postcolonial mask that appears to be committed to decolonization while in fact, it is a comforting word. By being a comforting word, transformation is used synonymously with decolonization to make people who fear decolonization and decoloniality a process of change.

Both transformation and decolonization have one thing in common, that is, change. Decoloniality is different from transformation because it is not changed for change's sake. It is a transformation that is based on the socio-political position that is influenced by the colonial transformation of the world. Often people fear and reach for their guns when we talk about decoloniality and blockchain technology and the things it has to offer. And others feel entitled to engage in forms of activism that involve attempting to decolonize the world through violence and burning down of things. Resistance is common to decolonization and blockchain technology, specifically the installation of 5G. And this has painted a bad picture about decoloniality from the position of people who want to still enjoy the privileges that come with white supremacy and white privilege. If one can take into consideration, "the goal of decolonial options does not take over, but to make clear, by thinking and doing, that global futures can no longer be thought of as one global future in which only one option is available; after all, when only one option is available, "option" entirely loses its meaning" (Mignolo 2011: 24). The contemporary modern global colonial world and its westernized universities including the curriculum humanities as it is, is the one which borders on absenteeism of the black body ontological as a human and academically as an object of study.

Whatever historical and political questions about the human subject are done at the abstraction and absenteeism of technology. The current colonial humanities are an embodiment and signifier of anything socially disgusting because it is inhumane most of the time led by anti-transformation and anti-decolonization management. To locate technology in an anti-transformed space the power of coloniality through coloniality of power is important to rethink. Decoloniality, therefore, borders on three registers namely coloniality of knowledge, coloniality of being, and coloniality of power.

Sabelo Ndlovu Gatsheni arges:

"…coloniality of power is in turn underpinned by colonial matrices of power that enables empire to take control… the process not only entails the reduction of defeated African chiefs into the lowest ranking colonial official responsible for supervision of Africans as providers of cheap labor during colonial encounters… it enables control of gender and sexuality… it enables control of subjectivity and knowledge, including the imposition of Euro-American epistemology and the sharping of formative processes of developing of black subjectivity (Ndlovu-Gatsheni 2013:31).

Therefore, to think of decolonizing not transforming the pedagogy, curriculum, and assessment we need to rethink deeply and be prepared, to be honest. The point of blockchain technology is to make things decentral, open, public, transparent, reusable, remixable, accessible, re-shareable, profitable, and most important, credible. As part of decentralization movement under blockchain technology, the metaverse can be a free space for the humanities that have been "defined by catalogues of deficits and series of lacks, lacking history, lacking writing, lacking souls, lacking civilization, lacking responsibility, lacking development, lacking human rights and lacking democracy" (Ndlovu-Gatsheni 2013: 4-5). The important pressing question about the construction of the globalizing world and its decolonial transformation is how to rid the colonial gap and the negative side of modernity, development, progress, and solidarity. Words or conceptions of modernity that are often thrown to suggest unity in the world, that can only exist beyond the technological abyssal line and traditional intelligence. Therefore, the metaverse shall present a world that is free from colonial/Eurocentric constructed deficits. Following the development of technology and the internet in the transforming "Pedagogical space" (Brown, Raymond 2005), the question of access and transformation of higher education should be at the center. While the dependence on technology grew even stronger during the time of the COVID-19 pandemic and they were changes in the ways work is done, teaching and learning are no exception. Many universities and institutions of learning that offered classroom-based learning were forced to adopt online education or e-learning.

In the South African context, few universities had already adopted online teaching and learning where open distance learning is conducted while the majority is still grappling with the idea of remote teaching and learning. Remote teaching and learning require a variety of technology, software, and an internet connection and as such, it becomes an expensive exercise. For many years the traditional classroom-based education offered its own experiences, benefits, and limits. Its benefits lie in the fact that it offered lived experience and learning that can be done through the tools that are offered in the classroom. It can be argued that although remote teaching and learning might come with the benefits of convenience and access, nothing that bit classroom-based learning. Looking at Leonardo da Vinci's Mona Lisa painting in a book or photograph is not the same as looking at its display on the wall of the Louvre Museum. However, the limit of the display is its demand for physical presence or face-to-face contact that requires the person to be at the gallery. It comes with cost and admin of booking many things including, traveling tickets, accommodation, viewing time with the museum and sometimes be prohibited to take photographs of the artworks displayed in the exhibition. Limits can be imposed by building maintenance, artwork loaned to another exhibition and unexpected lockdowns like during a pandemic like COVID-19.

Connecting to blockchain technology and the virtual space of the metaverse can overcome these limits by offering plug-and-go access to the viewing of the displayed artworks in the exhibition. The introduction of the metaverse, it is hoped to challenge the orthodox ways of teaching and learning. Therefore, nothing can overshadow the importance and value of what this chapter calls blended eLearning. Blended-eLearning can be identified as another key solution to obstacles that come with having to rely only on classroom-based learning. As a traditional practice, it has mostly favored those who are close to the university and its satellite compass. "Since the 1990s, several academic 'turns' have opened the academic and policy space to engage with alternative methodologies, as well as localised, everyday issues and their relevance for international politics (eg Lederach 1997; Mac Ginty and Richmond 2013, Bleiker 2001, 2009)". The development of blockchain technology potentially plays an important role to play in preparing the humanities for the offering of a decentralized and decolonized accessible education. Blockchain technology is a platform that hosts different digital tools including the metaverse. As a blockchain-based space, the metaverse is a virtual decentralized platform where users can create avatars to exist in this world.

To enter the metaverse, users create or chose their avatars that they will use as their login details to enter this digital virtual world. Just like in gaming, where a player needs some hardware device (Sony PlayStation, Microsoft Xbox, Nintendo, or Smartphone, etc.) and software (console games) to connect and play the game while sitting at home or the arcade games. The player chooses hardware based on preference and budget in as much as they can choose which game they want to play. Through playing a game, a player controls something that represents the player in the game they are playing, and the more they play the more they gain points while reaching the next level until the game is complete. In the strategic games, they will say until the mission is complete the player can keep playing according to the number of rounds (credits) that are given at the beginning of the game are finished. If the player finished their credits by coursing fouls before the mission is complete the game is over, and they get disqualified. However, if the player completes all the tasks at a given time and credit score they win the game and gain points. The metaverse operates similarly because it needs some hardware such VR headset, a computer, a tablet, and or a simple smartphone to be accessed. The difference between education in the metaverse from gaming is that the points will result in a qualification. Learning through the metaverse will mean the student (if we can use this term), will log in through an avatar that will be their representation throughout their life as a student. This means being a student one will have access to all the open-sources and free courses that will be available in the metaverse.

"Though coined quite some time ago, we use the term metaverse with the same semantics as... a collective virtual shared space, created by the convergence of virtually enhanced physical reality and physically persistent virtual space, including the sum of all virtual worlds, augmented reality, and the Internet... We use the term social metaverse to describe the above sorts of virtual realities in which a central purpose is socialization and interaction with other avatars — including both players and non-player characters (NPC's)" (Falchuk et al., 2018:53).

This definition of the metaverse means we must consider a virtual reality in which teaching and learning will operate to allow students/users to access open-resources, courses, and modules. Historically, the development of the metaverse introduced e-commerce, virtual reality (VR), and non-fungible tokens (NFTs) that contribute to the development of new ways of teaching and learning that will mean success for the students of the humanities. To understand some examples of the metaverse Falchuk et al., (2018:53) list the following.

"Examples of software systems considered social metaverses today include: Facebook Spaces, AltspaceVR, Sansar, High Fidelity, and many more. While the social metaverse may or may not include capabilities such as gamification, realistic physics, realistic 3D models, user-created content, or in-game economies, it is the complexity and nuance created by the presence of other avatars (human or not) that most motivates our work" (Falchuk et al., 2018:53).

The metaverse is a space that motivates lecturers or academics and curriculum developers to be open-minded about the different tools and services it can offer. The metaverse can work in a variety of ways for academics from researching, to developing study material, meeting students, setting, and marking exams, peer-review and publishing. The metaverse can work by making the process of peer-reviewing, co-writing, and publishing smooth and fast. This means the metaverse will be a platform where everyone can connect and log in to do their assignments anywhere they are in the world. Although there might be some concerns that "our privacy may be in jeopardy in ways we do not anticipate" (Falchuk et al., 2018:52) when we use the new internet let alone blockchain technology and the metaverse. Perhaps this is because this flexibility of the internet and open access to things is still a new phenomenon. Safeguarding and protecting personal information is still a matter of high concern.

CONCLUSION

Dealing with the COVID-19 pandemic and the different lockdown regulations made it tricky if not hard for many academics and educators who had to think about their students and how they can be able to finish their year syllabus. A pandemic such as COVID-19, which requires constant lockdown and quarantine, proved, and introduced a few things. The first of a few things it proved is that western modernity as an offering to the world is not complete. This is because western modernity was offered as a solution to many things that the knowledge of the so-called uncivilized non-European cultures cannot resolve, develop or dream of achieving even scientific. The influence of western modernity whitewashed everything in the globalizing world including knowledge, being, power, culture, education, and education about the history of those discoveries. Most specifically, science is at the top of epistemic weapons that were used to justify racism, slavery, and ethnic cleansing. As such, science proved not to be a panacea for all the problems of the world as it was presented. The second thing it proved is that classroom-based education and 8 to 5 workday cultures cannot be the only way of learning, working, or making money. This reveals that eLearning and most online learning platforms can offer more access in different ways. This chapter explores and contributes to the growing scholarship on blockchain technology, Web 3.0, and their possible solutions to teaching and learning in the humanities. The internet and its offerings are here to stay, and it will continually develop to be part of the human experiences at many different levels. Gardner's theory of multiple intelligence and decolonial epistemic perspective were deployed to foreground Artificial Intelligence and blockchain technology to understand how they can aid during teaching and learning. The new internet turn called Web 3.0 proves to be able to do more than what classroom-based education can offer. It will only require institutions of higher learning to be fully prepared and equipped with technology for the internet, and the academic staff and educators must constantly go under workshop training that will keep them updated with the new development of technology and new apps. The open resources and connectivity that blockchain technology and metaverse could provide the developing countries in the Global South are unlimited. Web 3.0 is not just the internet for surfing's sake, rather it is for surfing and creating content from one's position in the metaverse.

REFERENCES

Bleiker, R. (2001). The Aesthetic Turn in International Political Theory. *Millennium*, *30*(3), 509–533. doi:10.1177/03058298010300031001

Bleiker, R. (2009). *Aesthetics and World Politics*. Palgrave. doi:10.1057/9780230244375

Bod, R. (2022). History of the Humanities. *Histories, 2*, 178–184. 12020014 doi:0.3390/histories

Bod, R., Kursell, J., Maat, J., & Weststeijn, T. (2016). A New Field: History of Humanities. *History of Humanities*, *1*(1), 1–8. doi:10.1086/685056

Brown, R. (2005). *Exploring the notion of 'pedagogical space' through students' writings about a classroom community of practice*. Academic Press.

Descartes, R. (2004). A Discourse on Method: Meditations and Principles (J. Veitch, Trans.). Orion Publishing Group. (Original publication 1637)

Falchuk, B., Loeb, S., & Neff, R. (2018, June). The Social Metaverse: Battle for Privacy. *IEEE Technology and Society Magazine, 37*(2), 52–61. doi:10.1109/MTS.2018.2826060

Gardner, H. (2011). Frames of mind: The theory of multiple intelligences. New York: Basic Books. (Original publication 1983)

Gardner, H. (2013). *Frequently asked questions—Multiple intelligences and related educational topics.* https://howardgardner01.files.wordpress.com/2012/06/faq_march2013.pdf

Lederach, J. P. (1997). *Building Peace: Sustainable Reconciliation in Divided Societies.* United States Institute of Peace Press.

Mac Ginty, R., & Richmond, O. P. (2013). The local turn in peace building: A critical agenda for peace. *Third World Quarterly, 34*(5), 763–783. doi:10.1080/01436597.2013.800750

Mignolo, W. D. (2011a). *The darker side of Western modernity: global futures, decolonial options.* Duke UP.

Ndlovu-Gatsheni, S. J. (2013). *Empire, global coloniality, and African objection.* Berghahn Books.

Nevelsteen, K. J. L. (2017). Virtual world, defined from a technological perspective, and applied to video games, mixed reality and the meta-verse. *Comput Anim Virtual Worlds.* doi:10.1002/cav.1752

Oyewumi, O. (1997). *The invention of women: making an African sense of Western gender discourse.* University of Minnesota Press.

Tapping into multiple intelligences. (2004). Retrieved from https://www.thirteen.org/edonline/concept2class/mi/index.html

KEY TERMS AND DEFINITIONS

Blockchain Technology: This is a network of computers that oversee public Digital Ledger Technology which allows users to host various technologies and applications.

Coloniality of Knowledge: This is a second pillar of the decolonial epistemic perspective which means knowledge was colonized by placing European knowledge forward as the authority above all other non-European knowledge.

Decoloniality: This is a theoretical perspective and movement that stands to break the boundaries of modernity by revealing that there is no modernity without coloniality. It is a theoretical framework that represents and stands for new things, and new views and brings forth what was normally hidden by the Eurocentric and westernized oppressive system.

Metaverse: This is a virtual space that operates in blockchain technology to allow users to play games, buy virtual land, build galleries, and visit places with the click of a button.

Multiple Intelligence: This is a theory that was introduced by Howard Gardner to list 9 different intelligences that go beyond the traditional definition of intelligence.

Chapter 11

Supporting Student Success in Online Courses:
What COVID-19 Has Taught Us About Effective Teaching and Learning

Robert John Ceglie
https://orcid.org/0000-0002-1030-9568
Queens University of Charlotte, USA

ABSTRACT

The COVID-19 pandemic has offered many lessons for educators as this event has disrupted the lives of all students and teachers across the world. As all learning moved to some form of online instruction in early 2020, teachers and schools scrambled to modify current courses to move online and then to later design face-to-face courses to an online format. This shift to virtual instruction has not been easy, particularly for those teachers with little online teaching experience and for those courses that have not traditionally been offered online. This chapter offers some advice based on the author's experiences as well as an exploration of the current research, which suggests the best practices for online learning. It also offers three short cases that represent learning experiences that have helped shape the author's beliefs and actions.

INTRODUCTION

The worldwide pandemic caused by the COVID-19 virus has affected teaching and learning across the entire world. In early 2020, all students across the globe migrated from face-to-face instruction to some form of online learning. For most educators,

DOI: 10.4018/978-1-6684-4055-1.ch011

Copyright © 2023, IGI Global. Copying or distributing in print or electronic forms without written permission of IGI Global is prohibited.

this was an unfamiliar situation, as most teachers have had minimal training in how to teach in online environments (Forbes, 2020). Traditionally, teachers, particularly K-12 teachers, have seen online learning as an effective supplement to traditional face-to-face instruction. In 2020 however, online learning became the only viable way to continue learning for students across the world. Although this placed teachers in a new and uncomfortable position, it also left our students in unfamiliar territory. Many students encountered major challenges in adapting to online learning, and early evidence suggests that there will be major learning deficits in our students as a result of the move to online instruction (Angrist et al., 2021).

Even though the last few years have been among the most challenging times that educators at all levels have ever faced, it has also been a time for educators to reflect and evaluate their instructional practices. The necessary move to online teaching required educators to question what practices work the best for this mode of instruction. In addition, teachers needed to consider that their own traditional classroom practices which worked for in-school face-to-face instruction, might not transfer to an online environment. Thus, an entire new repertoire of teaching may have been necessary to effectively reach all students. This is particularly interesting because teachers are often very reluctant and slow to change their instructional practices (Weimer, 2016). In addition, not all online environments are the same, for example, synchronous learning is markedly different than asynchronous learning. Although these challenges have made the past few years extremely challenging, it has also offered opportunities for educators to learn and reflect upon their own teaching.

This chapter is an exploration of the changes in teaching and learning as educators transitioned to new instructional practices as a result of the COVID-19 Pandemic. The focus is primarily with those engaged in post-secondary education, however much of what has been uncovered applies across all levels of education. In this chapter, the aim to explore what practices have been most effective in online learning environments using available research as well as personal experiences to articulate some of the most valuable instructional strategies. While effective instructional practices often focus on what the teacher does, we do not want to minimize the student experience. Thus, we will also explore the learner experience in online environments, and what conditions and conditions students have found to be most conducive to their own learning. I will offer suggestions for ways to successfully modify instructional practices to better align with the current and future learning environments which are likely to continue to rely on some type of online instruction.

OVERVIEW OF EFFECTIVE INSTRUCTIONAL PRACTICES

Effective instructional practices are something that are acquired and refined over a long period of time (Kealey et al., 2000). At the collegiate level, teachers often experience some initial training in teaching in their graduate programs, some even as teaching assistants where they have received feedback on their practices. In many situations, teachers learn some of the key pedagogical tools from advisors and are able to "sample" these instructional practices in lower risk situations where they are often supervised by veteran faculty. As individuals begin university teaching positions, they further enhance their teaching practices. This is frequently complicated because college professors often teach a wide range of courses where different teaching styles are warranted. For example, what works in a large lecture introductory psychology course, is unlikely to succeed in a twenty-student discussion-based Ethics course. Over time, college faculty identify what strategies work best in their own discipline and context, and they utilize the evidence from their students' success to drive modifications in their practice.

One key feature of many effective teaching practices is that the teacher must design lessons which are student centered (Wright, 2011). In Maryellen Weimer's *Learner-Centered Teaching* (2002), she explains that instructional practices must consider the role of the following: 1) the power differential in a classroom, 2) the value or function of course content, 3) how the roles of teacher and student differ, 4) who is responsible for the learning, and 5) evaluation practices. She argues that good teachers provide lessons that require active participation by the student where they are required to reflect on the value and importance of the content. Instructors must find ways to promote interest and motivation to learn the content and help students take ownership of their learning. Good teachers show empathy, concern and respect for their students, all which help support modifications of teaching strategies when needed (Weimer, 2009). In addition to these ideas, other experts suggest additional factors that contribute to good teaching, these include providing a safe and organized learning environment, differentiating instruction for students, and the use of activating teaching styles (Noben et al., 2020).

The application of effective learning practices to online learning environments is not as simple as it sounds, as many of these factors can be challenging to implement. It is very likely that many teachers attempted to simply convert a face-to-face course to meet online without considering the implications for this change. In addition, most college faculty who may be experts in face-to-face learning, have limited training in online learning, although this has begun to change in recent years as more courses are being offered online (Roddy et al., 2017). The push to train and provide ongoing professional development to support college faculty as they increasingly engage in some form of online instruction has become a priority for many institutions,

228

especially ones with high enrollment in online courses (Gregory & Lodge, 2015). Additionally, online instructional practices have continued to evolve as Learning Management Systems and the tools they offer have changed. However, the COVID-19 Pandemic has not only accelerated the use of online teaching but necessitated it for all education. Unfortunately, for many teachers, the initial move online was a major challenge as there was virtually no time to plan and courses were also in the middle of the term in the Spring of 2020. When the following school year began in the Fall of 2020, faculty at colleges and universities were better prepared to teach online, and many colleges found opportunities to train their faculty over the summer. While this may have not been enough to truly support all faculty, it did offer professional development as well as needed time to plan and reorganize courses and consider alternative teaching strategies and activities to make the experience more beneficial for the learner (Telles-Langdon, 2020).

THEORETICAL FRAMEWORKS FOR ONLINE LEARNING

Constructivist learning theory offers the most commonly cited framework for understanding how students learn. If we also consider the social aspect of learning, we can explore how knowledge is fostered using socially based activities, the use of peer and instructor feedback, as well as related interactions in an online environment (Henning, 2004). Social learning theory provides the backbone for most relevant online learning theories, and it has a clear application to online learning (Ceglie, 2020).

A variety of scholars have attempted to design an inclusive framework which applies to all forms of online teaching and learning with the goal of helping teachers guide their instructional practices. One of the simpler models for online learning was created by Garrison, Anderson, and Archer (2000). In what they refer to as the Community Inquiry Model, they suggest they the key factors in online learning relate to the in-class interactions that occur and build social presence, teaching presence, and cognitive presence. The role of the instructor is to build presence though the climate, the transmission of content, and the use of discourse. This model for online learning was later revised by Anderson (2011), where he added additional details to account for the varying types of interactions that happen in an online class. These interactions include one that occur between student to student, student to content, teacher to content, and student to teacher. These forms of interactions are mediated by the types of tools used in online learning which serve as other related components within this theory. Anthony Picciano (2017) suggested one other relevant theory called the *Multimodal model for online education* which contains components similar to Anderson's initial work but also includes addition online elements such as social emotional learning and collaboration as important factors. One interesting feature of this model is the view that learning is dependent on a learning community being formed in the class. This learning community is similar to the work done by Wenger (2011) and posits that effective learning occurs when a community of learners is built and supported. Both Anderson and Picciano highlight the importance of the learning environment and the type of communities that are fostered in the virtual classroom, and these thus become essential to achieve student learning.

One more recent addition to current online learning theories suggests that effective online environments need to specifically build a sense of belonging which if often defined as an individual's perceived cohesion within a group and includes interactions that are academic and social (Hurtado & Carter, 1997). There is a wealth of studies that have used this framework to explore persistence and retention in college students (Hurtado & Carter, 1997; Pascarella & Terenzini, 2005). Sense of belonging appears to be supported when instructors serve as the mediators and design learning activities that engage all students and promote dynamic and socially based learning, which are sometimes absent in online environments. Work conducted by Peacock and Cowan (2019) concluded that student outcomes in online courses are often dependent on whether a teacher supports a strong sense of community of learners. They explained "Educational research suggests that students who feel accepted and valued, that they are important to the life and activity of the class, develop a strong SoB (sense of belonging), which is important for all" (p. 78). Since the idea of sense of belonging is linked to the types of activities and interactions that are fostered in a course, it is important to explore what activities are most supportive to foster student success. When we couple this idea with the other key factors highlighted by Anderson and Picciano, we get a sense for the type of critical factors that one must consider when teaching online courses.

EFFECTIVE ONLINE PRACTICES

The push to move to online instruction which occurred as a result of the COVID-19 Pandemic not only necessitated that faculty changed their usually preferred mode of instruction to an unfamiliar format, but also forced teachers to reconsider what teaching practices were most effective for them in an online environment. What works for one in the face-to-face classroom was unlikely to be easily transferred to the online learning environment. One key component to this beyond the obvious environment, is the fact that a great deal of online coursework is typically done in an asynchronous format. Thus, not only must an instructor consider that students are not physically in the same location, but also consider how one can consume information in an asynchronous environment.

230

Formatting Instruction: Asynchronous vs Synchronous Teaching and Learning

It is safe to assume that the typical college professor likely preferred teaching online using a synchronous environment. This, of course, would be the closest situation to the environment that they are most accustomed. Similarly, this is also likely the easiest way to modify one's usual lessons and still be able to create a supportive environment where collaboration and discussion is possible. However, for many instructors and students, the hectic environment caused by the pandemic disrupted many normal patterns both at school and at home. Because of this, it may have been better for instructors to utilize an asynchronous format to support the additional needs and challenges which occurred during the pandemic. Both synchronous and asynchronous environments have their merits and challenges and what works in one situation or content area may not be effective in all areas.

Synchronous Learning

In many ways, synchronous teaching and learning mimics what most teachers would classify as normal classroom practices. Many of the main advantages of synchronous learning relate to the ability to connect and engage with students in real-time. The new tools available such as the use of videoconferencing software such as Zoom and Microsoft Teams, provided a relatively stable medium for "meeting" as an online class. These tools support two-way audio and video, allow for the grouping of students, and also offer simultaneous text-based chat features. The learning curve for mastering these tools is not too steep and once learned, teachers may feel this is the best way to mimic the traditional classroom setting. There have been several studies that examined the types of interactions that occur in synchronous classrooms when compared to those in asynchronous environment. Chou (2002) compared the quality of discussions that occurred during the different class types. She found that in the synchronous learning environments, there was a higher percentage of social emotional interactions, the students spent more time on task-oriented discussions, and there was a higher amount of two-way interactive exchanges. Peterson and colleagues (2018) studied 52 undergraduate students who were assigned to synchronous or asynchronous interaction groups within an online course. They found that those who worked in the asynchronous groups struggled with cooperative group learning situations. In addition, they achieved a lower sense of belonging and more negative emotions arose during the activities. These and other studies (e.g., Mabrito, 2006; Martin et al., 2021; Molnar & Kearney, 2017) demonstrate that high quality discussions and interactions occur less frequently in asynchronous online courses.

Although research supports the value of synchronous learning and many teachers and students may even prefer this mode, lessons learned during the COVID-19 Pandemic may suggest that this is not the always best avenue for instruction. One of the biggest concerns for synchronous learning is the fact that it occurs at a specified time, and although one can record a live lesson for viewing at another time, this eliminates the real-time interaction and can minimize class to that of a YouTube video. As COVID disrupted the lives of all members of society and caused role changes for many, being available at a specific time to join class was a challenge. For some, new responsibilities changed schedules, for others, the ability to find a stable Internet connection was a challenge. In addition, teachers must also be careful to consider that not all students may be in the same time zone or even in the same country, and thus one must be careful to explore the potential impact of the timing of the live class and how this may influence a student's life or ability to participate. Given these disadvantages of the use of synchronous learning, it is important for faculty to consider if using this mode would put some students as a disadvantage and may make it impossible for others to participate. Although there is no correct answer for what format is best, many have found that the asynchronous model may be the best option given the drawbacks of the live class.

Asynchronous Learning

The use of asynchronous modes of "online instruction" has been around since the beginning of correspondence schools in the 1950s-60s (Ceglie, 2020). The progression from the early days of online instruction has been transformed with the advent of the current Learning Management Systems (LMS). The current platforms such as Blackboard, Canvas, and Moodle offer many teaching tools that support an active and engaging classroom environment. While these platforms cannot duplicate the personal nature of face-to-face instruction, tools such as discussion boards, video responses, and even live video chats can provide many similar experiences for both students and instructors. Research that has examined the effectiveness of asynchronous learning has found that in many cases is not significantly different than learning through the use of the asynchronous format (Roblyer, 2007; Skylar, 2009). However as discussed above, these types of courses can be more challenging to build a sense of community and some research suggests that they may be less effective in motivating students (Huang et al., 2015). Perhaps the greatest advantage of these platforms and asynchronous learning is the flexibility it offers to students. Depending on the layout of the course, students can complete their work at times that are convenient for them. With the disruptions that occurred during COVID-19, students may have found this option to work for their current needs (Basri et al., 2021).

Case 1: A Blend of Synchronous and Asynchronous Teaching

As the fall of 2020 was set to begin, many schools intended to return to some type of face-to-face instruction, however the continued pandemic forced many colleges to return to online only instruction. At my institution, this meant we would be online in the fall and students would not be returning to campus. For my classes, this forced me to again revise my course to online only. When I began to plan the course for online instruction, I had to consider whether to hold the classes synchronous or asynchronous. I was lucky because I already knew the students who would be in my classes. In addition, most of the students lived locally or within the same time zone, but I also had some students that were in different time zones, in addition I had one international student.

My experiences with these students informed me that they would prefer the flexibility of an asynchronous format, but I also knew that many complained about the lack of connection with faculty from the previous term. Several weeks prior to the start of the semester, I emailed the class and asked students if they had a preference for online format and asked them to explain their choice, so I had a better understanding of their circumstances. I knew that since the students were not on campus, it was likely that many would have additional responsibilities such as work, which they would now be adding to their schedule, thus making it harder to make class at a specific time. The responses to the email were mixed, and about half chose each format. The reasons for the choices were as expected. Many students noted that they would be working different hours now that they would be home. However, others were unhappy that we were online and preferred the synchronous format which more closely mimicked the traditional learning environment. I had a difficult choice to make.

I decided to make the class a mix between asynchronous and synchronous. This certainly made the planning and implementation of the course more challenging on my part, but I felt it was the right thing to do to meet the needs of my students. To make the synchronous portion more accessible to students I divided the class into two groups, so when we meet in a live format, the students could choose to attend the morning (9 am) or night (7 pm). In addition, I divided the course into six modules, which helped me better organize the material and activities. Thus, we meet live for six of the fifteen weeks, one for each of the modules. I also created groups of students for the collaborative work in the course. This allowed the scheduling of students when they had the best availability. Overall, I believe this format worked well. The response throughout the semester was positive as was a survey I sent to them at the end of the term. The students appreciated the flexibility and also found that the live sessions made the course feel more like a traditional face-to-face course.

There is not an abundance of research that has studied this issue, but the few studies that I found had similar results (e.g., Dickinson & Gronseth, 2020).

Supporting Community Building in Online Courses

The research is clear that one of the necessary conditions for effective online learning is that there is meaningful interaction between the students and the instructor (Harper, 2018). As discussed above, it is important that the instructor design courses that build the capacity for students to have a sense of belonging. Lewis and Abdul-Hamid (2006) explain that one of the most important parts of online teaching is "fostering an online atmosphere with vibrant interaction among students and between the instructor and the students" (p. 87). One of the easiest and most effective ways to initiate these qualities is to begin the course with an opening video by the instructor. In this video, it is best for the instructor to provide some background on themselves as well as discuss the importance for dialogue throughout the course. As a follow-up to the opening video, one can ask students to create their own video introduction to the class. This is much more personal than a simple "getting to know you" discussion post and this allows the students to get a better sense of who their classmates are. Using these strategies sets a positive and welcoming tone for the course which one aims to carry out throughout the semester.

The use of discussion boards has been the traditional choice that instructors use for adding some form of interaction in online courses (Swan, 2002). Studies have also found that high participation rates in online discussion boards is one indicator of better performance (Michinov, et al., 2011). In addition, the most effective use of discussion posting builds a community of learners (Ouyang & Scharber, 2017). In addition, there are a number of research-based strategies that support effective use of discussion board including:

a) Increasing social presence by modeling social cues and norms by being more personal and maintaining social norms.
b) Using discussion prompts which encourage structured interaction and critical thinking, including problem based, project based, and debate style prompts.
c) Prompt, personal, and engaging feedback and replies. This can occur through higher-level questioning strategies which facilitate critical thinking and reflection.
d) Consider using multimedia tools such as video and audio, in the feedback and posts.
e) Encourage students to facilitate peer interaction through sharing of knowledge and questioning strategies. (DeNoyelles et al., 2014)

The suggestions offered above have been studied and shown to be effective, but they rely heavily on the instructor to lead the way. In too many cases, discussion posting has become a tedious task which students may consider to be busywork (Cox, 2011). Instructors need to use these strategies to help build and support student engagement. Since we know that engagement increases satisfaction which then enhances motivation, finding ways to maximize meaningful interaction is critical (Martin & Bolliger, 2018). When interacting, it is also helpful to find ways to personalize the experience as this helps build ownership for the learner (Covelli, 2017). Sometimes simply using student's names in responses helps build connections. Additionally, effective discussion builds a supportive community in courses and ultimately improves a student's experience.

The key role of the instructor is to help model the types of interactions that one expects in the course, and this must be done in the first post or students will have a harder time following. It can also be helpful to share specific directions or exemplars with students. Judith Boettcher, the Executive Director of the Corporation for Research and Educational Networking at The University of Nevada-Reno, suggests that an effective strategy for discussion posts can be thought of as a three-part response. If the discussion asks an opened ended question related to a particular problem, there are a few steps in the reply. First, state your thoughts on the topic. Second, consider ones own personal connection or relationship to the question prompt. This can also be the knowledge that one has about the topic and may be a place where one cites references. Finally in the third part, the student states what they would like to know more about as related to the topic. This might also take the form of a question (Writing a successful discussion board post, n.d.). Using this type of model for the students assists them in conveying their thoughts on the topic while also drawing on their personal knowledge and connections to the topic. I have found that if I am very personal and curious in my initial posts, students gain some comfort and appear to open up more as they recognize that I am creating a safe and supportive environment for them to share. Asking a question at the conclusion of the post helps generate thoughts and interactions with their students who might be drawn into the conversation. When this positive environment is created and nurtured, the effect can be very similar to what one experiences in a live face-to-face classroom discussion.

Effective Use of Video

The use of video to supplement assignments in online courses comes in several different forms. The most obvious one is the use of video to record lectures, whether synchronous or asynchronous. There is strong research evidence to suggest that the use of video to deliver content in online courses does improve student learning. This is particularly true when courses are designed as self-paced modules where students can work at their own pace throughout the term. Brecht and Ogilby's (2008) study of a large lecture-based college course found that there was a positive impact on the students who used the video lectures to supplement their learning. In addition, they found that those who didn't watch the videos had a significantly higher failure rate than those who did watch them. One familiar idea is the use of videos that students would watch prior to class, and this has been described as the Flipped Model. Its primary goal is to free up class time for discussion or more in-depth study and thus idea has become popular over the past decade as video has become easier to create and share. Missildine and colleagues (2010) explored the flipped classroom model in a study of 589 nursing students where they compared the flipped model to both a traditional lecture only environment as well as a full video lecture. They found a significant exam score advantage for those in the flipped model as well as a significantly higher student satisfaction for this group when compared to the other two models. Scagnoli et al. (2019) studied student experiences of video lectures in an online environment. 96 college students participated in qualitative and quantitative surveys and the authors found "that VL (video lecture) play an influential role in students' online learning experience in terms of their satisfaction and learning impact" (p. 403). In addition, they found that the use of the video lecture enhanced the feelings of engagement with the course material. Collectively, these studies illustrate the progression of the use of video to supplement and provide the main instruction in online classes. Additionally, the positive outcomes suggest that its use can produce positive outcomes for engagement and achievement in students taking online courses. During the two years when COVID-19 had the greatest impact in the format of college courses, instructors increasingly used video both as the primary means to deliver content, as well as a way to supplement all forms of learning.

There are some situations where the use of video may not provide the effective learning outcomes we anticipate. The move of classes to an online format for all classes during COVID-19 led to the possibility that students would be watching live or recorded video all the time, something that even under the best circumstances is different from being face-to face in a classroom. Thus, some have suggested that "Zoom Fatigue" is having a negative effect on our students (Ramachanran, 2021). There have been some empirical studies that have explored if the length of video lectures had any impact on engagement and learning. Kinnari-Korpela (2015) surveyed college level math students and found that shorter lecture videos supported both student engagement and learning. In a second study, Pursel and Fang (2011) found that when they used video lessons for their lessons, students only watched select portions of the video lecture and not the whole videos. These and other studies suggest that there are some key practices that would best guide instructors in their use of video as a form of instruction or lecture. Guo et al. (2014) provide the following ideas based on the research of 6.9 million video sessions across four courses they had access to on their MOOC platform:

- It is better to plan video lessons to be in chunks shorter than six minutes to maximize student engagement.
- Filming in an informal setting (as oppressed to standing in front of a classroom) will provide a more personal experience for students.
- Teachers need to express their enthusiasm and excitement for the content while at the same time making sure they do not speak too quickly as to confuse students.
- Students tend to be more engaged in a "Talking head video" where they are watching the instructor as opposed to watching a slide or the teacher writing on a tablet or board.

The use of video for filming lessons does not only have to be used for the purpose of providing a lecture. In fact, Guo et al. (2014) found that teachers can effectively use video as a tutorial tool, particularly for classes such as math or performing arts. In these cases, the students are more likely watching some instructions which provide step by step directions which may be watched over and over. Another more novel use of video is in its application in discussion boards. As described earlier, discussion boards have traditionally been utilized as a way to build community within a course, however the majority of instructors likely have not considered using the newer video tools. In the last few years, Learning Management Systems (LMS) have embedded more user-friendly interfaces that enable the user and instructor to insert video throughout a course. A research team led by Clark compared the use of a text-based discussion to an asynchronous video-based discussion in an online course. They found that "video-enabled discussions were more effective at helping create social and teaching presence when compared with text-based discussion platforms." (Clarke et al., 2015, p. 60). Video discussion also rated higher for "teaching presence" which helped students view the teacher as a part of the discussion. Most instructors open their online courses with some type of personal or course introduction and often start the first discussion board where students introduce themselves to the class. One easy consideration is to open the class modeling an introduction video then have the students complete a similar video introduction instead of a text-based one. This practice has the potential to set the tone for the rest of the course and is something that I have personally used frequently in my courses with a great deal of success.

One other application of video can be in the way that instructors provide student feedback. The advent of tools such as Voicethread, have made it easier to provide student feedback directly on student work. Voicethread is an application which allows users to insert audio and video comments in a document in the same way one might insert text comments in a Word document. In addition to this application, all LMS's now have ways to add video and audio feedback to most of the work that students submit. While this may be a time-consuming endeavor, this has been shown to build instructor social presence and develop a closeness with students (Borup et al., 2014). Mahoney and colleagues (2019) completed a qualitative meta-analysis of the use of video feedback in higher education. They reviewed 37 studies which focused on the use of video feedback. The research implies that students appreciated the use of video feedback and that it also has a positive effect on student engagement and relationship building. What is less clear, is the impact that it has on student learning outcomes and the authors suggest that more larger scale studies are needed to better understand the impact.

A final suggested application of video in online courses is as an alternative medium to evaluate student performance. Fields that rely on some type of performance-based assessment such as teacher education, physical education, and health professions have been quicker to explore the value of video as a means to assess students. A literature review by Felthun et al. (2021) found that there are several studies that exist in the health profession fields where they have successfully used a form of video assessment to accurately evaluate student performance. They note that the results have been positive in terms of the reliability and validity of the assessment, but additional research is still needed as the research base is slim. Kramer et al. (2020) analyzed the use of video assessment on the evaluation of in-service biology teachers. The designed evaluation tool was found to be both valid and reliable in measuring the "professional vision" which is a "mediating situation-specific skill between cognitive dispositions and classroom performance" (p. 2). Although these examples are exploring the summative evaluation value of video, there are other studies that have found that video can be a valuable tool in the formative assessment of learning as well (Dohms, et al., 2020. Zheng, et al., 2021).

Case 2: Video as an Outlet for Reflection and Emotional Responses

Teaching controversial topics in any discipline can be a challenge on many fronts. In science, fostering discussions in areas such as climate change or vaccination requirements can range from environments where a few students dominate the discussion to situations where no one feels free to speak. In some cases, having students engage in difficult discussions in online platforms can be easier as some students feel freer to share because there is some level of anonymity when being online (Artanti, 2020). During a series of online classes within a science methods course, the issue of climate change was reviewed and studied. Following the viewing of the documentary *Before the Flood*, in which Leonardo DiCaprio explores climate change, the class engages in a reflective discussion. In past semesters, the effectiveness of the class discussion has been mediocre at best, as students typically appear hesitant to take a position on a controversial topic in front of their peers. COVID-19 necessitated that this course be taught online twice and instead of having a class discussion, I employed the use of video as a tool to share responses. I asked students to create a 5-minute video reflection on their personal opinions of climate change given all the material we had covered in class. I informed them that these videos would be shared with their classmates who would also have the ability to add text-based comments. In the two semesters that I have employed this method of "discussion," I had the most reflective and emotional responses from students. While this finding is subjective, this was not something I had planned nor expected. I used the video option because I expected a discussion post would not garner much of a meaningful response and I feared getting another lukewarm class discussion, albeit online, would be similar to what was traditionally done in class. Did the use of the video free students to speak more openly? Does simply being online reduce some of the fear for how peers may have responded? These and other questions suggest that this is something that needs to be explored, however, what is clear is that something about the use of online video leant itself to freeing student inhibitions in this particular situation.

Rethinking Delivery Of Course Content

Online teaching necessities that the instructor consider not only the way that a course is taught but also some consideration on the wide range of resources and tools that the online world affords to both the teacher and learner. Those who frequently teach online are likely aware of ways to modify one's teaching style to better utilize the Internet and related tools. In addition, the past decade has led to many innovations and features that have become available using the Learning Management Systems (LMS), including the ways that textbook publishers have designed course materials to support online teaching and learning. These course cartridges can be imported into ones LMS and they are able to offer additional material to support learning such as proprietary videos, interactive assignments, and readings. In addition, some companies have been able to add interactive case studies and even simulations for areas such as education and the health sciences. While these can often be found in other locations online, the LMS and cartridge allows for a streamlined experience for the user. Most of the publishers also offer assessment materials which can also be easily embedded into the online course. Instructors can also utilize these as forms of formative assessment to help students prepare for tests and quizzes. While these materials are separate from the actual LMS, most of these are so easily integrated it can be hard to distinguish them. Those who traditionally have taught using face-to-face formats may be unfamiliar with these tools but the move to online teaching during the past few years may have brought some awareness. As these materials are becoming increasingly utilized, it is safe to assume that many instructors will continue to use them even when a return to traditional in-class instruction occurs.

The LMS provide a wealth of tools beyond what textbook publishers have provided. The traditional tools include discussion boards, announcement pages, places to manage course assignments, and quizzes and tests. What has become more robust in recent years is the ease and sophistication of the available communication tools which can "help in providing space for rich online learning environment, and to utilize its tools and functionalities to improve pedagogy and to increase the quality of learning" (Al-Sharhan et al., 2020, p. 15). These tools can be applied in both synchronous and asynchronous environments and they often support communication within the course. Several LMS's now have an option for real-time video, audio, and text-based communication embedded into the course. Thus, a student can simply be logged into their online course and discuss virtually with a teacher or peer. An instructor can offer office hours by login into the LMS application. This tool also facilitates group interactions and space for group projects. These communication and collaborative tools would prove valuable as courses migrated online during COVID and would have allowed many of the usual dynamics and pedagogical strategies to continue in this environment. In addition, these also added a level of flexibility for students which was much appreciated as students' schedules became less predictable with new demands at home or work.

One of the advantages that I have learned as a result of the movement of courses online was the ease of integrating multimedia content and Internet resources into my instructional practices. Presenting material on the Internet, especially when scrolling or interacting with a website can be a challenge when in front of a classroom full of students. However, the ability to seamlessly scroll through website and resources online as students can view my screen opened a new world of material of which I would typically be hesitant to use in a face-to-face class. One example is the use of an animation which demonstrates the science behind force and motion. Using the animation, I can quickly change the settings and move objects to demonstrate the concepts. In addition, since all of the students are already online, they can easily interact with the application to practice on their own. This could be done in a traditional setting, but it would require more resources, more management issues, and more time.

As I have become more comfortable using the Internet in this way, I have found that I am also more freely able to use just-in-time teaching lessons. "Just-in-Time Teaching is a pedagogical strategy that employs the Internet to develop and utilize a feedback loop between students and instructors that exists both in class and out of class" (Formica, 2010, p. 2). This strategy often uses web-based resources to promote active learning by assigning an activity prior to class and then using class time to discuss and advance the ideas presented. Science teachers may utilize this method as it helps build conceptual understanding, especially when used in conjunction with Internet resources (Novak et al., 1999). A teacher may choose to start their class with a short online survey using one of the survey tools such as www.polleverywhere.com and gain immediate feedback which the directs the next part of the lesson. I have used this idea in both math and science courses where the in-class discussion of the topic leads to class ventures into online resources to build understanding. In my experience, I have found this strategy to be very effective as I moved these classes online. The flexibility and abundance of resources available online have deepened my use of the Internet in my lessons and I believe provided more active and engaging learning for my students.

Designing an Effective Online Classroom

If you ask an elementary teacher to get their classroom prepared for the first day of school, they will typically decorate and organize their classroom. They will have places to store student work and handouts. A calendar in the front of the room with children's birthdays and other important dates on it. All the neatly organized desks and cubbies provide students will places to do their work and store their lunches. And a class would not be complete with posters around the room, with at least one providing the class rules that all will observe. Can you apply these actions in an online class? If this type of order is so important in these classes, why is this any different when teaching a course online? While every student in college has now experienced some form of online learning, many were still new to this mode of instruction when the pandemic started. Thus, even those who had some online learning experience needed to gain access to their online courses, learn to navigate the LMS which their school was using, and learn or find all of the necessary tools utilized for online instruction. Unfortunately, this process is not straightforward for all students, especially those who have never taken online courses or have been out of college for some time. These new students need time adjusting to college, let alone trying to navigate an unfamiliar learning environment. It is likely that many teachers take the basic necessitates for online teaching for granted, especially as many were new to online teaching when COVID-19 pushed all courses online.

One of the major complaints that students have about online learning is that courses can be unorganized and difficult to find or navigate through the course content (Chen, 2016). Research has demonstrated that when students encounter these issues, it can lead to frustration, lack of focus, and even poor learning outcomes (Zeng & Wang, 2021). The majority of these problems likely stem from the lack of expertise in instructional or course design. This would be particularly problematic for teachers who had little online teaching experience prior to the pandemic (Abrahamsson &

Lopez, 2021). Luckily, studies have explored what qualities make course design better for student navigation which then can have a positive influence on their learning. There are a number of theories and models that suggest the best way to organize online classes and most have the theory of universal design as the foundation.

Universal design (UDL) began being applied for course design in the 1990s using the current learning theories as the background for its utilization. UDL provides a framework for how a learning environment can be best designed to be accessible to all learners, with special attention placed on this with disabilities (Dickinson & Gronseth, 2020). The key focus areas for the designer are providing multiple means for engagement with the course content, multiple representations of the material, and multiple opportunities for engagement with the material and assessments. In sum, "UDL principles can serve as a compass to identify barriers and to maximize learning experiences" (p. 1008) and has increasingly been used to design both online and face-to-face courses. One outgrowth of the UDL movement is the creation of guides for instructors and schools as they redesign their courses. With the increasing online offerings occurring this decade, other educators have applied the UDL principles to similar instructional design models. Perhaps the more relevant to online teaching is the work done by Quality Matters (QM), which is a non-profit organization who certifies online courses. Quality Matters has designed rubrics to assist schools as they design and implement online courses. They use a set of eight general standards and 42 specific review standards that are used to evaluate the design of both online and blended courses (Quality Matters, 2021). In addition, they certify courses as QM approved when they meet the requirements and are reviewed by a peer committee. QM does not evaluate the implementation of the teaching methods, rather they only focus on the design which in turn influences how courses are perceived and enacted by students.

Quality Matters is certainly not the only guide to support the building of effective course designs. Li-Ling Chen (2016) conducted a literature review and synthesis of research on effective online instructional designs. Chen proposes that there are five basic principles for designing and developing effective online courses. These five characteristics include Identify, Choose, Create, Engage, and Evaluate (ICCEE Model). These can also be viewed as steps in the design of a course. One identifies the course format and then identifies potential course objectives and content. This step also requires the instructor to explore the applicable technologies which may be beneficial to meeting the course objectives. In the Choose step, the instructor now chooses what elements will become part of the course, including the content, tools, and organization. Once these elements have been chosen, the instructor moves to the Create stage where they begin to build their course. At this point, one will develop materials, activities, assignments, and assessments. In order to support an effective learning environment, ways to keep the learner engaged in the course are employed. This step focuses on how communication and community building are supported in the course. The final step in the model is Evaluate, and Chen notes that instructors should utilize multiple strategies to assess students. Chen explains that this model "can provide online educators or instructors an effective guidance and checklist when designing online course materials. A proper implementation of the model can support online student's engagement, involvement, motivation, and focus on learning" (p. 2307). The ICCEE model can be used in conjunction with the rubrics provided by Quality Matters to provide guidance as one designs an online course. While there are other resources and models, many provide a very similar framework as presented in these examples (e.g. Kathuria & Becker, 2021). Regardless of the specific framework used, the COVID-19 Pandemic has forced so many courses to be taught online, and it is advisable for schools and educators to utilize these tools to support the main structural design of their courses.

Case 3: Applying Quality Matters to Online Courses

Several years ago, my institution began exploring the value of the Quality Matters certification for our online course offerings. As one of the more experienced and "expert" online faculty at our university, I was approached to complete training in the Quality Matters program. I did not anticipate learning much as I have been designing and teaching online courses for two decades. Over the course of a summer, I completed the entry level Quality Matters Peer Reviewer Training and the Quality Matters Applying the Rubric Training. This enabled me to be an official Quality Matters reviewer for any institution. The certification would provide me opportunities to support our university's new program offerings however, the greatest impact would be on my own courses. Despite my impression that I was an "expert" on online teaching, I quickly learned that I had a long way to go to make my online courses at the quality that they needed to be. Over the next year, which also coincided with the start of the COVID-19 Pandemic, I revised several of my courses to adhere to the QM guidelines. Although my courses were generally well organized, I lacked many of the accessibility requirements which would have hindered success for students with certain disabilities. In addition, I needed to reorganize some of my activities to better align with my intended objectives. The courses which I had been teaching online were once taught in a face-to-face format and as I converted this class to be an online course offering, I had failed to modify the course enough. As I was beginning the improvement process for my online courses, COVID-19 hit, and all my classes moved online. During the transition to complete the first semester courses using online only, I was in survival mode and did what I could to successfully complete those courses. However, when the following year started in an online format, I spent the extra time and effort to apply the QM Rubric to all my courses and believe that the enhancements have made a significant difference in improving the student experience. My advice to instructors is to review the rubrics provided by Quality Matters as they are freely accessible and are a great resource to support effective online learning. They can be found at the Quality Matters website. https://www.qualitymatters.org/qa-resources/rubric-standards/higher-ed-rubric

RECOMMENDATIONS AND DISCUSSION

The COVID-19 Pandemic which began in early 2020, may be the most significant event that has impacted how we educate students. The advent of more advanced technologies has made the option of online teaching and learning a necessary reality to students, only some who had already participated in online courses. The social distancing demands which forced us out of the classroom now necessitated that we use these technologies to move all learning to some type of online format. As the Pandemic eventually fades and allows face-to-face learning to return as the norm, many have questioned how much this will impact the future of schooling (Popa, 2020). Most argue that while virtual instruction is not necessarily the future of education, we are moving into a world where forms of online instruction will remain as one part of an individual's educational experience (Hu et al, 2021, Reuge et al., 2021).

What the COVID-19 Pandemic has taught us is that we can continue to deliver effective instruction using the online tools we have at our disposal. While we may not be able to perfectly mirror the face-to-face learning experience, we have a better understanding of how to support effective online learning. The implementation of an effective learning environment begins with the design of the course. The structure of the learning environment sets the stage for a learner and a well-organized and carefully thought-out design and layout of one's course is essential. Not only does this minimize student frustration but has clear implications for their outcomes (Jaggars& Xu, 2016). "Course design facilitates instruction by helping to structure content, engage learners, and simplify navigation. All decisions made about online courses and teaching should support student learning" (Baldwin & Ching, 2019). The use of the Quality Matters Rubrics and guides such as the ICCEE model, provide direction to help instructors in their design of online courses.

An extension of the design of a course is a consideration for the mode of instruction, namely whether one is using a synchronous or asynchronous design. It is important to realize that this is not an either-or choice. We can still design a course that is mindful of our students lives and build flexible learning in a blended format where we add some synchronous opportunities throughout a course. Depending on the familiarity with the students, a survey can be taken to gauge the availability of students and then plan accordingly, thus maintaining a great deal of flexibility for students. The instructor then can choose how to embed live teaching. This may take the form of duplicating a lecture or lesson for multiple groups or can occur how the instructor designs and implements groupwork or in-class activities. Although this is asking more work on the instructor's part, providing some form of live interaction can be important to many students' learning needs (Zydney, 2019).

Teachers are clearly experiencing how different online learning can be when compared to the traditional face-to-face environments. However, as a result of the experiences during the Pandemic, teachers have found that there are effective tools which can make the online experience much less sterile and impersonal. The environment and tone that the instructor sets at the beginning of an online course is only the starting point for building a supportive and inviting environment. Video is an excellent tool which can be effectively weaved throughout any online course. We suggest setting the tone for a class with a personal welcoming video to start a course and follow that by asking students to complete their own introductory videos to share with the class. In addition, video is an excellent tool to use throughout the course such an embedded it in discussion board posting, in assessing student work, and in announcement posts throughout the course. Video conferencing tools are also now readily available and opportunities to utilize live video adds engagement and teacher presence within a course (Bialowas & Steimel, 2019).

Building a community of learners is important in any course but this is particularly the case for online classes where students can become isolated from their courses and peers (Croft et al.,2010; Stepich & Ertmer, 2003). There are many strategies that an instructor can take to support student engagement and interaction. Meaningful reflective discussion posts which connect the course content to real-world applications can make the discussion forums more engaging and inviting (Nicholoson & Bond, 2003). It is best when instructors become part of discussion posts, not only to model posting, but also to build relationships and connections. In addition, it is supportive when using students' names and paying attention to specifics within their posts. Another strategy is to create assignments and activities that make the material relevant and personal to the learner, although this is no different than what one would typically do in a course, it can be a great way to support motivation and engagement in the course materials (Panigrahi et al., 2018). The range of resources available on the Internet can make lessons more engaging and active, and thus it is important to explore videos, animations, simulations, and other unique materials which the technology tools enable. Finally, feedback on student work is essential, not just in summative assignments but throughout the learning process. Experience and research support the view that frequent and timely feedback are important to student learning (Martin et al., 2018). Collectively, these ideas and activities can help support a positive and supportive learning environment and build a sense of ownership and community in one's courses.

This chapter has presented an amalgamation of personal and research-based practices to support effective online learning. The COVID-19 Pandemic has disrupted the lives of teachers and students, as we have collectively searched for resources to support the move to online instruction. We all have learned a great deal from the experience, and hopefully some of the ideas in this chapter resonate in your own experiences. What the future holds for schooling is uncertain, but most believe that some form of online learning will continue to be a part of our lives forever. The lessons that we learn along the way will make us better designers, teachers, and learners which promote positive outcomes for our students.

REFERENCES

Abrahamsson, S., & Dávila López, M. (2021). Comparison of online learning designs during the COVID-19 pandemic within bioinformatics courses in higher education. *Bioinformatics (Oxford, England)*, *37*(Supplement 1), i9–i15. doi:10.1093/bioinformatics/btab304 PMID:34252967

Al-Sharhan, S., Al-Hunaiyyan, A., Alhajri, R., & Al-Huwail, N. (2020). Utilization of learning management system (LMS) among instructors and students. In Z. Zakaria & R. Ahmad (Eds.), *Advances in Electronics Engineering, Lecture Notes in Electrical Engineering* (Vol. 619, pp. 15–23). Springer. doi:10.1007/978-981-15-1289-6_2

Anderson, T. (2011). *The theory and practice of online learning* (2nd ed.). AU Press.

Angrist, N., de Barros, A., Bhula, R., Chakera, S., Cummiskey, C., DeStefano, J., Floretta, J., Kaffenberger, M., Piper, B., & Stern, J. (2021). Building back better to avert a learning catastrophe: Estimating learning loss from COVID-19 school shutdowns in Africa and facilitating short-term and long-term learning recovery. *International Journal of Educational Development*, *84*, 102397. doi:10.1016/j.ijedudev.2021.102397

Artanti, Y. (2020). Online Content Sharing Behavior: A Review on the Social Psychology Perspective. *2nd International Research Conference on Economics and Business, Malang*, Indonesia.

Baldwin, S. J., & Ching, Y. H. (2019). An online course design checklist: Development and users' perceptions. *Journal of Computing in Higher Education*, *31*(1), 156–172. doi:10.100712528-018-9199-8

Basri, M., Husain, B., & Modayama, W. (2021). University Students' Perceptions in Implementing Asynchronous Learning During Covid-19 Era. *Journal of English Language, Literature, and Teaching*, *4*(3), 263–276. doi:10.31002/metathesis. v4i3.2734

Bialowas, A., & Steimel, S. (2019). Less Is More: Use of Video to Address the Problem of Teacher Immediacy and Presence in Online Courses. *International Journal on Teaching and Learning in Higher Education*, *31*(2), 354–364.

Borup, J., West, R. E., & Graham, C. R. (2013). The influence of asynchronous video communication on learner social presence: A narrative analysis of four cases. *Distance Education*, *34*(1), 48–63. doi:10.1080/01587919.2013.770427

Brecht, H., & Ogilby, S. (2008). Enabling a comprehensive teaching strategy: Video lectures. *Journal of Information Technology Education: Innovations in Practice*, *7*(1), 71–86.

Ceglie, R. (2020). Examining Theories which Support Online Learning: Ideas for a New Integrated Model. *Journal for the Advancement of Educational Research International*, *14*(1), 36–55.

Chen, L. L. (2016). A model for effective online instructional design. *Literacy Information and Computer Education Journal*, *6*(2), 2302–2308. doi:10.20533/licej.2040.2589.2016.0304

Chou, C. C. (2002). A comparative content analysis of student interaction in synchronous and asynchronous learning networks. In R. H. Sprague Jr. (Ed.), *Proceedings of the 35th Annual Hawaii International Conference on System Sciences* (pp. 1795–1803). IEEE. 10.1109/HICSS.2002.994093

Clark, C., Strudler, N., & Grove, K. (2015). Comparing asynchronous and synchronous video vs. text based discussions in an online teacher education course. *Online Learning*, *19*(3), 48–69. doi:10.24059/olj.v19i3.510

Covelli, B. J. (2017). Online discussion boards: The practice of building community for adult learners. *The Journal of Continuing Higher Education*, *65*(2), 139–145. doi:10.1080/07377363.2017.1274616

Cox, T. (2011). The absent graduate student: An A-B-A single-subject experiment of online discussion participation. *The Journal of Effective Teaching*, *11*(2), 96–109.

Croft, N., Dalton, A., & Grant, M. (2010). Overcoming isolation in distance learning: Building a learning community through time and space. *The Journal for Education in the Built Environment*, *5*(1), 27–64. doi:10.11120/jebe.2010.05010027

DeNoyelles, A., Mannheimer Zydney, J., & Chen, B. (2014). Strategies for creating a community of inquiry through online asynchronous discussions. *Journal of Online Learning and Teaching*, *10*(1), 153–165.

Dickinson, K. J., & Gronseth, S. L. (2020). Application of Universal Design for Learning (UDL) Principles to Surgical Education During the COVID-19 Pandemic. *Journal of Surgical Education*, *77*(5), 1008–1012. doi:10.1016/j.jsurg.2020.06.005 PMID:32576451

Dohms, M. C., Collares, C. F., & Tibério, I. C. (2020). Video-based feedback using real consultations for a formative assessment in communication skills. *BMC Medical Education*, *20*(1), 1–9. doi:10.118612909-020-1955-6 PMID:32093719

Felthun, J. Z., Taylor, S., Shulruf, B., & Allen, D. W. (2021). Assessment methods and the validity and reliability of measurement tools in online objective structured clinical examinations: A systematic scoping review. *Journal of Educational Evaluation for Health Professions*, *18*, 11. doi:10.3352/jeehp.2021.18.11 PMID:34058802

Forbes. (2020, March 26). *Most Teachers Say They Are 'Not Prepared' To Teach Online*. https://www.forbes.com/sites/dereknewton/2020/03/26/most-teachers-say-they-are-not-prepared-to-teach-online/?sh=6911b3627f2c

Formica, S. P., Easley, J. L., & Spraker, M. C. (2010). Transforming common-sense beliefs into Newtonian thinking through Just-In-Time Teaching. *Physical Review Special Topics. Physics Education Research*, *6*(2), 1–8. doi:10.1103/PhysRevSTPER.6.020106

Garrison, D. R., Anderson, T., & Archer, W. (2000). Critical inquiry in a text-based environment: Computer conferencing in higher education model. *The Internet and Higher Education*, *2*(2-3), 87–105. doi:10.1016/S1096-7516(00)00016-6

Gregory, M., & Lodge, J. M. (2015). Academic workload: The silent barrier to the implementation of technology-enhanced learning strategies in higher education. *Distance Education*, *36*(2), 210–230. doi:10.1080/01587919.2015.1055056

Guo, P. J., Kim, J., & Rubin, R. (2014, March). How video production affects student engagement: An empirical study of MOOC videos. In *Proceedings of the first ACM conference on Learning @ scale conference* (pp. 41-50). 10.1145/2556325.2566239

Harper, B. (2018). Technology and teacher–student interactions: A review of empirical research. *Journal of Research on Technology in Education*, *50*(3), 214–225. doi:10.1080/15391523.2018.1450690

Henning, W. (2004). Everyday cognition and situated learning. In Handbook of research on educational communications and technology (2nd ed., pp. 143–168). Erlbaum.

Hu, X., Chiu, M. M., Leung, W., & Yelland, N. (2021). Technology integration for young children during COVID-19: Towards future online teaching. *British Journal of Educational Technology: Journal of the Council for Educational Technology*. Advance online publication. doi:10.1111/bjet.13106

Huang, Y. M., Wang, C. S., & Liu, Y. C. (2015). A Study of Synchronous vs. Asynchronous Collaborative Design in Students Learning Motivation. *International Journal of Information and Education Technology (IJIET)*, 5(5), 354–357. doi:10.7763/IJIET.2015.V5.529

Hurtado, S., & Carter, D. F. (1997). Effects of college transition and perceptions of the campus racial climate on Latino college students' sense of belonging. *Sociology of Education*, 70(4), 324–345. doi:10.2307/2673270

Jaggars, S. S., & Xu, D. (2016). How do online course design features influence student performance? *Computers & Education*, 95, 270–284. doi:10.1016/j.compedu.2016.01.014

Kathuria, H., & Becker, D. (2021). Leveraging a Course Quality Checklist to Improve Online Courses. *Journal of Teaching and Learning with Technology*, 10(1), 400–407. doi:10.14434/jotlt.v10i1.31253

Kealey, K. A., Peterson, A. V. Jr, Gaul, M. A., & Dinh, K. T. (2000). Teacher training as a behavior change process: Principles and results from a longitudinal study. *Health Education & Behavior*, 27(1), 64–81. doi:10.1177/109019810002700107 PMID:10709793

Kinnari-Korpela, H. (2015). Using short video lectures to enhance mathematics learning- experiences on differential and integral calculus course for engineering students. *Informatics in Education-An International Journal*, 14(1), 69–83. doi:10.15388/infedu.2015.05

Kramer, M., Förtsch, C., Stürmer, J., Förtsch, S., Seidel, T., & Neuhaus, B. J. (2020). Measuring biology teachers' professional vision: Development and validation of a video-based assessment tool. *Cogent Education*, 7(1), 1–28. doi:10.1080/2331186X.2020.1823155

Lewis, C. C., & Abdul-Hamid, H. (2006). Implementing Effective Online Teaching Practices: Voices of Exemplary Faculty. *Innovative Higher Education*, 31(2), 83–98. doi:10.100710755-006-9010-z

Mabrito, M. (2006). A study of synchronous versus asynchronous collaboration in an online business writing class. *American Journal of Distance Education, 20*(2), 93–107. doi:10.120715389286ajde2002_4

Mahoney, P., Macfarlane, S., & Ajjawi, R. (2019). A qualitative synthesis of video feedback in higher education. *Teaching in Higher Education, 24*(2), 157–179. doi:10.1080/13562517.2018.1471457

Martin, F., & Bolliger, D. U. (2018). Engagement matters: Student perceptions on the importance of engagement strategies in the online learning environment. *Online Learning, 22*(1), 205–222. doi:10.24059/olj.v22i1.1092

Martin, F., Sun, T., Turk, M., & Ritzhaupt, A. D. (2021). A Meta-Analysis on the Effects of Synchronous Online Learning on Cognitive and Affective Educational Outcomes. *International Review of Research in Open and Distributed Learning, 22*(3), 205–242. doi:10.19173/irrodl.v22i3.5263

Martin, F., Wang, C., & Sadaf, A. (2018). Student perception of helpfulness of facilitation strategies that enhance instructor presence, connectedness, engagement and learning in online courses. *The Internet and Higher Education, 37*, 52–65. doi:10.1016/j.iheduc.2018.01.003

Michinov, N., Brunot, S., Le Bohec, O., Juhel, J., & Delaval, M. (2011). Procrastination, participation, and performance in online learning environments. *Computers & Education, 56*(1), 243–252. doi:10.1016/j.compedu.2010.07.025

Missildine, K., Fountain, R., Summers, L., & Gosselin, K. (2013). Flipping the classroom to improve student performance and satisfaction. *The Journal of Nursing Education, 52*(10), 597–599. doi:10.3928/01484834-20130919-03 PMID:24044386

Molnar, A. L., & Kearney, R. C. (2017). A comparison of cognitive presence in asynchronous and synchronous discussions in an online dental hygiene course. *Journal of Dental Hygiene, 91*(3), 14–21. https://jdh.adha.org/content/91/3/14. short PMID:29118067

Nicholson, S. A., & Bond, N. (2003). Collaborative Reflection and Professional Community Building: An Analysis of Preservice Teachers' Use of an Electronic Discussion Board. *Journal of Technology and Teacher Education, 11*(2), 259–279.

Noben, I., Folkert Deinum, J., & Hofman, W. H. (2020). Quality of teaching in higher education: Reviewing teaching behaviour through classroom observations. *The International Journal for Academic Development*. Advance online publication. doi:10.1080/1360144X.2020.1830776

Novak, G. M., Patterson, E. T., Gavrin, A. D., & Christian, W. (1999). *Just in Time Teaching: Blending Active Learning with Web Technology*. Prentice Hall. doi:10.1119/1.19159

Ouyang, F., & Scharber, C. (2017). The influences of an experienced instructor's discussion design and facilitation on an online learning community development: A social network analysis study. *The Internet and Higher Education*, *35*, 34–47. doi:10.1016/j.iheduc.2017.07.002

Panigrahi, R., Srivastava, P. R., & Sharma, D. (2018). Online learning: Adoption, continuance, and learning outcome—A review of literature. *International Journal of Information Management*, *43*, 1–14. doi:10.1016/j.ijinfomgt.2018.05.005

Pascarella, E. T., & Terenzini, P. T. (2005). *How College Affects Students: A Third Decade of Research* (Vol. 2). Jossey-Bass.

Peacock, S., & Cowan, J. (2019). Promoting sense of belonging in online learning communities of inquiry at accredited courses. *Online Learning*, *23*(2), 67–81. doi:10.24059/olj.v23i2.1488

Peterson, A. T., Beymer, P. N., & Putnam, R. T. (2018). Synchronous and asynchronous discussions: Effects on cooperation, belonging, and affect. *Online Learning*, *22*(4), 7–25. doi:10.24059/olj.v22i4.1517

Picciano, A. G. (2017). Theories and Frameworks for Online Education: Seeking an Integrated Model. *Online Learning*, *21*(3), 166–190. doi:10.24059/olj.v21i3.1225

Popa, S. (2020). Reflections on COVID-19 and the future of education and learning. *Prospects*, *49*(1-2), 1–6. doi:10.100711125-020-09511-z PMID:33012848

Pursel, B., & Fang, H.-N. (2011). *Lecture Capture: Current Research and Future Directions*. The Schreyer Institute for Teaching Excellence.

Quality Matters. (2021). *Course Design Rubric Standards*. https://www.qualitymatters.org/qa-resources/rubric-standards/higher-ed-rubric

Ramachandran, V. (2021, February 23). *Stanford researchers identify four causes for 'Zoom fatigue' and their simple fixes*. Stanford News. https://news.stanford.edu/2021/02/23/four-causes-zoom-fatigue-solutions/

Reuge, N., Jenkins, R., Brossard, M., Soobrayan, B., Mizunoya, S., Ackers, J., Jones, L., & Taulo, W. G. (2021). Education response to COVID 19 pandemic, a special issue proposed by UNICEF: Editorial review. *International Journal of Educational Development*, *87*, 102485. doi:10.1016/j.ijedudev.2021.102485 PMID:34511714

Roblyer, M. D., Freeman, J., Donaldson, M. B., & Maddox, M. (2007). A comparison of outcomes of virtual school courses offered in synchronous and asynchronous formats. *The Internet and Higher Education, 10*(4), 261–268. doi:10.1016/j.iheduc.2007.08.003

Roddy, C., Amiet, D. L., Chung, J., Holt, C., Shaw, L., McKenzie, S., ... Mundy, M. E. (2017, November). Applying best practice online learning, teaching, and support to intensive online environments: An integrative review. *Frontiers in Education, 2*, article 59.

Scagnoli, N. I., Choo, J., & Tian, J. (2019). Students' insights on the use of video lectures in online classes. *British Journal of Educational Technology, 50*(1), 399–414. doi:10.1111/bjet.12572

Skylar, A. A. (2009). A comparison of asynchronous online text-based lectures and synchronous interactive web conferencing lectures. *Issues in Teacher Education, 18*(2), 69–84.

Stepich, D. A., & Ertmer, P. A. (2003). Building community as a critical element of online course design. *Educational Technology*, 33–43.

Swan, K. (2002). Building communities in online courses: The importance of interaction. *Education Communication and Information, 2*(1), 23–49. doi:10.1080/1463631022000005016

Telles-Langdon, D. M. (2020). Transitioning University Courses Online in Response to COVID-19. *Journal of Teaching and Learning, 14*(1), 108–119. doi:10.22329/jtl.v14i1.6262

Weimer, M. (2002). *Learner-centered teaching: Five key changes to practice.* John Wiley & Sons.

Weimer, M. (2009). *Effective teaching strategies: Six keys to classroom excellence.* Faculty Focus. https://www.facultyfocus.com/articles/effective-teaching-strategies/effective-teaching-strategies-six-keys-to-classroom-excellence/

Weimer, M. (2016). *Why are we so slow to change the way we teach?* https://www.facultyfocus.com/articles/effective-teaching-strategies/why-are-we-so-slow-to-change-the-way-we-teach/

Wenger, E. (2011). *Communities of practice: A brief introduction.* Academic Press.

Wright, G. B. (2011). Student-centered learning in higher education. *International Journal on Teaching and Learning in Higher Education, 23*(1), 92–97.

Writing a successful discussion board post. (n.d.). Retrieved December 24, 2021 from https://www.unr.edu/writing-speaking-center/student-resources/writing-speaking-resources/writing-a-successful-discussion-board-post

Zeng, X., & Wang, T. (2021). College student satisfaction with online learning during COVID-19: A review and implications. *International Journal of Multidisciplinary Perspectives in Higher Education, 6*(1), 182–195.

Zheng, C., Wang, L., & Chai, C. S. (2021). Self-assessment first or peer-assessment first: Effects of video-based formative practice on learners' English public speaking anxiety and performance. *Computer Assisted Language Learning*, 1–34. doi:10.1080/09588221.2021.1946562

Zydney, J. M., McKimmy, P., Lindberg, R., & Schmidt, M. (2019). Here or there instruction: Lessons learned in implementing innovative approaches to blended synchronous learning. *TechTrends, 63*(2), 123–132. doi:10.100711528-018-0344-z

Compilation of References

Abrahamsson, S., & Dávila López, M. (2021). Comparison of online learning designs during the COVID-19 pandemic within bioinformatics courses in higher education. *Bioinformatics (Oxford, England)*, *37*(Supplement 1), i9–i15. doi:10.1093/bioinformatics/btab304 PMID:34252967

Adams, K. (2020). Research to resource: Developing a sense of community in online learning environments. *National Association for Music Education*, *39*(2), 5–9. 10.1177%2F8755123320943985

Adler, M. J. (1982). *The Paideia Proposal*. Macmillan.

Agievich, V. (2014). *Mathematical model and multi-criteria analysis of designing large-scale enterprise roadmap* [PhD thesis].

Alexander, A. S., & Murphy, E. R. (2020). "It started with this project": A mixed methods examination of a service learning project for preservice art educators. *Studies in Art Education*, *61*(4), 312–329. doi:10.1080/00393541.2020.1820833

Alfino, M., Pajer, M., Pierce, L., & O'Brien Jenks, K. (2008). Advancing Critical Thinking and Information Literacy Skills in First Year College Students. *College & Research Libraries*, *15*(1/2), 81–98.

Ali, T.T., & Herrera, M. (2020). *Distance learning during COVID-19: 7 equity considerations for schools and districts*. Southern Education Foundation.

Al-Sharhan, S., Al-Hunaiyyan, A., Alhajri, R., & Al-Huwail, N. (2020). Utilization of learning management system (LMS) among instructors and students. In Z. Zakaria & R. Ahmad (Eds.), *Advances in Electronics Engineering, Lecture Notes in Electrical Engineering* (Vol. 619, pp. 15–23). Springer. doi:10.1007/978-981-15-1289-6_2

Anastasiadis, L., Lampropoulos, G., & Siakas, K. (2018). Digital Game-based Learning and Serious Games in Education. *International Journal of Advances in Scientific Research and Engineering*, *4*(12), 139–144. doi:10.31695/IJASRE.2018.33016

Anderson, L. W., & Krathwohl, D. R. (Eds.). (2001). A taxonomy for learning, teaching and Assessing: A Revision of Bloom's Taxonomy of Educational Objectives: Complete Ed. New York: Longman.

Anderson, R. M., Heesterbeek, H., Klinkenberg, D., & Hollingsworth, T. D. (2020). How will country-based mitigation measures influence the course of the COVID-19 epidemic? *Lancet*, *395*(10228), 931–934. doi:10.1016/S0140-6736(20)30567-5 PMID:32164834

Anderson, T. (2011). *The theory and practice of online learning* (2nd ed.). AU Press.

Angel, S. L. (2018). If I would have learned this way! In A. K. Salmon (Ed.), *Authentic Teaching and Learning for PreK-Fifth Grade: Advice from Practitioners and Coaches* (pp. 32–49). Routledge. doi:10.4324/9781351211505-2

Angrist, N., de Barros, A., Bhula, R., Chakera, S., Cummiskey, C., DeStefano, J., Floretta, J., Kaffenberger, M., Piper, B., & Stern, J. (2021). Building back better to avert a learning catastrophe: Estimating learning loss from COVID-19 school shutdowns in Africa and facilitating short-term and long-term learning recovery. *International Journal of Educational Development*, *84*, 102397. doi:10.1016/j.ijedudev.2021.102397

Artanti, Y. (2020). Online Content Sharing Behavior: A Review on the Social Psychology Perspective. *2nd International Research Conference on Economics and Business, Malang, Indonesia*.

Artino, A. (2008). *A brief analysis of research on problem-based learning*. Retrieved April 12, 2009, from http://eric.ed.gov/ERICWebPortal/contentdelivery/servlet/ERICServlet?accno=ED501593

Artman, M., Frisicaro-Pawlowski, E., & Monge, R. (2010). Not Just One Shot: Extending the Dialogue about Information Literacy in Composition Classes. *Composition Studies*, *38*(2), 93–109.

Ash, K. (2012). Attention, videogames, and the retention economies of affective amplification. *Theory, Culture & Society*, *29*(6), 3–26. doi:10.1177/0263276412438595

Athens, W. (2018). Perceptions of the persistent: Engagement and learning community in underrepresented populations. *Online Learning*, *22*(2), 27–58. doi:10.24059/olj.v22i2.1368

Ayres Paul, K., & Tay, J. (2016). Critical conversations about big ideas in art using Paideia seminars. *Gifted Child Today*, *39*(2), 105–113. doi:10.1177/1076217516628567

Baek, Y. K. (2008). What hinders teachers in using computers and video games in the Classroom? Exploring factors inhibiting the uptake of computer and video games. *Cyberpsychology & Behavior*, *11*(6), 665–671. doi:10.1089/cpb.2008.0127 PMID:19006464

Baker-Bell, A. (2020). *Linguistic Justice: Black Language, Literacy, Identity, and Pedagogy*. Routledge. doi:10.4324/9781315147383

Bakhtin, M. M. (1986). *Speech genres and other late essays*. University of Texas Press.

Baldwin, S. J., & Ching, Y. H. (2019). An online course design checklist: Development and users' perceptions. *Journal of Computing in Higher Education*, *31*(1), 156–172. doi:10.100712528-018-9199-8

Baldwin, S. J., Ching, Y.-H., & Friesen, N. (2018). Online course design and development among college and university instructors: An analysis using grounded theory. *Online Learning*, *22*(2), 157–171. doi:10.24059/olj.v22i2.1212

Baran, E., Correia, A. P., & Thompson, A. (2011). Transforming online teaching practice: Critical analysis of the literature on the roles and competencies of online teachers. *Distance Education*, *32*(3), 421–439. doi:10.1080/01587919.2011.610293

Barratt, C. C., Nielsen, K., Desmet, C., & Balthazor, R. (2009). Collaboration Is Key: Librarians and Composition Instructors Analyze Student Research and Writing. *Portal*, *9*(1), 37–56.

Barton, K., McKellar, P., & Maharg, P. (2007). Authentic fictions: Simulation, professionalism And legal learning. *Clinical Law Review*, *14*, 143–193.

Basri, M., Husain, B., & Modayama, W. (2021). University Students' Perceptions in Implementing Asynchronous Learning During Covid-19 Era. *Journal of English Language, Literature, and Teaching*, *4*(3), 263–276. doi:10.31002/metathesis.v4i3.2734

Bayliss, J. D. (2012). *Teaching game A.I. through* Minecraft *mods*. Paper presented at the Games Innovation Conference (IGIC), 2012 IEEE International.

Bekoff, M., & Byers, J. A. (1998). *Animal Play: Evolutionary, Comparative and Ecological Perspectives*. Cambridge University Press. doi:10.1017/CBO9780511608575

Bennett & Milton J. (1993). Towards a Developmental Model of Intercultural Sensitivity. In R. Michael Paige (Ed.), *Education for the Intercultural Experience* (pp. 21–71). Intercultural Press.

Bennett & Milton. J. (2004). From Ethnocentrism to Ethnorelativism. In Toward Multiculturalism. Newton, MA: Intercultural Resource Corporation.

Betts, A., Thai, K. P., & Gunderia, S. (2021). Personalized Mastery Learning Ecosystems: Using Bloom's Four Objects of Change to Drive Learning in Adaptive Instructional Systems. In R. A. Sottilare & J. Schwarz (Eds.), Lecture Notes in Computer Science: Vol. 12792. *Adaptive Instructional Systems. Design and Evaluation. HCII 2021*. Springer. doi:10.1007/978-3-030-77857-6_3

Beymer, P. N., & Thomson, M. M. (2015). The effects of choice in the classroom: Is there too little or too much choice? *Support for Learning*, *30*(2), 105–120. doi:10.1111/1467-9604.12086

Bialowas, A., & Steimel, S. (2019). Less Is More: Use of Video to Address the Problem of Teacher Immediacy and Presence in Online Courses. *International Journal on Teaching and Learning in Higher Education*, *31*(2), 354–364.

Bickle, M. C., & Rucker, R. (2018). Student-to-student interaction. *Quarterly Review of Distance Education*, *19*(1), 1–11.

Birmingham, D., Calabrese Barton, A., Jones, J., McDaniel, A., Rogers, A., & Turner, C. (2017). "But the science we do here matters": Youth-authored cases of consequential learning. *Science Education*, *101*(5), 818–844. doi:10.1002ce.21293

Birmingham, E., Chinwongs, L., Flaspohler, M. R., Hearn, C., Kvanvig, D., & Portmann, R. (2008). Perceptions of Students' Information Literacy Competencies, and a Call for a Collaborative Approach. *Communications in Information Literacy, 2*(1), 6–24. doi:10.15760/comminfolit.2008.2.1.53

Blackburn, R., & Rosen, B. (1993). Total quality and human resources management: lessons learned from Baldrige Award-winning companies. *Academy of Management Perspectives, 7*(3).

Bleiker, R. (2001). The Aesthetic Turn in International Political Theory. *Millennium, 30*(3), 509–533. doi:10.1177/03058298010300031001

Bleiker, R. (2009). *Aesthetics and World Politics*. Palgrave. doi:10.1057/9780230244375

Bloom, B., & Krathwohl, D. R. (1956). *Taxonomy of educational objectives: the classification of educational goals by a Committee of College and University Examiners. Handbook 1: Cognitive Domain*. Longmans, Green.

Bod, R. (2022). History of the Humanities. *Histories, 2*, 178–184. 12020014 doi:0.3390/histories

Bod, R., Kursell, J., Maat, J., & Weststeijn, T. (2016). A New Field: History of Humanities. *History of Humanities, 1*(1), 1–8. doi:10.1086/685056

Borup, J., West, R. E., & Graham, C. R. (2013). The influence of asynchronous video communication on learner social presence: A narrative analysis of four cases. *Distance Education, 34*(1), 48–63. doi:10.1080/01587919.2013.770427

Boston University. (n.d.). *Center for Anti-Racist Research*. https://www.bu.edu/antiracism-center/

Botturi, L., & Belfer, K. (2014). *Pedagogical patterns for online learning*. ResearchGate.

Bourdieu, P. (1981). Structures, strategies, and the habitus. In C. C. Lemert (Ed.), *French sociology: Rupture and renewal since 1968* (pp. 86–96). Columbia University Press.

Bourdieu, P. (1983). The forms of capital. In J. G. Richardson (Ed.), *Handbook of theory and research for the sociology of Education* (pp. 241–258). Greenwood.

Boyd, F. B., Casey, L. L., & Galda, L. (2015). Culturally diverse literature: Enriching variety in an era of Common Core State Standards. *The Reading Teacher, 68*(5), 378–387. doi:10.1002/trtr.1326

Bozkurt, A., & Durak, G. (2018). A systematic review of gamification research: In pursuit of homo Ludens. *International Journal of Game-Based Learning, 8*(3), 15–33. doi:10.4018/IJGBL.2018070102

Brady, L., Singh-Corcoran, N., Dadisman, J. A., & Diamond, K. (2009). A Collaborative Approach to Information Literacy: First-Year Composition, Writing Center, and Library Partnerships at West Virginia University. *Composition Forum, 19*, 1-18.

Brecht, H., & Ogilby, S. (2008). Enabling a comprehensive teaching strategy: Video lectures. *Journal of Information Technology Education: Innovations in Practice, 7*(1), 71–86.

Brill, J. M. & Galloway, C. (2007). Perils and promises: University instructors' integration of technology in classroom-based instruction. *British Journal of Educational Technology, 38*(1), 95–105. .1467-8535.2006.00601.x doi:10.1111/j

Bronfenbrenner, U. (1979). *The Ecology of Human Development*. Harvard University Press.

Bronshteyn, K., & Baladad, R. (2006). Librarians as Writing Instructors: Using Paraphrasing Exercises to Teach Beginning Information Literacy Students. *Journal of Academic Librarianship, 32*(5), 533–536. doi:10.1016/j.acalib.2006.05.010

Brown, M. G. (2016). Blended instructional practice: A review of the empirical literature on instructors' adoption and use of online tools in face-to-face teaching. *Internet and Higher Education, 38*, 1–10. 1.iheduc.2016.05.001 doi:0.1016/j

Brown, R. (2005). *Exploring the notion of 'pedagogical space' through students' writings about a classroom community of practice*. Academic Press.

Budhai, S. S., & Skipwith, K. B. (2021). *Best practices in engaging online learners through active and experiential learning strategies* (2nd ed.). Routledge. doi:10.4324/9781003140405

Burgoyne, M. B., & Chuppa-Cornell, K. (2015). Beyond Embedded: Creating an Online-Learning Community Integrating Information Literacy and Composition Courses. *Journal of Academic Librarianship, 41*(4), 416–421. doi:10.1016/j.acalib.2015.05.005

Burke, J. (2022). *Group Work in the Classroom: Types of Small Groups*. Centre for Teaching Excellence, University of Waterloo. https://uwaterloo.ca/centre-for-teaching-excellence/

Cahapay, M. B. (2020). A Reconceptualization of Learning Space as Schools Reopen amid and after COVID-19 Pandemic. *Asian Journal of Distance Education, 15*(1), 269–276.

Calabrese Barton, A., Tan, E., & Birmingham, D. J. (2020). Rethinking high-leverage practices in justice-oriented ways. *Journal of Teacher Education, 71*(4), 477–494. doi:10.1177/0022487119900209

Campe, S., Denner, J., & Werner, L. (2013). Intentional computing: Getting the results you want from game programming classes. *Journal for Computing Teachers*. Retrieved on September 8, 2013 from http:// www.iste.org/store/product?ID=2850

Campe, S., Werner, L., & Denner, J. (2012). Game programming with *Alice:* A series of graduated challenges. In P. Phillips (Ed.), *Special Issue Computer Science K-8: Building a Strong Foundation*. Computer Science Teachers Association.

Canagarajah, S. (2011). Codemeshing in Academic Writing: Identifying Teachable Strategies of Translanguaging. *Modern Language Journal, 95*(3), 401–417. doi:10.1111/j.1540-4781.2011.01207.x

Cannon, K., & Jarson, J. (2009). Information Literacy and Writing Tutor Training at a Liberal Arts College. *Communications in Information Literacy, 3*(1), 45–57. doi:10.15760/comminfolit.2009.3.1.68

Carraway, C. (2019). *So, what does sisterhood really mean.* Retrieved from https://www. harpersbazaar.com/uk/culture/a26751347/cash-carraway-sisterhood-meaning-and-comment/

Casserly, A. M., Tiernan, B., & Maguire, G. (2019). Primary teachers' perceptions of multi-grade classroom grouping practices to support inclusive education. *European Journal of Special Needs Education, 34*(5), 617–631. doi:10.1080/08856257.2019.1580835

Caufield, M. (2016). Yes, Digital Literacy, but Which One? *Hapgood.* https://hapgood. us/2016/12/19/yes-digital-literacy-but-which-one/

Ceglie, R. (2020). Examining Theories which Support Online Learning: Ideas for a New Integrated Model. *Journal for the Advancement of Educational Research International, 14*(1), 36–55.

Center for Community Engaged Learning. (2020). Retrieved from https://communityengagedlearning. msu.edu/

Chang, A. W. (2013). Psyche's sisters: ambivalence of sisterhood in twentieth-century Irish women's short stories. *Estudios Irlandeses - Journal of Irish Studies,* (8), 1. Retrieved from https://search-ebscohost-com.ezproxy.snhu.edu/login.aspx?direct=true&db=edsglr&AN=edsg cl.336176159&site=eds-live&scope=site

Chatterjee, R., & Correia, A. (2020). Online students' attitudes toward collaborative learning and sense of community. *American Journal of Distance Education, 34*(1), 53–68. doi:10.1080 /08923647.2020.1703479

Chee, Y. S. (2011). Learning as *becoming* through performance, play, and dialog: A game-based learning model with the game Legends of Alkhimia. *Digital Culture & Education, 3*(2), 98–122.

Cheng, W.-L., Dohrmann, T., Kerlin, M., Law, J., & Ramaswamy, S. (2018). *Creating an effective workforce system for the new economy.* Retrieved from https:// www. mckin sey. com/ indus tries/ public- sector/ ourinsig hts/ creating- an- effective- workforce- system- for- the- new- Economy

Chen, L. L. (2016). A model for effective online instructional design. *Literacy Information and Computer Education Journal, 6*(2), 2302–2308. doi:10.20533/licej.2040.2589.2016.0304

Chesters, S. D. (2012). *The socratic classroom: Reflective thinking through collaborative inquiry.* Sense Publishing. doi:10.1007/978-94-6091-855-1

Chia, L. S., Khang, G. N., & Wah, L. K. (1983). A Piagetian-Based Programme for Learning "Elements and Symbols,". *Singapore Journal of Education, 5*(1), 20–24. doi:10.1080/02188798308548539

Chisholm, J. S., & Quillen, B. (2016). Digitizing the fishbowl: An approach to dialogic discussion. *English Journal, 105*(3), 88–91.

Chou, C. C. (2002). A comparative content analysis of student interaction in synchronous and asynchronous learning networks. In R. H. Sprague Jr. (Ed.), *Proceedings of the 35th Annual Hawaii International Conference on System Sciences* (pp. 1795–1803). IEEE. 10.1109/HICSS.2002.994093

Chou, Y.-S., Hou, H.-T., Chang, K.-E., & Su, C.-L. (2021). Designing cognitive-based game mechanisms for mobile educational games to promote cognitive thinking: An analysis of flow state and game-based learning behavioral patterns. *Interactive Learning Environments*. Advance online publication. doi:10.1080/10494820.2021.1926287

Clark, D., Tanner-Smith, E., Killingsworth, S., & Bellamy, S. (2013). Digital games for learning: A systematic review and meta-analysis (executive summary). Academic Press.

Clark, C., Strudler, N., & Grove, K. (2015). Comparing asynchronous and synchronous video vs. text based discussions in an online teacher education course. *Online Learning*, *19*(3), 48–69. doi:10.24059/olj.v19i3.510

Clark, I. (1995). Information Literacy and the Writing Center. *Computers and Composition*, *12*(2), 203–209. doi:10.1016/8755-4615(95)90008-X

Condon, F., & Young, V. A. (2016). *Performing Antiracist Pedagogy in Rhetoric, Writing, and Communication. Across the Disciplines Books*. The WAC Clearinghouse; University Press of Colorado.

Copeland, M. (2005). *Socratic circles*. Steinhouse.

Corbett, P. (2010). What about the 'Google Effect'? Improving the Library Research Habits of First-Year Composition Students. *Teaching English in the Two-Year College*, *37*(3), 265–277.

Covelli, B. J. (2017). Online discussion boards: The practice of building community for adult learners. *The Journal of Continuing Higher Education*, *65*(2), 139–145. doi:10.1080/0737736 3.2017.1274616

Cox, T. (2011). The absent graduate student: An A-B-A single-subject experiment of online discussion participation. *The Journal of Effective Teaching*, *11*(2), 96–109.

Cress, U., Moskaliuk, J., & Jeong, H. (2016). *Mass Collaboration and Education. Computer-Supported Collaborative Learning Series* (Vol. 16). CULS.

Croft, N., Dalton, A., & Grant, M. (2010). Overcoming isolation in distance learning: Building a learning community through time and space. *The Journal for Education in the Built Environment*, *5*(1), 27–64. doi:10.11120/jebe.2010.05010027

Cummins, J. (2001). *Negotiating identities: Education for empowerment in a diverse society* (2nd ed.). California Association for Bilingual Education.

Daniel, S. M., & Zybina, M. (2019). Resettled refugee teens' perspectives: Identifying a need to centralize youths "funds of strategies" in future efforts to enact culturally responsive pedagogy. *The Urban Review*, *51*(3), 345–368. doi:10.100711256-018-0484-7

Darvin, R., & Norton, B. (2014). Social Class, Identity, and Migrant Students. *Journal of Language, Identity, and Education*, *13*(2), 111–117. doi:10.1080/15348458.2014.901823

Davies, M., & Sinclair, A. (2014). Socratic questioning in the Paideia method to encourage dialogical discussions. *Research Papers in Education*, 29(1), 20–43. doi:10.1080/02671522.2012.742132

Davis, N., & Schaeffer, J. (2019). Troubling troubled waters in elementary science education: Politics, ethics, and black children's conceptions of water [justice] in the era of flint. *Cognition and Instruction*, 37(3), 367–389. doi:10.1080/07370008.2019.1624548

De Castell, S. (2011). Ludic epistemology: What game-based learning can teach curriculum studies. *Journal of the Canadian Association for Curriculum Studies*, 8(2), 19–27.

De Freitas, S., & Conole, G. (2010). The influence of pervasive and integrative tools on learners' experiences and expectations of study. In R. Sharpe, H. Beetham, & S. de Freitas (Eds.), *Rethinking Learning in the Digital Age*. Routledge.

De Freitas, S., & Jarvis, S. (2007). Serious Games – Engaging Training Solutions: A research and development project for supporting training needs. *British Journal of Educational Technology*, 38(3), 523–525. doi:10.1111/j.1467-8535.2007.00716.x

De Freitas, S., & Jarvis, S. (2009). Towards a development approach to serious games. Games-based learning advancements for multisensory human-computer interfaces. IGI Global.

De Freitas, S., & Neumann, T. (2009). The use of 'exploratory learning' for supporting immersive learning in virtual environments. *Computers & Education*, 52(2), 343–352. doi:10.1016/j.compedu.2008.09.010

De Freitas, S., & Oliver, M. (2006). How can exploratory learning with games and simulations within the curriculum be most effectively evaluated? *Computers & Education*, 46(Special Issue), 249–264. doi:10.1016/j.compedu.2005.11.007

Deitering, A.-M., & Jameson, S. (2008). Step by Step through the Scholarly Conversation: A Collaborative Library/Writing Faculty Project to Embed Information Literacy and Promote Critical Thinking in First Year Composition at Oregon State University. *College & Undergraduate Libraries*, 15(1/2), 57–79. doi:10.1080/10691310802176830

DeLoura, M., & Metz, E. (2013). *Games win big in education grants competition*. Retrieved August 18, 2013, from https://www.ed.gov/blog/2013/05/games-win-big-in-education-grants-competition/

Delpit, L. (2006). The Politics of Teaching Literate Discourse. In *Other People's Children: Cultural Conflict in the Classroom*. New Press.

Demmans Epp, C., Phirangee, K., & Hewitt, J. (2017). Student actions and community in online courses: The roles played by course length and facilitation method. *Online Learning*, 21(4), 53–77. doi:10.24059/olj.v21i4.1269

DeNoyelles, A., Mannheimer Zydney, J., & Chen, B. (2014). Strategies for creating a community of inquiry through online asynchronous discussions. *Journal of Online Learning and Teaching*, 10(1), 153–165.

Descartes, R. (2004). A Discourse on Method: Meditations and Principles (J. Veitch, Trans.). Orion Publishing Group. (Original publication 1637)

Devlin-Scherer, R., & Sardone, N. B. (2010). Digital simulation games for social studies classrooms. *The Clearing House: A Journal of Educational Strategies, Issues and Ideas*, *83*(4), 138–144. doi:10.1080/00098651003774836

Dickinson, K. J., & Gronseth, S. L. (2020). Application of Universal Design for Learning (UDL) Principles to Surgical Education During the COVID-19 Pandemic. *Journal of Surgical Education*, *77*(5), 1008–1012. doi:10.1016/j.jsurg.2020.06.005 PMID:32576451

Dill, B. T. (1994). Race, class, and gender: Prospects for an all-inclusive sisterhood. In L. Stone (Ed.), *The education feminism reader*. Routledge. doi:10.1515/9783110978919.401

DiRamio, D., & Wolverton, M. (2006). Integrating learning communities and distance education: Possibility or pipedream? *Innovative Higher Education*, *31*(2), 99–113. doi:10.100710755-006-9011-y

Directorate for Education, Education and Training Policy Division. (2011). *Teachers matter: Attracting, developing and retaining effective teachers, pointers for policy development*. Retrieved from https://www.oecd.org/education/school/48627229.pdf)

Dixson, M. D. (2012). Creating effective student engagement in online courses: What do students find engaging? *The Journal of Scholarship of Teaching and Learning*, *10*(2), 1–13. https://scholarworks.iu.edu/journals/index.php/josotl/article/view/1744

Dohms, M. C., Collares, C. F., & Tibério, I. C. (2020). Video-based feedback using real consultations for a formative assessment in communication skills. *BMC Medical Education*, *20*(1), 1–9. doi:10.118612909-020-1955-6 PMID:32093719

Driggs, C., & Brillante, J. (2020). Culture of attention and engagement. In D. Lemov (Ed.), *Teaching in the Online Classroom: Surviving and Thriving in the New Normal* (pp. 57–80). Jossey-Bass.

Edelman, G. (1992). *Bright Air and Brilliant Fire: On the Matter of the Mind*. Basic Books.

Elmborg, J. (2003). Information Literacy and Writing Across the Curriculum: Sharing the Vision. *RSR. Reference Services Review*, *31*(1), 68–80. doi:10.1108/00907320310460933

Engeström, Y. (1999). Activity theory and individual and social transformation. In Y. Engeström, R. Miettinen, & R.-L. Punamaki (Eds.), *Perspectives on Activity Theory* (pp. 19–38). Cambridge University Press. doi:10.1017/CBO9780511812774.003

Erstad, O., & Sefton-Green, J. (2013). Digital disconnect? The 'digital learner' and the school. In O. Erstad & J. Sefton-Green (Eds.), *identity, community, and learning live in the digital age* (pp. 87–106). Cambridge University Press. doi:10.3726/978-1-4539-1019-1

Falchuk, B., Loeb, S., & Neff, R. (2018, June). The Social Metaverse: Battle for Privacy. *IEEE Technology and Society Magazine*, *37*(2), 52–61. doi:10.1109/MTS.2018.2826060

Farmer, J. L., Leonard, A. E., Spearman, M., Quian, M., & Rosenblith, S. (2016). Picturing a classroom community: Student drawings as a pedagogical tool to assess features of community in the classroom. *Action in Teacher Education*, *38*(4), 299–314. doi:10.1080/01626620.2016.1226208

Fathema, N., Shannon, D., & Ross, M. (2015). Expanding the technology acceptance model (TAM) to examine faculty use of learning management systems in higher education institutions. *Journal of Online Learning and Teaching*, *11*(2), 210–232.

Faudler, T. R. (2011). *Technology integration: A research-based professional development program* [Unpublished master's thesis]. Mount Vernon Nazarene University.

Felfel, H., Ayadi, O., & Masmoudi, F. (2017). Pareto Optimal Solution Selection for a Multi-Site Supply Chain Planning Problem Using the VIKOR and TOPSIS Methods. *International Journal of Service Science, Management, Engineering, and Technology*. . doi:10.4018/IJSSMET.2017070102

Felthun, J. Z., Taylor, S., Shulruf, B., & Allen, D. W. (2021). Assessment methods and the validity and reliability of measurement tools in online objective structured clinical examinations: A systematic scoping review. *Journal of Educational Evaluation for Health Professions*, *18*, 11. doi:10.3352/jeehp.2021.18.11 PMID:34058802

Ferguson, C. J., & Garza, A. (2011). Call of (civic) duty: Action games and civic behavior in a large sample of youth. *Computers in Human Behavior*, *27*(2), 770–775. doi:10.1016/j.chb.2010.10.026

Fielding, J., Hans, J., Mabee, F., Tracy, K., Consalvo, A., & Craig, L. (2013). Integrated Information Literacy and Student Outcomes in Foundational First-Year Writing. *Journal of Assessment and Institutional Effectiveness*, *3*(2), 106–139. doi:10.5325/jasseinsteffe.3.2.0106

Fite, K. E., & Ross-Fordon, J. M. (2013). Carol Gilligan: Critical Voice of Feminist Thought. In J. D. Kirylo (Ed.), *A critical pedagogy of resistance: 34 pedagogues we need to know* (pp. 57–59). Sense Publ. doi:10.1007/978-94-6209-374-4_15

Fleming, J. (2021). *Teaching multicultural literature in the College classroom* (Publication No. 145) [Honors Thesis, Southeastern University]. Southeastern University. https://firescholars.seu.edu/honors/145

Forbes. (2020, March 26). *Most Teachers Say They Are 'Not Prepared' To Teach Online*. https://www.forbes.com/sites/dereknewton/2020/03/26/most-teachers-say-they-are-not-prepared-to-teach-online/?sh=6911b3627f2c

Formica, S. P., Easley, J. L., & Spraker, M. C. (2010). Transforming common-sense beliefs into Newtonian thinking through Just-In-Time Teaching. *Physical Review Special Topics. Physics Education Research*, *6*(2), 1–8. doi:10.1103/PhysRevSTPER.6.020106

Fowler, S., & Blohm, J. (2004). An analysis of methods for intercultural training. In *Handbook of intercultural training* (pp. 37-84). SAGE Publications, Inc. https://www.doi.org/10.4135/9781452231129.n3

Framework for Information Literacy for Higher Education. (2016). Association of Research and College Libraries. https://www.ala.org/acrl/sites/ala.org.acrl/files/content/issues/infolit/framework1.pdf

Gagne, R. M., & Briggs, L. J. (1974). *Principles of instructional design.* Holt, Rinehart, and Winston, Inc.

Garcia, N. M., & Delgado Bernal, D. (2021). Remembering and revisiting pedagogies of the home. *American Educational Research Journal, 58*(3), 567–601. doi:10.3102/0002831220954431

Gardner, H. (2011). Frames of mind: The theory of multiple intelligences. New York: Basic Books. (Original publication 1983)

Gardner, H. (2013). *Frequently asked questions—Multiple intelligences and related educational topics.* https://howardgardner01.files.wordpress.com/2012/06/faq_march2013.pdf

Garrison, D. R., Anderson, T., & Archer, W. (2000). Critical inquiry in a text-based environment: Computer conferencing in higher education model. *The Internet and Higher Education, 2*(2-3), 87–105. doi:10.1016/S1096-7516(00)00016-6

Gay, A. (2019). *How digital Literacy affects the modern workforce.* Retrieved from https:// the blog. Adobe. com/ how- digit al- literacy- affects- the- modern- workforce/

Gee, J. P. (1989). Literacy, Discourse, and Linguistics: Introduction and What Is Literacy? *Journal of Education, 171*(1), 5–25. doi:10.1177/002205748917100101

Gee, J. P. (2005). Learning by design: Good video games as learning machines. *E-learning, 2*(1), 5–16. doi:10.2304/elea.2005.2.1.5

Gee, J. P. (2007). *What video games have to teach us about learning and Literacy* (Revised edition). Palgrave Macmillan.

Gee, J. P. (2014). *An introduction to discourse analysis: Theory and method.* Routledge. doi:10.4324/9781315819679

Gentner, D., Rottermann, M. J., & Forbus, K. D. (1993). The roles of similarity intransfer: Separating retrievability from inferential soundness. *Cognitive Psychology, 25*(4), 524–575. doi:10.1006/cogp.1993.1013 PMID:8243045

Gilligan, C. (2003). *In a different voice. [electronic resource] : psychological theory and women's development.* Harvard University Press. Retrieved from https://search-ebscohost-com.ezproxy.snhu.edu/login.aspx?direct=true&db=cat04477a&AN=snhu.b1545291&site=eds-live&scope=site

Gobet, F., De Voogt, A., & Retschitzki, J. (2004). *Moves in Mind: The Psychology of Board Games.* Psychology Press. doi:10.4324/9780203503638

Gonzalez, N., Moll, L. C., & Amanti, C. (Eds.). (2005). *Funds of knowledge.* Routledge.

Green, T. (2020). Distance education in k-12: Guiding practice through a shared definition and framework. In J. P. Green (Ed.), *Thriving as an Online K-12 Educator* (pp. 1–16). Routledge. doi:10.4324/9781003127635-1

Gregory, M., & Lodge, J. M. (2015). Academic workload: The silent barrier to the implementation of technology-enhanced learning strategies in higher education. *Distance Education*, *36*(2), 210–230. doi:10.1080/01587919.2015.1055056

Griffiths, T., & Guile, D. (1999). Pedagogy in work-based contexts. In O. Mortimore (Ed.), *Understanding Pedagogy, and Its Impact on Learning*. Paul Chapman Publishing. doi:10.4135/9781446219454.n8

Griswold, J., Shaw, L., & Munn, M. (2017). Socratic seminar with data: A strategy to support student discourse and understanding. *The American Biology Teacher*, *79*(6), 492–495. doi:10.1525/abt.2017.79.6.492 PMID:29147033

Guangul, F. M., Suhail, A. H., Khalit, M. I., & Khidhir, B. A. (2020). Challenges of remote assessment in higher education in the context of COVID-19: A case study of Middle East College. *Educational Assessment, Evaluation and Accountability*, *32*(4), 519–535. doi:10.100711092-020-09340-w PMID:33101539

Guo, P. J., Kim, J., & Rubin, R. (2014, March). How video production affects student engagement: An empirical study of MOOC videos. In *Proceedings of the first ACM conference on Learning@ scale conference* (pp. 41-50). 10.1145/2556325.2566239

Halpern, D. F. (1998). Teaching critical thinking for transfer across domains: Dispositions, skills, structure training, and metacognitive monitoring. *The American Psychologist*, *53*(4), 449–455. doi:10.1037/0003-066X.53.4.449 PMID:9572008

Hammer, M. R., Bennett, M. J., & Wiseman, R. (2003). Measuring Intercultural Sensitivity: The Intercultural Development Inventory. *International Journal of Intercultural Relations*, *27*(4), 421–443. doi:10.1016/S0147-1767(03)00032-4

Han, J., Park, D., Hua, M., & Childs, P. (2021). Is group work beneficial for producing creative designs in STEM design education? *International Journal of Technology and Design Education*. Advance online publication. doi:10.100710798-021-09709-y

Harper, B. (2018). Technology and teacher–student interactions: A review of empirical research. *Journal of Research on Technology in Education*, *50*(3), 214–225. doi:10.1080/15391523.2018.1450690

Hayashi, K., Shibata, S., Inoue, E., Adachi, S., & Iba, T. (2022). Online Education Patterns, Part 1: Patterns for Linking Separate Worlds. *EuroPLoP'21: 26th European Conference on Pattern Languages of Programs,* 1–16. 10.1145/3489449.3490003

Helterbran, V. R., & Strahler, B. R. (2013). Children as global citizens: A socratic approach to teaching character. *Childhood Education*, *89*(5), 310–314. doi:10.1080/00094056.2013.830902

Henning, W. (2004). Everyday cognition and situated learning. In Handbook of research on educational communications and technology (2nd ed., pp. 143–168). Erlbaum.

Hine, G. S. C. (2013). The importance of action research in teacher education programs. In *Design, develop, evaluate: The core of the learning. environment. Proceedings of the 22nd Annual Teaching Learning Forum.* Murdoch University. http://ctl.curtin.edu.au/professional_development/conferences/tlf/tlf2013/refereed/hine.html

Holliday, W., & Fagerheim, B. (2006). Integrating Information Literacy With a Sequenced English Composition Curriculum. *Portal, 6*(2), 169–184.

Holliday, W., & Rogers, J. (2013). Talking About Information Literacy: The Mediating Role of Discourse in a College Writing Classroom. *Portal, 13*(3), 257–271. doi:10.1353/pla.2013.0025

Holroyd, J. (2015). Implicit bias, awareness and imperfect cognitions. *Consciousness and Cognition, 33*, 511–523. doi:10.1016/j.concog.2014.08.024 PMID:25467778

hooks, b., & McKinnon, T. (1996). Sisterhood: Beyond Public and Private. *Signs, 21*(4), 814-829. Retrieved from https://search-ebscohost-com.ezproxy.snhu.edu/login.aspx?direct=true&db=edsjsr&AN=edsjsr.3175025&site=eds-live&scope=site

Hu, X., Chiu, M. M., Leung, W., & Yelland, N. (2021). Technology integration for young children during COVID-19: Towards future online teaching. *British Journal of Educational Technology: Journal of the Council for Educational Technology.* Advance online publication. doi:10.1111/bjet.13106

Huang, Y. M., Wang, C. S., & Liu, Y. C. (2015). A Study of Synchronous vs. Asynchronous Collaborative Design in Students Learning Motivation. *International Journal of Information and Education Technology (IJIET), 5*(5), 354–357. doi:10.7763/IJIET.2015.V5.529

Huang, Z. Y., & Cappel, J. J. (2005). Assessment of a web-based learning game in an information systems course. *Journal of Computer Information Systems, 45*(4), 42–49.

Hunt, Shanda, & Riegelman. (2020). *Conducting research through an anti-racist lens.* University of Minnesota. https://libguides.umn.edu/antiracismlens

Hunt, L., & Yoshida-Ehrmann, E. (2016). Linking schools of thought to schools of practice. *Gifted Child Today, 39*(3), 164–172. doi:10.1177/1076217516644650

Hurtado, S., & Carter, D. F. (1997). Effects of college transition and perceptions of the campus racial climate on Latino college students' sense of belonging. *Sociology of Education, 70*(4), 324–345. doi:10.2307/2673270

Hussain, O., Dillon, Th., Chang, E., & Hussain, F. (2010). Transactional risk-based decision making system in e-business interactions. *International Journal of Comput Syst Sci & Eng, 2010*(1), 15–28.

Hussain, T. (2020). *Education and COVID-19 in Nigeria: Tackling the digital divide.* SOAS Blog.

Ingersoll, R. M., May, H., & Consortium for Policy Research in Education. (2011). *Recruitment, Retention and the Minority Teacher Shortage.* CPRE Research Report # RR-69. Consortium for Policy Research in Education. Retrieved from https://search-ebscohost-com.ezproxy.snhu.edu/login.aspx?direct=true&db=eric&AN=ED526355&site=eds-live&scope=site

Inoue, A. B., & Poe, M. (2012). Race and Writing Assessment. Academic Press.

Inoue, A. B. (2019). Classroom Writing Assessment as an Antiracist Practice: Confronting White Supremacy in the Judgments of Language. *Pedagogy*, *19*(3), 373–404. doi:10.1215/15314200-7615366

Inoue, A. B. (2019). *Labor-Based Grading Contracts: Building Equity and Inclusion in the Compassionate Writing Classroom. In Perspectives on Writing. The WAC Clearinghouse.* University Press of Colorado.

Isbell, D., & Broaddus, D. (1995). Teaching Writing and Research as Inseparable: A Faculty-Librarian Teaching Team. *RSR. Reference Services Review*, *23*(4), 51–62. doi:10.1108/eb049264

Jacobs, H. L. M. (2008). Information Literacy and Reflective Pedagogical Praxis. *Journal of Academic Librarianship*, *34*(3), 256–262. doi:10.1016/j.acalib.2008.03.009

Jacobs, H. L. M., & Jacobs, D. (2009). Transforming the One-Shot Library Session into Pedagogical Collaboration: Information Literacy and the English Composition Class. *Reference and User Services Quarterly*, *49*(1), 72–82. doi:10.5860/rusq.49n1.72

Jacoby, B. (1999). Partnerships for service learning. *New Directions for Student Services*, *87*, 18–35.

Jagers, R. J., Rivas-Drake, D., & Williams, B. (2019). Transformative social and emotional learning (SEL): Toward SEL in service of educational equity and excellence. *Educational Psychologist*, *54*(3), 162–184. doi:10.1080/00461520.2019.1623032

Jaggars, S. S., & Xu, D. (2016). How do online course design features influence student performance? *Computers & Education*, *95*, 270–284. doi:10.1016/j.compedu.2016.01.014

Jarvis, S. & De Freitas, S. (2009). *Evaluation of an Immersive Learning Programme to support.* Academic Press.

Jena, P. K. (2020). Impact of pandemic COVID-19 on education in India. *International Journal of Current Research*, 12.

Johnson, G. M. (2011). Internet activities and developmental predictors: Gender differences among digital natives. *Journal of Interactive Online Learning*, *10*(2), 64–76.

Jone, R., & Hafner, A. (2021). *Understanding Digital Literacy.* Routledge. doi:10.4324/9781003177647

Jonkers, H., Band, I., & Quartel, D. (2012a). *ArchiSurance Case Study.* The Open Group.

Kaffenberger, M. (2021). Modelling the long-run learning impact of the Covid-19 learning shock: Actions to (more than) mitigate loss. *International Journal of Educational Development*, *81*, 102326. doi:10.1016/j.ijedudev.2020.102326 PMID:33716394

Kahne, J., Middaugh, E., & Evans, C. (2009). *The civic potential of video games*. Massachusetts Institute of Technology Press. doi:10.7551/mitpress/8518.001.0001

Kambutu, J. (2016). Cultural Immersion Program Prepares Educators for Globalization Social Justice Teaching. In L. Nganga & J. Kambutu (Eds.), *Social Justice Education, Globalization, and Teacher Education* (pp. 271–290). Information Age Publishing, Inc.

Kaminski, K., & Bolliger, D. (2012). Technology, learning, and the Classroom: Longitudinal evaluation of a faculty development model. *Journal of Faculty Development*, *26*(1), 13–17.

Kathuria, H., & Becker, D. (2021). Leveraging a Course Quality Checklist to Improve Online Courses. *Journal of Teaching and Learning with Technology*, *10*(1), 400–407. doi:10.14434/jotlt.v10i1.31253

Kato, P. M., Cole, S. W., Bradlyn, A. S., & Pollock, B. H. (2008). A video game improves behavioral outcomes in adolescents and young adults with cancer: A randomized trial. *Pediatrics*, *122*(2), 305–317. doi:10.1542/peds.2007-3134 PMID:18676516

Katsara, O., & Witte, K. (2019). How to use Socratic questioning in order to promote adult's self-directed learning. *Studies in the Education of Adults*, *51*(1), 109–129. doi:10.1080/02660830.2018.1526446

Kautzman, A. M. (1996). Teaching Critical Thinking: The Alliance of Composition Studies and Research Instruction. *Reference Services Review*, *24*(3), 61–66. doi:10.1108/eb049289

Kealey, K. A., Peterson, A. V. Jr, Gaul, M. A., & Dinh, K. T. (2000). Teacher training as a behavior change process: Principles and results from a longitudinal study. *Health Education & Behavior*, *27*(1), 64–81. doi:10.1177/109019810002700107 PMID:10709793

Keengwe, J., & Kidd, T. T. (2010). Towards best-practices in online learning and teaching in higher education. *Journal of Online Learning and Teaching*, *6*(2), 533–539.

Kendall, S., Straw, S., Jones, M., Springate, I., & Grayson, H. (2008). Narrowing the Gap in Outcomes for Vulnerable Groups: A Review of the Research Evidence. National Foundation for Educational Research.

Kennedy, C. (2005). Teaching Information Literacy to the Advanced Writing Class in Three Sessions. *Electronic Journal of Academic & Special Librarianship, 6*(1).

Kersten, M. (2021). *Introducing SAFe® 5*. Your Operating System for Business Agility. Scaled Agile Inc.

Keynote address, multimodality, and learning conference. (2010). London Institute of Education. Retrieved from https://sites.google.com/a/lkl.ac.uk/cmr/conference-july-2010/keynote-Suzanne-de-castells- Jennifer-Jenson

Khanna, R., & Kareem, J. (2021). Creating inclusive spaces in virtual classroom sessions during the COVID pandemic: An exploratory study of primary class teachers in India. *International Journal of Educational Research Open, 2*, 100038. doi:10.1016/j.ijedro.2021.100038

Khlaif, Z. N., & Salha, S. (2020). The unanticipated educational challenges of developing countries in Covid-19 crisis: A brief report. *Interdisciplinary Journal of Virtual Learning in Medical Sciences, 11*(2), 130–134.

Kiili, K. (2005). Digital game-based learning: Towards an experiential gaming model. *The Internet and Higher Education, 8*(1), 13–24. doi:10.1016/j.iheduc.2004.12.001

Kim, C., Kim, M. K., Lee, C., Spector, J. M.. & DeMeester, K. (2013). Teacher beliefs and technology integration. *Teaching and Teacher Education, 29*, 76–85. .Tate.2012.08.005 doi:10.1016/j

Kim, A., & Lai, V. (2012). Rapid interactions between lexical-semantic and word form analysis during word recognition in context: Evidence from ERPs. *Journal of Cognitive Neuroscience, 24*(5), 1104–1112. doi:10.1162/jocn_a_00148 PMID:21981670

Kim, J., & Lennon, Sh. (2017). *Descriptive Content Analysis on E-Service Research. International Journal of Service Science, Management, Engineering, and Technology.* doi:10.4018/IJSSMET.2017010102

Kinnari-Korpela, H. (2015). Using short video lectures to enhance mathematics learning-experiences on differential and integral calculus course for engineering students. *Informatics in Education-An International Journal, 14*(1), 69–83. doi:10.15388/infedu.2015.05

Kiseleva, I., Karmanov, M., Korotkov, A., Kuznetsov, V., & Gasparian, M. (2018). Risk management in business: Concept, types, evaluation criteria. *Revista ESPACIOS, 798*, 1015.

Kolb, D. A. (1984). *Experiential learning.* Prentice-Hall.

Koppe, Ch., van Eekeleny, M., & Hoppenbrouwersz, S. (2015). Improving Student Group Work with Collaboration. Patterns: A Case Study. In *2015 IEEE/ACM 37th IEEE International Conference on Software Engineering.* IEEE. https://ieeexplore.ieee.org/document/7202977

Koruyan, K. (2016). *The influence of technology-enhanced task design on the development of language learner autonomy and motivation in an Anatolian high school; A case study.* The Open University.

Kraemer, E. W., Lombardo, S. V., & Lepkowski, F. J. (2007). The Librarian, the Machine, or a Little of Both: A Comparative Study of Three Information Literacy Pedagogies at Oakland University. *College & Research Libraries, 68*(4), 330–342. doi:10.5860/crl.68.4.330

Kramer, M., Förtsch, C., Stürmer, J., Förtsch, S., Seidel, T., & Neuhaus, B. J. (2020). Measuring biology teachers' professional vision: Development and validation of a video-based assessment tool. *Cogent Education, 7*(1), 1–28. doi:10.1080/2331186X.2020.1823155

Krischler, M., Powell, J. J., & Pit-Ten Cate, I. M. (2019). What is meant by inclusion? On the effects of different definitions on attitudes towards inclusion education. *European Journal of Special Needs Education, 34*(5), 632–648. doi:10.1080/08856257.2019.1580837

Kuhfeld, M., Soland, J., Tarasawa, B., Johnson, A., Ruzek, E., & Liu, J. (2020). Projecting the potential impact of COVID-19 school closures on academic achievement. *Educational Researcher, 49*(8), 549–565. doi:10.3102/0013189X20965918

Kumi-Yeboah, A., Dogbey, J., Yuan, G., & Smith, P. (2020). Cultural diversity in online education: An exploration of instructors' perceptions and challenges. *Teachers College Record, 122*(7), 1–46. doi:10.1177/016146812012200708

Kurt, G., Atay, D., & Ozturk, H. A. (2021). Student engagement in K-12 online education during the pandemic: The case of Turkey. *Journal of Research on Technology in Education.* Advance online publication. doi:10.1080/15391523.2021.1920518

Kutner, L. A., Olson, C. K., Warner, D. E., & Hertzog, S. M. (2008). Parents' and sons' perspectives on video game play - a qualitative study. *Journal of Adolescent Research, 23*(1), 76–96. doi:10.1177/0743558407310721

Ladson-Billings, G. (1995). Toward a theory of culturally relevant pedagogy. *American Educational Research Journal, 32*(3), 465–491. doi:10.3102/00028312032003465

Ladson-Billings, G. (2014). Culturally relevant pedagogy 2.0: Aka the remix. *Harvard Educational Review, 84*(1), 74–84. doi:10.17763/haer.84.1.p2rj131485484751

Laine & Lindberg, (2020). Designing engaging games for education: A systematic literature review on game motivators and design principles. *IEEE Transactions on Learning Technologies, 13*(4), 804-821. doi:10.1109/TLT.2020.3018503

Lankhorst, M. (2016). *Enterprise Architecture and Agile Development: Opposites Attract? Agile EA with TOGAF 9.1.* BizzDesign. https://bizzdesign.com/blog/enterprise-architecture-and-agile-development-opposites-attract/

Laur, D. (2019). *Authentic project-based learning in grades 9-12: Standards-based strategies and scaffolding for success.* Routledge. doi:10.4324/9780429275258

Lave, J., & Wenger, E. (1991). *Situated learning.* Cambridge University Press. doi:10.1017/CBO9780511815355

Lawyer, G. (2018). The dangers of separating social justice from multicultural education: Applications in higher education. *International Journal of Multicultural Education, 20*(1), 86–101. Advance online publication. doi:10.18251/ijme.v20i1.1538

Lederach, J. P. (1997). *Building Peace: Sustainable Reconciliation in Divided Societies.* United States Institute of Peace Press.

Lederman, D. (2020). Will shift to remote teaching be boon or bane for online learning. Inside Higher Ed.

Leibold, N., & Schwarz, L. M. (2015). The art of giving online feedback. *The Journal of Effective Teaching*, *15*(1), 34–46. https://uncw.edu/jet/articles/vol15_1/leiboldabs.html

Lemov, D., & Woolway, E. (2020). Remote teaching and the new normal. In D. Lemov (Ed.), *Teaching in the Online Classroom: Surviving and Thriving in the New Normal* (pp. 1–14). Jossey-Bass.

Lewis, C. C., & Abdul-Hamid, H. (2006). Implementing Effective Online Teaching Practices: Voices of Exemplary Faculty. *Innovative Higher Education*, *31*(2), 83–98. doi:10.100710755-006-9010-z

Lewis, K. A. (2018). A digital immigrant venture into teaching online: An autoethnographic account of a classroom teacher transformed. *Qualitative Report*, *23*(7), 1752–1772. doi:10.46743/2160-3715/2018.3036

Liu, X., Magjuka, R. J., Bonk, C. J., & Lee, S. (2007). Does a sense of community matter? An examination of participants' perceptions of building learning communities in online courses. *Quarterly Review of Distance Education*, *8*(1), 9–24.

Loewus, L. (2017). *The Nation's Teaching Force Is Still Mostly White and Female*. Retrieved from https://www.edweek.org/ew/articles/2017/08/15/the-nations-teaching-force-is-still-mostly.html

Lotherington, H., & Jenson, J. (2011). Teaching Multimodal and Digital Literacy in L2 Settings: New Literacies, New Basics, New Pedagogies. *Annual Review of Applied Linguistics*, *31*, 226–246. doi:10.1017/S0267190511000110

Lowe, N. K. (2019). What is a pilot study? *Journal of Obstetric, Gynecologic, and Neonatal Nursing*, *48*(2), 117–118. doi:10.1016/j.jogn.2019.01.005 PMID:30731050

Luckhurst, P. (2016). Reclaiming the biscuit; Crafting in the name of feminism, vagina-themed baking and safe spaces in the kitchen -- being a modern woman has never been such a complicated balancing act. Phoebe Luckhurst unpicks the new rules of the sisterhood. *The London Evening Standard*. Retrieved from https://search-ebscohost-com.ezproxy.snhu.edu/login.aspx?direct=true&db=edsbig&AN=edsbig.A465132119&site=eds-live&scope=site

Lyiscott, J. (2018). *Why English Class is Silencing Students of Color*. The Benjamin School.

Mabrito, M. (2006). A study of synchronous versus asynchronous collaboration in an online business writing class. *American Journal of Distance Education*, *20*(2), 93–107. doi:10.120715389286ajde2002_4

Mac Ginty, R., & Richmond, O. P. (2013). The local turn in peace building: A critical agenda for peace. *Third World Quarterly*, *34*(5), 763–783. doi:10.1080/01436597.2013.800750

Maharg, P. (2007). *Transforming Legal Education. Learning and Teaching the Law in the Early Twenty-first Century*. Ashgate Publishing.

Mahoney, P., Macfarlane, S., & Ajjawi, R. (2019). A qualitative synthesis of video feedback in higher education. *Teaching in Higher Education, 24*(2), 157–179. doi:10.1080/13562517.2018.1471457

Mangrum, J. R. (2010). Sharing practices through socratic seminar. *Kappan, 91*(7), 40–43. doi:10.1177/003172171009100708

Mann, S. J. (2001). Alternative Perspectives on the Student Experience: Alienation and Engagement. *Studies in Higher Education, 26*(1), 7–19. https://search-ebscohost-com.ezproxy.snhu.edu/login.aspx?direct=true&db=eric&AN=EJ628164&site=eds-live&scope=site

Manzone, J., & Peeples, R. (2021). Curated conversations: Transferring diverse literature to the K-12 classroom. In D. Hartsfield (Ed.), *Handbook of Research on Teaching Diverse Literature to Pre-Service Professionals* (pp. 257–275). IGI Global Publishing. doi:10.4018/978-1-7998-7375-4.ch013

Markides, C. (2011, March). Crossing the Chasm: How to Convert Relevant Research Into Managerially Useful Research. *The Journal of Applied Behavioral Science, 47*(1), 121–134. doi:10.1177/0021886310388162

Martens, R. L., Gulikers, J., & Bastiaens, T. (2004). The impact of intrinsic motivation on e-learning in authentic computer tasks. *Journal of Computer Assisted Learning, 20*(5), 368–376. doi:10.1111/j.1365-2729.2004.00096.x

Martin, F., & Bolliger, D. U. (2018). Engagement matters: Student perceptions on the importance of engagement strategies in the online learning environment. *Online Learning Journal, 22*(1), 205–222. doi:10.24059/olj.v22i1.1092

Martin, F., Sun, T., Turk, M., & Ritzhaupt, A. D. (2021). A Meta-Analysis on the Effects of Synchronous Online Learning on Cognitive and Affective Educational Outcomes. *International Review of Research in Open and Distributed Learning, 22*(3), 205–242. doi:10.19173/irrodl.v22i3.5263

Martin, F., Wang, C., & Sadaf, A. (2018). Student perception of helpfulness of facilitation strategies that enhance instructor presence, connectedness, engagement and learning in online courses. *The Internet and Higher Education, 37*, 52–65. doi:10.1016/j.iheduc.2018.01.003

Martirosyan, N. M., Kennon, J. L., Saxon, D. P., Edmonson, S. L. & Skidmore, S. T. (2017). Instructional technology practices in developmental education in Texas. *Journal of College Reading and Learning, 47*(1), 3–25. 1. 2016. 12188 06 doi:0.1080/10790195

Mayer, R. E. (2014). *Computer games for learning. An evidence-based approach.* MIT Press. doi:10.7551/mitpress/9427.001.0001

Mayer, R. E., & Johnson, C. I. (2010). Adding instructional features that promote learning in a game-like environment. *Journal of Educational Computing Research, 101*(3), 621–629. doi:10.2190/EC.42.3.a

Mayes, T., & De Freitas, S. (2007). Learning and e-Learning: the role of theory. In H. Beetham & R. Sharpe (Eds.), *Rethinking Pedagogy in the Digital Age*. Routledge.

McClure, R., Cooke, R., & Carlin, A. (2011). The Search for the Skunk Ape: Studying the Impact of an Online Information Literacy Tutorial on Student Writing. *Journal of Information Literacy*, *5*(2), 26–45. doi:10.11645/5.2.1638

McLuhan, M. (1964). *Understanding Media: The Extensions of Man*. Routledge.

Metcalfe, S. A., Aitken, M., & Gaff, C. L. (2008). The importance of program evaluation: How can it be applied to diverse genetics education settings? *Journal of Genetic Counseling*, *17*(2), 170–179. doi:10.100710897-007-9138-8 PMID:18247108

Michinov, N., Brunot, S., Le Bohec, O., Juhel, J., & Delaval, M. (2011). Procrastination, participation, and performance in online learning environments. *Computers & Education*, *56*(1), 243–252. doi:10.1016/j.compedu.2010.07.025

Mignolo, W. D. (2011a). *The darker side of Western modernity: global futures, decolonial options*. Duke UP.

Mishra, S. V. (2020). *COVID-19, online teaching, and deepening digital divide in India*. Academic Press.

Missildine, K., Fountain, R., Summers, L., & Gosselin, K. (2013). Flipping the classroom to improve student performance and satisfaction. *The Journal of Nursing Education*, *52*(10), 597–599. doi:10.3928/01484834-20130919-03 PMID:24044386

Moeller, V. J., & Moeller, M. V. (2002). *Socratic seminars and literature circles for middle and high school English*. Eye on Education.

Moffett, J. (1968). *Teaching the universe of discourse*. Heinemann.

Moldavan, A. M., Capraro, R. M., & Capraro, M. M. (2021). Navigating (and disrupting) the digital divide: Urban teachers' perspectives on secondary mathematics instruction during COVID-19. *The Urban Review*, 1–26. PMID:34276100

Molnar, A. L., & Kearney, R. C. (2017). A comparison of cognitive presence in asynchronous and synchronous discussions in an online dental hygiene course. *Journal of Dental Hygiene*, *91*(3), 14–21. https://jdh.adha.org/content/91/3/14.short PMID:29118067

Mounce, M. (2009). Academic Librarian and English Composition Instructor Collaboration: A Selective Annotated Bibliography 1998-2007. *Reference Services Review*, *37*(1), 44–53. doi:10.1108/00907320910934986

Muthuprasad, T., Aiswarya, S., Aditya, K. S., & Jha, G. K. (2021). Children' perception and preference for online education in India during COVID-19 pandemic. *Social Sciences & Humanities Open*, *3*(1), 100101. doi:10.1016/j.ssaho.2020.100101 PMID:34173507

Nagelhout, E. (1999). Pre-Professional Practices in the Technical Writing Classroom. *Technical Communication Quarterly*, 8(3), 285–299. doi:10.1080/10572259909364669

National Paideia Center. (2003). *The Paideia seminar: Active thinking through dialogue in the elementary grades*. Chapel Hill, NC: Author. www.paideia.org

Ndlovu-Gatsheni, S. J. (2013). *Empire, global coloniality, and African objection.* Berghahn Books.

Nelson, B. C., & Erlandson, B. E. (2008). Managing cognitive load in educational multi-user virtual environments: Reflection on design in practice. *Educational Technology Research and Development*, 56(5–6), 619–641. doi:10.100711423-007-9082-1

Nevelsteen, K. J. L. (2017). Virtual world, defined from a technological perspective, and applied to video games, mixed reality and the meta-verse. *Comput Anim Virtual Worlds*. doi:10.1002/cav.1752

New Media Consortium. (2012). *NMC Horizon Report 2012 K-12 Edition.* http://www.nmc.org/publications/2012-horizon-report-k12

Nicholson, S. A., & Bond, N. (2003). Collaborative Reflection and Professional Community Building: An Analysis of Preservice Teachers' Use of an Electronic Discussion Board. *Journal of Technology and Teacher Education*, 11(2), 259–279.

Nieto, S., & Bode, P. (2018). Affirming diversity: The sociopolitical context for multicultural education (7th ed.). New York, NY: Pearson.

Nikulin, D. (2006). *On dialogue.* Lexington Books.

Noben, I., Folkert Deinum, J., & Hofman, W. H. (2020). Quality of teaching in higher education: Reviewing teaching behaviour through classroom observations. *The International Journal for Academic Development*. Advance online publication. doi:10.1080/1360144X.2020.1830776

Noble, S. U. (2018). *Algorithms of oppression: How search engines reinforce racism.* New York University Press. doi:10.2307/j.ctt1pwt9w5

Norgaard, R., Arp, L., & Woodard, B. (2004). Writing information literacy in the classroom. *Reference and User Services Quarterly*, 43(3), 220–226.

Norton, B. (2013). *Identity and Language Learning: Extending the Conversation.* Multilingual Matters. doi:10.21832/9781783090563

Norton, B., & Toohey, K. (2011). Identity, language learning, and social change. *Language Teaching*, 44(4), 412–446. doi:10.1017/S0261444811000309

Novak, G. M., Patterson, E. T., Gavrin, A. D., & Christian, W. (1999). *Just in Time Teaching: Blending Active Learning with Web Technology.* Prentice Hall. doi:10.1119/1.19159

O'Brien, D. (2010). *Gaming for Classroom-Based Learning: Digital Role Playing as a Motivator of Study.* IGI Global.

O'Connor, L., Bowles-Terry, M., Davis, E., & Holliday, W. (2010). Writing Information Literacy: Revisited Application of Theory to Practice in the Classroom. *Reference and User Services Quarterly*, *49*(3), 225–230. doi:10.5860/rusq.49n3.225

Okojie, M. C., Olinzock, A. A., & Okojie-Boulder, T. C. (2006). The pedagogy of technology integration. *The Journal of Technology Studies*, *32*(2), 66–71.

Oliver, M., & Pelletier, C. (2004). *Activity theory and learning from digital games: implications for game design. Paper presented at Digital Generations: Children*, Young People and New Media.

Ouyang, F., & Scharber, C. (2017). The influences of an experienced instructor's discussion design and facilitation on an online learning community development: A social network analysis study. *The Internet and Higher Education*, *35*, 34–47. doi:10.1016/j.iheduc.2017.07.002

Ovadia, S. (2010). Writing as an Information Literacy Tool: Bringing Writing in the Disciplines to an Online Library Class. *Journal of Library Administration*, *50*(7), 899–908. doi:10.1080/01930826.2010.488990

Owston, R. D. (2012). Computer games and the quest to find their affordances for learning. *Educational Researcher*, *41*(3), 105–106. doi:10.3102/0013189X12439231

Oyewumi, O. (1997). *The invention of women: making an African sense of Western gender discourse*. University of Minnesota Press.

Palsson, F., & McDade, C. L. (2014). Factors Affecting the Successful Implementation of a Common Assignment for First-Year Composition Information Literacy. *College & Undergraduate Libraries*, *21*(2), 193–209. doi:10.1080/10691316.2013.829375

Panigrahi, R., Srivastava, P. R., & Sharma, D. (2018). Online learning: Adoption, continuance, and learning outcome—A review of literature. *International Journal of Information Management*, *43*, 1–14. doi:10.1016/j.ijinfomgt.2018.05.005

Pappas, C. (2022). *Cloud Based e-Learning Platforms: 10 Advantages eLearning Professionals Need To Know*. Docebo. https://www.docebo.com/learning-network/blog/cloud-based-elearning-platforms/

Paris, D. (2012). Culturally sustaining pedagogy: A needed change in stance, terminology, and practice. *Educational Researcher*, *41*(3), 93–97. doi:10.3102/0013189X12441244

Pascarella, E. T., & Terenzini, P. T. (2005). *How College Affects Students: A Third Decade of Research* (Vol. 2). Jossey-Bass.

Patterson, D. (2009). Information Literacy and Community College Students: Using New Approaches to Literacy Theory to Produce Equity. *The Library Quarterly*, *79*(3), 343–361. doi:10.1086/599124

Pea, R., & Lindgren, R. (2008). Video Collaboratories for Research and Education: An Analysis of Collaboration Design Patterns. IEEE Transactions on Learning Technologies, 1(4).

Peacock, S., & Cowan, J. (2019). Promoting sense of belonging in online learning communities of inquiry at accredited courses. *Online Learning, 23*(2), 67–81. doi:10.24059/olj.v23i2.1488

Perrotta, C., Featherstone, G., Aston, H., & Houghton, E. (2013). *Games-based learning: Latest evidence and future directions.* NFER.

Peterson, A. T., Beymer, P. N., & Putnam, R. T. (2018). Synchronous and asynchronous discussions: Effects on cooperation, belonging, and affect. *Online Learning, 22*(4), 7–25. doi:10.24059/olj.v22i4.1517

Picciano, A. G. (2017). Theories and Frameworks for Online Education: Seeking an Integrated Model. *Online Learning, 21*(3), 166–190. doi:10.24059/olj.v21i3.1225

Pisonia, G., Gijlersc, H., Ha Nguyend, T., & Chene, H. (2021). Collaboration patterns in students' teams working on business cases. *CEUR Workshop Proceedings.*

Plass, J. L., Homer, B. D., Kinzer, C. K., Chang, Y. K., Frye, J., Kaczetow, W., Isbister, K., & Perlin, K. (2013). Metrics in simulations and games for learning. In M. S. El-Nasr, A. Drachen, & A. Canossa (Eds.), *Game Analytics: Maximizing the value of player data* (pp. 297–729). Springer.

Popa, S. (2020). Reflections on COVID-19 and the future of education and learning. *Prospects, 49*(1-2), 1–6. doi:10.100711125-020-09511-z PMID:33012848

Porter, W. W., Graham, C. R., Spring, K. A., & Welch, K. R. (2014). Blended learning in Higher Education: Institutional adoption and implementation. *Computers & Education, 75,* 185–195. 10. 1016/j. Compe du. 2014. 02. 011 doi:https://doi.org/

Postle, G. (2003). Online Teaching and Learning in Higher Education: A Case Study. Department of Education, Science and Training. University of Southern Queensland.

Prensky, M. (2008). Students as designers and creators of educational computer games: Who else? *British Journal of Educational Technology, 39*(6), 1004–1019.

Pritchett, L., & Beatty, A. (2015). Slow down, you're going too fast: Matching curricula to child skill levels. *International Journal of Educational Development, 40,* 276–288. doi:10.1016/j.ijedudev.2014.11.013

Protopsaltis, A., Panzoli, D., Dunwell, I., & De Freitas, S. (2010). Re-purposing Serious Games in Health Care Education. *The 12th Mediterranean Conference on Medical and Biological Engineering and Computing – MEDICON 2010.*

Pugh, K. J., & Zhao, Y. (2003). Stories of teacher alienation: A look at the unintended consequences of efforts to empower teachers. *Teaching and Teacher Education, 19*(2), 187. https://doi-org.ezproxy.snhu.edu/10.1016/S0742-051X(02)00103-8

Pursel, B., & Fang, H.-N. (2011). *Lecture Capture: Current Research and Future Directions.* The Schreyer Institute for Teaching Excellence.

Putri, N., & Yusof, S. M. (2009). Critical success factors for implementing quality engineering tools and techniques in malaysian's and indonesian's automotive industries: An Exploratory Study. *Journal Proceedings of the International MultiConference of Engineers and Computer Scientists.*, *2*, 18–20.

Quality Matters. (2021). *Course Design Rubric Standards.* https://www.qualitymatters.org/qa-resources/rubric-standards/higher-ed-rubric

Ramachandran, V. (2021, February 23). *Stanford researchers identify four causes for 'Zoom fatigue' and their simple fixes.* Stanford News. https://news.stanford.edu/2021/02/23/four-causes-zoom-fatigue-solutions/

Ravel, K. (2021). Decluttering Our Technology [Sample Assignment]. Rockford University.

Reinitz, J. (2019, April 11). Sisterhood program building positive bonds. *Waterloo-Cedar Falls Courier.* Retrieved from https://search-ebscohost-com.ezproxy.snhu.edu/login.aspx?direct=true&db=nfh&AN=2W61417354456&site=eds-live&scope=site

Reuge, N., Jenkins, R., Brossard, M., Soobrayan, B., Mizunoya, S., Ackers, J., Jones, L., & Taulo, W. G. (2021). Education response to COVID 19 pandemic, a special issue proposed by UNICEF: Editorial review. *International Journal of Educational Development*, *87*, 102485. doi:10.1016/j.ijedudev.2021.102485 PMID:34511714

Reynolds, J., Caley, L., & Mason, R. (2002). *How Do People Learn?* Chartered Institute of Personnel Development.

Richardson, J. C., & Swan, K. (2003). Examining social presence in online courses in relation to student's perceived learning and satisfaction. *J. Asynchr. Learn.*, *7*(1), 68–88. doi:10.24059/olj.v7i1.1864

Richey, A., & Leena, H. (2016). Contesting Institutional Epistemologies of Diversity: The Shift to Global/Local Framework in Teacher Education. In L. Nganga & J. Kambutu (Eds.), *Social Justice Education, Globalization, and Teacher Education* (pp. 55–72). Information Age Publishing, Inc.

Rinto, E. E., & Cogbill-Seiders, E. I. (2015). Library Instruction and Themed Composition Courses: An Investigation of Factors that Impact Student Learning. *Journal of Academic Librarianship*, *41*(2), 14–20. doi:10.1016/j.acalib.2014.11.010

Rivas-Drake, D., Rosario-Ramos, E., McGovern, G., & Jagers, R. J. (2021). Rising up together: Spotlighting transformative SEL in practice with Latinx youth. CASEL: University of Michigan.

Roblyer, M. D., Freeman, J., Donaldson, M. B., & Maddox, M. (2007). A comparison of outcomes of virtual school courses offered in synchronous and asynchronous formats. *The Internet and Higher Education*, *10*(4), 261–268. doi:10.1016/j.iheduc.2007.08.003

Roddy, C., Amiet, D. L., Chung, J., Holt, C., Shaw, L., McKenzie, S., ... Mundy, M. E. (2017, November). Applying best practice online learning, teaching, and support to intensive online environments: An integrative review. *Frontiers in Education, 2*, article 59.

Roddy, C., Amiet, D. L., Chung, J., Holt, C., Shaw, L., McKenzie, S., Garivaldis, F., Lodge, J. M., & Mundy, M. E. (2017). Applying best practice online learning, teaching, and support to intensive online environments: An integrative review. *Frontiers in Education*, *2*(59), 1–10. doi:10.3389/feduc.2017.00059

Rogers, C. (1951). *Client-centered Therapy: Its Current Practice, Implications, and Theory*. Constable.

Roscoe, R., Russell, B., Snow, E., & McNamara, D. (2013). Game-based writing strategy practice with the *Writing Pal*. In K. E. Pytash & R. E. Ferdig (Eds.), *Exploring Technology for Writing and Writing Instruction*. IGIGlobal.

Roth, W. (2010). *Language, learning, context: Talking the talk*. Routledge.

Rovai, A. P. (2002). Development of an instrument to measure classroom community. *The Internet and Higher Education*, *5*(3), 197–211. doi:10.1016/S1096-7516(02)00102-1

Rubel, L. (2017). Equity-directed instructional practices: Beyond the dominant perspective. *Journal of Urban Mathematics Education*, *10*(2), 66–105.

Rugani, J., & Grijalva, K. (2020). Dissolve the Screen. In D. Lemov (Ed.), *Teaching in the Online Classroom: Surviving and Thriving in the New Normal* (pp. 36–56). Jossey-Bass.

Ryan, D. P. J. (2001). *Bronfenbrenner's ecological systems theory*. Retrieved from http://www.floridahealth.gov/AlternateSites/CMSKids/providers/early_steps/training/documents/bronfenbrenners_ecological.pdf

Sabatino, L. (2014). Improving Writing Literacies through Digital Gaming Literacies: Facebook Gaming in the Composition Classroom. *Computers and Composition*, *32*, 41–53. doi:10.1016/j.compcom.2014.04.005

Sadera, W., Robertson, J., Song, L., & Midon, M. (2009). The role of community in online learning success. *Journal of Online Learning and Teaching*, *5*(2), 277–284. https://jolt.merlot.org/vol5no2/sadera_0609.pdf

Sagheb-Tehrani, M. (2009). The Results of Online Teaching: A Case Study. *ISEDJ*, *7*(42). http://isedj.org/7/42/

Salmon, A. K. (2018). Frameworks that promote authentic learning. In A. K. Salmon (Ed.), *Authentic Teaching and Learning for PreK-Fifth Grade: Advice from Practitioners and Coaches* (pp. 1–31). Routledge. doi:10.4324/9781351211505-1

Samaras, A. P., & Freese, A. R. (2006). *Self-study of teaching practices: Primer*. Peter Lang.

Samson, S., & Millett, M. S. (2003). The Learning Environment: First-Year Students, Teaching Assistants, and Information Literacy. *Research Strategies*, *19*(2), 84–98. doi:10.1016/j.resstr.2004.02.001

Scagnoli, N. I., Choo, J., & Tian, J. (2019). Students' insights on the use of video lectures in online classes. *British Journal of Educational Technology, 50*(1), 399–414. doi:10.1111/bjet.12572

Scaled Agile. (2022). *Succeeding with AI in SAFe.* Scaled Agile, Inc. https://www.scaledagileframework.com/succeeding-with-ai-in-safe/

Schindler, L., Burkholder, J., Morad, A., & Marsh, C. (2017). Computer-based technology and student engagement: A critical review of the literature. *International Journal of Educational Technology in Higher Education, 14*(25), 1–28.

Schneider, J. (2013). Remembrance of things past: A history of the Socratic method in the United States. *Curriculum Inquiry, 43*(5), 613–640. doi:10.1111/curi.12030

Schrader, P. G., Lawless, K. A., & McCreery, M. (2009). Intertextuality in massively multiplayer online games. In R. E. Ferdig (Ed.), *Handbook of Research on Effective Electronic Gaming in Education* (Vol. 3, pp. 791–807). Information Science Reference.

Schrank, Z. (2020). Integrating the daily newspaper into the college classroom. *The Journal of Scholarship of Teaching and Learning, 20*(2), 122–126. doi:10.14434/josotl.v20i2.24386

Schultz, K. (2019). *There is rampant distrust in education. Here's how to fix that.* Retrieved from https://www.edweek.org/ew/articles/2019/06/20/there-is-rampant-distrust-in-education-heres.html

Seeman, M. (1959). On the Meaning of Alienation. *American Sociological Review, 24*(6), 783–791. https://doi-org.ezproxy.snhu.edu/10.2307/2088565

Service Architecture. (2022). *Education XML.* Service Architecture. https://www.service-architecture.com/articles/xml/education-xml.html

Sharma, R. N., & Sharma, R. K. (1996). *History of education in India.* Atlantic Publishers & Distributors.

Sheridan, J. (1992). WAC and Libraries: A Look at the Literature. *Journal of Academic Librarianship, 18*(2), 90–94.

Short, D. (2012). Teaching scientific concepts using a virtual world—*Minecraft. Teaching Science, 58*(3), 55–58.

Shute, V. J. (2008). Focus on formative feedback. *Review of Educational Research, 78*(1), 153–189.

Shute, V. J. (2013). *Stealth assessment: Measuring and supporting learning in video games.* MIT Press.

Şimşek, Ö., & Barto, A. (2006). An intrinsic reward mechanism for efficient exploration. *Proceedings of the 23rd International Conference on Machine Learning, 148*, 833–40.

Singh, R. N., & Hurley, D. C. (2017). The effectiveness of teaching-learning process in online education as perceived by university faculty and instructional technology professionals. *Journal of Teaching and Learning with Technology, 6*(1), 65–75. doi:10.14434/jotlt.v6.n1.19528

Sinicrope, C., Norris, J., & Watanabe, Y. (2007). *Understanding and assessing intercultural competence: A summary of theory, research, and practice* (Technical report for the Foreign Language Program Evaluation Project). SLS Papers. http://hdl.handle.net/10125/40689

Skylar, A. A. (2009). A comparison of asynchronous online text-based lectures and synchronous interactive web conferencing lectures. *Issues in Teacher Education*, *18*(2), 69–84.

Smith, D. G. (2009). *Diversity's promise for higher education: Making it work*. Johns Hopkins University.

Smitherman, G. (1976). 'God Don't Never Change': Black English from a Black Perspective. *College English*, *34*(6), 828–833. doi:10.2307/375044

Smith, G., Li, M., & Drobisz, J., Park, K. D., & Smith, S. (2013). Play games or study? Computer games in eBooks to learn English vocabulary. *Computers & Education*, *69*, 274–286.

Soflano, M. (2011). *Modding in serious games: Teaching Structured Query Language (SQL) using Neverwinter*. Academic Press.

Spencer, M. (2016). *Agile EA – the MVP – enterprise architect-Building the Business Value Chain…* https://enterprisearchitect.wordpress.com/2016/04/11/agile-ea-the-mvp/1/2

Squire, K. (2006). From content to context: Videogames as designed experience. *Educational Researcher*, *35*(8), 19–29. doi:10.3102/0013189X035008019

Steinkuehler, C., & Williams, D. (2006). Where everybody knows your (screen) name: Online games as third places. *Journal of Computer-Mediated Communication*, *11*(4), 26. doi:10.1111/j.1083-6101.2006.00300.x

Stepich, D. A., & Ertmer, P. A. (2003). Building community as a critical element of online course design. *Educational Technology*, 33–43.

Stieler-Hunt, C., & Jones, C. M. (2015). Educators who believe: Understanding the enthusiasm of teachers who use digital games in the classroom. *Research in Learning Technology*, *23*, 1–14. doi:10.3402/rlt.v23.26155

Stojanov, I. (2015). *Scaling agile using scaled agile framework [Master's thesis]*. Eindhoven University of Technology.

Strong, M. (1996). *The habit of thought: From Socratic seminars to Socratic practice*. New View.

Sturgeon, C. (2011). *Faculty perceptions of the factors enabling and facilitating their integration of instructional technology in teaching* [Doctoral dissertation]. University of Tennessee.

Subotnik, R. F., Olszewski-Kubilius, P., & Worrell, F. C. (2021). The talent development megamodel: A domain-specific conceptual framework based on the psychology of high performance. In R.J. Sternberg & D. Ambrose (Eds.), Conceptions of Giftedness and Talent (pp. 425-442). Palgrave Macmillan. doi:10.1007/978-3-030-56869-6_24

Sult, L., & Mills, V. (2006). A blended method for integrating information literacy instruction into English composition classes. *RSR. Reference Services Review*, *34*(3), 368–388. doi:10.1108/00907320610685328

Swan, K. (2002). Building communities in online courses: The importance of interaction. *Education Communication and Information*, *2*(1), 23–49. doi:10.1080/1463631022000005016

Sweeney, M. (2012). The Wikipedia Project: Changing Students from Consumers to Producers. *Teaching English in the Two-Year College*, *39*(3), 256–267.

Tannen, D. (1998). *The argument culture: Moving from debate to dialogue*. Random House.

Tapping into multiple intelligences. (2004). Retrieved from https://www.thirteen.org/edonline/concept2class/mi/index.html

Teaching Tolerance. (2016). *Social justice standards: The teaching anti-bias framework*. Author.

Telles-Langdon, D. M. (2020). Transitioning University Courses Online in Response to COVID-19. *Journal of Teaching and Learning*, *14*(1), 108–119. doi:10.22329/jtl.v14i1.6262

Terlecki, M., Brown, J., Harner-Steciw, L., Irvin-Hannum, J., Marchetto-Ryan, N., Ruhl, L., & Wiggins, J. (2011). Sex differences and similarities in video game experience, preferences, and self-efficacy: Implications for the gaming industry. *Current Psychology (New Brunswick, N.J.)*, *30*(1), 22–33. doi:10.100712144-010-9095-5

The Open Group. (2011a). *Architecture Development Method*. The Open Group. https://pubs.opengroup.org/architecture/togaf9-doc/arch/chap05.html

The Open Group. (2011b). *TOGAF 9.1*. The Open Group.

Thune, T. (2011). Success Factors in Higher Education–Industry Collaboration: A case study of collaboration in the engineering field. *Tertiary Education and Management*, *17*(1), 31–50. doi:10.1080/13583883.2011.552627

Toohey, K., Dagenais, D., & Schulze, E. (2012). Second Language Learners Making Video in Three Contexts. *Language and Literature*, *14*(2), 75–96. https://doi.org/10.20360/G2S59R

Trad, A. & Kalpić, D. (2022c). Business Transformation Project's Holistic Agile Management (BTPHAM). *CBER 2022*.

Trad, A. (2022a). Transformation Projects and Virtual Military Strategy. *CBER 2022*.

Trad, A., & Kalpić, D. (2022a). Business Transformation Projects based on a Holistic Enterprise Architecture Pattern (HEAP)-The Basics. IGI.

Trad, A., & Kalpić, D. (2022b). Business Transformation Projects based on a Holistic Enterprise Architecture Pattern (HEAP)-The Implementation. IGI.

Trad, A. (2015a). *A Transformation Framework Proposal for Managers in Business Innovation and Business Transformation Projects-Intelligent aBB architecture*. Centeris.

Trad, A. (2015b). *A Transformation Framework Proposal for Managers in Business Innovation and Business Transformation Projects-An ICS's atomic architecture vision*. Centeris.

Trad, A., & Kalpić, D. (2014). The Selection and Training Framework for Managers in Business Innovation and Transformation Projects-An applied mathematics hyper-heuristics model. *Proceedings of the 2014 International Conference on Mathematical Methods, Mathematical Models and Simulation in Science and Engineering (MMSSE 2014)*.

Trad, A., & Kalpić, D. (2017a). *An Intelligent Neural Networks Micro Artefact Patterns' Based Enterprise Architecture Model*. IGI-Global.

Training, T. (n.d.). *Proceedings of the 1st IEEE International Conference in Games and Virtual Worlds for Serious Applications*. IEEE Computer Society.

Turner, S. A. (2010). Teaching research to teachers: A self-study of course design, student outcomes, and instructor learning. *The Journal of Scholarship of Teaching and Learning*, *10*(2), 60–77. https://files.eric.ed.gov/fulltext/EJ890719.pdf

U.S. Department of Education. (1996). *Getting America's students ready for the 21st century: Meeting the technology literacy challenge*. Author.

U.S. Department of Education. (2017). *Reimagining the role of technology in Education: 2017 national education technology plan update*. Retrieved from https:// tech. ed. gov/ files/ 2017/ 01/ NETP17. pdf

U.S. Department of Education. (2017). *Reimagining the role of technology in Education: 2017 national education technology plan update*. Retrieved from https:// tech. ed. gov/ files/ 2017/ 01/ NETP17. Pdf

U.S. Department of Education. (2020). *Student enrollment*. https://nces.ed.gov/ipeds/ TrendGenerator/app/build-table/2/42?rid=6&cid=85

UNESCO. (2020). *COVID-19 educational disruption and response*. UNESCO.

University of Minnesota. (n.d.). https://libguides.umn.edu/antiracismlens

Valkenburg, P., Schouten, A., & Peter, J. (2005). Adolescents' identity experiments on the Internet. *New Media & Society*, *7*(3), 383–402. doi:10.1177/1461444805052282

Vanduhe. (2020). Continuance intentions to use gamification for training in higher education: Integrating the technology acceptance model (TAM), social motivation, and task technology fit (TTF). *IEEE*, *8*, 21473 21484. doi:10.1109/ACCESS.2020.2966179

Vesely, P., Bloom, L., & Sherlock, J. (2007). Key elements of building online community: Comparing faculty and student perceptions. *Journal of Online Learning and Teaching*, *3*(3), 234–246. https://jolt.merlot.org/vol3no3/vesely.pdf

Vora, S. (2020). *Approaching Writing with an Antiracist Perspective*. Contributions by Writing Center Antiracism Working Group.

Vygotsky, L. (1978). *Mind in society: The development of higher psychological processes.* Harvard University Press.

Vygotsky, L. (1978). *Mind in Society: The Development of Higher-Order Psychological Processes.* Harvard University Press.

Walsh-Moorman, B. (2016). The socratic seminar in the age of the common core: A search for text-dependent discourse. *English Journal, 105*(6), 72–77.

Wang, Q., & Huang, C. (2017). Pedagogical, social and technical designs of a blended synchronous learning environment. *British Journal of Educational Technology, 49*(3), 451–462. doi:10.1111/bjet.12558

Warburton, S. (2008). Defining a framework for teaching practices inside immersive virtual environments: The tension between control and pedagogical approach. *Proceedings of RELIVE '08 Conference.*

Waters, K. R. (2011). The importance of program evaluation: A case study. *Journal of Human Services, 31*(1), 83–93.

Watson, A. P. (2012). Still a Mixed Bag: A Study of First-Year Composition Students' Internet Citations at the University of Mississippi. *Reference Services Review, 40*(1), 125–137. doi:10.1108/00907321211203685

Watson, S., Rex, C., Markgraf, J., Kishel, H., Jennings, E., & Hinnant, K. (2013). Revising the "One-Shot" through Lesson Study: Collaborating with Writing Faculty to Rebuild a Library Instruction Session. *College & Research Libraries, 74*(4), 381–398. doi:10.5860/crl12-255

Waycott, J., Sheard, J., Thompson, C., & Clerehan, R. (2013). Making students' work visible on the social web: A blessing or a curse? *Computers & Education, 68*, 86–95. doi:10.1016/j.compedu.2013.04.026

Webb, H., & Rosson, M. B. (2013, March). Using scaffolded examples to teach computational thinking concepts. In*Proceedings of the 44th ACM technical symposium on Computer science education* (pp. 95-100). ACM.

Weimer, M. (2009). *Effective teaching strategies: Six keys to classroom excellence.* Faculty Focus. https://www.facultyfocus.com/articles/effective-teaching-strategies/effective-teaching-strategies-six-keys-to-classroom-excellence/

Weimer, M. (2016). *Why are we so slow to change the way we teach?* https://www.facultyfocus.com/articles/effective-teaching-strategies/why-are-we-so-slow-to-change-the-way-we-teach/

Weimer, M. (2002). *Learner-centered teaching: Five key changes to practice.* John Wiley & Sons.

Wenger, E. (2011). *Communities of practice: A brief introduction.* Academic Press.

Wergin, J. F. (2001). Beyond Carrots and Sticks: What Really Motivates Faculty. *Liberal Education, 87*(1), 50–53.

283

West, D., & Bleiberg, J. (2013). Education technology success stories. *Issues in Governance Studies.* http:// www.insidepolitics.org/brookingsreports/education_technology_success_stories.pdf

Wickersham, L., & McElhany, J. (2010). Bridging the divide: Reconciling administrator and faculty concerns regarding online Education. *Quarterly Review of Distance Education, 11*(1), 1–12.

Williams, D., Consalvo, M., Caplan, S., & Yee, N. (2009). Looking for gender: Gender roles and behaviors among online gamers. *Journal of Communication, 59*(4), 700–725.

Witeck, G. R., Alves, A. C., & Bernardo, M. H. S. (2021). Bloom Taxonomy, Serious Games and Lean Learning: What Do These Topics Have in Common? In D. J. Powell, E. Alfnes, M. D. Q. Holmemo, & E. Reke (Eds.), Learning in the Digital Era. ELEC 2021. IFIP Advances in Information and Communication Technology (Vol. 610). Springer. https://doi.org/10.1007/978-3-030-92934-3_31.

World Bank. (2020). *The COVID-19 Pandemic: Shocks to Education and Policy Responses.* Author.

World Economic Forum. (2020). *How COVID-19 deepens the digital education divide in India.* Author.

Wright, G. B. (2011). Student-centered learning in higher education. *International Journal on Teaching and Learning in Higher Education, 23*(1), 92–97.

Writing a successful discussion board post. (n.d.). Retrieved December 24, 2021 from https:// www.unr.edu/writing-speaking-center/student-resources/writing-speaking-resources/writing-a-successful-discussion-board-post

Wu, Y. (2016). Factors impacting students' online learning experience in a learner-centered course. *Journal of Computer Assisted Learning, 32*(5), 416–429. doi:10.1111/jcal.12142

Wynter-Hoyte, K., Braden, E. G., Rodriguez, S., & Thornton, N. (2019). Disrupting the status quo: Exploring culturally relevant and sustaining pedagogies for young diverse learners. *Race, Ethnicity and Education, 22*(3), 428–447. doi:10.1080/13613324.2017.1382465

Yang, H., & Wang, C. (2008). Product placement of computer games in cyberspace. *Cyberpsychology & Behavior, 11*(4), 399–404. doi:10.1089/cpb.2007.0099

Yosso, T. (2005). Whose culture has capital? A critical race theory discussion of community cultural wealth. *Race, Ethnicity and Education, 8*(1), 69–91. doi:10.1080/1361332052000341006

Young, M., Schrader, P., & Zheng, D. P. (2006). MMOGs as Learning environments: an ecological journey into Quest Atlantis and the Sims Online. *Innovate, 2*(4). Retrieved March 20, 2006, https://www.innovateonline.info/index. php?view=article&id=66

Young, S. (2006). Student views of effective online teaching in higher education. *American Journal of Distance Education, 20*(2), 65–77. doi:10.120715389286ajde2002_2

Young, V. A. (2010). Should Writers Use They Own English? *Iowa Journal of Cultural Studies, 12*(1), 110–117. doi:10.17077/2168-569X.1095

Yun, S., & Shin, H. Y. (2021). Social justice-oriented activity models for young learners illiteracy development in a Korean language classroom. *NABE Journal of Research and Practice*, *11*(1-2), 13–21. doi:10.1080/26390043.2021.1950518

Zahua, J. (2014). Peering Into the Writing Center: Information Literacy as a collaborative conversation. *Communications in Information Literacy*, *8*(1), 1. doi:10.15760/comminfolit.2014.8.1.160

Zaky, H. (2022). Emotional Intelligence and Professional Development: The Impact of Affective Competence on Teacher Performance. In A. El-Amin (Ed.), Implementing Diversity, Equity, Inclusion, and Belonging in Educational Management Practices (pp. 174–202). IGI Global. https://doi.org/10.4018/978-1-6684-4803-8.ch009

Zaky, H. (2021). Self-Regulation and Adult Learners: Investigating the Factors Enhancing Deliberate Practice in Composition Classes. *International Journal of Curriculum Development and Learning Measurement*, *2*(2), 45–60. https://doi.org/10.4018/IJCDLM.2021070104

Zeng, X., & Wang, T. (2021). College student satisfaction with online learning during COVID-19: A review and implications. *International Journal of Multidisciplinary Perspectives in Higher Education*, *6*(1), 182–195.

Zheng, C., Wang, L., & Chai, C. S. (2021). Self-assessment first or peer-assessment first: Effects of video-based formative practice on learners' English public speaking anxiety and performance. *Computer Assisted Language Learning*, 1–34. doi:10.1080/09588221.2021.1946562

Zinn, J. E., Bloodworth, M. R., Weissberg, R. P., & Walberg, H. J. (2007). The scientific base linking social and emotional learning to school success. *Journal of Educational & Psychological Consultation*, *17*(2-3), 191–210. doi:10.1080/10474410701413145

Zoetewey, M. W., & Staggers, J. (2003). Beyond 'Current-Traditional' Design: Assessing Rhetoric in New Media. *Issues in Writing*, *13*(2), 133–157.

Zydney, J. M., McKimmy, P., Lindberg, R., & Schmidt, M. (2019). Here or there instruction: Lessons learned in implementing innovative approaches to blended synchronous learning. *TechTrends*, *63*(2), 123–132. doi:10.100711528-018-0344-z

About the Contributors

Julie Tatlock currently chairs the Department of Justice, Sociology and History at Mount Mary University in Milwaukee, WI. She has presented and published several articles/chapter on best practices in online pedagogy. In addition, Julie Tatlock was part of a Mellon Foundation grant to take an in-depth look at digital learning in the humanities. Her interests are primarily in finding new and creative ways to engage students in good online research and writing as well as creating unique online education spaces. Her other primary research areas are in British History and World History.

* * *

Robert Ceglie primarily teaches science education and instructional technology courses. He was previously an assistant professor at Mercer University in Macon, Georgia where he taught across many programs including graduate and doctoral programs. His interests include many areas of science education, including under-representation of women and minorities, the achievement gaps in science and math, and persistence and retention of students entering STEM majors. He has published and presented works related to science and math education and is an editorial reviewer for several scholarly journals including Journal of Science Teacher Education and Higher Education. Dr. Ceglie is a enthusiastic Atlanta Braves fan even though he grew up in Boston, Mass. He has two children, Robbie and Jenny, and a wife Nicole who are all thrilled to have relocated to Charlotte.

Jannat Fatima Farooqui works at the Research, Monitoring and Evaluation Department of Room to Read India, a global organization working towards a world free of illiteracy and gender inequality. Jannat holds a PhD in Social Work from the Department of Social Work, University of Delhi. She has attained her Masters in Social Work from Tata Institute of Social Sciences. Her research interests lies in areas of child rights, education, minority identities, race and ethnicity. She has published and presented her work at several national and international conferences like Joint World Conference on Social Work, Education and Social Development, Conference on Child Rights & Sight, Yale University, Asia-Pacific Joint Regional Social Work Conference etc. She has also worked in different social work organizations like UNICEF, University of Delaware, Pratham Education Foundation, and India Vision Foundation.

DuEwa M. Frazier, Ed.D., is an Assistant Professor of English. She is the author of a recent book chapter titled, Blooming Where We Land: HBCU Writing Programs and Literary Legacies. Frazier's scholarly writing was also published in a Routledge series in 2021. Frazier gave a TEDx talk in 2019 focused on education and hip hop titled, "Word is Bond." She earned the B.A. degree in English at Hampton University, the M.S. degree in Curriculum and Teaching at Fordham University, the Ed.M. degree in Educational Leadership at Columbia University, the M.F.A. degree in Creative Writing at The New School, and the Ed.D. degree in Higher Education Leadership at Maryville University. Frazier's research interests include digital humanities, culturally responsive pedagogy, literacy studies, and hip-hop pedagogy. Visit her website at www.duewafrazier.com.

Stepanka Korytova-Magstadt is an educator, an interdisciplinary and an international scholar, former director of the Center for the Study of Human Trafficking and Interpersonal Violence, and the director of Global Studies at Semesteratsea. org. Areas of expertise include teaching introductory and upper level courses in Sociology, History, International and Global Studies, Criminal Justice and Behavioral Studies (face to face, and online). Publications include a book titled: To Reap A Bountiful Harvest: Czech Emigration Beyond the Mississippi River, 1850-1900.

Jessica Manzone is an Assistant Professor of Practice in the College of Education at Northern Arizona University. She was a classroom teacher and instructional coach before entering higher education. Jessica currently serves as lead faculty for the Arizona Teacher Residency where she works to prepare graduate students for future careers serving their local communities. Jessica's research interests include curriculum and instruction for diverse gifted and advanced students. She co-authored and was awarded two US Department of Education grants that focused specifically on differentiation and non-traditional means of identification for young learners. Jessica speaks at state, national, and international conferences on gifted education and provides demonstration lessons for school districts related to curriculum and instruction. Jessica is also the co-creator of the Home and Community Connections Model, which provides teachers with a means of modifying curriculum through a culturally sustaining lens.

Pradeep Mishra is currently working as a Manager of Research, Monitoring and Evaluation unit of Room to Read India. He holds an Ph.D. in Education, M.Phil. in Education with specialization in Educational Measurement and Evaluation from RIE (NCERT) and B.Ed from Kurukshetra University. Before joining Room to Read, he worked at NMRC in the area of multilingual education, Jawaharlal Nehru University (JNU), New Delhi. He is a former UGC Junior Research Fellow (JRF) and as part of the grant he has done research on assessment approaches of in-service teacher training programs in South Asian region. His research focuses on professional development of teachers, pedagogical intelligence and its construct and assessment, assessment of literacy experience of children and reading motivation.

Zingisa Nkosinkulu is an artist, art historian, and curator whose areas of study and practice include contemporary African art, black radical tradition, decolonial aesthesis, Hip Hop and Free Jazz, graffiti/street art, decolonial epistemic perspective, Xhosa indigenous culture and art, and black existentialism. He is especially concerned with the depiction of the black lived experience and its social formation in black creative expression practices, in particular, as well as the relation between art and history. Nkosinkulu is interested in the relation between decolonial thought and black existential art and has been preoccupied with fusing these fields to illuminate the power of their synergy. He addresses these concerns by way of art-making, art exhibitions and criticism with special focus on Mary Sibande's visual artworks, Fanonian discourse, Jean Michel Basquiat, Tupac Shakur, and Édouard Glissant. He is determined to contribute to the decolonization of art history by deconstructing and decolonizing aesthetics. Nkosinkulu completed his Ph.D. in Art at Unisa where he is also a Research Post Doctoral Fellow.

Paula Reiter currently chairs Mount Mary University's English Department. She has presented and published widely on best practices in online pedagogy. She emphasizes strong reflection on curriculum, student learning outcomes, and innovative teaching strategies.

Hany Zaky is an international scholar. His diverse teaching capacities throughout his career have provided him with the ability to work effectively with diverse linguistic learners. His research interests include using Technology to enhance Teacher Reflection, Action Research, Reflective Teaching, Educational Technology, Literacy Assessment and Evaluation, Professional Development for Diversity, Culturally Responsive Pedagogy, and Language Teachers' Identity.

Index

Recommended Reference Books

IGI Global's reference books can now be purchased from three unique pricing formats:
Print Only, E-Book Only, or Print + E-Book.
Shipping fees may apply.

www.igi-global.com

ISBN: 9781522589648
EISBN: 9781522589655
© 2021; 156 pp.
List Price: US$ 155

ISBN: 9781799840756
EISBN: 9781799840763
© 2021; 282 pp.
List Price: US$ 185

ISBN: 9781799855989
EISBN: 9781799856009
© 2021; 382 pp.
List Price: US$ 195

ISBN: 9781799864745
EISBN: 9781799864752
© 2021; 271 pp.
List Price: US$ 195

ISBN: 9781799875710
EISBN: 9781799875734
© 2021; 252 pp.
List Price: US$ 195

ISBN: 9781799857709
EISBN: 9781799857716
© 2021; 378 pp.
List Price: US$ 195

Do you want to stay current on the latest research trends, product announcements, news, and special offers?
Join IGI Global's mailing list to receive customized recommendations, exclusive discounts, and more.
Sign up at: **www.igi-global.com/newsletters.**

Publisher of Timely, Peer-Reviewed Inclusive Research Since 1988

www.igi-global.com   ✉ Sign up at www.igi-global.com/newsletters   f facebook.com/igiglobal   t twitter.com/igiglobal

Ensure Quality Research is Introduced to the Academic Community

Become an Evaluator for IGI Global Authored Book Projects

Premier Reference Source

Stabilizing Currency and Preserving Economic Sovereignty Using the Grondona System

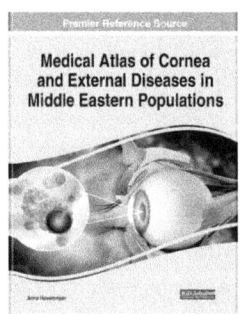

Premier Reference Source

Medical Atlas of Cornea and External Diseases in Middle Eastern Populations

Premier Reference Source

Examining Biophilia and Societal Indifference to Environmental Protection

Premier Reference Source

Using Narratives and Storytelling to Promote Cultural Diversity on College Campuses

The overall success of an authored book project is dependent on quality and timely manuscript evaluations.

Applications and Inquiries may be sent to:
development@igi-global.com

Applicants must have a doctorate (or equivalent degree) as well as publishing, research, and reviewing experience. Authored Book Evaluators are appointed for one-year terms and are expected to complete at least three evaluations per term. Upon successful completion of this term, evaluators can be considered for an additional term.

If you have a colleague that may be interested in this opportunity, we encourage you to share this information with them.

Easily Identify, Acquire, and Utilize Published
Peer-Reviewed Findings in Support of Your Current Research

IGI Global OnDemand

Purchase Individual IGI Global OnDemand Book Chapters and Journal Articles

For More Information:

www.igi-global.com/e-resources/ondemand/

Browse through 150,000+ Articles and Chapters!

Find specific research related to your current studies and projects that have been contributed by international researchers from prestigious institutions, including:

- Accurate and Advanced Search
- Affordably Acquire Research
- Instantly Access Your Content
- Benefit from the InfoSci Platform Features

It really provides an excellent entry into the research literature of the field. It presents a manageable number of highly relevant sources on topics of interest to a wide range of researchers. The sources are scholarly, but also accessible to 'practitioners'.

- Ms. Lisa Stimatz, MLS, University of North Carolina at Chapel Hill, USA

Interested in Additional Savings?

Subscribe to

IGI Global OnDemand *Plus*

Learn More

Acquire content from over 128,000+ research-focused book chapters and 33,000+ scholarly journal articles for as low as US$ 5 per article/chapter (original retail price for an article/chapter: US$ 37.50).

6,600+ E-BOOKS.
ADVANCED RESEARCH.
INCLUSIVE & ACCESSIBLE.

IGI Global e-Book Collection

- **Flexible Purchasing Options** (Perpetual, Subscription, EBA, etc.)
- Multi-Year Agreements with **No Price Increases** Guaranteed
- **No Additional Charge** for Multi-User Licensing
- No Maintenance, Hosting, or Archiving Fees
- Transformative **Open Access Options** Available

Request More Information, or Recommend the IGI Global e-Book Collection to Your Institution's Librarian

Among Titles Included in the IGI Global e-Book Collection

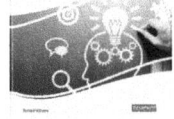

Research Anthology on Racial Equity, Identity, and Privilege (3 Vols.)
EISBN: 9781668445082
Price: US$ 895

Handbook of Research on Remote Work and Worker Well-Being in the Post-COVID-19 Era
EISBN: 9781799867562
Price: US$ 265

Research Anthology on Big Data Analytics, Architectures, and Applications (4 Vols.)
EISBN: 9781668436639
Price: US$ 1,950

Handbook of Research on Challenging Deficit Thinking for Exceptional Education Improvement
EISBN: 9781799888628
Price: US$ 265

Acquire & Open

When your library acquires an IGI Global e-Book and/or e-Journal Collection, your faculty's published work will be considered for immediate conversion to Open Access *(CC BY License)*, at no additional cost to the library or its faculty *(cost only applies to the e-Collection content being acquired)*, through our popular **Transformative Open Access (Read & Publish) Initiative**.

For More Information or to Request a Free Trial, Contact IGI Global's e-Collections Team: eresources@igi-global.com | 1-866-342-6657 ext. 100 | 717-533-8845 ext. 100

Have Your Work Published and Freely Accessible

Open Access Publishing

With the industry shifting from the more traditional publication models to an open access (OA) publication model, publishers are finding that OA publishing has many benefits that are awarded to authors and editors of published work.

| Freely Share Your Research | Higher Discoverability & Citation Impact | Rigorous & Expedited Publishing Process | Increased Advancement & Collaboration |

Acquire & Open

When your library acquires an IGI Global e-Book and/or e-Journal Collection, your faculty's published work will be considered for immediate conversion to Open Access (*CC BY License*), at no additional cost to the library or its faculty (*cost only applies to the e-Collection content being acquired*), through our popular **Transformative Open Access (Read & Publish) Initiative**.

Provide Up To
100%
OA APC or
CPC Funding

Funding to
Convert or
Start a Journal to
**Platinum
OA**

Support for
Funding an
**OA
Reference
Book**

IGI Global publications are found in a number of prestigious indices, including Web of Science™, Scopus®, Compendex, and PsycINFO®. The selection criteria is very strict and to ensure that journals and books are accepted into the major indexes, IGI Global closely monitors publications against the criteria that the indexes provide to publishers.

WEB OF SCIENCE™   €) Compendex   Scopus®

PsycINFO®    Inspec

Learn More Here:

For Questions, Contact IGI Global's Open Access Team at openaccessadmin@igi-global.com

IGI Global
PUBLISHER of TIMELY KNOWLEDGE
www.igi-global.com

Lightning Source UK Ltd.
Milton Keynes UK
UKHW032033141122
412210UK00007B/134